Middle East Politics and International Relations

The contemporary Middle East has been defined by political crises and conflict. The interplay of internal and external factors have set the region on a path of turmoil and crisis with devastating outcomes for its people. The absence of political accountability and representation, and policies pursued by the United States to keep US-friendly regimes in power have been two key factors that have contributed to the seemingly insoluble Middle East politics.

This book provides a detailed exploration of the forces, internal and external, that have shaped today's Middle East. The book follows a chronological order and provides context to major political milestones. Topics explored include:

- Imperialism in the Middle East
- The formation of the State of Israel
- The Arab -Israeli wars
- Palestinian politics and the failure of the 'peace process'
- The Iranian Revolution and pan-Shi'ism
- Superpowers in the Middle East
- The US-led 'War on Terror'
- The Arab uprisings
- The Syrian War and the rise of the 'Islamic State'
- US -Iranian relations

This study puts recent developments in historical context, and will serve as a core reference tool for students and researchers of Middle Eastern Politics and International Relations.

Shahram Akbarzadeh is Research Professor of Middle East and Central Asian Politics and held the prestigious ARC Future Fellowship (2013–2016). He is Deputy Director (International) at the Alfred Deakin Institute for Citizenship and Globalization, Deakin University, Australia.

Kylie Baxter is a Lecturer in Islamic Studies at Asia Institute, University of Melbourne, Australia.

Middle East Politics and International Relations

Crisis Zone

Shahram Akbarzadeh and Kylie Baxter

Routledge
Taylor & Francis Group

LONDON AND NEW YORK

First published 2018
by Routledge
2 Park Square, Milton Park, Abingdon, Oxon OX14 4RN

and by Routledge
711 Third Avenue, New York, NY 10017

Routledge is an imprint of the Taylor & Francis Group, an informa business

British Library Cataloguing-in-Publication Data
A catalogue record for this book is available from the British Library

Library of Congress Cataloging-in-Publication Data
Names: Akbarzadeh, Shahram, author. | Baxter, Kylie, author.
Title: Middle East politics and international relations : crisis zone / Shahram
Akbarzadeh and Kylie Baxter.
Description: Milton Park, Abingdon, Oxon ; New York, NY : Routledge,
2018. | Includes bibliographical references and index.
Identifiers: LCCN 2017060139| ISBN 9781138056268 (hbk) | ISBN
9781138056275 (pbk) | ISBN 9781315165455 (ebk)
Subjects: LCSH: Middle East--Politics and government--20th century. |
Middle East--Politics and government--21st century. | Middle East--Foreign
relations--20th century. | Middle East--Foreign relations--21st century.
Classification: LCC DS62.8 .A39 2018 | DDC 327.56--dc23
LC record available at https://lccn.loc.gov/2017060139

ISBN: 978-1-138-05626-8 (hbk)
ISBN: 978-1-138-05627-5 (pbk)
ISBN: 978-1-315-16545-5 (ebk)

Typeset in Bembo
by Taylor & Francis Books

Contents

Figures

Boxes

Acknowledgements

The authors would like to acknowledge the support of the Alfred Deakin Institute for Citizenship and Globalization, Deakin University, and the Asia Institute, University of Melbourne. We would also like to acknowledge the many graduate and undergraduate students we have taught over the years. This book reflects their interest and enthusiasm for the politics, religions and cultures of the Middle East. Finally, thanks also to Ms Renee Davidson, whose hard work and dedication immeasurably enhanced this volume.

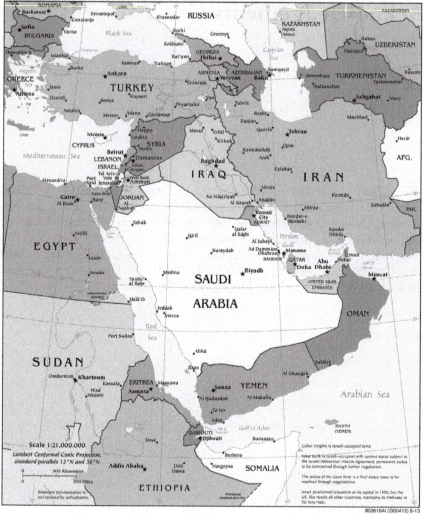

Map 1 Map of the Middle East
docs/refmaps.html

1 Introduction

The colonial background

The Middle East has been defined by political crises for the last 100 years. In the political halls of power, the media, popular culture and the educational institutions of Western countries, the term 'Middle East' conjures a confused imagery of religion, resources, foreign interference and politics that can be hard to untangle. In the twentieth century, the establishment of nation-states and the framework of the Cold War moderated not just the political environment of the region, but the lens through which outsiders came to understand events. For much of the century, authoritarian stability was the dominant form of politics in the Middle East. As the Cold War receded, a new, chaotic sense of globalization penetrated the region and this system of political organization began to falter.

Despite these changes, few observers foresaw the magnitude of the shifts underway in this region. For generations, the gap between the political elites and the people they ruled had grown not just in terms of economic opportunity, but in terms of political and social capital. This led to a build-up of resentment and discontent that had no legal avenue of expression. The pent-up energy erupted into mass protests in some cases (the 1979 revolution in Iran, the 2011 Arab uprisings). In other cases, deep social and political tensions turned into violent inter-community conflict. Recent events in the Middle East have thrown into sharp relief the legitimacy of the political elites and the system that sustains their power: the system of nation-states. In the Middle East, the nation-state has lacked institutional capacity and popular legitimacy. The political entities that emerged out of the colonial experience were unrepresentative of the masses they governed. Lack of transparency and accountability, mixed with the inability to provide or foster social and economic mobility, on the one hand, and authoritarian practices which were aimed at silencing dissent, on the other, made states in the Middle East vulnerable to combustible resentment. Anti-systemic energy kept building up in a pressure-cooker environment, ready to erupt.

Social and political tensions in the Middle East were exacerbated by the continuing involvement of colonial and post-colonial superpowers in the region. In the following pages, an overview of the colonial impact will be provided. But what will become clear in the course of this book is that the Cold War rivalry between the Soviet Union and the United States made a devastating impression on the region and deepened the divide between society and the political elite. Each superpower sought to strengthen its links with ruling regimes that aligned with its global interests. This experience stood out markedly in relation to the United States as Washington turned a blind eye to the authoritarian nature of the ruling regimes in Iran, Egypt and Saudi Arabia in the latter half of the twentieth century. Washington helped prop up these regimes to counter Moscow's influence at the expense of popular wishes. The consequence was US-sponsored regimes that were not responsive to their own populations. This political divide ran through the region and set the Middle East on course for seismic shocks, long after the end of the Cold War. As will be explored in detail, the underlying reasons for the Arab uprisings of 2011 may be traced to the political system that emerged in the Cold War era.

This book offers readers a detailed, contextualized exploration of the forces, internal and external, that have shaped today's Middle East. It charts colonial intervention, political and religious movements, state formation, conflicts, international involvement and the role of global institutions. Most importantly, it places the conflicts of the twenty-first century in their appropriate historical, political and international context. Foreign intervention is a fact of history for most, if not all, parts of the world. However, in the Middle East the dynamic of colonial intervention, superpower bipolarity and occupation have played out in distinctive ways. The question of foreign influence has become a point of reference in the political discourse. The authors have previously written on anti-Americanism in the region. However, foreign intervention is not the only determinant of events. Rapid structural change, urbanization, education and enhanced access to information, in a context of economic and political stagnation, have contributed to the volatility of the region. In the twenty-first century, a new dynamic of instability has emerged which connects internal fissures with external pressures. Iran and Saudi Arabia have emerged as two regional arch-rivals, with competing agendas and diametrically opposed interests. Their behaviour prior to the 2011 uprisings and even more in the wake of those momentous events has proven extremely destabilizing. This regional rivalry and how it interacted with ethnic and sectarian fault-lines has become a feature of Middle East politics, especially in the Persian Gulf region.

This book will examine a series of interconnected themes and issues, some of which are noted here. First, external interference is a key theme of Middle Eastern politics. This is not a static issue. In the twentieth century, external interference in the form of colonialism dominated the political landscape. Having set the contours of new institutions by drawing new territorial boundaries, the colonial experience turned the Middle East into a playground of superpower rivalry during the Cold War before it became subject to unipolar American hegemony by the end of the last century. In the twenty-first century, US influence in the region has come under strain as Russia seeks to regain its former position as a global power, China seeks entry into the Middle East, and regional powers, such as Iran and Saudi Arabia, aim to enhance their own competing spheres of influence. This dynamic has highlighted how external influences can have significant impacts on the course of history in each Middle Eastern state. The political crisis in the Middle East in the twenty-first century is linked to more powerful states' efforts to project their influence in the region through soft and/or hard power. This external factor has invariably led to conflict and the entrenchment of social, political and religious divisions in the target country. The US occupation of Iraq in 2003, the NATO-led action in Libya in 2011 and the West's calls for regime change in Syria – in unison with Saudi Arabia, Turkey and a number of Arab sheikhdoms in the Persian Gulf – have opened social, ethnic and religious fault-lines that have dragged the region into open conflict and widespread misery. Popular coverage of these conflicts often blames primordial communal grievances. But if sectarian tensions have been ever present, why didn't they flare up long ago? Why now? Coming to grips with the interplay between external and internal factors is an important aspect of making sense of the Middle East.

Second, a consideration of the modern nation-state underpins many of the chapters in this book. What does it mean to be a nation-state? What is nationalism and how does it interact with other regional identities? Why is the power of the state used to coerce rather than protect its citizens? In the contemporary Middle East, the nation-state has been seriously challenged. Libya is a failed state. Syria, still in the grips of civil war at the time of writing, is likely to become one. These vital case-studies are, however, exceptions. In most cases, the revolutionary zeal of 2011 was matched by a determined assertion of top-down authority as the political elites sought to solidify their control in the name of preserving state sovereignty. This has been mirrored beyond the Arab environment, with Iran, Turkey and Israel surging from strength to strength as sovereign powers. Since the post-colonial period, the Middle Eastern state model has been prone to authoritarianism, often (but not always) with religion used – to some degree – to justify the centrality of the structure. Consequently, any study of the nation-state in the Middle East is by definition a study of authoritarianism.

Third, political manifestations of Islam have been integral to political developments in the Middle East. Religion has played a significant role in the politics of the region. Islam has been used to justify the position of political elites and, in the case of the Islamic Republic of Iran or the Kingdom of Saudi Arabia, the actual structure of state itself. Islam has also often been instrumentalized as a framework for the expression of dissent and opposition to the ruling regimes. Some branches of political Islam which emerged in the 1970s originally as alternative models to many Western-oriented ruling regimes later morphed into terrorist groups that target the West, such as al-Qaeda and the Islamic State of Iraq and Syria (ISIS), which have added a new layer of sectarian warfare to the established anti-Western ideology.

Fourth, the theme of popular desire for self-rule, representative government and justice runs through many chapters in this book. Many of the political upheavals in the twentieth-century Middle East may be traced to the political divide between the ruling elite and the masses – a feature that continues to undermine the region even today. The absence of accountability has meant that incumbent regimes act with impunity and represent their interests as national interests. Frustration and anger with this unresponsive political system have led to popular revolts that have shaken the region. The 1979 revolution in Iran was one such episode. This popular revolt toppled the US-backed regime and raised the mantle of political accountability. In 2011 the same ideals inspired a number of Arab uprisings that challenged the ruling elites over their arrogance and unresponsiveness to popular wishes. This universal desire for justice has rarely borne fruit because of the intersection of other factors, most notably the ability of the ruling elites to use a combination of coercion and adaptation to pacify dissent.

This is the tragedy of the Middle East, a region where popular movements have pushed for reform but are held back by well-entrenched incumbents who owe their authority to a system that was put in place by colonial powers and upgraded by post-colonial superpowers. This dynamic has put the Middle East on a path of recurring social, political and religious crisis.

Chapter outline

This book begins its investigation of the Middle East with a brief exploration of the fall of the Ottoman Empire, the role of local elites and the impact of colonial interventions in the early twentieth century. This is a vital undertaking for the contextualization of regional views of Western policy. This foundational history is our starting point. The remainder of this introductory chapter will examine the impact of the competing identities that emerged in response to challenges with roots in foreign intervention.

The book then turns to a detailed exploration of Arab–Israeli politics, bringing in discussions of diverse issues such as Zionism, large-scale war, popular uprisings and self-determination. Chapter 2 provides an account of Zionism, the movement which created the modern State of Israel. It also covers the 1948 Arab–Israeli War, which consecrated this new state in the Muslim-majority Middle East. The analysis of Israel continues in Chapter 3, in which we chart Israeli experiences through the major conflicts of the twentieth and early twenty-first centuries – 1967, 1973, 1982 and 2006 – taking into account the experience of Palestinian refugees. To complete this section of the book, Chapter 4 engages directly with the Palestinian political experience, including the experience of occupation, civil conflict and the prevalence of HAMAS in the contemporary arena.

Chapter 5 looks at the impact of broader identities in the region as we focus on the role of pan-Arab nationalism and the articulation of political Islam. This chapter is integral to understanding the transnational affiliations, such as the Salafi-jihadist movement, which were mobilized throughout the twentieth century, often as a challenge to the emergent political elites.

Chapter 6 shifts the focus to the Iranian context with an exploration of the seminal 1979 revolution. This chapter charts the events of that year and explores the consequences of this upheaval on Iran and the region as a whole. It also begins to flesh out the consequences of Shia mobilization in the late twentieth century. Chapter 7 functions as a capstone to the exploration of the twentieth century, considering the role of superpowers in the region throughout that century and beyond.

In Chapter 8 we begin our analysis of the contemporary Middle East, with special focus on understanding the consequences of political decision-making, foreign interference and poor governance as detailed through the earlier chapters. This chapter explores the watershed moment of 9/11 and the launching of the 'War on Terror', with its disastrous occupation of Iraq. This provides the framework for understanding the events of the Arab uprisings of 2011. This series of interrelated, yet distinct, political upheavals are explored across the next two chapters. Chapter 9 explores the events of the revolutionary, and counter-revolutionary, period in Egypt, Libya and Bahrain. The devastation of the Syrian conflict – and the rise of the ISIS militia – is detailed in Chapter 10.

The key outcome of the post-2003 period is the resurgence of Iran as a regional heavyweight, and this is investigated in Chapter 11, which focuses on the Iranian–US relationship and the important emergent dynamic of Iranian–Saudi competition which underscores the contemporary regional political scene. Finally, Chapter 12 offers a summation of the book with a review on the political experiences, inter-state tensions and major challenges facing the modern Middle East.

This book provides a contextualized insight into nearly 100 years of political turmoil in the Middle East. The chapters are designed as stand-alone insights into particular places or aspects of the Middle East. However, the interlocking nature of regional politics means the chapters build upon each other to provide a comprehensive picture of the political terrain. To this end, it is useful to provide a brief account of the early twentieth century and the colonial machinations of the Great Powers. Three major documents – the Husayn–McMahon Correspondence of 1915, the Sykes–Picot Agreement of 1916 and the Balfour Declaration of 1917 – are key to understanding the region under consideration.

The colonial period

The early twentieth century was a time of unparalleled change in the Middle East. The fall of the Ottoman Empire and the establishment of a system of distinct nation-states signalled a new phase in regional history. While local agency played some role in this process, especially in relation to elite participation, it is reasonable to view this period through the lens of Western intervention.

The external imposition of territorial boundaries irrevocably changed the Middle East. Under the Ottoman Empire, and even prior to this period, while formal governance was implemented at a supra-level, the lived experience of politics was local, influenced by the immediate considerations of geography, tribal politics and religion. The imposition of new 'states' by Western powers sought to overturn these traditions and bind the region's peoples to a series of distinct nation-states. It was this division of the region into territorial entities, often implemented with little regard for pre-existing identities such as ethnicity or religious affiliation, which created a system of states that were plagued by endemic political instability. This new political configuration, endorsed in the post-colonial period by emergent leaderships often of secular orientation, worked to override ethnic and tribal identities. Throughout the twentieth century these new national identities interacted with existing norms and traditions, which sometimes worked to reinforce the new nation-states, but often complicated the formation of strong national identities. As the national projects in the Middle East began to falter in the mid to late twentieth century, these identities – especially religious and sectarian loyalties – re-entered the public and political domains.

The United Kingdom was the key colonial player in regional politics at the dawn of the twentieth century. From the perspective of the Arab world, it was British involvement that set the scene for a history of Western influence and intervention that spanned the century. It is therefore useful to begin our analysis of the modern Middle East in this period.

The contemporary geopolitical landscape of the Middle East is the product of direct colonial administration, client protectorate systems of governance and the Mandate system established by the League of Nations. With the notable exception of Iran, Saudi Arabia and Turkey, the fledgling states of the Middle East all experienced various degrees of colonial administration. This was a significant impediment to the region's political development within the international system. At the time, the preference for direct administration by colonial powers created a situation in which the local leaderships were limited in their exposure to the international stage, the consequences of which are most clearly evident in the Palestinian–Zionist conflict of the early twentieth century. Moreover, long after the period of formal colonial rule had ended, Britain and France continued to manipulate key aspects of state sovereignty, such as trade and security issues.

In the Western discourse, the colonial period has been largely relegated to history. In the Middle East, however, the situation is different. The colonial period fundamentally shaped the political system of the region, and many of the regional delineations created in this period continue to cause instability. The experience of colonialism is now deeply internalized and continues to serve as a point of reference in the political discourse in the region. The subsequent intervention of superpowers in the post-colonial Middle East then served to keep memories of subjugation alive, with much of the anti-Western animosity now directed towards the United States. It is important to note, however, that the United States was not a major player in the colonial divisions of the Middle East. In the early decades of the twentieth century, it was a predominantly isolationist power. Indeed, the US position was governed by the Wilsonian idealism of self-determination for colonized people. Over time, however, this idealistic approach was increasingly tempered by Cold War pragmatism and self-interest before it was finally supplanted by policies of direct intervention, making the United States a focus of both admiration and spite.

Collapse of the old order

Ottoman rulers, buoyed by the merging of temporal and Islamic authority in the structure of the Caliphate, had maintained centralized control over the entire Middle East for hundreds of years. However, in the first two decades of the twentieth century, the Ottoman Empire became increasingly vulnerable to internal tensions and external pressures. In October 1914 the empire concluded a treaty with Germany that led to its entry into the First World War against Russia and, by extension, the United Kingdom and France. Geopolitical considerations at the time pushed the Ottomans into action, and their commitment to the German alliance set in motion a chain of events that led to the eventual downfall of their system of centralized governance, the disintegration of the Ottoman Empire and the emergence of new states.

London was well aware of the geographical and historical importance of the Middle East, and the German–Ottoman alliance only solidified a determined and sustained British interest in the region. As the war developed, British military and political leaders sought opportunities to weaken and destabilize Germany's Ottoman ally. In small pockets of the Arab world, this new alignment of forces was also seen as an opportunity. For some regional leaders, Ottoman rule, although imbued with Islamic legitimacy, was increasingly perceived as domination by non-Arab forces. Encouraged by this predisposition towards anti-Ottoman rebellion, Britain began to look for allies within the Arab world. It was in this climate that a handful of Arab tribal leaders began to view their own interests and those of the British state as aligned. The Hashemite family emerged as the major player in this delicate and complex political scene. Descended from the Prophet Mohammed, this central Arabian tribal family had both historical legitimacy and political ambitions. Emboldened by the war, the Hashemite clan, in league with the British, made its play for regional influence and prestige, advancing its aims with the language of Arab nationalism and self-determination.

> **Box 1.1 The Hashemite family**
>
> The Hashemite family originate from Hijaz, in the western part of the Arabian Peninsula, and have traditionally wielded great religious influence in the Arab world. Their political and religious legitimacy is derived from their lineage to the Prophet Mohammed, through his daughter Fatima. During the Ottoman Empire, the Hashemites were the guardians of the two Muslim holy sites of Mecca and Medina. At the beginning of the twentieth century, they endeavoured to translate their religious legitimacy into political power via their leadership of the Arab nationalist movement that sought freedom from the Ottoman Empire. The Hashemite family have ruled Jordan since it gained independence from British Mandate power in 1946.

Traditional views of Islam

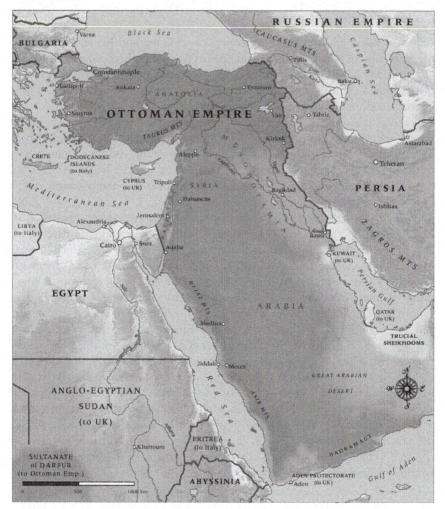

Map 2 The Ottoman Empire
Source: https://nzhistory.govt.nz/media/photo/map-ottoman-empire-1914

The first major international involvement of the Hashemites occurred in the context of the Ottomans' entry into the First World War. The 'Husayn–McMahon Correspondence' was a series of letters exchanged between Sharif Husayn of Mecca and the United Kingdom's High Commissioner in Egypt, Henry McMahon. Aware of Britain's interest in destabilizing the Ottoman Empire from the east, Husayn approached the British authorities with an outline of the conditions under which he would lead an Arab revolt against Ottoman rule in the Hijaz. In return, Husayn aimed to secure land for Arab – or, more correctly, Hashemite – self-rule.

In many ways, the Hashemite proposal reflected the broader international system of the time. Recourse to Great Power patronage became a key theme of international relations in this period as nationalist movements sought to improve their positions within a fluid international environment. However, the Hashemite negotiations with the British were far from clear cut, and the exact tract of land slated for Arab self-rule in the Husayn–McMahon Correspondence has long been the subject of academic and political conjecture. At the centre of this debate is the future of the land known as Palestine. As will be discussed, the disposition of Palestine in the Husayn–McMahon deliberations became an issue of increasing importance to all actors, particularly as Zionist settlement in the region intensified. Despite the ambiguity of his arrangement with the British, Husayn initiated a rebellion in the Hijaz, and the British aided it significantly. This became known as the Arab Revolt of 1916.

The Arab nationalist movement has sparked much controversy among modern academics. The role played by political beliefs in academic enquiry is evident in an analysis of the various positions taken regarding the nature of the Hashemite movement. Among others, the Israeli historians Efraim and Inari Karsh assert that Husayn 'was not an Arab nationalist but an aspiring imperialist bent on empire-building' (Karsh and Karsh 1999: 232). The tribal and dynastic intentions of the Hashemite family are indeed evident. However, in the all-important popular historiography of the region, the Hashemite movement is often presented as an Arab nationalist uprising against Ottoman rule. Mary C. Wilson (1991: 189) argues that Arab nationalism 'was spawned in the cities of the Fertile Crescent among a class of provincial notables that had lost power because of changes in Istanbul between 1908 and 1914'. The most constructive interpretation may well be that the Arab Revolt of 1916 was caused by a blend of political opportunism, nationalist inclinations, financial incentive (which was provided by the British) and dynastic ambition. The degree to which the broader Arab world embraced nationalist self-determination became a matter of lively political and academic debate largely because of the significant implications the question has had in the Arab–Israeli battle for historical legitimacy.

It is important to remember that at this point the entire region was still under Ottoman rule; therefore, McMahon's letters constitute nothing more than a vague statement of future British intent. The British framers of the correspondence allowed themselves significant room to manoeuvre. Nevertheless, the letters also constitute – and more importantly were perceived by future observers to have constituted – a promise, made explicit in the text: 'Great Britain is prepared to recognize and uphold the independence of the Arabs' ('Hussein–McMahon Correspondence' 1915–1916). Yet the drafters of the documents were careful not to specify precisely what regions along the Mediterranean coastal plain were considered 'not purely Arab' and thus excluded from support for Arab self-rule. The Syrian coastal plain was an area long coveted by the French because of the presence of their regional allies, the Maronite Christians. Seen in this light, the wording of the McMahon letters appears to relate less to the ethnic composition of the region than it does to the British desire to keep their wartime allies on their side. Such motives were typical of the colonial powers' decisions regarding the Middle East. In any case, in the post-war period the lack of a clearly defined fate for Palestine became one of the central points of contention arising from the correspondence, as from 1920 the British held that Palestine was excluded from the area intended for Arab independence. This position was hotly – if, as some argue, retrospectively – contested. As the fall of the Ottoman Empire loomed, regional and international interest in the fate of Palestine continued to grow.

The Sykes–Picot Agreement (1916) and the Balfour Declaration (1917)

The Husayn–McMahon Correspondence was not the only negotiation conducted by Britain during this period. Concurrent plans were afoot among the wartime allies. The British diplomat Mark Sykes and his French counterpart François Georges-Picot reached an accord in February 1916, known as the 'Sykes–Picot Agreement', to subdivide the defunct Ottoman Empire. The plan received Russian endorsement in late 1916, and became public when it was revealed by the anti-imperialist Bolsheviks after the 1917 Russian Revolution. The agreement carved up the Middle East on the basis of the economic and geostrategic interests of France and the United Kingdom. The two colonial powers sought to assure their maritime access to and political domination of the areas of the Middle East that were already under their influence. The Sykes–Picot Agreement is usually understood by pro-Arab historians as a contradiction of the spirit, if not the letter, of the Husayn–McMahon Correspondence, which at a minimum provided a generalized endorsement of Arab self-determination.

The Middle East envisaged in this agreement was a markedly different geo-political entity from that 'promised' by the British in 1915 and was premised on the solidification of external influence. Imperial Russia was also set to benefit from this agreement due to its acquisition of Armenia and Istanbul as well as the complete demise of its arch enemy, the Ottoman Empire. The agreement delineated French and British areas of control. In contrast to the ambiguous treatment of Palestine in the Husayn–McMahon Correspondence, this area was clearly marked for joint administration by the allies. This demonstrated an increasing awareness of the region's controversial status and an acknowledgement of the Russian Orthodox Church's interest in the cities of the Holy Land. Once Britain had secured its own interests and appeased its wartime allies, the amount of land left with which to honour the Husayn–McMahon Correspondence was considerably smaller and basically limited to the Arabian Peninsula.

The Husayn–McMahon and Sykes–Picot negotiations were conducted by a handful of local and international power-brokers. This reality supports the depiction of the Arab nationalist movement as a limited, elitist movement rather than a grassroots expression of popular will. However, the existence of

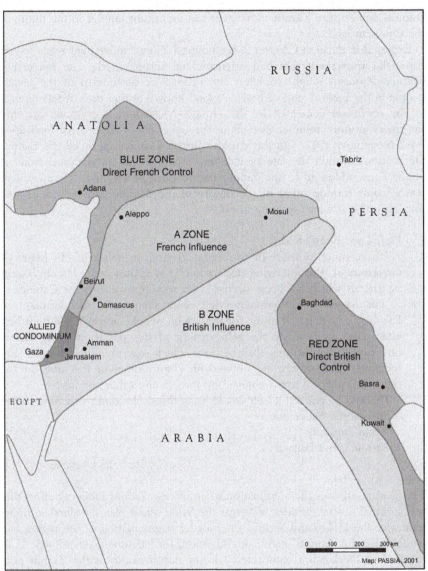

Map 3 The division of the Middle East under the terms of the Sykes–Picot Agreement
Source: http://passia.org/maps/view/4

the agreements reflects a broad-based awareness that the geopolitical future of the region was an open question at this juncture. It is instructive to view the agreements as demonstrating two trends: the notional desire for autonomy within the Middle East and the determination of external powers to maintain their interests. Yet these trends were not the sole factors influencing the political processes of the Middle East at this time. In addition to the Arabs and the colonial powers, the Zionist movement had significant interest in the future of the Ottoman lands.

Explored in detail in Chapter 2, the political Zionist movement was a Jewish nationalist movement that had originated in Europe in the late nineteenth century. Zionism sought to effect the national reconstitution of the Jewish people in the biblical land of Israel – a land known at that time as Palestine.

The confusion generated by the Husayn–McMahon Correspondence and the interventionist mindset evident in the Sykes–Picot Agreement intensified on 2 November 1917. On this day the British Cabinet approved the Balfour Declaration, turning the fate of Palestine into a major international issue. A public letter addressed to the Zionist patron Lord Rothschild, this document was a major turning point in the history of the Middle East. Given its vital importance, it is worth quoting in full:

> Dear Lord Rothschild,
>
> I have much pleasure in conveying to you, on behalf of His Majesty's Government, the following declaration of sympathy with Jewish Zionist aspirations which has been submitted to, and approved by, the Cabinet.
>
> 'His Majesty's Government view with favour the establishment in Palestine of a national home for the Jewish people, and will use their best endeavours to facilitate the achievement of this object, it being clearly understood that nothing shall be done which may prejudice the civil and religious rights of existing non-Jewish communities in Palestine, or the rights and political status enjoyed by Jews in any other country.'
>
> I should be grateful if you would bring this declaration to the knowledge of the Zionist Federation.
>
> Yours sincerely
> Arthur James Balfour
>
> (Balfour Declaration 1917)

This declaration was the culmination of an intense Zionist lobbying effort that had spanned several decades. Whereas the Sykes–Picot plan for allied adminis-tration of the Holy Land and for the broader fragmentation of the region had confounded the Zionists' nationalist intentions for Palestine (Sachar 2005: 353), the Balfour Declaration constituted a major step forward for the Zionist pro-ject. However, it was rife with inherent contradictions. As Avi Shlaim points out, at the time of its release, Palestine was home to around 690,000 Arabs and 85,000 Jews (Shlaim 1995: 24). The United States was emerging into the international spotlight, and the ideal of self-determination of peoples, as expressed in the proclamation of President Woodrow Wilson's Fourteen Points, was becoming a feature of Western political discourse. Considering the low ratio of Jews to Arabs in Palestine, the Balfour Declaration could be seen as at odds with that principle of self-determination. In fact the Balfour Declaration marks the beginning of a political struggle for Israeli versus Palestinian legiti-macy that spanned the twentieth century. For example, Alan Dershowitz refers to the same figures as Shlaim to argue against the opposing view that Jewish self-determination, in the area inhabited by Jews, was in line with Wilsonian self-determination. Reflecting traditional Zionist discourse, Dershowitz (2003: 32) also makes the point that 'a Jewish homeland would not be carved out of a pre-existing Palestinian state ... after all there had never been a Palestinian state in this area'. Yet, as this chapter has shown, a *pre-existing state system* was simply not present in the Middle East in this period.

The demographic 'facts on the ground' go some way to explaining the furore the document sparked in Arab political circles at the time. Sahar Huneidi (2001: 28) contends that the depth of Arab anger towards the Balfour Declaration was well understood by the British authorities, who delayed the formal release of the text in Palestine for several years. For Britain, the declaration functioned as a public endorsement of the Zionist movement, but more importantly it solidified in the eyes of the global community London's post-war dominance over Palestine (Sachar 2005: 357). By assuming the role of regional power-broker, London was staking its claim in the post-war Middle East.

In a clear acknowledgement of the increasing role of the United States, the declaration was floated in Washington and received the support of the Wilson administration on 16 October 1917. The passage of this brief yet historically explosive document was aided at different times by factors as diverse as individual sentiment, geostrategic considerations and alliance-building. In addition to the issues surrounding the reality of demographic imbalance, the problematic term 'national home' was unknown in the parlance of international relations at this time. The term had first been employed by the Zionists in lieu of the more explicit terminology of statehood at the 1897 World Zionist Conference (Sachar 2005: 360) in order to allay Ottoman concerns about the Zionist enterprise in Palestine. Yet, with the drafting of the Balfour Declaration, it entered the international system. Dershowitz (2003: 32) argues that the debates generated by the controversial declaration effectively helped incorporate the notion of 'national home' into international law. The actual intentions of Britain, beyond yet another broad-brush statement of support for a people, are difficult to ascertain. Like other foreign policy statements before it, the declaration was careful not to bind the British government to exact outcomes. For instance, it did not compel the British government to endorse a specific, territorially defined Jewish 'national home'. Rather, it functioned as a statement of support for the existence of a 'national home' *somewhere* in the already contested land of Palestine.

Self-interest among influential players set the course of history in the Middle East. From Husayn's self-interested launching of the Arab Revolt to secure the prosperity of his lineage to the British manoeuvrings to improve their position against their wartime enemies, the Middle East was manipulated for the benefit of political elites. In this way, the early twentieth-century experience of the Middle East mirrors that of most developing regions. In the period after the First World War, local resentment of the colonial powers and the enforced status quo took on strong anti-Western overtones, and culminated in calls for national self-determination.

These trends were aided by changes in the international system that resulted from the actions of a new player on the international scene – the United States. As a result of its entry into the First World War, the United States also entered the politics of the Middle East. President Woodrow Wilson's Fourteen Points, proclaimed in 1918, signalled a new phase in international relations, with the US endorsement of self-determination made explicit. Many contemporaries believed that the new era would be defined by a sense of transparency in international relations and self-determination for the ex-Ottoman regions. Throughout the Middle East, Arabs were keen to wrest the future from external forces. They were not to succeed.

The King–Crane Commission and the Mandates

In the post-war period, the spirit of the imperial carve-up evident in the Sykes–Picot Agreement was ascendant, albeit with concessions to the idealism of the Wilsonian worldview dominant in Washington. This blending of worldviews became expressed in the Mandate system, which was confirmed on 28 June 1919. The following year, the League of Nations conference at San Remo effectively divided the remains of the Ottoman Empire among the Allied victors. In line with the intentions of the wartime negotiators, France retained its influence in Syria and the United Kingdom was assured of a continuing presence in Mesopotamia and Palestine.

The United States played an often overlooked role in the immediate post-war period. As tensions flared between the Arabs and the colonial powers, the United States suggested a fact-finding commission to investigate the popular will of the region's people. Initially envisaged as a tripartite initiative, the tour of the King–Crane Commission to the Middle East in 1919 was completed by just two US delegates because of increasing tensions between the French and the British. The commission tendered its report on 28 August 1919; it was the intention of Washington that this report would play a role in deciding the region's fate at the San Remo Conference. During this period the United States publicly renounced territorial ambitions in the region, as the report's preamble stated clearly:

> The American people – having no political ambitions in Europe or the Near East; preferring, if that were possible, to keep clear of all European, Asian, or African entanglements but nevertheless sincerely desiring that the most permanent peace and the largest results for humanity shall come out of this war – recognize that they cannot altogether avoid responsibility for just settlements among the nations following the war, and under the League of Nations.
>
> (King–Crane Commission 1919)

However, the body of the report clearly suggests that the United States could act as a major player in the region, taking on a role that would eclipse those of the colonial powers. By the time it reaches its conclusion, the report appears to be little more than a call for a US Mandate in Syria.

This controversial document, leaked to the public several years after its submission, was predominantly concerned with the French role in Syria and the local response there to the looming implementation of the Mandate system. Retrospectively, however, the report has gained attention for its clear indication of the opposition of Palestinian Arabs to the implementation of the Balfour Declaration and the establishment of the envisaged 'national home' in Palestine for the Jewish people. Overall, the King–Crane Commission found that the region's people rejected the idea of Mandate rule, and that they instead desired independent Arab rule and an immediate end to Zionist settlement. In specific relation to Zionism, the report found that, in order to preserve the Wilsonian vision of self-determination, a positive stance on Zionism should be reconsidered. It stated that, 'if the wishes of Palestine's population are to be decisive as to what is to be done with Palestine, then it is to be remembered that the non-Jewish population of Palestine – nearly nine tenths of the whole – are emphatically against the entire Zionist program' (King–Crane Commission 1919). The report acknowledged the Balfour Declaration, but stressed the caveat in it that 'nothing shall be done which may prejudice the civil and religious rights of existing non-Jewish communities' ('Balfour Declaration' 1917).

In conclusion, the report recommended that 'only a greatly reduced Zionist program be attempted by the Peace Conference, and even that, only very gradually initiated ... Jewish immigration should be definitely limited, and ... the project for making Palestine distinctly a Jewish commonwealth should be given up' (King–Crane Commission 1919).

The submission of the report caused uproar among America's allies, France and the United Kingdom, both of which were close to securing their interests through the post-war negotiations. In the end, the report's recommendations were not adopted by the US government. This prompted denouncements of the US administration for falsely raising hopes among the Arab participants in the fact-finding mission regarding their ability to avoid the imposition of Mandate rule (Helmreich 1974: 139).

The Mandates for the Middle East were officially adopted by the Allied powers at the San Remo Conference in 1920. After discussions with the United States, the Mandates were confirmed by the United Nations in 1922 and came into effect in September of the following year. The French received the Mandate for Syria, and subsequently approved the creation of Lebanon as a distinct entity. This decision was designed to assure the political dominance of the Christian majority. Under Ottoman rule, the Maronite Christians enjoyed some degree of autonomy in the region of Mount Lebanon. In the rapidly changing post-war climate, the Maronites pushed their claim under the French for a greater tract of land, which was to house a Christian majority and be independent from the predominantly Muslim area of Greater Syria. The State of Greater Lebanon was therefore created on 1 September 1920, with Beirut as its capital. However, the expansion of territory assigned for Lebanon meant that the Maronite Christian community held a thin demographic majority, so a political system was created in order to preserve the status quo. The seeds of Lebanon's future instability were sown in this period as a system of governance based on proportional sectarian representation, or confessionalism, emerged.

Box 1.2 Confessionalism

Lebanon's confessional system of governance was established in 1943 after the state gained independence. It was agreed by Lebanon's Maronite President and Sunni Muslim Prime Minister under the National Pact. Representation in the parliament and political posts were allocated on the basis of religious identity, as declared in a 1932 census conducted by the French Mandate authorities. Under this system, the role of President was allocated to the Maronite Catholics, the role of Prime Minister was allocated to Sunni Muslims and the role of Speaker of the House was allocated to Shia Muslims. The division of parliamentary seats allocated six Christian members to every five Muslims members. This structure was amended in 1990 but remains the basis of the Lebanese system of governance today.

This system was confirmed in the so-called National Pact that accompanied Lebanon's formal independence in 1943. This unwritten agreement served to institutionalize the power relationships. The Christian-to-Muslim proportion of representation in parliament was set at six to five. It was decided that the President was always to be a Maronite Christian, the Prime Minster a Sunni Muslim and the Speaker of the House (a largely ceremonial role) a Shia Muslim. The increasing politicization of the Lebanese Shia in the late twentieth century was, in part, a response to their institutionalized under-representation and marginalization. The power-sharing system crumbled in 1975 with the onset of the Lebanese Civil War and was problematically renegotiated in the Taif Accords of 1990, which reset the parliamentary representation balance at five-to-five – a proportion that many Muslims argue is still unrepresentative of the demographic make-up of Lebanon. The seeds of dissent sown in the Mandate period have therefore continued to have a profound effect on Lebanon's history. The same is true of the neighbouring Mandate for Palestine.

Post-war negotiations assured the British of their dominant position in Palestine, and the Balfour Declaration was incorporated into the wording of the British Mandate. In an acknowledgement of the increasing influence of the United States and its ideals of self-determination, the League of Nations conferred the Mandates in accordance with the Type A allocation system, which required the Mandatory powers to provide tutelage for independent statehood and not simply continue under the model of colonial exploitation. In order to provide some overarching governance, the newly established League of Nations was given the power to oversee the administration of the Mandates, and the Mandatory powers were required to report to the international body. In reality, as Leon

Carl Brown points out, the League of Nations did little to constrain the actions of the Mandatory powers. This was not surprising as the League of Nations was drawn from European powers with their own colonial traditions (Brown 1984: 250).

Tension between France and the United Kingdom over the spoils of war was a major factor in the post-war period. The United Kingdom, duty bound to honour at least some of its wartime promises, attempted to appease the Hashemites. Although London was not in any position to offer the independence discussed in the deliberations with Husayn during the early years of the war, the Hashemite sons, Abdullah and Faisal, were rewarded with positions of power in the new British Mandates. Despite these concessions, Husayn entered the post-war period an embittered and still divisive figure in regional politics. He remained in the Hijaz, where he had declared his kingship in 1916. However, he was not the only British ally in the region. Abdul-Aziz ibn Saud, the Wahhabi Emir of Riyadh, had also nurtured links with the British. Ibn Saud was a leading figure in the al-Saud tribal family, which also had political ambitions in the Arabian Peninsula (Kostiner 1995: 47). As the period of Saudi ascendency commenced in the early 1920s, the British did nothing to prevent the Hashemite fall. Al-Saud rule of the Arabian Peninsula was recognized in 1929. Kamal Salibi suggests that, compared to Husayn, the Hashemite sons and the al-Saud family were more 'practical men who were willing to give and take, and settle for what was ultimately achievable in given circumstances' (Salibi 1993: 24).

In Palestine, the League of Nations had charged the British authorities with the creation of 'self-governing institutions'. As mentioned, the Balfour Declaration was incorporated into this Mandate, thus securing a place for the notion of a Jewish 'national home' among the international legal norms that related to this region. However, the Arab population of Palestine were also to be protected under the guidelines established by the Balfour Declaration and, more explicitly, under the terms of the Mandate. In 1921 the United Kingdom designated a section of Mandatory Palestine as a protectorate under Husayn's son Abdullah. This region, the Kingdom of Transjordan, was immediately closed to Zionist settlement from Europe, an act that some Zionists criticized as a contradiction of the Balfour Declaration. The State of Jordan did not become a member of the United Nations until December 1955.

The map of the Middle East changed rapidly in the first few decades of the twentieth century. The fall of the Ottoman Empire, widely seen as a moment of opportunity for self-determination in the Arab world, led instead to the imposition of external, Western rule. Although the agency of local leaders and the intentions of the Zionist movement played a part in this process, the region was shaped primarily by the external power-brokers of the time, and all of the actors were beholden to the will of distant European powers. This is evident in the creation of states such as Jordan and Lebanon, both results of the colonial desire to appease and endorse local constituencies. The colonial masters continued through the Mandate system to act for the new Arab states on the international stage, retaining control over foreign relations and security. The formal objectives of the Mandates explicitly included the notion of a transition to sovereignty, yet the implementation of the Mandate system clearly limited exposure to statecraft and diplomacy in the Arab world. This was to become strikingly evident as the new Arab states struggled to deal with the ascendancy of Zionism in the region and the emergence of the State of Israel.

Conclusion

The historical account provided above is important for understanding the Middle East today. It is significant because it documents the establishment of existing political demarcations that continue to serve as points of reference or dissension, and because the local population continues to interpret current events through this historical prism. As a result, local views of the West are tinged with suspicion and distrust. But this has not prevented the people of the Middle East from aspiring to the same ideals of liberty and self-determination that are now celebrated in the West and enshrined in international treaties. Memories of past experiences and aspirations for a better future present the people of the region with difficult choices. Can they look to the United States and Europe to facilitate their advance towards their ideals? Or will the Great Powers betray them again? Is there hope for the Middle East to break out of recurring crises and attain a level of stability and prosperity? This book may not have the answers to these questions, but we have tried to highlight some key episodes and factors that have pushed the region into a spiral of crisis.

References

'Balfour Declaration' (1917) available at http://avalon.law.yale.edu/20th_century/balfour.asp.

Brown, Leon Carl (1984) *International Politics and the Middle East: Old Rules, Dangerous Game* (London: IBTauris).

Dershowitz, Alan (2003) *The Case for Israel* (New York: John Wiley and Sons).

Helmreich, Paul C. (1974) *From Paris to Sevres: The Partition of the Ottoman Empire at the Peace Conference of 1919–1920* (Athens, OH: Ohio State University Press).

Hughes, Matthew (1999) *Allenby and the British Strategy in the Middle East 1917–1919* (London: Frank Cass).

Huneidi, Sahar (2001) *A Broken Trust: Herbert Samuel, Zionism and the Palestinians* (London: IBTauris).

'Hussein–McMahon Correspondence' (1915–1916), available at www.mideastweb.org/mcmahon.htm.

Karsh, Efraim and Karsh, Inari (1999) *Empires of the Sand: The Struggle for Mastery in the Middle East 1789–1923* (Cambridge, MA: Harvard University Press).

King–Crane Commission (1919) 'The King–Crane Commission Report 1919', available at www.mideastweb.org.

Kostiner, Joseph (1995) 'Prologue of the Hashemite Downfall and Saudi Ascendency: A New Look at the Khurma Dispute 1917–1919', in Asher Susser and Aryeh Shmuelevitz (eds), *The Hashemites in the Modern Arab World* (London: Frank Cass).

League of Nations (1919) 'Covenant of the League of Nations 1919', available at www. mideastweb.org/leaguemand.htm.

Rogan, Eugene L. (1999) *Frontiers of the State in the Late Ottoman Empire* (Cambridge: Cambridge University Press).

Sachar, Howard (2005) *A History of the Jews in the Modern World* (New York: Vintage Books).

Salibi, Kamal (1993) *A House of Many Mansions: The History of Lebanon Reconsidered* (London: IBTauris).

Shlaim, Avi (1995) *War and Peace in the Middle East* (London: Penguin).

Wilson, Mary C. (1991) 'The Hashemites, the Arab Revolt and Arab Nationalism', in Rashid Khalidi (ed.), *The Origins of Arab Nationalism* (New York: Columbia University Press).

2   The formation of the State of Israel

Introduction

The establishment of a Jewish state in the Middle East was a turning point in twentieth-century politics. Israel was created by the determined momentum of the Zionist movement, a modern nationalist manifestation of the Jewish faith. The Zionist mission was given added urgency by the events of the Second World War and the Holocaust. The systematic murder of European Jewry under-scored the link between national self-determination and human security for many in the Jewish Diaspora community. This led to a fierce focus on the need to establish a Jewish state. The biblical land of Israel roughly corresponds to the tract of territory in which modern political Zionism sought to found that state. Since the expulsion of the Jews in biblical times, this land (known as Palestine) had been settled by Arabs of both Christian and Muslim faiths, as well as Druze, Bedouin and various other communities. In the Ottoman years, Palestine had been administered as a province of the Empire with an overwhelmingly Arab and largely Muslim population.

At the end of the Second World War, the Zionist focus on settling European refugees in Palestine became critical. It is without question that European history influenced the international community's responses to Zionism and its vision for Palestine.

In 1947 the United Nations recognized the rights of *both* the Jewish and the Arab nationalist communities in Palestine. It passed Resolution 181, which endorsed a two-state solution in the Mandate of Palestine. Israel, uti-lizing Resolution 181, made a unilateral declaration of independence in 1948. This declaration was then approved by the emergent superpowers of the United States and the Soviet Union. Almost immediately the new State of Israel was challenged by Arab states which saw this move as illegal and a usurpation of Arab lands. The War of Independence of 1948–1949 – known as al-Nakba (the Catastrophe) by the Palestinians – created 700,000 Palestinian refugees. Some Palestinians remained within the borders of the new State of Israel and took up citizenship; they are known as the Arab citizens of Israel. However, the bulk of Palestine's residents became refugees, displaced throughout the Gaza Strip, the West Bank and the neighbouring Arab states.

These people were denied the right to return to their homes in the aftermath of the 1948–1949 war.

Israel has a series of Basic Laws which function in lieu of a formal constitution (Masri 2017: 162). First among these is the assertion that Israel is a Jewish and a democratic state. The Jewish character of the State of Israel was further codified through the Law of Return (July 1950) and legislation that aimed to shore up the Jewish nature of the state. This fundamentally excludes the Palestinians, with whom Israel has engaged in a sporadic and unsuccessful 'peace process' for seventy years.

This chapter explores the Zionist movement and the establishment of Israel, the 1948–1949 conflict and the composition of the new Israeli society, with special focus on the Arab citizens, and their implications for Israel's Jewish and democratic character.

Box 2.1 The creation of Israel

In November 1947 the United Nations' General Assembly passed UN Resolution 181 which called for Palestine to be partitioned into Arab and Jewish states. The resolution designated the city of Jerusalem as a separate entity to be internationally administered. Since 1922, Palestine had been governed under British Mandate, which witnessed growing Jewish immigration. This led to tension and physical clashes between the Arab and Jewish peoples. Resolution 181 was in part designed to address this communal tension. It was also a response to the Holocaust. The Palestinian community rejected the resolution and viewed it as another colonial act, whereas the Jewish population of Palestine interpreted it as a blueprint for their future State of Israel.

The road to statehood

Israel has its origins in the Eastern European nationalist movement known as Zionism. Crystallizing around the Hungarian-born Viennese Jew Theodor Herzl, political Zionism sought to reconstitute Jewish life on a national basis. Although often understood as the father of modern Zionism, Herzl was part of a pre-existing tradition of Jewish thought. In formulating his position, he drew on previous work such as that of the Russian Jew Leo Pinsker (1821–1891), who had articulated the importance of a national territory for the Jewish people. Pinsker had initially endorsed assimilation as the most appropriate method for securing Jewish rights in Europe. However, a wave of anti-Semitic violence in the 1870s and 1880s led him to the belief that it was only within a national homeland that Jews would be safe from persecution. His 1882 text *Auto-emancipation* was controversial in European Jewish circles, because proactive political action to secure a Jewish homeland was seen by many as a challenge to traditional Jewish teachings regarding exile and redemption. Nevertheless, the

Zionist movement grew quickly in the 1880s and 1890s and soon spanned the European continent. Its early advocates were motivated by a range of concerns, depending on their national and socio-political situations. In Eastern Europe, Zionist thinkers emphasized that violent anti-Semitism in the form of pogroms and massacres was threatening the physical existence of the Jewish people. In Western Europe, the situation was more complex, with both institutionalized anti-Semitism and increasing assimilation obstructing progression while also threatening the spiritual and cultural uniqueness of the Jewish community.

An assimilated Jew, Herzl, whose 1896 publication *The Jewish State* is one of modern Zionism's foundational texts, reacted strongly against the increasing anti-Semitism in Europe. The emergence of a Jewish nationalist movement in Europe at this time is unsurprising, for nationalism was both a curse and an opportunity for the Jewish people. As European nationalisms intensified, Jews were increasingly marginalized, although simultaneously Jewish thinkers assimilated nationalist doctrines into their own worldviews. The term 'Zionism' (Zion is a biblical name for Jerusalem) was coined in 1885 to describe a movement that was first and foremost nationalist and, although fleeting consideration was given to nationalist reconstitution in places such as Western Australia and Africa, it generally focused on the right of the Jewish people to reclaim a national existence in the biblical land of Israel, which for two thousand years had been known as Palestine.

The Zionist claim to the land of Palestine is based on several key points, each given varying degrees of emphasis depending on the orientation of individual proponents. First, there is a biblical connection between the Jewish people and the land. According to Jewish tradition, God promised a geographically defined tract of land to the Jewish patriarch Abraham and his descendants. During the biblical era, there were periods of Jewish sovereignty over this land, symbolized historically by the construction of the First and Second Temples in Jerusalem, the holiest location in the Jewish tradition. With the destruction of the Second Temple in 70 CE, the period of Jewish sovereignty ended and the Roman rulers exiled the majority of Jews. The latter were scattered throughout Europe, the Middle East and Asia in what became known as the Jewish Diaspora. The region, then known as Palestine, passed under the rule of Arabs, Crusaders and, finally, the Ottomans. However, the historical and religious memory of the land, and particularly of the city of Jerusalem, became ritualized within the Jewish tradition and remained a focal point of Jewish identity. In this sense, the ideas of exile and return are central to Jewish culture. Although the vast majority of Jews resided in the Diaspora, a small contingent remained in the region of Palestine, many of them in or around Jerusalem. The latter community fluctuated drama-tically throughout history, ranging from a few thousand to nearly a quarter of a million, often due to upheavals such as the Crusades (Sachar 2005: 260–263). The political value of the continual presence of a Jewish community in Palestine was, however, significant and has been utilized throughout Israeli history as a justification for the establishment of the modern state.

Driven by the central belief that Jews could not prosper without a state, Zionism was in many ways as much a nationalist as a religious movement. Its

Birth place

leaders called for a revival of Hebrew as the national language of the Jewish people, rejecting the more commonly spoken Yiddish as the language of the ghettos of Europe. This focus on linguistics as a communal unifying force had clear nationalist overtones. Indeed, some Zionists, heavily influenced by socialism, paid little attention to the religious connotations of their movement. The very diversity of the 'Zionist' label itself is striking, as the movement was flexible enough to hold within it socialist, nationalist, religious and secular imaginings. It is important to note that Zionism was only one aspect of a diverse and dynamic Jewish political scene in Europe at the end of the nineteenth century. In some ways, the emergence of political Zionism can be seen as a consequence of the period of Jewish intellectual renewal known as the Haskalah which commenced in the 1770s. This movement sought to modernize Jewish identity, supplementing traditional religious teachings with secular traditions and European cultural norms to aid the integration and assimilation of Jewish communities in Europe. The focus on the regeneration of Hebrew as the language of the Jewish people has its roots in this period. It was from this active intellectual tradition, which collided with an increase in virulent anti-Semitism in the late nineteenth century, that thinkers began to turn to more nationalistic conceptions, such as Zionism. Even so, Zionism was not universally embraced in Jewish circles. Various organizations, such as the Bund, initially opposed the Zionist programme of national reconstitution in Palestine, advocating alternative strategies to enhance the standing of Europe's Jews.

Nevertheless, by the late 1880s, the Zionist movement, given further impetus by increasing persecution, was sending Jews to Palestine to rebuild a communal presence. Often the Jews most attracted to emigration, whether because of religious belief or political conviction, were young and single. This led to a dynamic and youthful mindset in the early Zionist community in Palestine. Moreover, the experience of persecution in Europe led many to adopt an assertive posture in relation to securing Jewish rights in Palestine. Socialism was a powerful political ideology in early twentieth-century Europe, and its influence can be identified in the central Zionist focus on working or reclaiming the land itself in Palestine. That legacy is most powerfully evident in the Kibbutz movement.

Box 2.2 Kibbutz movement

The kibbutz – meaning 'communal settlement' in Hebrew – is a socio-economic system based on the socialist principles of economic and social equality, joint ownership of property and cooperation in the fields of education, production and consumption. The founders of the kibbutz movement in Israel arrived in the early twentieth century, with the first kibbutz established in the Galilee in 1909. In Israel today, there are over 270 kibbutzim, with approximately 120,000 members, totalling around 2.8 per cent of the Israeli population. While agriculture fuelled the early kibbutz movement's economy, today it is industrial based, with agriculture, tourism and entrepreneurial businesses providing additional income.

Buoyed by the Balfour Declaration in 1917, Zionist leaders began a serious international campaign to build and legitimize a viable community in Palestine. The Western origins and mindset of the movement's founders were reflected in its political methodology, and a fundamental characteristic of Zionism became its supporters' determination to form an alliance with a powerful external actor. The movement's leaders worked in the international arena to achieve this aim. Given the realities of the international system at the time, British support was particularly valuable to Zionist ambitions.

In the aftermath of the First World War, the League of Nations had conferred upon the United Kingdom a Mandate for Palestine. This was a Type A Mandate, meaning the region was to receive interim tutelage in preparation for independent statehood. Reflecting the political mindset of the United Kingdom, a pivotal state in the League of Nations, the Balfour Declaration, with its support for a 'national home' for the Jewish people, had been incorporated into the Mandate. This had given the Zionist dream of securing a national community for Jews in the region some degree of international legitimacy. However, since the historical scattering of Jews in the Diaspora, the land of Israel had been populated by Arabs, a reality that was a serious obstacle to the Zionist dream of Jewish sovereignty in the region. Under the terms of the Mandate, the United Kingdom was theoretically required to assist the areas under its influence to develop the capacity for self-governance. Moreover, the Balfour Declaration itself had stipulated that the civil and religious rights of the non-Jewish communities were to be protected. Arguably, the British had set themselves up for failure, as the task of preparing a region for self-rule while also endorsing the existence of two competing nationalisms was fraught with difficulties. As a result, the Mandate authorities found themselves increasingly engaged in attempts to manage the disintegrating relationship between two rival and increasingly nationalist communities.

Box 2.3 The Balfour Declaration, 1917

On 2 November 1917, United Kingdom issued the Balfour Declaration, which declared its support for 'the establishment in Palestine of a national home for the Jewish people'. The declaration was issued in a letter, signed by UK's Foreign Secretary Arthur Balfour, to the president of the British Zionist Federation, Lord Rothschild. At that time, the demographics of Mandated Palestine were 90 per cent Arab and 10 per cent Jewish. While the declaration supported the establishment of a Jewish homeland, it also pledged to protect the civil and religious rights of the non-Jewish community in Mandated Palestine.

Global politics significantly influenced the United Kingdom's administration of the Mandate for Palestine. After the conclusion of the First World War, the European powers hoped to avoid further bloodshed. However, in the 1920s and 1930s further conflict appeared increasingly inevitable, and managing the Nazi threat became a growing preoccupation of the British political elite. At the same time the United Kingdom, fettered by its contradictory promises to both Arabs and Jews, found its authority seriously challenged in Palestine. Both communities intensified their commitment to their competing claims to the land and to national self-determination.

Despite the inclusion of the Balfour Declaration in the Mandate, the British were soon placed in a position in which they sought to reassess their alliances in this pivotal region. The first of many British policy volte-faces occurred in 1922 with the publication of a government White Paper that imposed economic criteria for immigration to Palestine. This edict was clearly aimed at stemming the flow of young Jews from Europe and designed to appease Arab concerns regarding the future of Palestine. Perceived by Zionists as a repudiation of Balfour's promise, the White Paper stepped away from the implicit promise of support for statehood that many Zionists had assumed would be the eventual outcome of the rather ambiguous notion of a national home: '[T]he status of all citizens of Palestine in the eyes of the law shall be Palestinian, and it has never been intended that they, or any section of them, should possess any other juridical status' ('White Paper' 1922). This document was a public acknowledgement by the British government that a communal conflict was brewing in Palestine. Members of the Zionist movement, although bitterly disappointed, remained largely committed to a diplomatic resolution through the auspices of its relationship with the United Kingdom. This policy of political adaptation was a vital component of the early Zionist movement. The European roots of the movement helped immeasurably as the Zionist leadership, familiar with Western applications of international relations, sought to develop their case for Palestine through the Western corridors of power.

Intellectually, early Zionism displayed an often naive belief that the dual claim to the land would resolve itself over time. Overall, the Arab question was minimized by many early Zionists. The Arab understanding of Zionism, and indeed Zionism's understanding of itself, was as a predominantly nationalist movement of Western origins. For the Arab population in Palestine, the Zionists were foreign settlers. Consequently, it was difficult for many Arabs not to see Zionism as just another form of colonization of Arab lands.

Palestinian political identity is one of the more complex dimensions of this political history. Issues of Western-centric and Orientalist thought need to be addressed in any exploration of Palestinian nationalism in the inter-war period. As mentioned above, Arabs, both Muslim and Christian, had resided as a majority in the land of Palestine since the Jewish expulsion in 70 CE. Some tribes, such as the Bedouin, were nomadic; some had settled in villages and pursued an agrarian lifestyle; and others had become traders and merchants. The concept of nationalism, as espoused by the Zionist movement, was an inherently Western one, spawned and nurtured in late nineteenth-century Europe and expressed in the language of European political thought. By contrast, the identity of the Arabs of Palestine can be understood as organic, premised on the relationship between the land, the tribe and the community. This highlights the complexity of a collision between different forms of political identity.

The religious dimensions of Palestine, and specifically Jerusalem, made the contrasting claims of its communities extremely complicated and difficult to resolve. Jerusalem is a holy site in the Islamic faith, surpassed in importance only by Mecca and Medina; it is the most sacred location in the Jewish tradition; and it is central to the Christian tradition. It is reasonable to view Jewish and Palestinian identities as having a symbiotic relationship throughout the pre-state period, with each reinforcing and intensifying the other. As Zionist immigration increased, Arabs began to organize politically to counter the perceived threat. This in turn caused a hardening of Zionist claims to Palestine.

This reality was acknowledged by certain members of the Zionist movement. Some, often those of a more socialist persuasion, called for a federation-style approach – a uniting of the Arab and Jewish workers – to construct a new state. Others, such as Ze'ev Jabotinsky (1880–1940), who led a splinter faction called Revisionist Zionism, demanded a more hardline response. This group broke from the broader Zionist movement over the mainstream's acceptance of the terms of the 1922 White Paper. Revisionist Zionism advocated a territorial understanding of a future Jewish state that corresponded with the biblical promise (that is, both banks of the River Jordan) and called for an immediate declaration of Jewish sovereignty over the land. Although understanding the need for Great Power patronage, this faction was dissatisfied with the diplomatic man-oeuvrings of the Zionist Executive and demanded urgent action to achieve the dream of a Jewish state in Palestine. The precursor to the modern Israeli right wing, Revisionist Zionism focused on the need for a strong military capability to secure the borders of a future state. Although Jabotinsky's line was rejected as too extreme by many within the Zionist movement, he was one of the few to acknowledge the reality of Palestinian identity and foresaw the inevitability of conflict between the two nationalisms:

> Every indigenous people will go on resisting alien settlers as long as they see the hope of ridding themselves of the danger of foreign settlement. This is how the Arabs will behave and go on behaving so long as they possess a gleam of hope of preventing 'Palestine' from becoming the Land of Israel.
>
> (Jabotinsky 1923)

As Jabotinsky predicted, the situation in Mandated Palestine grew progressively worse. The Arab Revolt of 1936–1939 demonstrated the intractable determination of the Palestinians and their increasing willingness to resist Zionist intentions. The British government, sliding towards another European conflict, struggled to resolve the situation. The 1937 Peel Commission is the most well known of a number of British fact-finding missions that attempted to extricate the United Kingdom from the tangle of the competing claims in Palestine. It recommended partition, accompanied by transfer of land and populations, as the only feasible solution. Publication of its report sparked controversy within the Zionist camp and outright condemnation from the Arab states. Yet, for most Zionist leaders, partition offered the pinnacle of the Zionist dream: the legitimacy of statehood in place of the ambiguous status of a 'national home'. Despite internal differences regarding the land allocated, the Zionist mainstream eventually accepted the plan. The Arab position was, however, unequivocal. Representing both the Palestinian Arab and wider Arab perspectives, seen in this period as indivisible, the Arab states declared the partition of Palestine unacceptable and decried the proposal as illegitimate – an example of an imperial power promising to a Western minority land that was not theirs to give. The Arab position also held that force would be used to resist any implementation of partition in Palestine. That the British proposed partition – a project they knew was fraught with uncertainty and logistical challenges – revealed their awareness that nationalism on both sides was intense and growing.

Zionism during the Second World War

As another European war loomed, the United Kingdom identified gaining Arab support against Germany as more important than maintaining its commitment to the small transnational Jewish minority. Thus, in a new White Paper published in 1939, London reversed the partition plan. Crushing the hopes of the Zionists, this document was clearly an attempt to secure Arab support on the eve of the Second World War. It asserted that Jews were to remain a minority without the security of statehood in the land of Palestine:

> It has been urged that the expression 'a national home for the Jewish people' offered a prospect that Palestine might in due course become a Jewish State or Commonwealth ... His Majesty's Government therefore now declare unequivocally that it is not part of their policy that Palestine should become a Jewish State. [It is] contrary to their obligations to the Arabs under the Mandate, as well as to the assurances which have been given to the Arab people in the past, that the Arab population of Palestine should be made the subjects of a Jewish State against their will.
>
> ('White Paper' 1939)

Despite this devastating setback, most Zionist organizations called a truce against the Mandate authorities and assisted the United Kingdom and its allies in the confrontation with Hitler's Germany. Many Jews from Palestine fought in Britain's Jewish battalions, gaining vital military experience throughout the course of the war. This strengthened an already well-developed Zionist military capability. Military organization and experience were key components of the Zionist experience in the pre-state period. For example, the Haganah had been established in 1920 as a clandestine force for the defence of Jewish settlements.

Various splinter groups also existed, such as the fiercely nationalist Irgun, the armed wing of Revisionist Zionism, which had been established in 1931 and advocated a policy of armed reprisals against both Arab and British targets. The Irgun elected to hold to the wartime truce, however, and consequently a further splinter group emerged: Lehi, also known as the Stern Gang, was established in 1940 and exhorted its followers to refuse to serve in the Jewish battalions against the Axis powers (Heller 1995: 70–76).

By the close of the Second World War, many in the Zionist community had gained significant combat experience and military training and were already organized into various efficient fighting structures. With the Allied victory came awareness of the full scale of the devastation of the Holocaust, and Zionist determination to establish a Jewish state became absolute. Outrage and desperation among international Jewry had grown steadily throughout the final years of the war, as information about the systematic destruction of Europe's Jewish communities seeped out. This can be seen in initiatives such as the Biltmore Program of 1942, developed in the United States. Given the contradictions and confusion evident in the position of the United Kingdom, it was not surprising that the Zionist community agitated against British rule as the war ended. The Haganah undertook sabotage missions and maintained its defence of Jewish settlements against Arab attacks, while marginal groups such as the Irgun adopted a more violent programme, including acts of terrorism that culminated in a bomb attack against the British authorities in their headquarters at Jerusalem's King David Hotel in 1946.

By 1947 Palestine was in a state of chaos. Zionist factions were waging a war of rebellion while Palestinian militias launched raids on Jewish settlements and British military installations. The violence had assumed the form of a cyclical, communal war of attrition, with civilians dying on either side. The United Kingdom, recovering from its own war of survival and realizing that the sun was setting on the British Empire, referred the matter of Palestine to the United Nations, which in turn formed the eleven-member Special Committee on Palestine to consider the situation. The committee interviewed Zionists, but Palestinians boycotted the process following an Arab declaration that Palestinian rights were self-evident. After deliberation, on 29 November 1947 the UN passed Resolution 181, which advocated the partition of Palestine into two states. A redevelopment of the Peel Commission's recommendation, the resolution was plagued by the same challenges and shortcomings.

The partition would have been a geographic and demographic disaster, with the security of neither community assured. The planned Jewish state included a population of approximately 500,000 Jews and just under 400,000 Arabs, so in reality it would have been binational, with Jerusalem placed under UN-administered trusteeship (Galnoor 1995: 285). Furthermore, at the time of the resolution the Zionist community owned only some of the land allotted to Jews. The structural weaknesses of the partition plan may have been deliberate, with the United Nations attempting to ensure that neither the Zionists nor the Palestinians were in a position to exercise absolute dominance over the other.

Resolution 181, like the Peel Commission before it, caused some dissent within Zionist ranks, but since it offered international recognition of statehood, they eventually accepted it. Flapan suggests that David Ben Gurion and many others in the Zionist leadership viewed acceptance as a logical and pragmatic move, citing Ben Gurion's statement that 'in the wake of the establishment of the state, we will abolish partition and expand to the whole of Palestine' (quoted in Flapan 1987: 22). This indicates that the Zionist leadership's support for partition was premised on the expectation that their territory would be expanded in the coming conflict that they viewed as inevitable, and for which they had prepared since the mid-1940s.

The Palestinians, represented by the Arab Higher Committee (which had been formed by the Arab League to address the question of Palestine), completely rejected Resolution 181. The Arab League declared the partition plan illegal and threatened force if it were implemented. The role played by non-Palestinian regional Arab actors in this period is extremely problematic, and set a precedent for the exploitation of the Palestinian political perspective. The Arab states, reacting with hyperbole and propaganda that exaggerated their ability to defeat the Zionist community in armed conflict, were hasty to take the mantle of representation from the Palestinian people. The decision to reject Resolution 181 had disastrous consequences, with the resulting conflict establishing only one of the two states envisaged by the United Nations.

Al-Nakba/Israeli War of Independence

The Zionist leadership, drawing on the legitimacy offered by the UN partition plan, declared independent statehood on 14 May 1948. This was a brave move, cautioned against by Washington and London. The level of international trepidation about the potential for conflict was so high that on the eve of Israel's independence the United States called for a ten-year cooling-off period on Resolution 181, with Palestine placed under a trusteeship administered by the United Nations or the United States itself (Tal 2004: 83). The possibility of coming so close to statehood only to see it delayed for a decade may have spurred the Zionist leadership into action. The Israeli declaration, although citing the new state's desire for peace, did not stipulate borders, an omission that has been seen as a clear indication of the leadership's awareness of the inevitability of regional conflict.

The declaration initiated a chain of events that revealed the importance of Palestine in the global order at this time. The emergent post-war superpowers – the United States and the Soviet Union – both immediately recognized the new state. When added to the UN mandate established by Resolution 181, the dual superpower endorsement effectively established the international legitimacy of the new State of Israel. The dynamics of the early Cold War period may well have prompted the superpowers' recognition. Some sources indicate that President Truman, viewed by some historians as the 'midwife' at Israel's birth, struggled with the decision to endorse Israel immediately, but domestic pressures, splits within the administration itself and intelligence indicating that

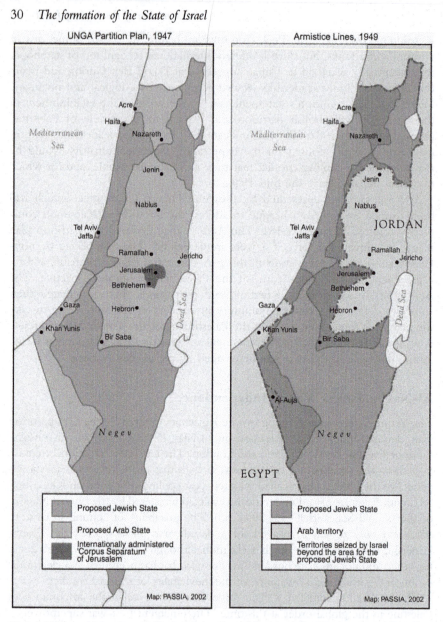

Map 4 UN partition plan, 1947; Armistice lines following the 1948 Arab–Israeli War
Source: http://passia.org/maps/view/15

the Soviet Union would do so may have forced his hand (Ganin 1979). Concerns regarding the new state's possible Soviet leanings were intensified by the socialist underpinnings of the Zionist movement. Put simply, in the context of a rapidly developing Cold War, Washington was worried about the possibility of a pro-Soviet state in the Middle East.

The day after Israel's declaration of independence a combined Arab force invaded the new state, launching the first major Arab–Israeli war. The invasion of 15 May 1948 was the culmination of the low-intensity conflict that had already engulfed Mandated Palestine. In effect, it signalled a new phase in the conflict between Arabs and Zionism as this became a regional inter-state war. With varying degrees of intensity, the two communities had been locked in a struggle over the land and its future political status since the turn of the century. While this situation was inexorably heightened by the Second World War, it is important to note that the struggle pre-dated the 1940s. More recently, the Zionist and Arab communities in Palestine had been conducting a low-intensity war since the announcement of Resolution 181 on 29 November 1947. This period of conflict between Zionist and Arab militias can be understood as a guerrilla war, with significant loss of civilian life. Palestinian fighters, ill-equipped and unable to muster a regular army, engaged in commando raids and incursions against Zionist settlements. Initially, the Zionist forces limited themselves to containment operations, but in April 1948, only a month before the declaration of independence, the inevitability of a broader regional conflict triggered a significant tactical change.

Plan Dalet, also known as Plan D, was a highly contested Zionist military operation in the pre-state period. To the Zionists, it was an aggressive defence measure aimed at securing the areas allocated to the Jews under Resolution 181 from hostile or *potentially* hostile Arab factions – a designation that often included Arab civilians. By contrast, Arabs identified Plan D as a Zionist attempt to expropriate their land. The objectives of Plan D included the capture of Arab villages, a tactic that the Haganah had not previously attempted. As David Tal (2004: 100) points out, Palestinian civilians were already fleeing the region, and the goal of Plan D to 'seize territory and impose Jewish authority' only reinforced this trend. Therefore, the roots of the Palestinian refugee crisis can be traced back to this period, prior to the May 1948 war.

Palestinian civilians were most affected by this conflict. In addition to the possibility of Zionist military action, many traditional community leaders, including landowners and the leaders of the Arab Higher Committee, fled Palestine in this period (Flapan 1979). Such losses only added to the sense of panic as the Palestinian community found itself lacking stable leadership in a time of crisis. In April 1948, a Zionist militia operation resulted in the deaths of civilians in the Arab village of Deir Yassin, a community that had signed a non-aggression pact with its Jewish neighbours. News of the killings spread quickly. Although the Zionist Executive issued a formal apology, fears of further massacres at the hands of Zionist forces clearly contributed to the exodus of Palestinians from the region and may even have precipitated the Arab states' entry into the conflict (Hogan 2001: 332). However, it is important to note that violence against civilians was perpetrated by both sides. For example, Palestinian factions responded to the massacre at Deir Yassin by killing medical staff at Hadassah Hospital on Mount Scopus.

In addition to the climate of fear and violence, some Zionist accounts have suggested that regional Arab leaders, influenced by overestimates of their own military strength, encouraged Palestinians to leave and return after the Arab armies had defeated the Zionists. There is, however, little evidence for this and it remains highly contested (Flapan 1987). The range of arguments and interpretations regarding the origins of the Palestinian exodus are complex because this period is central to the nationalist self-images of the Israeli and Palestinian communities to this day. At the time, for the Palestinian fighting forces, the impact of the population's instability was significant. By the end of April 1948, the irregular military capabilities of the Palestinian fighters had been seriously degraded, if not destroyed (Elam 2002: 52). As Rashid Khalidi (2001: 12–14) comments, by the time of the Israeli declaration on 15 May 1948, the Palestinian people were in a state of chaos: 'weak political institutions, factionalism and a lack of leadership', compounded by international ambivalence and Arab self-interest, rendered the community unable to maintain a military position against the better-organized Zionists. The collapse of local resistance to partition triggered, or perhaps forced, an Arab tactical switch from supporting the Palestinian irregular fighters to committing regular national army deployments. Thus, the Arab states, bound by pan-Arab solidarity and their own propaganda regarding their ability to defeat an emergent Jewish state, declared war on Israel. Egypt, Transjordan, Syria, Lebanon and Iraq all committed troops and regional conflict began in earnest.

The perspectives of the superpowers would have been a serious consideration for the invading Arab states. It bears remembering that the United States and the Soviet Union had both recognized Israel's declaration of independence, thus affirming their support for the existence of the new state. The potential willingness of one – or both – superpowers to intervene to protect Israel was unknown and could not have been discounted by the Arab war planners. Although the 1948 war has been understood in Israeli historiography as a struggle for survival, some modern Israeli historians suggest that, given the position of the superpowers, the Arab military campaign may have been waged with more limited objectives. Different understandings of aim and objective, as well as contradictory interpretations of events, are significant features in any study of the Arab–Israeli wars. This is especially the case in the 1948 war, which is at the heart of myth-making and the creation of national identity for both communities.

The 1948 war has traditionally been understood by Israelis as a 'David and Goliath' conflict. However, in the 1980s a number of Israeli academics who became known as the 'new historians' challenged this narrative. Although political geography lends itself to the traditional interpretation, it has been suggested that 'the Arab Goliath was suffering from extreme poverty, domestic discord and internal rivalries' (Thomas 1999: 81). The revisionist, new historian school, spearheaded by figures such as Avi Shlaim and Simha Flapan, asserted that the 'David and Goliath' paradigm was not reflected in the combat strength of the two sides in the actual fighting. Despite its much smaller size, Israel was able to match and then increase its numerical strength vis-à-vis the Arab armies. Poor leadership and coordination also affected the Arab armies, with individual states – especially Transjordan and Egypt – seeking to improve their own positions. In the field, an Arab tendency to underestimate and then over-estimate the combat strength and capabilities of the Israelis had a devastating effect on troop morale.

As the new historians contended, the morale differential on the battlefield was another important factor: Israel's soldiers were volunteers who fought fiercely for their new homeland whereas the Arab troops were predominantly conscripts who simply followed their governments' orders. The contrast in the extent of political will and military training, the impact of the apparent and public superpower support for the State of Israel and the need for the new Arab states to hold back some of their forces to protect the status quo at home all contributed to the Arab defeat. In addition, Western arms embargoes limited the ability of all parties to rearm their forces. All of the states involved received smuggled weapons from various quarters, but the Israeli forces clearly benefited from a major arms lift from Czechoslovakia (Elam 2002: 57). This arms deal, which originated in the Soviet Union, pointed to the Cold War dimension of the conflict, an inherent aspect of subsequent Arab–Israeli wars.

At the conclusion of the inter-state conflict in January 1949, the State of Israel emerged victorious. Moreover, it had gained control of significantly more territory, and attained greater strategic depth, than had been stipulated in the 1947 partition plan. Israel proudly terms this conflict its 'War of Independence'. As a baptism of fire for the new state, it occupies a central position in the national history. The memorialized experience of the war also serves as an important counter to the imagery of persecution, victimhood and devastation which many felt had characterized the Jewish experience in Europe (Waxman 2006: 29). In this sense, the new Israeli identity, secured through conflict, was seen as an assertion of collective pride and strength.

The Arabs have a very different view. They see the 1948 war as the Palestinian people's 'Catastrophe' – al-Nakba. A mirror image of the Israeli perspective, al-Nakba lies at the heart of the Palestinian account of collective history and, similar to Zionism, the focus is on exile, loss and persecution.

The Palestinian experience in this conflict can be simplified in three main outcomes. First, hundreds of thousands of people either remained in or were displaced into Gaza and the West Bank. After the decisive Israeli victory, the Gaza Strip and its 200,000 to 300,000 Palestinian residents came under the adminis-tration of Egypt. Meanwhile, the West Bank, with its population of between 400,000 and 450,000, was controlled by Transjordan. Neither state had a vested interest in encouraging Palestinian independence. Thus, the refugees became 'double victims', displaced from their land as a result of the Zionist dream of a Jewish state in Palestine and then failed by their fellow Arabs.

Second, this period saw the creation of a refugee community that fled the area of Mandated Palestine. By 1949, between 600,000 and 700,000 Palestinians were refugees (Flapan 1987: 83). Whereas the conventional Zionist discourse blames Arab leaders for the dislocation, asserting that the latter encouraged Palestinians to leave their homes, revisionist historians and Arab sources place greater weight on the implementation of Plan D and the dynamics of the conflict. The central 'cause' of the Palestinian exodus aside, the reality was that hundreds of thousands of people were displaced and herded into refugee camps along Israel's borders with Arab states. In response, the United Nations passed Resolution 302, which created an organization to manage the provision of aid and assistance – the United Nations Relief and Works Agency (UNRWA). This was controversial even at the time because the UN also created the United Nations High Commissioner for Refugees (UNHCR) in 1949. The focus of UNRWA was the provision of humanitarian and educational assistance to the Palestine refugees *until a political situation could be found*. While it was originally established with a three-year renewable mandate, to this day it – rather than the UNHCR – remains the key provider of assistance to Palestinian refugees.

UNRWA has attracted much controversy over the years. Israel, in particular, has heavily criticized the nature of its mandate, its relationship to Palestinian political groups and its role in cementing the centrality of refugeehood in the Palestinian political identity. This final point can be understood in more conceptual terms, as UNRWA's focus on service provision to assist refugees as they await the conclusion of the conflict is seen as perpetuating and entrenching a belief in the inevitability and 'right' of a return to their pre-1948 homes (Bocco 2009: 232). Much of this controversy is directly attributable to UNRWA's definition of the Palestinian refugee community:

> persons whose regular place of residence was Palestine during the period 1 June 1946 to 15 May 1948, and who lost both home and means of livelihood as a result of the 1948 conflict ... The descendants of Palestine refugee males, including adopted children, are also eligible for registration as refugees. When the Agency began operations in 1950, it was responding to the needs of about 750,000 Palestine refugees. *Today, some 5 million Palestine refugees are registered as eligible for UNRWA services.*
>
> (UNRWA 2017a; emphasis added)

In 1948, UNRWA was envisaged as an interim measure and thus no time limit was set on the inclusion of descendants. This means that, without a political resolution, the number of people entitled to UNRWA assistance grows every year. Indeed, by 2030, current projections suggest UNRWA will be providing services to over 8.5 million people (Rosen 2012: 5). Moreover, UNRWA was created with an apolitical mandate, which simply means it was not designed as an advocacy body. As a result, it cannot engage in a political process to alleviate Palestinian suffering; rather, it is reliant on international actors (which have proven manifestly inadequate in this area) to secure a resolution to the conflict. Israel's opinion of UNRWA is largely negative and it repeatedly calls for its abolition. It views the organization as a political actor and, more powerfully, an obstacle to Israel's preferred option of Palestinian resettlement in the Arab world.

Supporters of UNRWA point out that it was created to provide assistance to Palestinian refugees and their descendants until a political resolution could be found; hence, as a political solution has not been forthcoming, the organization is required to meet the basic humanitarian needs of the refugee communities. This is especially compelling in the face of humanitarian crises for Palestinians in Gaza and, more recently, Syria. Indeed, UNRWA's status has been further complicated by the contemporary refugee crisis sparked by the Syrian Civil War, which has served to de-exceptionalize the Palestinian refugee experience with negative consequences in terms of both political and financial focus (UNRWA 2017b).

The debate on UNRWA and its role in the formation of Palestinian political identity notwithstanding, the 'right of return' of the refugee community became a foundational component of Palestinian political identity, especially through the remainder of the twentieth century. In contemporary times, this focus has declined as Palestinian leaders within the West Bank have struggled to manage the differences between their own agendas and those of Gaza and the external refugee community. As the decades have unfolded, the logistics of any 'return', let alone the political viability of such a step, have become ever more complicated. The Palestinian leadership has long been accused of failing the external refugee community, a situation which came dramatically to light with the release of the 'Palestine Papers' by Arab news station al-Jazeera in 2011. The Arab states have held to the 'right of return' both as a statement of historical justice and as a political tool against Israel. In some cases, most notably Lebanon, this stance has also been required to allay domestic fears regarding mass inclusion of the Palestinian refugee community in a national political structure. In the midst of these political manoeuvres, the Palestinian refugees, especially those still housed in camps in Arab states, remain trapped, isolated and hamstrung by dire political, humanitarian, educational and economic challenges.

Box 2.4 The Palestinian Papers

In January 2011 over 1,600 confidential Palestinian documents were leaked by the al-Jazeera news agency. These records, including emails, minutes from private meetings and strategy papers, covered eleven years (1999–2010) of Palestinian negotiations with Israel and the United States. Controversial issues were highlighted in the Palestinian Papers regarding East Jerusalem, Jewish settlements, the Palestinian Authority's security cooperation with Israel and various concessions the Authority was willing to grant on Palestinian refugees and their 'right to return'.

The 'right of return' holds a formidable place in the Palestinian narrative as it speaks directly to Israel's refusal to take accountability for the consequences of the 1948 war. Conversely, strengthened by the swelling of the Palestinian refugee community to some 5 million registered refugees, Israel has been determined to resist the 'right of return' lest it destroys the Jewish aspect of the state's identity.

Third and finally, while the bulk of the Palestinian population fled the conflict in 1948–1949, some 150,000 people stayed within the territory claimed by the new state. These people became known as the Arab – or Palestinian – citizens of Israel. This community has strong familial and social ties with the Palestinian communities in Gaza and the West Bank. Arab citizens of Israel have the right to political organization and a strong history of partici- pation in Israel's electoral process. Unlike Jewish citizens of the state, they are not subject to compulsory military service. As the military network remains a backbone of the Israeli state, this means that this community is excluded from the many advantages of military service, including access to a range of veterans' networks and employment opportunities (International Crisis Group 2012). This is often presented as a factor in the comparative disadvantage experienced by Arab citizens in relation to education, healthcare, welfare and employment. Today, the Arab community within Israel constitutes roughly 20 per cent of the total population. This sizeable minority has, at differing times, proved a challenge to Israel as the state navigates the intersection between its 'Jewish' and 'democratic' identities. These tensions became more pronounced in times of heightened conflict between Israel and the Palestinian community under occupation. For example, in recent years, the Israeli government has insisted that the Palestinian Authority must recognize Israel as a specifically *Jewish* state, rather than simply a legitimate state body (Netanyahu 2009). Israel argues that this recognition is vital for the continuation of the 'peace process' with the Palestinians. The Palestinians counter that recognizing Israel as a Jewish state would entail an implicit rejection of 20 per cent of the population who identify as Arab. This demonstrates that the challenges created at the establishment of Israel in the mid-twentieth century remain central to the conflict today.

To return to the events of 1948–1949, despite its clear military victory, this was a costly war for Israel, with 1 per cent of the population, some 6,000 people, dying in the conflict (Shlaim 2000: 34). Moreover, there was no comprehensive peace: the key issues of borders and refugees remained unresolved in 1949, as they do even today. Israel insisted that its responsibility was first and foremost to the resettlement of Jewish refugees from the Holocaust and the Second World War. In addition to this challenge, hundreds of thousands of Jews who had lived throughout the Arab world poured into Israel as a result of increased persecution in the aftermath of the establishment of the Jewish state. In terms of nation-building, Israel's creation of a cohesive national identity from the disparate mix of local Jewish people, Jews from throughout the Arab world, European refugees and Holocaust survivors was nothing short of remarkable. The role of repeated state-to-state conflicts in forging this identity should not be underestimated.

Meanwhile, in the aftermath of the 1948 war, the Arab states called for resettlement of the Palestinians who had been displaced during the conflict. The Arab League, still representing the Palestinian people, forced the pan- Arab position on the refugees: return or compensation, and the acknowl- edgement of Israel liability. Israel, for its part, argued that the Arabs were the aggressors in the conflict. This dynamic did nothing to alleviate political uncertainty among the refugees.

Conclusion

The 1948 Arab–Israeli War is one of the most controversial wars in modern history. The centrality of this conflict in the formulation of a cohesive national identity for both Israelis and Palestinians is undeniable. For the Arab citizens of Israel, a differing set of challenges are evident as they navigate their place within a state that is premised on its Jewish identity. For Israel and the Palestinians, the oppositional narratives forged in the conflict have served to perpetuate tensions and complicate any form of political settlement between what have become two very unequal parties. Much has changed since 1947 – from the relative parity of UN Resolution 181, with its call for two states within Palestine, to the contemporary situation of an empowered Israeli state and a 'cantonized' and dismembered Palestine.

In both symbolic and literal terms, the refugee crisis sparked by the 1948 war remains central to the Arab–Israeli dispute, at least in terms of the rhetoric of international players. As Flapan (1979: 301) asserted long ago, resolution of this key point, historically speaking, has been complicated by the fact that the two national narratives are 'diametrically opposed and equally inadequate'. The traditional Israeli discourse has asserted a lack of Israeli culpability and focused on the supposed role of the Arab leaderships, whereas the Arab historiography glosses over the concept of self-flight and the internal dissolution of political structures and focuses instead on forced expulsion. Unfortunately, both of these interpretations, which leave little room for reconciliation, remain influential in the political and public mind and have been entrenched by decades of conflict and occupation. For the Palestinians, caught up in a conflict and then a political game of blame attribution, the events of this period were an unmitigated disaster, with even the unsatisfactory promise of partition lost. For Israel, its establishment was assured with the military victory, but the peace that its founders called for in the declaration of statehood proved elusive.

References

Bocco, R. (2009) 'UNRWA and the Palestinian Refugees: A History within a History', *Refugee Studies Quarterly*, Vol. 28, No 2/3, pp. 229–252.

Elam, Yigal (2002) 'On the Myth of the Few against the Many', *Palestine–Israel Journal of Politics, Economics and Culture*, Vol. 9, No. 4, pp. 50–57.

Flapan, Simha (1979) *Zionism and the Palestinians* (London: Croom Helm).

Flapan, Simha (1987) *The Birth of Israel: Myths and Realities* (New York: Pantheon Books).

Galnoor, Itzhak (1995) *The Partition of Palestine: Decision Crossroads in the Zionist Movement* (Albany: State University of New York Press).

Ganin, Zvi (1979) *Truman, American Jewry and Israel 1945–1948* (New York: Holmes & Meier).

Heller, Joseph (1995) *The Stern Gang: Ideology, Politics and Terror 1940–1949* (London: Frank Cass).

Hogan, Matthew (2001) 'The 1948 Massacre at Deir Yassin Revisited', *Historian*, Vol. 63, No. 2, pp. 309–333.

International Crisis Group (2012) 'Report on Israel's Arab Minority and the Israeli–Palestinian Conflict', *Journal of Palestine Studies*, Vol. 41, No. 4, pp. 185–191.

Jabotinsky, Ze'ev (1923) 'The Iron Wall', available at www.mideastweb.org/ironwall.htm.

Khalidi, Rashid (2001) 'The Palestinians and 1948: The Underlying Causes of Failure', in Eugene Rogan and Avi Shlaim (eds), *The War for Palestine: Rewriting the History of 1948* (Cambridge: Cambridge University Press).

Masri, Mazen (2017) *The Dynamics of Exclusionary Constitutionalism: Israel as a Jewish and Democratic State* (Oxford: Bloomsbury).

Netanyahu, Benjamin (2009) 'Address by PM Netanyahu at Bar-Ilan University', 14 June, available at http://mfa.gov.il/MFA/PressRoom/2009/Pages/Address_PM_Netanyahu_Bar-Ilan_University_14-Jun-2009.aspx.

Rosen, Steven J. (2012) 'Why a Special Issue on UNRWA?', *Middle East Quarterly*, Vol. 19, No. 4, pp. 412–437.

Sachar, Howard (2005) *A History of the Jews in the Modern World* (New York: Vintage).

Shlaim, Avi (2000) *The Iron Wall: Israel and the Arab World* (London: Penguin).

Tal, David (2004) *War in Palestine 1948: Strategy and Diplomacy* (London: Routledge).

Thomas, Baylis (1999) *How Israel Was Won: A Concise History of the Arab–Israeli Conflict* (Lanham, MD: Lexington Books).

United Nations Relief and Works Agency (UNRWA) (2017a) 'Palestinian Refugees', available at www.unrwa.org/palestine-refugees.

United Nations Relief and Works Agency (UNRWA) (2017b) 'Syria Emergency Appeal for 2017', available at www.unrwa.org/resources/emergency-appeals/syria-emergency-appeal-2017.

Vital, David (1982) *Zionism: The Formative Years* (Oxford: Clarendon Press).

Vital, David (1987) *Zionism: The Crucial Phase* (Oxford: Clarendon Press).

Waxman, Dov (2006) *The Pursuit of Peace and the Crisis of Israeli Identity: Defending/Defining* (New York: Palgrave).

'White Paper' (1922), available at www.mideastweb.org/1922wp.htm.

'White Paper' (1939), available at www.mideastweb.org/1939.htm.

3 The Arab–Israeli wars

Introduction

The establishment of Israel in 1948 fundamentally altered the political balance of the Middle East. The creation, and early military victories, of a Jewish state in the Muslim-dominated region presented new challenges and opportunities for local and international players alike. In some ways, Israel's creation sharpened regional identities as the Arab states, also newly established, were forced to respond to the new Israeli presence from a political, ideological and religious viewpoint. From the end of the 1948 conflict, Israel commenced a period of intense nation-building as it sought to cement a new national identity which both drew from and rejected previous notions of Jewishness which were shrouded in the legacy of European anti-Semitism and the Holocaust. This, along with the dynamics of regional politics, led to a militarization of identity. In turn, this gave symbiotic focus to the emergent discourses of Arab national and transnational political identities.

As Israel found its feet in the Middle East its identity became intrinsically linked to conflict and, increasingly, isolation. Throughout the twentieth century and beyond, Israel fought a series of conventional wars with its neighbours. Despite continual references to primordial conflict and religious imperatives, these wars were fought for overtly temporal reasons: territory, national legitimization, security, access to resources and political ambition. These root causes of conflict are evident throughout Arab–Israeli history.

The establishment of Israel and prospects of conflict with the Arab states offered important new opportunities for regional influence to the two super-powers as the Cold War took hold post-1945. As demonstrated, initially both the Soviet Union and the United States were keen to capitalize on this new player in the region. However, as the decades unfolded, Israel became ever more closely entwined with the United States, while the Arab states moved into the Soviet sphere of influence. This proved to be a drawback for Palestinian political ambitions as the close of the Cold War saw the emergence of a unipolar superpower with a distinct pro-Israel orientation.

This chapter explores Israel's major conflicts. It will first examine the Six-Day War of 1967 and the transformative impact this had on the region and superpower dynamics. It will then explore the Yom Kippur/Ramadan conflict of 1973, which led to the politicization of the oil trade and acceleration of the Israeli settlements in the Palestinian Occupied Territories. Next, it will examine the Palestine Liberation Movement's (PLO's) resistance against Israel and how this led the latter to invade and occupy southern Lebanon in the early 1980s. It will then investigate the antagonistic relationship between Israel and the Lebanese Islamist group Hezbollah, which solidified in response to this occupation. Finally, the chapter will explore the ongoing hostilities between Israel and Hezbollah, which erupted into all-out war in July 2006. This comprehensive analysis will also shed light on the development of Israel's close alliance with the United States in the post-war period and beyond.

The Six-Day War, 1967

The 1950s was a decade of intense international interest in the Middle East. The colonial period was coming to a close, which provided unprecedented opportunities for new international influences. This trend was exemplified in the 1956 Suez Crisis, which saw the old guard of the United Kingdom and France firmly supplanted by the principal Cold War players of the United States and the Soviet Union. While much attention is given to superpower interest in the region, it is important to note that this period also saw a willingness among regional actors, notably Egypt and Israel, to engage within the Cold War paradigm to secure and enhance their own interests.

Box 3.1 The Suez War, 1956

In a controversial move, the Egyptian President, Gamal Abdel Nasser, nationalized the Suez Canal in 1956. The canal is a lifeline in the largely landlocked Middle East. Built by Egyptian labour in the late 1880s, it had historically been under the control of a French and English consortium, the Suez Canal Company. Nasser's decision to nationalize it had two consequences: it deprived France and the United Kingdom of profits, and Israel of waterway access. This infuriated the colonial powers, leading to the formation of an alliance of convenience. A secret tripartite operation, codenamed Operation Musketeer, was launched by Israel, France and the United Kingdom, and the canal was seized by a combined military force on 29 October 1956. Although the assault was a military success, it was a political disaster for the allied forces. Both the United States and the Soviet Union condemned the tripartite aggression and applied political and economic pressure against Israel, France and the UK to withdraw. Between 2,500 and 3,500 people, mainly Egyptians, had been killed by the war's conclusion in March 1957. In the aftermath of the Suez War, Nasser's prestige soared inside Egypt and the rest of the Arab world.

As the 1960s unfolded, President Nasser's Egypt became increasingly entrenched in the Soviet camp. In the wider Arab world, the idea of pan-Arab nationalism, or pan-Arabism (explored in detail in Chapter 6), became increasingly prominent. Influenced by socialism, pan-Arabism sought to unify the whole Arab world and focused on the ideal of a shared Arab destiny. The socialist flavour of this movement and its Soviet orientation led to a frosty reception from the United States. By the mid-1960s, Nasser was at the peak of his power and his role as undisputed leader of the Arab world heightened his sense of Egypt's invincibility. Moreover, a central tenet of pan-Arab nationalism focused on Israel as the chief enemy of the Arab states. In this sense, Nasser sought to facilitate greater unification of the Arab states in the face of a common threat.

Regional tensions had been escalating throughout the decade, with Israel and its Arab neighbours engaging in border skirmishes and low-level hostilities. In May 1967, the situation reached a climax as Nasser ordered the withdrawal of the United Nations Emergency Forces that had provided a security buffer between Israel and Egypt since 1957 (Krasno 2004: 232). Then, on 22 May, Egypt declared its intention to blockade Israeli goods from shipment through the Strait of Tiran. Simultaneously, Syria increased its border clashes with Israel in the north, and Arab rhetoric regarding the imminent destruction of Israel intensified. Israel saw all of these acts as ominous. From its perspective, the unfolding situation had all the hallmarks of an imminent two-front conflict.

Box 3.2 The Strait of Tiran

The Strait of Tiran is a six-kilometre-wide channel between Egypt and Tiran Island that separates the Gulf of Aqaba from the Red Sea. It is of great strategic importance because it gives large ships access to ports in Israel and Jordan.

In late May, Egypt moved tanks into the Sinai, complete with press coverage that was transmitted throughout the Arab world. As a result, Israel saw itself as increasingly besieged. In Tel Aviv, the political and military leadership reacted to the combination of confrontational Arab rhetoric, the removal of UN troops and the closure of the waterway with increasing unease. Many academics have suggested that Egyptian moves in this period were mere posturing, aimed at boosting its leaders' prestige among the domestic and broader Arab audience, rather than a clear threat to Israel (Mutawi 2002: 94). Israel, however, could not afford to assume it was in no danger. Moreover, when faced with such provocation, Israeli planners may well have seen a strategic opportunity to alter the state's borders and thus address long-standing concerns regarding Israeli security through the Tel Aviv corridor while also gaining access to, and control over, water resources in the Jordan Valley. Egypt then inflamed the situation by signing mutual defence pacts with other Arab states (Jordan on 30 May 1967 and Iraq on 4 June 1967). Despite calls for caution from the United States, Israeli leaders viewed conflict as imminent and acted. Concerned that Israel would not survive an Arab first strike or a protracted war, Tel Aviv launched a pre-emptive assault. On 5 June 1967, conflict began with the much-vaunted Operation Focus, in which Israel deployed nearly its entire air force in a surprise strike on Nasser's airports. A mere six days later Israel had accomplished one of the twentieth century's most stunning military victories – a victory that would dramatically alter the political landscape of the Middle East.

At the close of the Six-Day War, Israel had captured the Arab Palestinian territories of the West Bank (including Jerusalem) and Gaza, Egypt's Sinai and Syria's Golan Heights. Over a million Palestinians living in the West Bank and Gaza were forced to accept Israeli military occupation. This reality moved them even further from the intent of UN Resolution 181 and its vison of a two-state solution. The territorial gains increased Israel's size by six times. Israel presented this as an unintended consequence of a war of anticipatory self-defence. This interpretation, however, was challenged in Arab and Muslim societies, which saw the occupations as evidence of Israel's expansionism.

Box 3.3 The Golan Heights

The Golan Heights is an elevated landmass between Syria and Israel. It became Syrian territory in 1941, but was occupied by the Israeli Defence Forces (IDF) in the 1967 war. Because of its strategic importance, the Golan has been a point of contention among regional states since 1948. The UN established a buffer zone around it after the 1973 conflict, but Israel uni-laterally annexed the parts of the Golan under its control in 1981. This annexation is viewed as illegal by many in the region and the wider interna-tional community, including the UN Security Council. At various times, including in 2000 and 2007, Israel has raised the future of the Golan Heights in an attempt to draw Syria to the negotiating table.

Israeli intelligence played a significant role in this important conflict and was henceforth relied upon as a central component of Israel's military doctrine. The relative ambivalence of the international community assisted the Israeli military planners, who found it easy to convince the Israeli public that they faced a moment of existential crisis. In the words of Abba Eban (1988: 22), Israelis perceived 1967 in stark terms: 'defend the national existence or lose it for all time'. Decisive military leadership was also of great importance. Despite the regional awareness of imminent conflict, Arab leaders, especially Nasser, appeared unprepared for an Israeli attack and responded to the outbreak of war in a confused and disorganized manner, which served to enhance the Israeli position.

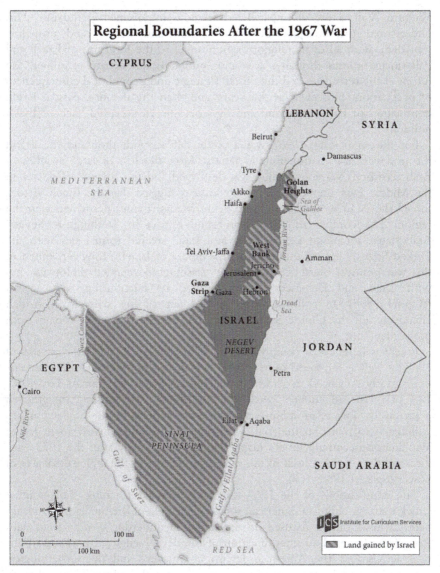

Map 5 Post-1967 borders
Source: www.icsresources.org/maps

One of the most important political outcomes of the war was Israel's capture of Jerusalem. Most sources indicate that this objective did not feature strongly in the Israeli Defence Force's war plans. However, when Jordan entered the conflict Israel was presented with an opportunity to claim the city. Once in control of Jerusalem, the Israelis immediately moved to shore up their control of this symbolic site, razing Palestinian houses to create a plaza around the

Western Wall, a site of unparalleled religious importance in Judaism. This underscored the interplay between religion and politics and propelled Jerusalem, with all of its religious significance, to the forefront of Israeli and Palestinian politics. Initially, a vibrant public Israeli debate examined the future of the territories and the moral, strategic and geopolitical consequences of occupation. However, as the years, and then the decades, passed, Israeli domination of Palestinian land and lives became an accepted 'fact' of Israeli politics.

For the Arab states, 1967 was a costly defeat, with thousands dead and the pride of Arab nationalism in tatters. After the loss of large swathes of Arab territory, Nasser's prestige was destroyed and the balance of power in the Middle East altered. Many Arab sources suggest that the Israeli victory forced the Arab world belatedly to acknowledge Israel's permanence in the region. The conflict also had a profound impact in Washington. Several Arab states, including Egypt, Syria and Iraq, severed formal ties with the United States, alleging interference in support of Israel. However, much of this was political bluster, as in reality Washington retained diplomatic ties with Cairo and Damascus and intensified its relationship with Jordan (Raphel 1988). In contrast, Moscow did cut all ties with Israel, which effectively left the United States as the only external power in contact with both sides.

Israel's willingness to comply with calls for restraint in the early months of 1967, as well as the speed of its victory, which had not required US intervention, greatly enhanced its stature in the United States (Bar-Siman-Tov 1987: 143–144). In subsequent years, the Israeli–US relationship strengthened dramatically. This relationship was given extra impetus by the Soviet Union's willingness to replenish the Arab war arsenal. The Soviet involvement led to Washington becoming Israel's major supplier, particularly after the 1973 conflict, and thus assuring itself of the role of moderator in the regional balance of power (Spiegel 1988: 118).

The ramifications of the 1967 war have been far reaching. This conflict struck a strong chord in American society. The role of the media is significant here, as news outlets focused on the supposed underdog's 'miraculous' victory. This triggered an intensification of the deeply engaged pride and political activism of the American Jewish community and the eschatological assumptions of Christian factions which called for the return of Jerusalem to Jewish control. These factors led to a significant increase in Israel's public profile in the United States. However, 1967 also had a polarizing effect in the United States. The conservatives rallied to Israel's cause, but the Palestinian national movement attracted support from US liberals (although not to the same levels seen in Europe).

For the Palestinians, 1967 was an unmitigated disaster. Having endured repressive Arab rule in the enclaves of Gaza and the West Bank, they were now subjected to Israeli military occupation. The seizure of Jerusalem was a distinct blow. For Palestinian Muslims, who make up 98 per cent of the Palestinian population, the city is of great religious significance. It is home to the al-Aqsa Mosque, considered the third-holiest religious site in Islam. The loss of Jerusalem to a newly established non-Muslim power was a cause of devastation not only for Palestinians but for the Muslim community as a whole. In the immediate aftermath of the conflict, Israel moved to alter the status of the city to incorporate it into the Jewish state, an act which was condemned in the UN General Assembly (Resolution 2253). Despite this, Jerusalem was effectively annexed by the Israeli state. Israel's control over the city increased with the subsequent – bipartisan – programmes of Israeli settlement, which encircled Jerusalem and effectively excised it from the West Bank. The changed status of Jerusalem was therefore a key outcome of 1967 and it remains at the forefront of the conflict to this day.

At the time, the effects of this military defeat were extensive for Palestinian political activism. An increasingly assertive national movement began to move away from a unified 'Arab' position and to claim independence in the struggle against Israel. The Palestine Liberation Organization (PLO) had been established by Nasser in 1964 largely as a token gesture of Arab political support for the Palestinian cause. Following the disaster of 1967, though, the PLO became more aggressive in its approach. In many ways, its leaders indigenized the responsibility for the liberation of Palestine. In terms of political psychology, it is interesting to note the resonance of similar themes in the Arab and Israeli camps. After decades of humiliating battlefield defeats, the concept of the 'new Arab man' became embodied in the imagery of the determined Palestinian fighter (Sinora 1988). The notion of the revolutionary Palestinian, tired of waiting for distant Arab deliverance and willing to rise up against dispossession, had emotive parallels with the concept of the 'new Jew', triumphing after 'centuries of powerlessness, persecution and humiliation' (Shlaim 2001: 79), a concept that had been forged on the battlefields of 1948. This symbiotic trend is often seen in Israeli and Palestinian narratives, which have hardened and sharpened in a responsive fashion throughout the conflict.

Box 3.4 The PLO

The Palestine Liberation Organization (PLO) was established by the Arab League in 1964 after a proposal from Egypt's President Nasser. The organization was conceived as a body dedicated to the cause of Palestinian national liberation and drew strongly on the structure of the Fatah group. A secular–nationalist organization, the PLO was most closely associated with Yasser Arafat. It became more militant as a result of the crushing Arab defeat in 1967, and its leaders began to pursue a dedicated agenda of agitation, including the use of military tactics against Israel. Its leadership was exiled from the Middle East in the early 1980s and was based in Tunis until it was reconstituted as the Palestinian Authority under the Oslo Peace Accords in 1993.

Box 3.5 Fatah

The Fatah movement was established by Palestinians working in Kuwait and the Gulf states in the late 1950s. The group was committed to the liberation of Palestine and moved away from the broader pan-Arab movement to focus on national self-determination. Yasser Arafat was a key force in the establishment of Fatah, which became the dominant faction in the PLO. Over the course of its history, Fatah has produced numerous armed splinter groups. In the Oslo Accords of 1993, the Fatah leadership transformed into the Palestinian Authority. HAMAS defeated Fatah in the 2006 elections, and the June 2007 split between the two organizations has left Fatah as the recognized leadership in the West Bank.

On 22 November 1967, the UN Security Council adopted Resolution 242 in response to the Six-Day War. This controversial document led to vigorous debate, and to this day it remains unimplemented. It called for 'withdrawal of Israeli armed forces from territories occupied in the recent conflict'. However, the territories from which Israel was expected to withdraw were not explicitly stipulated, leaving room for varied interpretations. The resolution also linked the question of withdrawal to other matters arising from the conflict, calling for

> termination of all claims or states of belligerency and respect for and acknowledgement of the sovereignty, territorial integrity and political independence of every State in the area and their right to live in peace within secure and recognized boundaries free from threats or acts of force while affirming the need for a just settlement for the refugee problem.
>
> (United Nations Security Council 1967)

To the Arab states, this resolution was intended to enforce a complete withdrawal of Israel from the territories it had seized during the war. However, to Israel and its increasingly close ally the United States, the call for withdrawal was to be read in conjunction with the assertion of the right of a state to security. As US President Lyndon Johnson affirmed on 10 September 1968:

> We are not the ones to say where other nations should draw lines between them that will assure each the greatest security. It is clear, however, that a return to the situation of 4 June 1967 will not bring peace. There must be secure and there must be recognized borders. Some such lines must be agreed to by the neighbors involved.
>
> (Cited in Rostow 1975: 284)

The difficulties associated with achieving a resolution's safe passage through the Security Council were evident in this situation, and the result was a resolution that did not meaningfully compel Israel to return its wartime acquisitions. The importance of this document should not be underestimated as it still forms an integral part of peace negotiations today. On the one hand, supporters of the Palestinians consider Israel's withdrawal from the Occupied Territories as the document's primary focus. On the other hand, Israeli and US discourses continue to link the question of withdrawal to Israel's right to security. These two perspectives conflict, with the notion of Palestinian resistance imbued by Israel's refusal to withdraw, and Israel's refusal to withdraw grounded in continued Palestinian resistance that undermines Israeli security. This mutually reinforcing cycle has been a central feature of the Israeli–Palestinian conflict since 1967 and continues to obstruct all conflict resolution strategies between the two peoples. Furthermore, the continued international determination to focus on Resolution 242 as a basis for negotiation is open to significant critique, especially as the reality of Israeli and Palestinian presence on the land has changed dramatically since 1967. Since this time, Israeli governments of both right- and left-wing orientations have undertaken significant state-sponsored settlement of Palestinian land by Israeli citizens. Indeed, Israeli control of many Palestinian areas in the slated two-state solution is so entrenched that the international determination to retain Resolution 242 as a point of reference for the peace process could be described as an obstacle to peace in itself.

The aftermath of 1967 also marked an ideological turning point in the Arab–Israeli conflict. With this victory, minority elements in Israel, the Arab world and even the United States increasingly exhibited a tendency to view events in the Middle East through the paradigm of divine intervention. For the Muslim world, 1967 marked a moment of intense reassessment, with some organizations positing that the Middle East's acceptance of Western ideologies, such as secular nationalism, was to blame for the crushing losses on the battlefield. An important manifestation of this ideological re-evaluation was the emergence and consolidation of political Islam, a movement that is explored in Chapter 4. Underscoring the symbiotic elements of the conflict, a similar trend occurred within Israel, where some individuals construed the victory as a divine reward for the Jewish people (Rubenstein 1984: 98–126). The re-establishment of the Jewish people's sovereignty in the land of Israel is, in some Christian interpretations a precondition for the Second Coming. Consequently, this trend was mirrored in the United States, where right-wing Christians began to expound the theory that Israel was on a divinely sanctioned and directed path. This potent intertwining of religion and politics served to inflame the situation on the ground.

Egypt was a major loser in the 1967 war and refused to accept the loss of territory; instead, it engaged in a 'war of attrition'. Sporadic skirmishes broke out between Egypt and Israel between 1968 and 1970 with no clear victor. The major outcome of these hostilities was the increasingly close relationship between Egypt and the Soviet Union, which provided high-tech equipment such as surface-to-air missiles (SAM-3s) and MiG-21 fighters, complete with Soviet crew, to assist Egypt in its attacks on Israel (Bregman 2003: 132). The deepening Soviet–Egyptian ties were an important factor in the strengthening of Israeli–US relations. But Israel was not content to rely on international alliances for security and sought self-sufficiency in its national defence doctrine. Hence, Tel Aviv forged ahead with its own defence programme in this period and subsequently refused to sign the Nuclear Non-Proliferation Treaty (NPT) of 1968. This raised the spectre of nuclear conflict in the region. It also triggered the first clear 'double standard' in US foreign policy as it related to the Arab–Israeli conflict. Washington demanded explanations for Israel's refusal to sign the treaty, but was satisfied with the response that Israel would not be the first to introduce nuclear weapons to the region: that is, that the state would not publicly declare or test nuclear weapons unless another state did so first. From the Arab perspective (and in years to come the Iranian perspective), Israel received special treatment and the United States turned a blind eye to a flagrant breach of international law.

The Yom Kippur/Ramadan War, 1973

In the aftermath of the 1967 conflict, a meeting of the Arab League which became known as the Khartoum Conference laid out a clear stance on Israel: 'no peace, no recognition, no negotiation'. Determined to break the status quo established in the aftermath of 1967, Arab leaders began planning a surprise attack. In this period, Israel relied on the notion of *active deterrence*, which is best understood as the belief that superior military capacity will deter attack. This perception was enhanced by the reality of Israel's military control over substantial tracts of Palestinian land, meaning the Israeli forces had an effective 'early warning' system regarding Arab troop movements. Moreover, Arab rhetoric, which was ramped up against Israel in both 1971 and 1972 did not lead to an attack, which may have contributed to Israel's sense of security in this period. The dynamics of the Cold War also influenced Israeli planners in their assessment of Egyptian strategy. The Israelis relied on a strategy known as the Conception. This referred to Israeli assumptions that Egypt would not launch a full-scale attack against the Jewish state without a significant material increase in Soviet support. (Bregman 2000: 74), In the context of détente, Israel knew that the Soviet Union was unwilling to supply high-calibre weaponry to an Arab client for use against a state that was closely aligned with Washington. However, while the overall Israeli interpretation of Egyptian military planning may have been correct, Sadat still planned a 'limited war' to break the status quo.

On Yom Kippur, the Jewish Day of Atonement, a combined 'surprise' assault by Egypt and Syria penetrated Israel's borders. The Arab objective in this conflict was to recapture territory lost in the 1967 conflict, namely the Golan Heights and the Sinai Peninsula. In addition to the obvious link between territory and national pride, both tracts of land held strategic value for the Arab states and Israel. Moreover, should the attack fail to recapture the lands in question, Egypt and Syria hoped to provoke an international crisis that would force Israel to the negotiating table. Israeli academic Uri Bar-Joseph (2005, 2008), among other modern scholars, has tested the accepted post-war consensus that an Israeli intelligence failure was the cause of the state's early defeats in this conflict. He found that Israeli planners were in fact well aware of Arab troop movements in the days leading up to the assault, and a mixture of overconfidence, flaws in the IDF's war planning and tensions in the military and political leadership of the day may have had a greater impact on the course of the conflict (Bar-Joseph 2008: 511–514). In addition, a misplaced belief in Israeli political circles that the Arab states were willing to accept the status quo indefinitely may have contributed to Israel's failure to predict the assault. So, although the Israeli government knew what was happening in the hours before 2 p.m. on 6 October 1973, a combination of indecisive leadership, poor coordination and possibly a simple lack of time prevented an effective early defence. Arab advances in war planning also aided the momentum of the initial attack. After a tense beginning, however, the Israeli Defence Force (IDF) first regained parity on the field and then secured another Israeli victory, albeit on a level far removed from the stunning outcome of 1967.

The events of 1973 forced Israel into a sober reassessment of its position in both political and military terms. The war had been comparatively costly in terms of Israeli lives, and the sense of invincibility which had permeated Israeli politics since 1967 had been compromised. Despite this, Israel was well served by some of the outcomes of this conflict. For instance, the Yom Kippur War helped consolidate Israel's valuable international alliances. The United States could not allow its most significant regional ally to be overwhelmed by a coalition of Soviet-backed states. Despite initial hesitation, Washington launched a massive airlift of military hardware on 13 October 1973, known as Operation Nickle Grass. This provided 22,395 tonnes of military hardware to Israel, a full resupply of its losses in the conflict. While only 9,000 tonnes arrived before the ceasefire in 1973, the symbolism of this policy was significant as it explicitly underscored the depth of the Israeli–US alliance. Indeed, Operation Nickle Grass can be seen as a turning point in US engagement in the Arab–Israeli conflict, a moment with far-reaching consequences for all involved. The United States was forced into action as, in the first few days of the war, Israel's 'capacity for self-defence' was seriously tested. To capitalize on this, the Soviet Union kept up its military aid to Egypt and Syria (Bar-Siman-Tov 1987: 205–207).

Given the dynamics on the ground, the United States saw little option but to support Israel's defence and preserve the post-1967 status quo. The influential US Secretary of State Henry Kissinger admitted as much when he observed that the US policy was largely reduced to 'support for Israel and for the status quo' (Shlaim 2000: 321). The Israelis had begun to turn the tide of this conflict even before the US airlift, and the resupply of arms then allowed them to recover from their initial setbacks and gain another decisive victory. However, the political outcomes were more complex, with Kissinger calling the end of the war a 'strategic defeat' for Israel (Bar-Siman-Tov 1987: 206). The initial delay of military aid hurt Israel and implied Washington's willingness to formulate policy to ensure its role vis-à-vis the Arabs. Yet the eventual decision to resupply the Israeli arsenal triggered Arab perceptions that Washington had directly intervened to protect Israel from imminent disaster. In this sense, the 1973 conflict altered the playing field between Israel and the Arab world as the 'special relationship' between Israel and the United States was now a fact of regional politics. The Arab world, faced with this reality, changed its strategy and turned to another form of pressure to achieve its territorial aims.

The 1973 war led to the politicization of the oil trade. Led by Saudi Arabia, the Organization of Petroleum Exporting Countries (OPEC) placed an embargo on the West and Israel. This was the first time that oil was used as a geostrategic tool. Implicit self-confidence governed this bold step. Arab leaders must have been pondering the extent to which economic muscle might achieve results where brute force had repeatedly failed. But their plan was too ambitious and its consequences were serious. Israel was not prepared to give up territory captured on the battlefield because of economic imperatives and Washington was unwilling to force Israel's hand. If the objective of the oil embargo was to force an Israeli withdrawal from the territories occupied in 1967, the strategy was a complete failure. But it did have an unintended – and extremely negative – consequence for the Arab world. It demonstrated to the US administration that the Arab states would go to political and economic extremes to pursue their objectives, a perspective that increasingly situated Israel as Washington's leading partner in the region. Thus, the oil embargo, which was designed and implemented in a bid to affect Israel's regional behaviour, merely forced Israel and the United States closer together.

The embargo caused major price increases and contributed to a worldwide energy crisis. It also confirmed the economic and strategic importance of the Middle East to US policy-makers. It was lifted in March 1974, but the ripple effects continued to generate serious global economic impacts, precipitating the economic slump of 1974. In addition, the Gulf states emerged as stronger regional power-brokers, having enriched themselves through the embargo process. In turn, US strategy, while now coalesced around Israel, moved to anchor the Arab regimes of OPEC more firmly within Washington's sphere of influence. In this sense, American rhetoric regarding democratization and human rights took a back seat to building relationships with the undemocratic and repressive Arab regimes which controlled energy resources. Following the events of 1973–1974, US policy was increasingly designed to ensure that the United States was protected from further instances of economic warfare, such as the oil embargo.

In Israel, the trend towards a theologically derived interpretation of events was strengthened by the close call of 1973. The religious settler movement, led by the ultra-nationalist Gush Emunim, solidified in this period (Sprinzak 1999). The Likud Party was also formed as elements within Israeli society took a more hardline approach towards the need to populate the Occupied Territories with Israeli citizens. This was justified on either theological or geostrategic grounds.

Meanwhile, despite the reality of another military defeat, the events of 1973 were viewed within the Arab world as a restoration, or at least a partial restoration, of Arab pride. Indeed, if viewed as a 'limited war' that was undertaken to propel resolution of the Arab–Israeli conflict to the forefront of international relations, it was a success, and post-war negotiations were launched in an atmosphere of parity. However, as Israel regained its self-assurance through the 1970s, this slowly changed.

Box 3.6 Likud

Likud is a right-wing political party that was formed in late 1973, in the aftermath of the 1973 Arab–Israeli War. The fractious Israeli political scene has meant that even when it is not the ruling party in government, Likud has often been a decisive force within 'unity government' arrangements. It has traditionally followed a conservative, nationalist ideology and has been known for its tough stance on security matters and relations with the Palestinians. It moved further to the right as a result of the Palestinian Intifadas, and in the twenty-first century it is characterized by its overt rejection of the establishment of a Palestinian state.

The United States, particularly in the aftermath of the oil crisis, was clearly aligned with Israel and centrally involved in attempts to negotiate 'peace in the Middle East'. As part of this agenda, the 1978 Camp David Accords were signed between Israel and Egypt, a treaty that marked the beginning of 'cold peace' between the two former combatants (Quandt 2001: 205–245). From the Israeli perspective, the return of the Sinai, including the forced evacuation of the settler community at Yamit, was a taste of things to come. It also served to underpin an Israeli perspective that the return of the Sinai fulfilled Israel's obligations under UN Resolution 242, as the return of the desert region to Egypt was presented as meeting the vague UN requirement of withdrawal from territories seized in 1967. Initially touted as the start of regional peace, Camp David largely failed to trigger a wave of peace deals. Egypt's President Anwar Sadat was assassinated by an Islamist group, Egyptian Islamic Jihad, for his role in the Accords and perceived acquiescence to Israeli and US interests at the expense of the Palestinian cause. On similar grounds, Egypt was subsequently suspended from the Arab League and frozen out of Arab politics until the 1990s.

The increasing bond between Israel and its superpower backer was formalized on 30 November 1981 with the signing of the first Israeli–US strategic cooperation agreement. This was contracted despite (or perhaps because of) an international drama in June 1981, when the Israeli Air Force launched a raid, known as Operation Orchard, against a nuclear facility in southern Iraq. Israel's willingness to act as a regional policeman clearly aided the US agenda in the Middle East.

Box 3.7 The Camp David Accords, 1978

The Camp David Accords were brokered by US President Jimmy Carter and signed by Egyptian President Anwar Sadat and Israeli Prime Minister Menachem Begin on 17 September 1978. They led to an Egypt–Israeli peace treaty the following year. The signing of the Accords was a watershed event in contemporary Middle Eastern history as they brought an end to Egypt and Israel's thirty-year state of war and meant Egypt became the first Arab state to normalize relations with Israel. Sadat and Begin were jointly awarded the 1978 Nobel Peace Prize for their roles in the process. The treaty has been criticized for detailing Palestinian territory without Palestinian participation in the creation of the Accords. Egypt was consequently suspended from the Arab League from 1979 until 1989.

The Lebanese War, 1982

Israel's northern neighbour has long played a significant role in the security calculations of the Tel Aviv. Lebanon, formed from the French Mandate from Syria, was governed under a delicate and dysfunctional model of consociationalism. In this model of governance different groups share power within a system of assured representation. In Lebanon, these groups reflected the different ethnic, religious and sectarian communities that were present in the state, but the Christian community enjoyed a privileged position. This model was historically shaky, with an explosion of tension in 1958 which led to a brief US military deployment at the request of the Christian-led government. These tensions resurfaced dramatically in the early 1970s and triggered a brutal civil war which raged between the country's various militia from 1975 to 1990. The civil conflict was heavily influenced by outside forces, from Syria's deployment into Lebanon in the late 1970s to Israel's willingness to spend US$150 million between 1975 and 1977 arming the Lebanese Maronite Christians (Black and Morris 1996: 581).

In 1948, Lebanon had been a key destination for Palestinian refugees, with approximately 100,000 people crossing the border. This refugee community had proved challenging for a state such as Lebanon, where traditional Arab demands regarding Israeli acceptance of accountability for the refugee crisis were exacerbated by the domestic balance of power. The influx of Sunni Muslim Palestinians threatened to upset this delicate balance. In the wake of the 1967 defeat, PLO activism became increasingly troublesome for Arab states. Jordan, in particular, was faced with a restless Palestinian population, a large majority of whom were refugees. PLO agitation in Jordan and armed incursions into Israel threatened Jordan's domestic stability and risked Israeli retaliation. Tension reached boiling point in September 1970 when the Jordanian government moved to crack down on PLO training camps. Following a bloody conflict between Jordanian soldiers and PLO militia in this month, known henceforth as 'Black September', PLO fighters were expelled from Jordan and moved to southern Lebanon. Yasser Arafat, the chairman of the PLO, who was committed to keeping the pressure on Israel, saw this area as a suitable base from which to launch continued armed incursions into Israel. Indeed, there were frequent PLO cross-border raids in the 1970s. In 1978, Israel launched Operation Litani against Lebanon's Bekka Valley in the hope of uprooting the militants. However, international pressure and the arrival of the United Nations forced a retreat. This did not relieve the tension, though, as the UN forces proved ineffective in preventing PLO cross- border attacks on Israel.

This situation was clearly unacceptable to Israel, and the attempted assassination of its ambassador to the United Kingdom on 3 June 1982 offered an opportune pretext for decisive action against the PLO. Three days later, the Israeli Defence Force moved into Lebanon. The Israeli Defence Minister, Ariel Sharon, was in charge of planning and executing the military operation, which was designed to occupy southern Lebanon, break the back of Palestinian nationalism and secure Israel's northern borders. The plan was initially presented to the Israeli Cabinet as a 'Litani-type operation, namely a short and small scale invasion directed against the PLO only' (Bregman 2000: 105). As the conflict unfolded, however, the significant Israeli ground force advanced and laid siege to the Muslim quarter of Beirut for ten weeks. This expansive move raised suspicions about Israel's strategic objectives. The relationship between Bachir El-Gemayal, an ambitious Christian Maronite leader, and the authorities in Tel Aviv had been a poorly kept secret in Lebanese political circles. From Israel's perspective, the installation of a pro-Israeli Christian leadership at the expense of Muslim representation would advance Tel Aviv's geostrategic position.

This conflict is often retrospectively understood as a war between 'greater Israel and greater Syria'. However, it is a difficult conflict to analyse as the relationships between the various Lebanese factions changed constantly and external players, such as Syria, supported different factions at different times. It is important to note that, in this period, both Israel and Syria were flexing their regional muscles and attempting to redesign the region, and especially the destabilized and devastated Lebanon, to suit their own interests. Despite the usual US calls for restraint, elements in the Israeli military leadership were clearly committed to the conflict. In contrast to previous battles, the war in Lebanon was seen as one of choice rather than necessity, and it proved deeply unpopular with the Israeli public. However, as Bregman (2000: 115–116) points out, although 1982 'broke the national consensus on defence', it was not Israel's first war of choice, as the wars in 1956 and, to some extent, 1967 had also been undertaken on Israel's terms.

Much of the planning for the 1982 invasion of Lebanon was conducted in the murky world of intelligence and counter-intelligence, and the alliances between civil war-hardened Lebanese militias and the Israeli state proved disastrous. The siege of Beirut sparked international condemnation. Saudi Arabia, Egypt and the Gulf states all refused to offer refuge to PLO fighters. Eventually, the remnants of the PLO forces were evacuated to Tunisia under a

US-sponsored deal, an operation that saw nearly 11,000 people relocated. The departure of the fighting men of the PLO set the scene for a gruesome final chapter in this ill-fated conflict. The massacres of Sabra and Shatila in September 1982, while under Israeli occupation, left a lasting stain on Israel's international reputation and served to entrench the Palestinian narrative of loss, dispossession and political abandonment.

Box 3.8 Sabra and Shatila

Sabra and Shatila were two Palestinian refugee camps under the jurisdiction of the Israeli Defence Force in the 1980s. During the siege of Beirut, Israeli forces allowed the Phalange, a Lebanese Christian militia, into the camps, resulting in a massacre of Palestinian men, women and children. The death toll estimates vary widely, from several hundred to over 2,500. News of the massacre triggered mass protests by hundreds of thousands of Israelis, confirming the fundamentally unpopular nature of the war in Lebanon. Israel held its military accountable and established the Kahane Commission to investigate the massacres. On the basis of the concept of reasonable foresight, the investigation found that the IDF was 'indirectly responsible' for the deaths.

The 1982 war had potent effects on Israel's domestic politics. In Israeli academic circles, the conflict itself and the shattering of the national consensus on defence created a climate in which revisionist, 'new' historians could emerge. These academics controversially re-examined Israel's foundational myths. The conflict also divided the usually united Israeli public on the necessity of armed conflict and challenged popular notions of Israel's exercise of military power as defensive and legitimate.

Despite its eventual departure from the central regions of Lebanon, Israel retained an occupying force in the south of the country. This decision dragged the IDF into a sporadic guerrilla conflict with the Lebanese Hezbollah, a group that emerged to challenge the dominant Lebanese Shia organization, Amal. Hezbollah was formed as a resistance movement to the Israeli occupation and drew on Iranian inspiration (Qassem 2005). In its militant campaign, it employed suicide bombers, a development that grew to become a feature of the Palestinian resistance. It engaged Israel throughout the following decades and proved an intractable enemy. In a regional first, Israel withdrew completely from Lebanon on 25 May 2000 without a peace accord or any concessions from Hezbollah.

The 1982 invasion of Lebanon constitutes a significant page in Israel's military history. Domestically, the image of the Israeli soldier as a symbol of power was weakened due to the political turmoil surrounding the IDF's deployment in a fragile neighbouring state. In some ways, this war can be identified as a turning point in Israeli political history: battles were no longer clear cut and defence of the Zionist dream became, even in the popular psyche, entangled with the oppression and exclusion of Palestinians.

Fighting Hezbollah, 2006

The IDF's withdrawal from southern Lebanon in May 2000 did not mark the end of hostilities between Israel and the Shia militias, which had solidified in response to Israel's occupation. Rather, it constituted a significant opportunity for the militias, which for nearly two decades had legitimized their presence by the need to confront Israel. In this political context, the withdrawal did not mean a rejection of armed action by Hezbollah, which continued to launch sporadic, small-scale rocket attacks against Israel's northern communities.

On 12 July 2006, a thirty-four-day conflict erupted that, once again, engulfed Lebanon. Tensions had been simmering between the two parties throughout the early years of the twenty-first century. In the months leading up to the Israeli attack, Israel had faced increased HAMAS activity in the Gaza Strip, which included kidnapping IDF reservists. Similarly, in July, Hezbollah, amid an ongoing campaign of Katyusha rocket attacks against northern Israel, launched a cross-border raid and captured two Israeli soldiers. Several more IDF soldiers died in an unsuccessful rescue attempt. Israel responded with air strikes against Hezbollah targets and civilian infrastructure and a new conflict opened in the Middle East.

An Israeli air and naval blockade preceded a ground invasion of southern Lebanon. Thereafter, the conflict dragged on for over a month while an increasingly horrified international community appealed for a cease-fire. Israel drew the ire of that international community by launching a military campaign that included 'more than 7000 air strikes, the deaths of 1183 people and the displacement of a further 970,000' (Amnesty International 2006). The damage inflicted on Lebanon was staggering, with 120 bridges destroyed and the total bill amounting to approximately US\$3.5 billon. The impact of this conflict on Israel was also significant, with the deaths of 43 civilians and 117 soldiers, and the temporary displacement of 300,000 to 500,000 civilians. It bears mentioning that Israel's ability to protect its citizens through a system of shelters and evacuations helped to keep the civilian death toll relatively low.

The global reaction to the conflict revealed much about the balance of power in the international system. The United States, supported by its allies the United Kingdom and Australia, linked the conflict to the broader 'War on Terror' and endorsed Israel's right to self-defence. Other voices pointed out that Israel's conflict was with the Shia Hezbollah, yet it was the people of Lebanon who were paying the price. The political schisms in the Arab world, and the increasing fear of Shia activism, led many Arab states to criticize both Hezbollah's provocative actions and Israel's response.

A UN-endorsed cease-fire came into effect on 14 August 2006, and Israel's naval blockade of Lebanon was lifted on 8 September. There was no clear victor in the war of 2006. Israel failed to eradicate Hezbollah, while Hezbollah celebrated this as a victory and consequently increased its standing significantly in the region.

Conclusion

Israel's sweeping victory over the Arab states in the Six-Day War fundamentally altered the political and ideological landscape of the Middle East and the lives of millions of Palestinians and Israelis in the decades to come. Israel's capture of Arab territory, which increased its size by six times, firmly entrenched Israel as a powerful actor within the region. Nasser's pan-Arab nationalist vision was severely discredited as a result and subsequently eclipsed by the emerging ideology of political Islam (discussed in Chapter 5). In an attempt to save face, the Arab states once again went down the path of war to reclaim their lost land. This led to the 1973 Yom Kippur/Ramadan War, which once again saw Israel emerge triumphant over the Arab states. This victory had a significant impact on religious discourses within segments of Israel's Jewish community. The emerging Israeli settler movement viewed the victory through the lens of divine intervention and moved forward in populating occupied Palestine with Israeli citizens. Ever since, Israeli settlement expansion has continued unabated in the Occupied Territories and, as will be explored in the following chapter, it continues to undermine attempts to establish an independent Palestinian state as stipulated under UN Resolution 181 (1947).

Israel's acquisition of Palestinian territory in 1967 left the Palestinians with little hope that the Arab states would help them secure their liberation and statehood. This ultimately indigenized the Palestinian struggle and saw the PLO gain precedence within Palestinian society as it mobilized support for armed resistance against Israel. Throughout the 1970s and 1980s, the PLO represented a significant security threat to Israel. With its headquarters in southern Lebanon, PLO fighters engaged in cross-border raids against Israel. The ramifications of PLO resistance were far reaching as it led Israel to launch an offensive against the group in 1982 which saw southern Lebanon fall under Israeli occupation. The PLO was consequently forced to relocate to North Africa, which undermined its reach and influence in the Occupied Territories. Meanwhile, Israel's continued military occupation had a profound impact on war-torn Lebanon, specifically in regards to the Lebanese Hezbollah that emerged in 1982 with a relentless anti-Israeli agenda. Hezbollah, backed by Iranian military and ideological support, developed into a serious fighting force. It not only survived repeated Israeli attempts to quash it, but managed to force Israel to withdraw its forces from southern Lebanon in 2000.

The short history of the State of Israel is characterized by war. Arab–Israeli conflicts, however, are based not on primordial hatred but on temporal issues such as territorial concerns, access to waterways, strategic planning and, finally, the personal agendas of politicians. Although they are often underscored by the ever-present reality of competing Israeli and Palestinian claims to the same land, the broader issues mentioned above have been at the heart of many of the region's wars.

References

Amnesty International (2006) 'Israel/Lebanon: Deliberate Destruction or "Collateral Damage"? Israeli Attacks on Civilian Infrastructure', 23 August, available at www.amnesty.org/en/documents/MDE18/007/2006/en/.

Bar-Siman-Tov, Yaaov (1987) *Israel, the Superpowers and the War in the Middle East* (London: Praeger).

Bar-Joseph, Uri (2005) *The Watchmen Fell Asleep: The Surprise of Yom Kippur and Its Sources* (Albany: State University of New York Press).

Bar-Joseph, Uri (2008) 'Strategic Surprise or Fundamental Flaws? The Sources of Israel's Military Defeat at the Beginning of the 1973 War', *Journal of Military History*, Vol. 72, No. 2, pp. 509–530.

Black, Ian and Morris, Benny (1996) *Israel's Secret Wars: A History of Israel's Intelligence Services* (Cambridge: Cambridge University Press).

Bregman, Ahron (2000) *Israel's Wars, 1947–1993* (London: Routledge).

Bregman, Ahron (2003) *A History of Israel* (London: Palgrave Macmillan).

Eban, Abba (1988) 'Israel's Dilemmas: An Opportunity Squandered', in Stephen Roth (ed.), *The Impact of the Six Day War: A Twenty Year Assessment* (London: Macmillan).

El Badri, Hassan, El Magdoub, Taha and Dia El Din Zohdy, Mohammed (1978) *The Ramadan War, 1973* (New York: Dupuy Associates).

Krasno, Jean E. (2004) 'To End the Scourge of War: The Story of UN Peace Keeping', in Jean E. Krasno (ed.), *United Nations: Confronting the Challenges of a Global Society* (Boulder, CO: Lynne Rienner Publishers).

Kurz, Anat (2005) *Fatah and the Politics of Violence: The Institutionalization of a Popular Struggle* (Brighton: Sussex Academic Press).

Mutawi, Samir (2002) *Jordan in the 1967 War* (Cambridge: Cambridge University Press).

Nasser, Jamal R. (1991) *The Palestine Liberation Organization: From Armed Struggle to the Declaration of Independence* (New York: Praeger).

Qassem, Naim (2005) *Hizbullah: The Story from within* (London: Saqi).

Quandt, William B. (2001) *Peace Process: American Diplomacy and the Arab–Israeli Conflict since 1967* (Berkeley: University of California Press).

Raphel, Gideon (1988) 'Twenty Years in Retrospect: 1967–1987', in Stephen Roth (ed.), *The Impact of the Six Day War: A Twenty Year Assessment* (London: Macmillan).

Rostow, Eugene V. (1975) 'The Illegality of the Arab Attack on Israel of October 6, 1973', *American Journal of International Law*, Vol. 69, No. 2, pp. 272–289.

Rubenstein, Amnon (1984) *The Zionist Dream Revisited: From Herzl to Gush Emunim and Back* (New York: Schocken Books).

Sahliyeh, Emile F. (1986) *The PLO after the Lebanon War* (Boulder, CO: Westview Press).

Shlaim, Avi (2000) *The Iron Wall: Israel and the Arab World* (London: Penguin).

Shlaim, Avi (2001) 'Israel and the Arab Coalition in 1948', in Eugene Rogan and Avi Shalaim (eds), *The War for Palestine* (Cambridge: Cambridge University Press).

Sinora, Hanna (1988) 'A Palestinian Perspective', in Stephen Roth (ed.), *The Impact of the Six Day War: A Twenty Year Assessment* (London: Macmillan).

Smith, Charles D. (2004) *Palestine and the Arab–Israeli Conflict* (Boston: Bedford/St Martin's).

Spiegel, Steven (1988) 'American Middle East Policy', in Stephen Roth (ed.), *The Impact of the Six Day War: A Twenty Year Assessment* (London: Macmillan).

Sprinzak, Ehud (1991) *The Ascendance of Israel's Radical Right* (New York: Oxford University Press).

Sprinzak, Ehud (1999) *Brother against Brother: Violence and Extremism in Israeli Politics from Altalena to the Rabin Assassination* (New York: Free Press).

United Nations Security Council (1967) 'UNSC Resolution 242', 22 November, available at www.mideastweb.org/242.htm.

4   Palestinian politics

The failure of the 'peace process'

Introduction

The Palestinian predicament has served as one of the major flashpoints in regional politics since the early twentieth century. As we have explored in the preceding chapters, the Palestinian community has suffered as a result of Zionist settlement, indecisive international policy and Arab state politics. By the mid-2000s, the Israeli–Palestinian 'peace process' was in freefall. In its place was an endless cycle of internationally led negotiation and discussion. This process occurred against the backdrop of Israeli settlement expansion in occupied West Bank territory, Palestinian terrorism against Israeli civilians and, increasingly, armed conflict between factions in Gaza and the Israeli military. Finally, the situation was further complicated by political conflict among Palestinians themselves. As Arab politics transitioned into the 'Arab Spring', further challenges emerged. Palestinian factions were forced to navigate the changing currents in regional alliances, and international attention was drawn to emergent conflicts, such as the Syrian Civil War.

Throughout this history, the Palestinian people have seen the promises of self-determination which the international community offered to Jews and Arabs in Palestine in the mid-twentieth century dissolve. Israel, backed by the United States, remains rhetorically committed to a bilateral 'peace process', yet this is a process in which Tel Aviv rarely honours its commitments. Instead, Palestinian land is confiscated, settlements increase and disunity plagues Palestinian politics.

This chapter explores the contemporary state of play for Palestinians. It will consider the 'peace process' of the late twentieth century, the Gaza withdrawal of 2005, the civil conflict between HAMAS and the Palestinian Authority, Palestinian appeals to international bodies such as the UN and the International Criminal Court and, finally, the impact of the Arab uprisings on Palestinian politics.

Background

Israel's relationship with its Arab neighbours has been marked by sporadic conflict, with major regional wars in 1956, 1967, 1973 and 1983. However, this context of large-scale inter-state warfare should not obscure the conflict that has concurrently unfolded between Israel and the Palestinians. While some Palestinian academics point to 1948 as the moment of occupation, most Western sources contend that Israeli occupation of Palestinian land commenced in 1967, because this was when the areas slated by the United Nations for a Palestinian state were occupied in the Six-Day War. Ever since, occupation has been the basic premise of Israel's engagement with the Palestinians. This is a profoundly hierarchical relationship in which one side physically, economically and politically dominates the other. It also carries legal implications as the occupier must guarantee the rights and safety of those living under its authority and, crucially in this context, must not move its own citizens into the occupied land (United Nations 1949).

Similar to Arab–Israeli politics more broadly, Palestinian–Israeli tensions are fundamentally temporal issues. Sovereignty, security, self-determination, territory, refugees, leadership, access to resources, international recognition and borders are the factors which have informed the conflict. Jerusalem, as a symbol of the religious aspect of the conflict, is of course central. However, a reading of Israeli–Palestinian politics which privileges religion as the main driver of antagonism runs the risk of excusing the failures of leaderships, both local and international, to reach a meaningful resolution.

The first Intifada (1987)

The status quo established by the sweeping Israeli victory of 1967 was challenged in the Occupied Territories in the late 1980s. The seething discontent over two decades of occupation and political stagnation merely required a spark, which was provided by a traffic accident in Gaza on 9 December 1987. This incident triggered a grassroots uprising that rocked Israel and the international community. It is commonly known by its Arabic name: the Intifada.

As the civil unrest spread to the West Bank it became clear to all observers, Israeli and international, that a new phase in the conflict between Palestinians and Israelis had begun. First and foremost, the uprising was an expression of anti-occupation sentiment. As Sami Farsoun and Jean Landis point out, the Intifada was similar in conceptualization to other rebellions against occupation (Farsoun and Landis 1999: 16). Seen in this way, it can be understood as a manifestation of the national liberation struggle of the Palestinian people. However, the events of 1987 were also a powerful critique of internal Palestinian politics, which had stagnated since the exile of the PLO to North Africa in the early 1980s. As the PLO's leadership languished in Tunis, the grassroots outburst of discontent which drove the Intifada con-stituted a significant challenge to the organization's claim to the leadership mantle of Palestinian politics. Therefore, the first Intifada can be understood as both a challenge to Israel's occupation and an expression of 'frustration at the PLO's failure to stop the occupation and the abuses that occurred within it' (Meir 2001: 65).

Israel viewed the Intifada as a serious threat. Its political and military leadership ordered a strong military response, and images of Israeli soldiers beating unarmed Palestinian civilians led to international calls for resolution. Inside Israel, the inability of the Israeli Defence Force to suppress the Intifada reignited the debate over the moral and political costs of occupation. According to Azmay Bizhara (1999: 217), this led to a 'polarization which ... penetrated all of Israel's political parties'.

In the midst of the growing popular unrest and street mobilization, the various Palestinian leadership structures merged into loose coalitions. Over time, the PLO-backed organizations began to gain ground (Milton-Edwards 1999: 145). However, the influence of the Islamic political alternatives was significant, and a complicated power-sharing relationship began to emerge. The PLO, long the accepted representative of the Palestinian community, was challenged from within. The rise of an Islamic alternative was a key outcome of this shift in the balance of power in Palestinian politics.

HAMAS

The emergence of Islamic groups in the Palestinian political scene was not a new phenomenon, as the Muslim Brotherhood had been active in the Palestinian territories for decades. By the late 1980s, the traditionally apolitical stance of the Brotherhood was under challenge, with more militant and proactive Islamist alternatives, such as Palestinian Islamic Jihad, attracting the support of young Palestinians.

Sheikh Yassin, a factional leader of the Brotherhood, pushed his organization's leadership to declare itself a leading participant in the struggle against Israel, both as an expression of ideological intent and as a strategy to re-engage disaffected young supporters. His pursuit of his cause resulted in the creation of a new wing of the Brotherhood – Harakat al-Muqawama al-Islamiyya – better known by its acronym, HAMAS. With Yassin at the theological helm, HAMAS declared itself through its covenant in 1988 and soon became a major player in Palestinian politics. As noted by Rashad al-Shawwa, Mayor of Gaza at the time, the appeal of HAMAS was theological, ideological and situational:

> One must expect these things after twenty years of debilitating occupation. People have lost hope. They are frustrated and don't know what to do. They have turned to religious fundamentalism as their last hope. They have given up hoping that Israel will give them their rights. The Arab states are unable to do anything, and they feel that the PLO, which is their representative, has also failed.
>
> (Cited in Hroub 2000: 37)

HAMAS quickly overtook the Muslim Brotherhood in terms of relevance. As the Intifada continued, the traditionally fractious Palestinian political scene became increasingly dominated by two organizations: HAMAS and the PLO.

The former's popularity hinged on its capacity and willingness to organize militarily and its support for the Palestinian people through welfare organizations. In this way, the organization became central to both the resistance against Israel and the day-to-day functioning of Palestinian society.

The peace process

The Intifada marked a significant turning point in the Palestinian struggle and was widely supported in the Palestinian Diaspora. Yet, as the years passed with little in the way of tangible progress, both Israelis and Palestinians grew increasingly weary of conflict. The Oslo Accords, which emerged from this experience, were the major political outcome of the 1987 Intifada. Both the Israeli and Palestinian leaderships perceived that there was much to be gained from taking their seats at the negotiating table. Israel's international prestige had been profoundly damaged by its heavy-handed military tactics during the Intifada. Meanwhile, for the PLO, exiled in North Africa, the dynamic surge in local political leadership meant that its position as chief representative of the Palestinian cause was no longer unchallenged. Therefore, securing safe passage back into the Occupied Territories became an overriding consideration. In addition, Yasser Arafat's international reputation required some polish after his ill-advised articulation of support for Iraq in the 1991 Gulf War.

The Oslo Accords, signed in 1993, laid out a structure of staged steps. This approach to conflict resolution, dubbed 'phased reciprocal negotiation', was intended to build confidence and establish a firm foundation for discussion of the so-called 'final status' issues: the future of the refugees, Jerusalem and borders. Although often vague, the Accords implied – or, more importantly, were perceived by the Palestinian community to advocate – a two-state solution.

Washington's role in the Accords was initially limited. However, once the potential of these meetings to resolve one of the greatest political issues of the twentieth century became clear, the Clinton administration seized a central role. As Manuel Hassassian (2004: 125) points out, with its entry into the Oslo process, the United States came to play 'the contradictory roles of arbiter, staunch supporter of Israel and promoter of peace and regional stability'. At the time, however, these conflicting trends were submerged, and the Oslo Accords were regarded as a triumph for all involved. The handshake between Yasser Arafat and Yitzhak Rabin on the White House lawn was a defining moment of the Clinton presidency. For the PLO's Arafat, the Accords signalled a return to the international stage. More importantly, they marked the end of the PLO's exile in North Africa. The organization returned to the Occupied Territories, where it transformed itself into the Palestinian Authority (PA).

Retrospective accounts of the Oslo Accords reveal that all parties had their doubts that the process would bring lasting peace. However, in 1994, Rabin and Arafat shared the Nobel Peace Prize for their efforts, and there was a sense of hope that a new chapter in Israeli–Palestinian relationships had begun.

Box 4.1 Yitzhak Rabin

Yitzhak Rabin was born in Palestine on 1 March 1922 and served as a general in the Israeli army before becoming a politician. He was the Prime Minister of Israel from 1974 to 1977 and again from 1992 until his death in 1995. In 1994, he shared the Nobel Peace Prize with fellow Israeli politician Shimon Peres and the Palestinian leader, Yasser Arafat. He was assassinated by Yigal Amir, a right-wing Israeli extremist, on 4 November 1995.

However, the promise of the Oslo period slid into overt confrontation during the latter part of the decade. By the 1990s, settlement had become an entrenched feature of the Israeli approach to the disputed territories. Under Oslo, the fate of the territories was a 'final status' issue, but it was agreed that neither party would take steps to change the status of these areas prior to the final negotiations (Hass 2004: 48). This was widely interpreted as meaning a freeze on the expansion and development of the settlements. More explicitly, the Accords divided Palestinian land into three distinct administrative areas: Area A was turned over to exclusive Palestinian administration; Area B fell under dual Israeli and Palestinian control; and, most controversially, Area C, some 60 per cent of West Bank territory, was placed under sole Israeli authority. However, the Accords stated that Area C would be gradually turned over to Palestinian jurisdiction.

Box 4.2 Yasser Arafat

Yasser Arafat was born in 1929 into a Palestinian family and became active in post-1948 factional Palestinian politics. He completed his education at Cairo University, and was initially a supporter of Nasser's vision for the Arab world. Along with other Palestinians in exile, he formed Fatah in 1957 in Kuwait. After the defeat of 1967, Arafat became more strongly committed to Palestinian self-determination outside the auspices of pan-Arabism. He was elected Chairman of the Executive Committee of the PLO in February 1969 and proceeded to push the PLO agenda from pan-Arabism to national liberation. His major political misstep was his public support for Saddam Hussein in the 1991 Gulf War, which placed him at odds with almost the whole international community. Nevertheless, after the Oslo Accords, Arafat re-entered the Occupied Territories as the accepted leader of the Palestinian people. In 1994 he shared the Nobel Peace Prize with Yitzhak Rabin and Shimon Peres. He then consolidated the Palestinian Authority and was elected President in 1995. From 1995 to 2000, Arafat fulfilled his side of the Oslo bargain in an erratic fashion, and he was frequently accused of corruption and nepotism. He died of an undisclosed illness on 11 November 2004.

Among the Palestinian population, the Accords and Israel's willingness to adhere to both the letter and the spirit of the negotiations were increasingly called into question. From the perspective of the Israeli government, the Accords were intended to ensure Israel's internal security. However, Palestinian terrorism against Israeli civilians occurred throughout the 1990s as organizations such as HAMAS attempted to derail the process. April 1994 marked the advent of suicide bombings against Israeli targets, with a HAMAS press release citing a recent massacre of Palestinians by an Israeli settler as justification for the attack. Over a hundred Israelis died in similar attacks between 1994 and 2000, and a climate of fear permeated the lives of the Israeli public. Under the Oslo Accords, the newly created Palestinian Authority was charged with dismantling the terrorist infrastructure of organizations such as HAMAS. However, the PA was plagued by nepotism and corruption, which led to frequent deployment of its forces in vendettas and revenge attacks; therefore, its ability to counter HAMAS's security threat was highly questionable. Moreover, its capacity to temper HAMAS's political power was limited as the latter had built up a significant support base, secured as a result of its leadership of the Intifada, its willingness to take the fight to Israel and its welfare activities. Indeed, moving decisively against HAMAS could well have led the PA into open confrontation. Thus, the game of cat and mouse between the two major power-brokers in Palestinian society continued. The Oslo process was amended in a series of subsequent meetings: in Cairo in 1994; Taba in 1995; and Wye River in 1998. However, these summits achieved little and Area C remained firmly under Israeli jurisdiction.

This fundamental failing led many Palestinians to question the efficacy of the formal peace process. Conversely, as the voices of reconciliation were drowned out by extremist action on both sides, many Israelis saw the terrorist campaign against civilian targets as proof that the Palestinian community as a whole had reneged on the peace process. It is, however, vital to view these trends through the very real power imbalance that existed and continues to exist between Israel and the Palestinian community. Indeed, as Sara Roy (2012: 74) points out, Oslo proved extraordinarily costly to the Palestinians: 'the denial of territorial contiguity, which came to define the status quo after Oslo, remained unchallenged by the international community'.

In 1999 an Israeli Labour government came to power under Ehud Barak. Like many before him, Barak attempted to resolve the Israeli–Palestinian conflict. The failings of Oslo had called the effectiveness of phased reciprocal negotiations into question. Moreover, the bloodshed of the 1990s had created a climate in which neither side could afford another long, drawn-out political process while the situation on the ground worsened. At the same time, the Clinton presidency was mired in controversy due to the Monica Lewinksy affair, so the administration was casting around for a dramatic political victory. A peace agreement in the Middle East seemed the perfect fit.

The ensuing Camp David 2000 summit was arguably doomed from the outset. Clinton's team pushed both camps to the negotiating table on the basis of a one-time, 'all or nothing' approach. This tactic had significant drawbacks. Clinton was correct in surmising that both communities would reject another prolonged process. However, the level of distrust that had built up over the 1990s was a serious obstacle. A common criticism of Camp David is that Clinton assumed he could forge a lasting agreement simply by force of his own will. However, for both the Israeli and Palestinian teams, there were other considerations. A decade of broken promises had generated severe discontent within the Palestinian community, HAMAS had gained strength as a result, and Arafat's own position was far from secure. Indeed, he had resisted the idea of a summit and, as the negotiations progressed, his position became increasingly precarious. At the talks, the Israeli Prime Minister, Ehud Barak, made the Palestinian team an offer. The exact nature of this proposal is not on the public record, but it is commonly accepted that it included: Israeli retreat from 95 per cent of the West Bank and 100 per cent of the Gaza Strip; the creation of a Palestinian state in the areas of Israeli withdrawal; and Palestinian control over East Jerusalem, including most of the Old City, as well as 'religious sovereignty' over the Temple Mount, replacing the Israeli jurisdiction that had been in effect since 1967. These terms constituted a stunning transgression of traditional Israeli 'red lines', and as word of them filtered out there was shock and surprise in Israel.

Barak's ability to actually implement such expansive terms in practice remains one of the open questions of Camp David. However, this question was overshadowed by the reality that Arafat rejected the proposal and failed to issue a counter-offer. This response reinforced the dominant American and Israeli perception of Palestinian intransigence and Arafat's personal commitment to conflict. In the following years, the Israelis insisted that Arafat 'critically failed' as he was not committed to a lasting peace and that he negotiated on the assumption that any political agreement would be no more than 'a temporary tactical tool' (Sher 2005: 60–61). This interpretation of Arafat, which fails to engage with the reality that the Palestinian leader simply did not have the power to accept the Israeli proposal, remained dominant throughout the remainder of his life. A more nuanced reading of his actions would take into account his initial unwillingness to attend the summit because of his clear understanding of the fractious and volatile nature of his own community at the time. As Barak himself pointed out, a peace negotiation takes two, and at Camp David 'the other side was not a willing partner *capable* of making the necessary decisions' (Barak 2005: 117; emphasis added). Indeed, the ability of both Arafat and Barak to convince the more extreme elements in their communities to abide by the terms on the table is open to serious question. In the Palestinian community, many factions already viewed the situation as one of outright conflict and thus viewed any peace agreement as 'surrender'. After the decade of compromise under Oslo, the feeling in the Occupied Territories was that enough concessions had already been made. Indeed, Naseer Hasan (2003: 15) argues that 'Oslo had become a symbol of diplomatic paralysis and economic impoverishment for the Palestinian people'. The summit ended in a stalemate, and the situation in the Occupied Territories was ripe for another explosion of discontent.

The spark for the second Intifada came on 28 September 2000, when the Likud Party's Ariel Sharon visited the al-Aqsa Mosque in Jerusalem. Sharon had played a central and controversial role in Israeli politics for several decades before his accession to the position of leader of Likud (which was in opposition at the time) in 1999. He had a particularly tense history with the Palestinian people, largely due to his role in the siege of Beirut in the early 1980s. Consequently, when he visited the mosque, he was accompanied by a sizeable armed security cohort. Israeli Arabs rioted in response to his presence, and the unrest spread quickly throughout Gaza and the West Bank.

Box 4.3 Settlement policy

Israel's settlement policy refers to the construction of settlements – secured Israeli communities – in the Occupied Territories of Palestine. Their existence on occupied Palestinian land defies Article 49 of the Fourth Geneva Convention, which states that it is illegal for an occupying power to 'deport or transfer parts of its own civilian population into the territory it occupies'. Between 2009 and 2014, Israeli construction commenced on over 12,000 new settlement units in the Occupied Territories. By 2015, the total settler population in the West Bank and East Jerusalem stood at 570,000 – double the 1993 figure (Middle East Quartet 2016). In December 2016, the United Nations Security Council adopted Resolution 2334 by fourteen votes to nil, with the United States abstaining. This reaffirmed that settlement construction has 'no legal validity' and constitutes a 'flagrant violation of international law'. Hence, it demanded that Israel must immediately and completely cease all settlement activities in the Occupied Territories, including East Jerusalem.

The new Intifada was different from the grassroots activism of 1987, and Israel and the Palestinians were quickly dragged into the bloodshed. Palestinian militia groups, including the armed wing of the ruling Fatah Party, commenced a campaign of suicide attacks against Israeli civilian targets. The Israelis responded with targeted killings and helicopter gunships. This horrific cycle of violence seemed self-perpetuating as collective punishment, house demolitions and detentions were matched by firearm attacks against settlements and terrorist attacks against cafés, buses and shopping precincts. Furthermore, regional opinions were inflamed as the newly founded al-Jazeera TV channel beamed images of Palestinian suffering into people's homes throughout the Arab world.

The election of Likud in 6 February 2001 was another major development. Israelis voted for Sharon, who campaigned under the slogan 'Sharon alone can bring peace', largely on the basis of the very attributes that so disturbed the Palestinian community. Sharon, as part of the 1948 generation, was seen as a man of action who would take whatever steps were necessary to protect Israeli lives. As Itamar Rabinovich (2003: 182) points out, the fact that Sharon had sparked the 2000 Intifada and was then elected with a mandate to resolve it is highly ironic. However, the urgent need to counter terrorism drove the Israeli electoral process. In this context, the events of 11 September 2001 had a profound impact. The launching of a 'War on Terror' allowed Sharon's government to position Israeli actions within the broader paradigm of 'fighting terrorism'. However, the blending of Israeli and American suffering at the hands of suicide bombers served to obscure the very real differences between legitimate Palestinian grievances and the agendas of transnational terrorist groups such as al-Qaeda.

The Intifada dragged on, albeit punctuated by various attempts at peace, including the ill-fated 'Saudi Peace Plan' of 2002 and the Bush administration's 'Roadmap to Peace'. As the unrest continued, Arafat began a steady fall from grace within the international community. In contrast to the warm welcome he had received from the Clinton administration on the lawn of the White House in 1993, he was marginalized by the Bush administration, which tightened its ties with Tel Aviv. Traditionally, the Palestinians had been careful to walk a comparatively moderate line on all matters relating to the United States. Policy in the Occupied Territories was dictated by a long-standing awareness of the pivotal role Washington played in forcing concessions from Tel Aviv.

Box 4.4 Ariel Sharon

Ariel Sharon was born in Palestine in 1928, so he was a *sabre* – a member of a generation of locally born Jews who were committed to founding the State of Israel. He fought in all of Israel's early wars and was the driving force behind the settlement programme in Gaza after the 1967 conflict. His political career stalled in the 1980s when he was forced to resign after the Kahane Commission found him indirectly responsible for the massacres of Palestinian civilians in the Sabra and Shatila refugee camps. However, he returned to politics as Housing Minister in the 1990s, when he presided over the most intense period of Jewish settlement building in the West Bank and Gaza in Israeli history. He went on to become leader of the right-wing Likud Party after it lost the general election in 1999. Like his nemesis Yasser Arafat, Sharon was a fascinating politician, and few public figures tapped into more elements of Israel's national mythology. He won general elections in 2001 and 2003, largely on the basis of a single factor: Israelis trusted him to take whatever measures were necessary to protect them from the ongoing campaign of Palestinian suicide attacks, even though many blamed him for sparking the Intifada. He suffered a massive stroke in January 2006 and was entirely incapacitated until his death eight years later.

However, in 2002 Arafat's international standing suffered a serious blow from which he never recovered. During Operation Defensive Wall, the IDF seized documents that indicated Arafat had personally approved payments to the families of terrorists (Karsh 2000: 7). This led the IDF to confine Arafat in his headquarters in Ramallah, where the Israelis claimed he was hiding several wanted terrorists. Two years later, media reports suggested that Arafat might be the next target of an Israeli assassination plot. The ensuing debate over the potential murder of an elected national official revealed a whole new side to the 'War on Terror' in which all traditional norms of political behaviour seemed to have been rendered obsolete, at least according to many Arab commentators.

Israel's treatment of Arafat merely served to increase his popularity among Palestinians. There had been widespread dissatisfaction with his authoritarian style and the rampant corruption of the Palestinian Authority. However, he had played the central role in Palestinian politics since the 1970s, and, perhaps more than any other individual, he was seen as the personification of a national cause. The massive outpouring of public grief over his death in 2005, despite his highly controversial status, underscored the sense of solidarity the Palestinian people felt with him.

Palestinian political rupture, Gaza and the security wall

It was within this tense environment and its seemingly unending cycle of violence that Israel commenced its building of a 'security wall'. This decision was condemned by the Vatican and the European Union (2003) and even cautioned against by Washington. The Israeli official line remains that the barrier is a necessary security measure and may be removed should the security situation allow. The construction of this physical barrier between Israel and the West Bank was a unilateral measure, so it was decried by the Palestinians as a violation of the bilateral process, which the international community insisted was the only path to Palestinian self-determination. From an Israeli perspective, any ethical concerns raised by segregating the Palestinians were balanced against national security requirements.

The decision to go ahead was validated for many in Israel by the results: during the wall's first year of existence, there was a significant decline in terrorist attacks against Israel. As Tami Jacoby (2005: 35) points out, this led to a 'widespread belief in Israel that the separation barrier is an effective counter-terrorist strategy'. However, other security measures, such as the assassination of several senior HAMAS figures, including the organization's spiritual leader and founder, Sheikh Yassin, may have contributed to this outcome, too.

Box 4.5 The security wall

Israel commenced construction of its security wall in 2002 in response to a string of Palestinian suicide attacks against Israeli citizens. The ruling Likud Party proposed the wall with a view to regulating the entry of Palestinians from the West Bank into Israel. Despite international condemnation, Israel's Supreme Court ruled that it was a legal enterprise. The wall, which is now 710 kilometres long and up to 8 metres high, is constructed out of concrete slabs topped by barbed wire, and it features a number of watchtowers and checkpoints.

On 9 July 2004, the International Court of Justice delivered its advisory opinion on the legality of the separation barrier. Israel refused to cooperate in the proceedings, contending that the court had no jurisdiction over the issue. In a document it submitted to the court, the Israeli government argued that the barrier was a political, as opposed to a legal, matter. Thus, it should have been dealt with bilaterally between Israel and the Palestinians. This stance was problematic given that the erection of the wall was an entirely unilateral undertaking.

This sharpens the focus on the questions of unilateralism and bilateralism, which are of paramount importance in the Israeli–Palestinian 'peace process' and can be explored through a multitude of specific case-studies. For a start, the establishment of Israel in 1948 was, in effect, a unilateral declaration of statehood. It was premised, in part, on the validity of UN Resolution 181 pertaining to partition, which offered sovereignty to both Jews and Arabs in Palestine. Since the Oslo Accords, Israel and the international community have insisted that the Palestinians must adhere to a process of bilateral negotiation, despite the evident power imbalance, the failure of this process to secure tangible gains for the Palestinians and Israel's own propensity for unilateral action. The security wall is but one example of this trend.

A further example of the tension between the rhetoric of bilateralism and the unilateral nature of Israeli policy is the withdrawal from Gaza in 2005. Ariel Sharon's government announced the removal of all Israeli settlements from the Gaza Strip in a move that received the blessing of the Bush administration, but this was done with little coordination with the Palestinian authorities and critics were quick to point out that Gaza held little appeal for Israel from a strategic, natural resources or religio-political perspective. The Gazan settlements were small (especially in comparison with those on the West Bank), had to be defended by the IDF and were situated in the middle of one of the most densely populated tracts of land in the world. While the evacuation – some of which was forced – was heralded in Tel Aviv and Washington as proof of Israel's willingness to disengage, this was not an end to the occupation in any meaningful sense because Israel retained access to and control over all Gazan air and sea space. Hence, the removal of the settlers merely created what was, in effect, a giant, open-air Palestinian prison (United Nations General Assembly 2006: 7).

The withdrawal continued amid a larger unfolding crisis in Palestinian politics. In the Occupied Territories, the elections of 25 January 2006 marked an important turning point. By this point, HAMAS had played a significant but largely unofficial role in Palestinian politics for nearly two decades. As an Islamist organization committed to the establishment of an Islamic state, it had a limited relationship with the formal Palestinian political process, which had long been dominated by the secular–nationalist Fatah movement. Despite some internal dissent, in the 1996 elections HAMAS did not field any candidates, as its leaders felt participation would signal implicit endorsement of the 'peace process' (Nusse 1999: 161). However, over the subsequent decade, dissatisfaction with Fatah grew and HAMAS decided to test the electoral waters in 2006. The result was a landslide victory: HAMAS won 74 of the 123 parliamentary seats.

This was a significant challenge to several global players, most notably the United States, where a cornerstone of the Bush doctrine had been the call for democratization in the Middle East. The 2006 Palestinian elections were widely acknowledged as free and fair, yet the expression of popular Palestinian will was the election of an Islamist organization with an explicitly anti-Israel stance. HAMAS's rise to power reflected the Palestinian people's frustration with two decades of stagnation and failure in the peace process under the leadership of the Fatah-dominated authorities, and it left Washington with a difficult choice: either adhere to the official US policy of supporting the democratization of Arab societies by endorsing the victory of a movement it regarded as a terrorist organization or reject the results of a clearly democratic process. It decided to follow the latter course. US funding to the Occupied Territories ceased, Arab countries were warned against supporting the new HAMAS government and, in what would become a common tool against the Palestinians, Israel withheld customs revenue (Elhadj 2006: 147).

Tensions between the Palestinian factions intensified until they exploded into civil conflict between the Palestinian Authority and HAMAS in 2007. Consequently, Gaza fell under HAMAS control and the West Bank was governed by the internationally backed PA. The two factions have not been meaningfully reconciled since, with HAMAS refusing to renounce its confrontational position on Israel. In return, Israel and the international community have refused to engage with a Palestinian governance structure which includes HAMAS. This has proven a terminal stumbling block for the Palestinian people. There have been numerous attempts at reconciliation since 2007, often with the involvement of Arab mediators, notably Egypt and Qatar, but both factions have much to lose by pursuing a power-sharing arrangement. Public opinion polls indicate that, while a majority of Palestinians support the principle of reconciliation, few believe that either the PA or HAMAS will agree to it (Davis 2016: 158).

The shifting alliances in the wake of the Arab uprisings have further complicated the Palestinian political environment. The counter-revolutions of 2012 and beyond have seen HAMAS further isolated in the Gaza Strip. The PA, meanwhile, has tied its credibility to a two-state solution, yet it continues to emerge from discussions 'empty-handed and without a strategy on how to end the Israeli occupation' (Pogodda and Richmond 2015: 894). This stand-off works in Israel's favour as it forges ahead with increased settlement activity in the West Bank, particularly around the highly contested site of Jerusalem.

HAMAS and Israel

The Israeli withdrawal from Gaza in 2005 and the subsequent establishment of a security ring around the Gaza Strip prepared the ground for an escalation of the conflict between Israel and HAMAS with a costly civilian toll. While Israel presented the withdrawal as an effort to fulfil its obligations under UN

Resolution 242, the Palestinians countered that the Israelis' true intention was to set up a blockade and start the process of strangling a besieged population. On the other hand, some Israeli voices have argued that the withdrawal has compromised their country's security, with the Strip becoming a base for HAMAS militancy, including rocket attacks into southern Israel and cross-border incursions. These have been answered by major Israeli military assaults against the Strip in 2008, 2012 and 2014, which Israel itself labelled 'wars'. However, as Sara Roy (2012: 77) points out, this terminology is problematic as it suggests, on some level, two equal parties engaging in a conflict. In Gaza, Israel's actions are better understood through the lens of military operations against a militia group embedded in an urban, civilian setting.

The first of these Israeli incursions, in 2008, was codenamed Operation Cast Lead. The subsequent three-week conflict left over 1,400 Palestinians dead, including more than 300 children and 110 women, with a further 5,000 injured (United Nations General Assembly 2009: 17, 91). Thirteen Israelis died, too. In addition to the death toll, this conflict caused momentous damage to the infrastructure of Gaza. According to Human Rights Watch (2010), 'overall, some 3,540 homes, 268 factories and warehouses, as well as schools, vehicles, water wells, public infrastructure, greenhouses and large swathes of agricultural land, were destroyed, and 2,870 houses were severely damaged'. The assault also incurred a significant political cost in terms of its damage to Palestinian perceptions of international conflict resolution and its efficacy. The United Nations, moved by significant international condemnation of the devastation in Gaza, established an independent fact-finding mission under the leadership of a South African judge, Richard Goldstone, who published his report in September 2009. It concluded that both Israel and HAMAS had violated international law by indiscriminately targeting innocent civilians (United Nations General Assembly 2009). It also drew attention to the imbalance in military capacity and thus the consequent suffering of Palestinians during Israeli operations in the Strip. These findings generated an immediate and strong backlash, particularly from Israel and the United States. Meanwhile, the Palestinians and their supporters welcomed the criticism of Israeli violations of international law. However, despite the report, and the sworn testimonies of thirty-eight Gazans, little was done in relation to holding either side accountable for their actions. In consequence, Palestinian confidence in the international community declined further.

In 2012, the situation flared up again, with a marked increase in HAMAS missiles into Israel and the subsequent assassination of HAMAS's security chief in Gaza. Over an eight-day period, 174 Palestinians were killed and 1,269 injured, while 6 Israelis lost their lives (OHCHR 2013: 4). This conflict, which is usually known by its Israeli military codename – Operation Pillar of Defence – served to enhance HAMAS's previously waning prestige in the Strip (Davis 2016). Similar to the dynamic evident in Lebanon in 2006, HAMAS's ability to withstand an Israeli onslaught was construed as a 'victory'.

Two years later, Israel launched a much broader incursion, known as Operation Protective Edge. The catalyst for this assault was the kidnap and murder of three Israeli teenagers, while the main military objective was the eradication of a tunnel system which militants were using to penetrate Israeli territory. In the ensuing conflict, 2,251 Palestinians were killed, including 299 women and 551 children, and a further 11,231 injured (United Nations General Assembly 2015). The Gaza Strip, already economically devastated by international isolation, the Israeli blockade and previous conflicts, lost a further '18,000 homes, in whole or in part, much of the electricity network and of the water and sanitation infrastructure were incapacitated; and 73 medical facilities and many ambulances were damaged' (United Nations General Assembly 2015). Protective Edge was also a more costly conflict for Israel, with 74 Israelis killed and 1,600 injured (United Nations General Assembly 2015). The exchanges were much more fierce, with 2,000 Israeli air strikes and over 1,500 HAMAS rockets launched against Israel (Davis 2016: 182). The focus on the tunnel system was significant as it was, in effect, 'dual purpose'. Its use by militants was well established and certainly constituted a significant security threat to Israel's civilian population. However, the tunnels that linked the Strip to Egypt also served a vital economic purpose because they allowed the blockaded residents of Gaza to gain access to vital food, construction and medical supplies. Indeed, it has been suggested that up to US$700 million worth of supplies entered the Strip by this route each year (Piven 2014). The new Egyptian government was an enthusiastic supporter of this aspect of Operation Protective Edge because it was keen to isolate HAMAS in light of the latter's ties with the Muslim Brotherhood.

In many ways, Protective Edge can be seen as a 'bare-knuckled' expression of the Israeli–HAMAS dynamic that has been in play since 2008. By 2014, the destabilized regional and international situation, especially the fact that the Arab world was still in a state of flux, gave Israel an opportunity to undertake a more dramatic operation against Gaza. The whole HAMAS–Israeli relationship can be characterized as a series of actions and reactions, with both sides more than willing to take up arms in the face of provocation. HAMAS militants assuredly constituted a serious security threat to Israel throughout this period, undertaking attacks against Israeli civilians that were commensurate with their comparatively limited capacity. Israel would then deploy its vastly superior military capabilities against an organization that was operating within a densely populated and besieged civilian space. The HAMAS–Israel dynamic can be viewed through political, military, security, humanitarian and ethical lenses, and it raises significant questions about the right to self-defence and the proportionality of military retaliation. The international community's response to the history of Israeli military operations in Gaza reflects, at differing times, all of these perspectives.

In 2014, the Arab world was deeply immersed in the Arab uprisings, and international attention was focused on the internal conflicts in Syria and Libya. In this sense, the devastation in Gaza was often dismissed as yet another episode in an increasingly difficult saga. The US perspective on the conflict was clear: President Obama called for restraint, yet Congress authorized an additional aid package of US$225 million to Israel for missile defence (Bermant 2014). In the West Bank, tensions flared with protests and attacks against settlements, civilians and the presence of the IDF. As the cycle of action and reaction continued, Israel stepped up its security measures and, in a move decried by Amnesty International, claimed yet more Palestinian land. The situation remains unchanged at the time of writing, with the UN warning that Gaza will be unliveable by 2020 and a solution, or even the possibility of progress, seemingly as far out of reach as ever (al-Monitor 2017).

HAMAS and the Arab Spring

In addition to its physical situation inside Gaza, HAMAS faced further challenges in this period as the Arab uprisings served to empower and then isolate the organization. As an offshoot of the Muslim Brotherhood, committed to confrontation with Israel, HAMAS's regional alliances had always been clear. The short-lived rise to power of the Brotherhood's Freedom and Justice Party (FJP) in Egypt was a major development for HAMAS. It placed a sympathetic government in Cairo, with the FJP's President Morsi even able to intervene in the 2012 Gaza conflict (alongside the Americans) to secure a cease-fire (Milton-Edwards 2016a: 85). This brief upswing in Brotherhood influence suggested the opening of a new chapter of increased regional support for HAMAS. However, the real political game for HAMAS was not to occur in Egypt but within the realm of its other external alliances. In 1999, HAMAS had been expelled from Jordan as that state moved closer to a security understanding with Israel. Since then, HAMAS's external structure had been hosted in Syria, under the protection of the Assad regime. This gave HAMAS important access to Tehran, which, while a Shia power-broker, supplied and supported HAMAS on the basis of a shared antipathy for Israel. Put simply, the rejection of Israel was common ground which facilitated a cross-sectarian alliance between Sunni HAMAS and Shia Iran.

Box 4.6 The Muslim Brotherhood and the Freedom and Justice Party

The Muslim Brotherhood is a Sunni Islamist organization founded in Egypt in 1928 by the Egyptian schoolteacher Hassan al-Banna. It emerged in response to the British colonial legacies of secularization and Westernization, with al-Banna advocating the Islamization of Egyptian society from the 'bottom up'. The Brotherhood's religious teachings and practices have conflicted with the secular leadership of successive Egyptian presidents. Under the presidency of Gamal Abdel Nasser, the group was violently persecuted and outlawed in 1954. It has since experienced various degrees of persecution and coercion by the Egyptian government, forcing many members into exile in surrounding Arab states. Consequently, Brotherhood branches have been established in Syria, Jordan, Palestine and throughout the wider region. Inside Egypt, the Brotherhood maintained a prominent position via its provision of a vast welfare system and ability to bypass electoral restrictions. In the aftermath of the 2011 Egyptian uprisings, the group reached its zenith with the success of its Freedom and Justice Party in Egypt's first free and fair elections. Held in 2012, these elections brought the FJP's leader Mohamed Morsi to power, but he was overthrown the following year and the Brotherhood has since experienced high levels of persecution by the Egyptian state.

As the protests in Syria unfolded and Assad's repression of Sunni rebels hardened, HAMAS was faced with a stark choice: remain in Damascus, allied to the regime, and thus implicitly endorse its actions against its fellow Sunnis' resistance, or break with Assad and, by extension, Syria's Iranian backers. In many ways, HAMAS's predicament serves as the most powerful example of the complexities of the uprisings period itself, when strategic alliances throughout the region were subjected to new challenges and sectarian considerations complicated, but rarely eclipsed, political realities.

HAMAS made its choice and its leaders departed for Doha, Qatar. This was a significant moment in the 'Arab Spring'. HAMAS's rejection of Assad laid bare the emergence of the sectarian axis in regional politics, cemented Qatar's emergence as a power-broker linked to the Muslim Brotherhood and its affiliates, and signalled a rupture in the Iranian–Syrian–HAMAS relationship, which had provided significant financial support for HAMAS for decades. Despite these consequences, HAMAS's leadership stood in solidarity with the Syrian Sunni community, stating, 'no political considerations will make us turn a blind eye to what is happening on the soil of Syria' (Fahmy and al-Mughrabi 2012). This cannot have been an easy choice for HAMAS, which was already physically and economically besieged in Gaza. The consequences of the breach were predictable, with Iran responding by cutting its reported US$150 million in annual aid to HAMAS by 60 per cent (Davis 2016: 156).

As the Syrian Civil War unfolded, there were signs of a rapprochement between HAMAS and its former backers. For HAMAS, this was made more urgent by the fall of the Morsi government in Egypt in 2013. This had clear strategic and practical implications for HAMAS. Following Morsi's fall, the new military government in Cairo moved decisively against the organization. It closed or destroyed 80 per cent of the tunnels into Gaza, so,

> from around the middle of June to the middle of July 2013, the Gaza Strip lost around $225 million due to the decline of imports, namely fuel and construction materials … By early August 2013, the loss reportedly increased to a quarter of a billion dollars. As a result, 20,000 construction workers lost their jobs.
>
> (Roy 2013: 265)

This dire situation forced HAMAS's hand and the organization moved to mend ties in the region. By mid-2013, observers reported the restoration of Iranian aid to HAMAS, albeit below previous levels (Roy 2013: 227), and the re-establishment of direct channels of communication between the organization and Hezbollah. As detailed above, the devastation of the 2014 Israeli operation against Gaza also played a significant role in HAMAS's changing attitude, with reports of a formal request for enhanced assistance from Tehran (Fars News Agency 2014). In this sense, the 2014 conflict was an opportunity for Tehran to draw focus away from its role as a sectarian driver of conflict in Syria, Yemen and Iraq and re-establish its credentials as a regional power committed to one of the most enduring popular causes in Arab politics: the liberation of Palestine. From HAMAS's perspective, the fall of the Brotherhood, marginalization of Qatar by other Arab sheikhdoms in the Persian Gulf and the solidification of Iran's regional role dictated the need to mend its relationship with Tehran (Amer 2014). By 2017, this reconciliation seemed to be complete, with high-level Iranian leaders pointing to a new chapter in HAMAS–Iranian relations (Amer 2017).

The Palestinian Authority, the United Nations and the bid for statehood

HAMAS was not the only Palestinian faction struggling in this period. While it navigated its confrontations with Israel and its regional challenges, the Palestinian Authority was also placed in a seriously compromised position. Ironically, as HAMAS attempted to mitigate its isolation as a result of its rejection of Israel and the peace process, the PA was suffering blow after blow to its legitimacy because of its commitment to the same process. However, as the bilateral process dragged on with little in the way of tangible gains for the Palestinian community, the PA moved to circumvent it through direct appeals to international institutions. As part of this strategy, it made a bid for formal recognition at the United Nations. Since 1974, the Palestinians had held observer status in the international body. This ambiguous status reflected both the UN General Assembly's goodwill towards the Palestinians and the capacity of Israel's principal ally, the United States, to block a more formal endorsement through its permanent membership of the Security Council. In concert with Tel Aviv, Washington has long cautioned that the road to Palestinian self-determination lies solely through bilateral negotiation with Israel.

The catalyst for more overt Palestinian action came in 2011 when the United States vetoed a UN draft resolution that classified Israeli settlements illegal (United Nations 2011). This triggered a robust statement by Palestinian officials that 'the current peace process, as it has been conducted so far, is over' (Elgindy 2011: 105). The continued US endorsement of Israel's position (even under the Obama administration, which was perceived as sympathetic to Palestinians) pushed the PA into unilateral action (Elgindy 2011: 105). For the PA, the pursuit of international recognition was an attempt to demonstrate its capacity to secure legitimacy for the Palestinian people, despite the realities of territorial and political division and Israel's continued occupation.

This brought to the fore the need for Palestinian unity, which stands as a precondition for statehood.

In 2012, the PA secured an 'upgrade' from 'non-member observer entity' to 'non-member observer state' in the United Nations. As Pogodda and Richmond (2015: 890) suggest, this may well 'demonstrate growing international support for Palestinian sovereignty'. Despite this upswing in international support, however, the change in status falls short of recognizing a Palestinian state and, more importantly, it did little to address the very real, daily challenges of Palestinian life. Moreover, this symbolic victory came at a substantial cost, as both Israel and the United States moved to punish the Palestinian Authority by effectively 'weaponizing' aid. For example, Washington withheld approximately US$147 million in FY 2011 Economic Support Funds (ESF) approved by Congress for USAID's humanitarian and socioeconomic programmes in the West Bank and Gaza (Roy 2012: 84), while Israel withheld US$100 million in tax funds to the PA (Rozen 2012). In a further indication of the determination of Israel's allies, the United States and Australia then blocked a 2014 UN Security Council resolution which called for Israel to withdraw from Palestinian territory occupied since 1967 and for the parties to reach a negotiated solution within a year (United Nations Security Council 2014).

In addition to its efforts at the United Nations, the PA signed up to twenty international conventions, including the Rome Statute of the International Criminal Court. This gave the court jurisdiction over crimes committed on Palestinian land and opened an unprecedented new chapter in Israeli–Palestinian relations. In retaliation, Israel announced it would withhold US$125 million in monthly tax funds that it collects on the Palestinians' behalf (al-Jazeera 2015). Public opinion polls in the Palestinian community indicate significant support for the strategy of bypassing Israel and directly approaching international organizations (Palestinian Center for Policy and Survey Research 2016b). It bears reiteration, however, that in the current situation, with the peace process stagnating, significant numbers of polled Palestinians also support a resumption of armed resistance against Israel (Palestinian Center for Policy and Survey Research 2016b)

The Palestinian Authority remained committed to its internationalization strategy, arguably because it lacked any viable alternatives. In late 2015, Palestinian anger manifested in a new, macabre fashion with the emergence of the so-called 'knife intifada' – a nine-month wave of deadly violence between Palestinians and Israelis. In this period, Palestinian militants, possibly copying a spate of 'lone wolf' incidents around the world, attacked civilians in shared public spaces, killing thirty-five Israelis and two foreign nationals. Israel responded by stepping up its security measures and increasing penalties (Knesset 2015). Between October 2015 and July 2016, Israeli security forces killed over 200 Palestinians (Amnesty International 2016) in a brutal crackdown that generated sustained criticism from both international pressure groups (Amnesty International 2015) and the US government (United States Department of State 2015).

The 2015 upsurge in violence was indicative of a situation at breaking point. In the words of one Likud politician, Israel needed to 'internalize the fact that terror cannot be fought with democratic tools' (Knesset 2015). In the Palestinian arena, polling suggested popular support for stabbing attacks as a method of resistance had waned by 2016, yet over 50 per cent of those questioned still supported such actions (Palestinian Center for Policy and Survey Research 2016a). In the midst of this, the PA, pressed by Israel to control militancy in the West Bank and increasingly politically exposed in the Palestinian arena for its failure to secure progress, cast about for options. The US veto of the 2016 resolution on settlements, informed by the reality of boiling popular anger, triggered another concerted push for international recognition.

In each of these examples, Israel, backed by the United States and its allies, rejected the Palestinian right to seek unilateral recognition of statehood outside the parameters of the bilateral peace process. In this sense, Palestinians have been politically and financially coerced to remain within a process that has provided little in the way of tangible benefits over the course of the last two decades. International awareness of this reality has increased in recent years, with the Middle East Quartet reporting:

> The continuing policy of settlement construction and expansion in the West Bank and East Jerusalem, designation of land for exclusive Israeli use, and denial of Palestinian development, including the recent high rate of demolitions, is steadily eroding the viability of the two-state solution. This raises legitimate questions about Israel's long-term intentions, which are compounded by the statements of some Israeli ministers that there should never be a Palestinian state. In fact, the transfer of greater powers and responsibilities to Palestinian civil authority ... has effectively been stopped.
>
> (Middle East Quartet 2016)

Despite this, the dynamics of global and regional politics serve to enable Israeli policy, especially in relation to settlement expansion. In this sense, to speak of a 'peace process' is to participate in a charade which continues to legitimize the stagnation of the Palestinian cause and continued conflict between Israel and the Palestinians.

Two states or one?

The failure of the peace process has triggered other political responses. The viability of a two-state resolution, the bedrock of international engagement with this conflict, has now been seriously compromised and discussions about alternative models of resolution have emerged. In particular, some Palestinian and international voices have floated the idea of a one-state solution (Karmi 2011). This is a complex notion, as national identity is paramount to both the Palestinian and Israeli communities. More practically, Israel is the dominant actor in the relationship and it has vehemently rejected this option (O'Leary 2016). While one-state advocates position this approach within a narrative of justice, egalitarianism and securing democratic norms, most Israelis see it through the lens of national suicide, given the demographic reality that they would be outnumbered by the Arab population. Yet, as each round of peace talks leads nowhere and the land historically slated for Palestinian self-determination continues to be eroded by ever more Jewish settlement, there is little reason for the Palestinians to pursue the idea of a two-state solution. Even the United States has acknowledged the challenge, with Secretary of State John Kerry pointing out in 2016:

> [I]f the choice is one state, Israel can either be Jewish or democratic – it cannot be both – and it won't ever really be at peace … How does Israel reconcile a permanent occupation with its democratic ideals? How does the US continue to defend that and still live up to our own democratic ideals? Nobody has ever provided good answers to those questions because there aren't any.
>
> (Kerry 2016)

It was within this context that the United Nations passed Security Council Resolution 2334 in another bid to address the settlement question. It reaffirmed that Israeli settlements on Palestinian land constitute flagrant violation of international law and called for the immediate cessation of the settlement programme (United Nations Security Council 2016). This resolution's safe passage through the Security Council was seen by many as President Obama's parting shot to the Likud-run Netanyahu government. However, while much has been made of the fractured relationship between Israel and the United States during Obama's presidency, the reality was more nuanced. While Obama certainly took a much stronger line than the traditional trite endorsement of the 'special relationship' between America and Israel, his administration attempted to adopt a broader, regional perspective. For example, Washington was determined to push through the controversial Iran nuclear deal over sustained Israeli objections (see Chapter 11), so it offered Israel an unprecedented aid package – some US\$38 billion in military assistance over a ten-year period (Spetalnick 2016a).

At the end of 2016, officials from the incoming Trump administration proclaimed an even more supportive stance towards Israel, including the assertion that the United States would endorse Israel's proposal to transfer its national capital to Jerusalem (Spetalnick 2016b). On the ground, Trump's election triggered a predictable increase in state-sponsored settlement construction, with many projects that had been delayed in the Obama era receiving authorization in Tel Aviv (Kershner 2017). UNSECO responded by expressing its concern over the new excavations and building works in East Jerusalem (UNESCO 2017). In this sense, the very real dismemberment of Palestinian land has intensified, while the political process which aims to achieve a resolution has stalled.

Conclusion

Since 1967, Israel has been an occupying power. In the aftermath of the Six-Day War, some Israelis warned that occupation or annexation was tantamount to 'national suicide' (Eban 1988: 27), as it would harm both the Palestinian people and the moral fabric of Israel itself. However, as the years passed and the Palestinian resistance became more intractable, occupation became an accepted 'fact' of Israeli politics. While Israeli opinion polls suggest security remains important, domestic concerns such as education and employment regularly outrank the continued occupation of Palestinian land as paramount political issues within Israel. This is matched by international fatigue over the 'peace process', and in recent years a lack of interest in the Palestinian refugee crisis, which risks becoming a historical footnote in a region that remains engulfed in conflict.

All of this provided very little room for the Palestinian political narrative. Continued international insistence that Palestinians must abide by the 'rules of the game' and commit to a bilateral process is difficult to reconcile with the reality of stagnation and disempowerment which has characterized the last fifty years. The role of the United States has been problematic due to the incompatibility between its close relationship with Israel and its self-proclaimed role as 'peace-maker'. Yet, given the asymmetries of political power between Israel and the Palestinian factions, international involvement in this conflict is clearly required. As Israel's unilateral disengagement from Gaza has shown, the dynamic between Israel and the Palestinians remains as toxic as ever. The 2005 withdrawal brought little in the way of prosperity to the people of Gaza, while security for Israel was not enhanced. Palestinian political reunification is central to these challenges, but regional and international attempts to broker a resolution have been complicated by the factions' divergent positions on matters such as resistance, recognition of Israel and the role of religion in the public sphere. The international community appears powerless to resolve this crisis, yet it is well aware of the consequences of continual and sustained inaction. As ex-Secretary-General of the United Nations Ban Ki-moon (2016) has stated, 'as oppressed peoples have demonstrated throughout the ages, it is human nature to react to occupation, which often serves as a potent incubator of hate and extremism'. In this sense, the 'Palestinian issue' may well continue to serve as an important focal point of regional and political destabilization for some time to come.

References

Al-Jazeera (2015) 'Abbas to Renew Bid for Palestinian Statehood', 5 January, available at www.aljazeera.com/news/middleeast/2015/01/abbas-renew-bid-palestinian-statehood-20151423844267227.html.
Al-Monitor (2017) 'Gaza May Already Be "Unlivable": UN Official', 7 July, available at http://fares.al-monitor.com/pulse/afp/2017/07/israel-palestinians-conflict-gaza-health-un.html.

Amer, Adnan Abu (2014) 'Hamas Asks Iran for Money, Weapons', *al-Monitor*, 14 December, available at www.al-monitor.com/pulse/ru/contents/articles/originals/2014/12/iran-hamas-repair-ties-with-visit-to-theran.html.

Amer, Adnan Abu (2017) 'In Eye of Regional Storm, Hamas Pushed Closer to Tehran', *al-Monitor*, 2 June, available at www.al-monitor.com/pulse/originals/2017/06/hamas-iran-relations-improve-elections.html#ixzz4khn0g1E0.

Amnesty International (2015) 'Israeli Forces in Occupied Palestinian Territories Must End Pattern of Unlawful Killings', 27 October, available at www.amnesty.org/en/latest/news/2015/10/israeli-forces-must-end-pattern-of-unlawful-killings-in-west-bank/.

Amnesty International (2016) 'Lethal Force and Accountability for Unlawful Killings by Israeli Forces in Israel and the Occupied Palestinian Territories', 28 September, available at www.amnesty.org/en/documents/mde15/4812/2016/en/.

Barak, Ehud (2005) 'The Myths Spread about Camp David Are Baseless', in Shimon Shamir and Bruce Maddy-Weitzman (eds), *The Camp David Summit: What Went Wrong?* (Brighton: Sussex Academic Press).

Bermant, Azriel (2014) 'Does Israel's US-Funded Iron Dome Make the World Safer?', *Guardian*, 6 August, available at www.theguardian.com/commentisfree/2014/aug/06/iron-dome-israel-gaza-defence-usa.

Bizhara, Azmay (1999) 'The Uprising's Impact on Israel', in Joel Beinin and Zachary Lockman (eds), *Intifada: The Palestinian Uprising against Israeli Occupation* (London: South End Press).

Davis, Richard (2016) *Hamas, Popular Support and War in the Middle East: Insurgency in the Holy Land* (London: Routledge).

Eban, Abba (1988) 'Israel's Dilemmas: An Opportunity Squandered', in Stephen Roth (ed.), *The Impact of the Six Day War: A Twenty Year Assessment* (London: Macmillan).

Elgindy, Khaled (2011) 'Palestine Goes to the UN: Understanding the New Statehood Strategy', *Foreign Affairs*, Vol. 90, pp. 102–113.

Elhadj, Elie (2006) *The Islamic Shield: Arab Resistance to Democratic and Religious Reforms* (Boca Raton, FL: BrownWalker Press).

European Union (2003) 'Statement to the Tenth Emergency Special Session of the General Assembly of the United Nations by H.E. Ambassador Marcello Spatafora, Permanent Representative of Italy to the UN on Behalf of the European Union', 20 October, available at www.eu-un.europa.eu/articles/articleslist_s7_en.html.

Fahmy, Omar and al-Mughrabi, Nidal (2012) 'Hamas Ditches Assad, Backs Syrian Revolt', Reuters, 24 February, available at www.reuters.com/article/us-syria-palestinians-idUSTRE81N1CC20120224.

Fars News Agency (2014) 'Hamas Asks for Iranian Support of Palestinians against Israel's Increasing Aggression', 30 June, available at www.globalresearch.ca/hamas-asks-for-iranian-support-of-palestinians-against-israels-increasing-aggression/5389152.

Farsoun, Sami and Landis, Jean (1999) 'The Sociology of an Uprising: The Roots of the Intifada', in Jamal Raji Nassar and Roger Heacock (eds), *Intifada: Palestine at the Crossroads* (New York: Praeger).

Gross, Aeyal (2017) *The Writing on the Wall: Rethinking the International Law of Occupation* (Cambridge: Cambridge University Press).

Hasan, Naseer (2003) *Dishonest Broker: The US Role in Israel and Palestine* (London: South End Books).

Hass, Amira (2004) 'Israeli Colonialism under the Guise of the Peace Process, 1993–2000', in Dan Leon (ed.), *Who's Left in Israel? Radical Political Alternatives for the Future of Israel* (Brighton: Sussex Academic Press).

Hassassian, Manuel (2004) 'Why Did Oslo Fail? Lessons for the Future', in Robert Rothstein, Moshe Ma'oz and Khalil Shikaki (eds), *The Israeli–Palestinian Peace Process: Oslo and the Lessons of Failure* (Brighton: Sussex Academic Press).

Hroub, Khaled (2000) *HAMAS: Political Thought and Practice* (Washington, DC: Institute for Palestinian Studies).

Human Rights Watch (2010) '"I Lost Everything": Israel's Unlawful Destruction of Property during Operation Cast Lead', 13 May, available at www.hrw.org/report/2010/05/13/i-lost-everything/israels-unlawful-destruction-property-during-operation-cast-lead.

Jacoby, Tami Amanda (2005) *Bridging the Barrier: Israeli Unilateral Engagement* (London: Ashgate).

Karmi, Ghada (2011) 'The One-State Solution: An Alternative Vision for Israeli–Palestinian Peace', *Journal of Palestine Studies*, Vol. 40, No. 2, pp. 62–76.

Karsh, Efraim (2000) *Arafat's War: The Man and His Battle for Israeli Conquest* (New York: Grove).

Kershner, Isobel (2017) 'Emboldened by Trump, Israel Approves a Wave of West Bank Settlement Expansion', *New York Times*, 24 January, available at www.nytimes.com/2017/01/24/world/middleeast/israel-settlement-expansion-west-bank.html.

Kerry, John (2016) 'Kerry Blasts Israeli Government, Presents Six Points of Future Peace Deal', *Haaretz*, 28 December, available at www.haaretz.com/israel-news/1.76188.

Ki-moon, Ban (2016) 'Secretary-General's Remarks to the Security Council on the Situation in the Middle East', 26 January, available at www.un.org/sg/en/content/sg/statement/2016-01-26/secretary-generals-remarks-security-council-situation-middle-east.

Knesset (2015) 'Approved in First Reading: Harsher Punishments for Stone Throwers, Fines on Parents of Minors who Committed Related Offenses', 13 October, available at http://knesset.gov.il/spokesman/eng/PR_eng.asp?PRID=11706.

Meir, Hatina (2001) *Islam and Salvation in Palestine: The Islamic Jihad Movement* (Tel Aviv: Tel Aviv University).

Middle East Quartet (2016) 'Report of the Middle East Quartet', July, available at www.un.org/News/dh/infocus/middle_east/Report-of-the-Middle-East-Quartet.pdf.

Milton-Edwards, Beverley (1999) *Islamic Politics in Palestine* (London: IB Tauris).

Milton-Edwards, Beverley (2016a) *Muslim Brotherhood* (London: Routledge).

Nusse, Andrea (1999) *Muslim Palestine: The Ideology of HAMAS* (London: Routledge).

Office of the High Commissioner for Human Rights (OHCHR) (2013) 'Human Rights Situation in Palestine and Other Occupied Arab Territories', 6 March, available at www.ohchr.org/Documents/HRBodies/HRCouncil/RegularSession/Session22/A.HRC.22.35.Add.1_AV.pdf.

O'Leary, Brendan (2016) 'Power-Sharing and Partition amid Israel–Palestine', *Ethnopolitics*, Vol. 15, No. 4, pp. 345–365.

Palestinian Center for Policy and Survey Research (2016a) 'Palestinian Public Opinion Poll (59)', 17–19 March, available at www.pcpsr.org/en/node/636.

Palestinian Center for Policy and Survey Research (2016b) 'Palestinian Public Opinion Poll (62)', 31 December, available at www.pcpsr.org/en/node/676.

Piven, Ben (2014) 'Gaza's Underground: A Vast Tunnel Network that Empowers Hamas', al-Jazeera, 23 July, available at http://america.aljazeera.com/articles/2014/7/23/gaza-undergroundhamastunnels.html.

Pogodda, Sandra and Richmond, Oliver P. (2015) 'Palestinian Unity and Everyday State Formation: Subaltern "Ungovernmentality" versus Elite Interests', *Third World Quarterly*, Vol. 36, No. 5, pp. 890–907.

Rabinovich, Itamar (2003) *Waging Peace: Israel and the Arabs 1948–2003* (Princeton, NJ: Princeton University Press).

Roy, Sara (2012) 'Reconceptualizing the Israeli–Palestinian Conflict: Key Paradigm Shifts', *Journal of Palestine Studies*, Vol. 41, No. 3, pp. 71–91.

Roy, Sara (2013) *Hamas and Civil Society in Gaza: Engaging the Islamist Social Sector* (Princeton, NJ: Princeton University Press).

Rozen, Laura (2012) 'E1 Zone No-Build Policy "No Longer Relevant" for Israel', *al-Monitor*, 2 December, available at www.al-monitor.com/pulse/originals/2012/al-m onitor/israel-pa-e-1-zone-settlements.html#ixzz4n3TSddhX.

Sher, Gilead (2005) 'Lesson from the Camp David Experience', in Shimon Shamir and Bruce Maddy-Weitzman (eds), *The Camp David Summit: What Went Wrong?* (Brighton: Sussex Academic Press).

Spetalnick, Matt (2016a) 'US, Israel Sign $38 Billion Military Aid Package', Reuters, 15 September, available at www.reuters.com/article/us-usa-israel-statement-idUSKC N11K2CI.

Spetalnick, Matt (2016b) 'Israeli Ambassador Backs Trump Pledge to Move US Embassy to Jerusalem', Reuters, 21 December, available at www.reuters.com/article/us-usa -trump-israel-idUSKBN14A06I.

United Nations (1949) 'Geneva Convention Relative to the Protection of Civilian Persons in Time of War', 12 August, available at www.un.org/en/genocidepreven tion/documents/atrocity-crimes/Doc.33_GC-IV-EN.pdf.

United Nations (2011) 'United States Vetoes Security Council Resolution on Israeli Settlements', 18 February, available at www.un.org/apps/news/story.asp?NewsID= 37572#.WUw7gROGMWo.

United Nations Educational Scientific Cultural Organization (UNESCO) (2017) 'UNESCO Resolution on "Occupied Palestine"', 1 May, available at www.timeso fisrael.com/full-text-of-may-2017-unesco-resolution-on-occupied-palestine/.

United Nations General Assembly (2006) *Report of the Special Rapporteur on the Situation of Human Rights in the Palestinian Territories Occupied since 1967*, 5 September, available at https://documents-dds-ny.un.org/doc/UNDOC/GEN/G06/138/12/PDF/G061 3812.pdf.

United Nations General Assembly (2009) *Report of the United Nations Fact-Finding Mission on the Gaza Conflict*, 25 September, available at www2.ohchr.org/english/bodies/ hrcouncil/docs/12session/A-HRC-12-48.pdf.

United Nations General Assembly (2015) 'Report of the Independent Commission of Inquiry Established Pursuant to Human Rights Council Resolution S-21/1', 24 June, available at www.ohchr.org/EN/HRBodies/HRC/CoIGazaConflict/Pages/Report CoIGaza.aspx.

United Nations Security Council (2014) 'Resolution in Security Council to Impose 12-Month Deadline on Negotiated Solution to Israeli–Palestinian Conflict Unable to Secure Nine Votes Needed for Adoption', 31 December, available at www.un.org/ press/en/2014/sc11722.doc.htm.

United Nations Security Council (2016) 'Security Council Resolution 2334', 23 December, available at www.un.org/webcast/pdfs/SRES2334-2016.pdf.

United States Department of State (2015) *Israel 2015 Human Rights Report*, available at www.state.gov/documents/organization/253139.pdf.

5   Ideologies and supra-state identities

Introduction

The modern Middle East has witnessed the ascendancy and decline of several competing ideologies. Regional and global trends have played a key role in this process. The colonial dismemberment of the Ottoman Empire opened the door to expressions of national self-determination by groups and individuals whose vision was not always consistent or complementary. Over the past century, certain events and experiences have been critical in shaping ideas and influencing the political, social and theological trends in the region. Among them stand the legacies of colonialism, the failure of secular–nationalism to deliver economic and social prosperity, the establishment of Israel and the interventionist policies of the United States, especially in the wake of the 9/11 terror attacks.

This chapter will first examine the rise of pan-Arabism through the lens of its principal proponents – the Ba'ath Party and the Egyptian President Gamal Abdel Nasser. This discussion of pan-Arabism will provide context for the driving factors and events that influenced the rise of Islamism. A brief account of Islam and its politicization in the mid-twentieth century will be provided before examining the specific circumstances that led to its utilization as a revolutionary political doctrine. Two of Islamism's key thinkers, the Egyptian Sayyid Qutb and the Iranian Ayatollah Ruhollah Khomeini, will be discussed to explore these issues. Finally, the chapter will examine the impact of the Afghan conflict (1979–1989) on political Islam and its later evolution into transnational Salafi-jihadism.

Pan-Arabism spreads across the region

Pan-Arabism, also known as pan-Arab nationalism, was the dominant ideology of the Arab world in the 1950s and 1960s. The term refers to the desire for Arab unification under a single political structure, an ideology that draws on elements of shared history, language and culture. Pan-Arabism was developed in resistance to colonial domination and its various manifestations focused on the need for self-determination. Its two leading proponents were the Ba'ath Party, which was formalized in Syria in 1947, and Egyptian

President Gamal Abdel Nasser, who emerged as the unrivalled champion of pan-Arabism in the 1950s.

Pan-Arabism gained significant traction after the Arab states gained independence in the 1940s as a new generation of Arab thinkers explicitly rejected the grave economic and social legacies of the colonial period. In many ways, the ideology was propagated as a secular modernizing programme that aimed to deliver economic and social prosperity to the Arab world. In this sense, and in the context of the Cold War climate, pan-Arabism may be viewed as a modernizing ideology which borrowed ideas from socialism about state responsibility for the welfare of the population. The Ba'athists and Nasser adopted some socialist principles from the Soviet Bloc and then 'indigenized' them to meet local economic concerns. This centred on bridging the gap between the rich and the disenfranchised and eliminating the influence of the political and social elite who had been the chief beneficiaries of colonial rule. It is important to note that while pan-Arabism's proponents recognized the importance of Islam as a basis of identity in the region, the movement was avowedly secular in orientation, with religion relegated firmly to the private domain. In this sense, pan-Arabism was a unifying ideology which sought to bring together all Arab communities, regardless of religious or sectarian affiliations. As will be explored below, as the twentieth century unfolded, some Muslim thinkers from across the region attributed the failure of the pan-Arab project to its refusal to adopt Islamic jurisprudence as the principal source of governance.

Pan-Arabism was widely credited for the formation of the League of Arab States in 1945. This organization was established by Egypt, Iraq, Syria, Saudi Arabia and Lebanon with a view to safeguarding their new-found independence against the old colonial powers. It became even more relevant in the context of the Cold War as the United States and the Soviet Union competed for regional influence. The League, however, was a compromise solution between the notion of political unity of the Arab people and newly established political regimes in demarcated territories. Respect for national sovereignty was a central principle of the organization, as was non-interference in domestic affairs (League of Arab States 1945). In other words, the members of the League borrowed the notion of Arab unity from pan-Arabism to advance their own nationalist agendas and consolidate their territories.

The Ba'ath Party in Syria offered an alternative vision for the Arab world. Ba'athism – meaning 'renaissance' in Arabic – sought to reinvigorate the Arabs into a unified, modern nation based on their shared language, history and culture. The movement's ideological foundations were formulated by the Syrian Christian Michel Aflaq and the Sunni Muslim Saleh al-bin Bitar. Both men had been exposed to European ideas of secular–nationalism and sought to renew the Arab world along those lines. Syria's colonial history under a French Mandate (1920–1945) that emphasized secularism and the bonds of language and culture as the foundations of political expression clearly informed the Ba'athist outlook. The Ba'ath Party developed a revolutionary vision to unify the Arab world and free it from foreign influence, as stipulated by the group's 1947 constitution:

The Party, although based in Damascus, belongs to the whole Arab nation. It is a socialist and popular party, whose socialism derives from Arab nationalism. It is revolutionary, since revolution is the only means to its declared ends. This entails a struggle to destroy colonialism, unite the Arabs and overthrow the social and political system in the Arab world.

(Cited in Roberts 2013: 63)

Although the Ba'ath Party recognized the intrinsic link between Islam and the Arab world, its ideology was explicitly secular. Defining themselves in opposition to Syria's existing social and political structures, the Ba'athists were committed to ending 'class exploitation, and tyranny and to establish[ing] freedom, democracy and socialism' (Cleveland 2000: 316). Social justice and socialism became defining features of the pan-Arab movement and the Ba'athists consequently merged with the Arab Socialist Party in 1952. By 1954, the Ba'athists were the second-largest political party in Syria. The movement's revolutionary message of revitalizing the Arab world proved highly influential, and it established branches in Lebanon, Jordan and Iraq. Against this background, the region was soon to experience the pan-Arab aspirations of the Egyptian Gamal Abdel Nasser, who had risen to power by virtue of the Egyptian Revolution.

On 22 July 1952, Nasser, a former colonel in the Egyptian Army, had led his 'free officers' in a military coup to overthrow the monarchy, forcing the King into exile. This was a momentous occasion for Egypt. While the country had gained independence in 1919, Egyptian society had long viewed the monarch as subservient to British interests. By 1953, Nasser and his cohorts had declared Egypt a republic, and by 1956 he had begun his rule as President.

A year earlier, Nasser had called for the political unification of all twenty-two Arab states in order to achieve economic and social prosperity in the Arab world. In his 1955 manifesto, he declared that it was 'impossible to ignore that there is an Arab circle surrounding us and this circle is as much as part of us as we are a part of it, that our history has been mixed with it and that [its] interests are linked with ours' (Nasser 1955: 54). This worldview clearly informed Egypt's 1956 constitution: 'We, the people of Egypt, realising that we form an organic part of a greater Arab entity, and aware of our responsibilities towards the common Arab struggle for the glory and honour of the Arab nation ...' (Middle East Institute 1956: 300). Nasser's experience as an officer during the 1948 Arab–Israeli War shaped his perspective. He attributed the Arab defeat to the Arab states' 'lack of coherence and unity', which he felt was more destructive to the Palestinian cause than 'anything the enemy could do' (Nasser 1955: 61). The establishment of Israel in the heart of the Arab Middle East offered significant impetus for greater Arab unity, while the subsequent refugee crisis, with some 700 000 Palestinians congregating in refugee camps throughout the Arab region, proved highly traumatic for all concerned. These experiences galvanized Arab public opinion and Nasser focused on the formation of Israel on Arab land and a shared sense of injustice over the Palestinians' plight as a key element of his pan-Arab position.

Nasser's public standing in the region soared following the 1956 Suez War against the colonial powers of Britain and France. With his growing prestige and charisma in the Arab world, his foreign policy trajectory took a distinctive pan-Arabist turn. In 1958 he announced the formation of the United Arab Republic (UAR), which merged Egypt and Syria into a single state. This move was acclaimed throughout the Arab world, as it was seen as the first step in the creation of unitary Arab state. At the time, Syria's political landscape was marred by political instability, with power drifting between the Ba'athists and the communists. The pan-Arab project afforded the Ba'athists an opportunity to bolster their position against their communist rivals. However, it was frustrated by Nasser's self-interest and the Syrians became increasingly dissatisfied with the arrogance of the Egyptian armed forces. Moreover, the socialist economic policies implemented by Nasser in Syria marginalized the country's urban business community and landlord class, while the Ba'athists in Damascus were increasingly sidelined as all of the important political decisions were made in Cairo (Jankowski 2002: 172). The UAR collapsed in 1961 after a coup in Syria. This constituted a major setback for the pan-Arab cause.

The decline of pan-Arabism in Egypt may be largely attributed to Nasser's adventurist policies abroad. He was committed to projecting military power in defence of various Arab movements, which compromised Egypt's economy. This point was underscored by Nasser's involvement in the Yemeni Civil War. Egypt threw its full economic and military weight behind the Yemeni 'free officers' who had overthrown the newly crowned monarch Imam Muhammad al-Badr on 26 October 1962 (Gerges 1995: 299). The ensuing five-year conflict was fought between the Arab nationalists, backed by Egypt, and the Yemeni royalists, supported by Saudi Arabia and Britain. In turn, Egypt was backed by the Soviet Union (Ferris 2008: 7), but this support came at a cost. Relations with the United States deteriorated in this period, which served to push Nasser further into Moscow's camp. His increasing reliance on the Soviet Union undermined his appeal, and the Yemeni conflict put tremendous strain on the Egyptian economy. With Egyptian casualties mounting, public discontent grew. By the mid-1960s, the Egyptian public was ready for a change.

The turning point came in the Six-Day War of 1967. Israel's ability to crush the Arab armies in just 132 hours humiliated Nasser and the rest of the region's Arab leaders. As a result of this military defeat, Egypt lost control of its oil fields in the Sinai; tourism and investment in development and infrastructure declined, resulting in a severe drop in Egypt's national income (Meital 2000: 66); and the Palestinian territories of Gaza and the West Bank, previously under Egyptian and Jordanian jurisdiction, respectively, fell under Israeli military control. The defeat also dealt a devastating blow to pan-Arabism. Some critics saw it as divine punishment for rejecting an Islamic agenda in favour of pan-Arabism's nationalism and socialism. The shock of defeat therefore allowed a religiously inspired alternative ideology to gain ground and become a serious political force.

The founding of political Islam

Islamist movements in the Middle East have presented a challenge to the ruling secular regimes of the region. As explored above, between the 1950s and 1970s, pan-Arabism was the dominant ideological force. However, the failure of the Arab states to liberate Palestine during the 1967 Arab–Israeli War shattered the region's psyche and laid pan-Arabism open to criticism from religiously minded thinkers. Before examining the fervour of Islamism in the post-1970 period, a brief exploration of Islam itself is in order.

The religiously inspired opposition to secular ruling regimes gained momentum in the late 1960s and 1970s. Often called Islamism or political Islam, this movement ascribed the failure of nationalist and/or pan-Arabist projects to their rejection of Islam as a complete body of social and political knowledge and its role in the governance of Muslim societies. It drew inspiration from the early experience of Islam and sought to apply its principles in the modern Middle East. Islam is a monotheistic belief system that is understood by Muslims as the culmination of a series of revelations that began with the biblical patriarch Abraham. The holy book of Islam, the Qur'an, was revealed by God to the Prophet Mohammed (570–632 CE). The Qur'an and the Sunnah (the tradition, custom or practices of the Prophet) set out the foundations of the Sharia, often translated as 'law' but more correctly interpreted as a complete code of Muslim behaviour. In the contemporary context, any attempt to implement the Sharia is contentious because it is closely linked to the formation of a state based solely on Islamic principles. Throughout Islamic history, political power has often been won and lost through force. In itself, this is not unusual, as many empires have risen or fallen as a result of their military strength or weakness. However, in the Islamic world, political ideas have been linked directly to war, most notably the concept of jihad, which has gained considerable attention in modern theatres of conflict (as explored in other chapters in relation to Afghanistan and Syria).

In the Qur'an, jihad is described in numerous contexts and it can be interpreted in two distinct ways (Bonney 2004). It can refer to a personal, internal struggle for piety and closeness with God (known as the greater jihad) or to a public or communal striving to implement Islamic norms, which may culminate in an armed struggle (the lesser jihad). Throughout Islamic history, the militarized understanding of the concept has competed with other, non-martial interpretations. Modernist thinkers have displayed a tendency to focus on the latter, arguing that the lesser jihad of physical, often military, action can only follow the greater jihad of 'spiritual, political, social, economic and intellectual forms of struggle' (Sadiki 1995: 20).

This debate is pertinent to the political upheavals of the twentieth century. The concept of militant jihad was adopted by those seeking the supremacy of what they claimed to be the 'true' Islam. As a result, some Islamists embraced a militant interpretation of jihad as the ultimate force for the sovereignty of God. The political movement known as Islamism emerged in the mid-twentieth century in a context of growing frustration with the shortcomings of secular nationalism in the Muslim world. It was also deeply affected by the regional struggle to redefine politics and society as the Middle East emerged from its colonial past. In this way, Islamism became an expression of desire for revolutionary change (Akbarzadeh and Saeed 2003: 11). This political movement instrumentalized Islam as a doctrine of political action. In the mid-twentieth century, Islamism was often labelled 'Islamic fundamentalism', a term that originated in the context of US Christianity (Denoeux 2002), but this designation is misleading as it implies that members of this movement are distinguished by an atypical focus on the 'fundamentals' of the Islamic faith. Yet, almost all Muslims share that focus and adhere to the fundamentals of their faith, known as the Five Pillars: recognition of God; prayer; fasting; charity; and pilgrimage to Mecca. By contrast, the term 'Islamism' more correctly implies a political movement that claims to act with the religion of Islam as its core. Islamism, however, is not a unified movement, and different groups exhibit diverse interpretations, aims and methods. Although it draws on the rich intellectual and theological history of Islamic civilization, the movement has been influenced and informed by various socio-political experiences in the Middle East and throughout the Muslim world, especially in the early and mid-twentieth century.

As has been explored in earlier chapters, Western colonialism had a traumatic effect on the Middle East. The defeat and occupation of Arab lands, the creation of new states and the imposition of new systems of governance all contributed to a serious rupture in the political development of the region. Secularization crept into Middle Eastern societies as a social response to these changes; or, as in the case of Turkey and Iran, it was forced upon them from above by pro-Western regimes. For some Muslims, these rapid changes were unwelcome, as they were seen as leading the community away from its own traditions. Intellectuals and activists cast about for a response – a political programme that was better suited to and more representative of the Muslim experience. At the core of the Islamist movement is a sense of reactive pride. Although there are major variations in interpretation, objectives and methodology, Islamism essentially hinges on a desire to reorganize Muslim societies, and the lives of individual Muslims, so that they conform to the directives of the Islamic faith.

It is interesting to note that Islamism has always been sustained by educated, middle-class individuals. Historically speaking, the ranks of the Islamist movement swelled when a generation of university-educated graduates attempted to climb the socioeconomic ladder, only to discover that the ruling elite had no interest in sharing the spoils of power. The authoritarian and closed elites of Egypt, Iran and Pakistan, to name just three, were too slow to modernize, absorb the growing class of technocrats, and allow their countries' rapidly increasing wealth to extend beyond their own small family circles. This generated great disillusionment among upwardly mobile groups, especially the middle classes, who have proved to be the most fertile ground for Islamist recruitment. The Islamist response to corruption and nepotism has therefore been to call for a return to Islam: 'Islam is the solution' became a common slogan in societies where avenues to development and progress seemed to be closed. As Manuel

Castells (2004: 17) points out, in such contexts Islamism became the oppositional doctrine to 'capitalism, to socialism, and to nationalism, Arab or otherwise, which are [in the view of Islamists] all failing ideologies of the post-colonial order'. Thus, it is hardly surprising that the early Islamist organizations frequently accused the region's secular regimes of corruption, nepotism and an anti-Muslim, pro-Western orientation.

In the 'revival' period of the 1950s to the 1970s, the modern Islamist movement was pioneered by the Muslim Brotherhood-affiliated thinker Sayyid Qutb and the Iranian Ayatollah Ruhollah Khomeini. These two men drew on an existing tradition of Islamic political thought and adapted the doctrines of their faith to form the basis of revolutionary socio-political movements. A core aspect of the movement in this period was its responsive and reactive nature. Islamism did not emerge in an intellectual or ideological vacuum and, although it is an indigenous response to the experiences of the Middle East, it was greatly affected by the political trends that were sweeping across the world at this time. In this way, Islamism can be understood as a movement that is partly anchored in the Islamic tradition but also highly reactive and responsive to external stimuli. Its major theorists drew on the ancient traditions of Islam to formulate a response to the realities of the early and mid-twentieth- century Middle East. Importantly, although the life and teachings of the Prophet are venerated and held as the ultimate blueprint for society, only a small minority of activists advocate a 'return' to the early years of Islamic history. Indeed, Yvonne Haddad (1992: 272) asserts that most Islamist organizations hope to 'Islamize modernity' rather than return to some idealized past. Islamism is therefore a modern political movement born of the historical experience of the mid-twentieth century.

State secularization played a central role in the rise of political Islam. This is most evident in the history of organizations like the Muslim Brotherhood, an Egyptian movement that was pivotal in the development of Islamism. It was founded in 1928 by a schoolteacher, Hasan al-Banna. Initially, it was not established as a force for radical change; rather, it followed an 'evolutionary path of preaching and socio-political action' (Esposito 1999: 140). Its leaders advocated a return to Islamic authenticity in the face of the increasing secular-ization of Egyptian society. However, as the Muslim Brotherhood spread throughout the region, its doctrine of grassroots activism was often interpreted, or utilized, as a challenge to the ruling elite. Although conceived as an apolitical organization committed to the Islamization of society through education, splinter factions increasingly pursued a political agenda. This trend continued after the Egyptian secret police assassinated Hasan al-Banna in 1949.

One of the most influential and controversial theorists of the Muslim Brotherhood was Sayyid Qutb, who joined the organization in 1951. Qutb was well educated and spent a period of time in the United States at the behest of the Egyptian government. Observers often focus on his negative experiences in that country as the trigger for his subsequent hardline views. However, his philosophy was clearly a response to the behaviour of Arab leaders vis-à-vis their own societies rather than a reaction to the relationship between Muslims and the West. His radicalization during his decade-long incarceration in Nasser's jails supports this interpretation. During this period, Qutb's worldview hardened considerably and his belief in Islam as a revolutionary political doctrine crystallized. In this way, his thinking was clearly and definitively a product of, and a reaction to, his own historical epoch – the period of Arab nationalism.

Qutb wrote several pivotal texts that are now seen as blueprints for Islamist action. His most influential major work was *Milestones*, first published in 1960 (Qutb 1978). In this text, Qutb presented his greatest innovation – a reworking of the Islamic concept of *jahiliyyah*, the 'Age of Ignorance', which is how Muslims refer to pre-Islamic Arabia. Qutb argued that the modern Muslim world had plunged back into a state of *jahiliyyah* as society was now governed without knowledge of God's divine law. This argument was premised on his observation of Muslim societies, which he believed 'openly declare secularism and negate all their relationships with religion' (Qutb 1978: 55). He was critical of his own country (Egypt) as well as the broader Muslim world for harming Muslim dignity by not adhering to Islamic principles in politics (Qutb 1978: 55) and insisted on the need to 'revive the Muslim community which is buried under the debris of the man-made traditions of several generations, crushed under the weight of false laws and customs' (Qutb 1978: 3). He viewed Islam as a revolutionary doctrine in opposition to existing political structures and against the West, and played a key role in articulating the parameters of political Islam as a distinct ideology which continues to inspire many people in the Middle East. The most controversial aspect of this worldview was his advocacy of jihad as a political tool to bring about the idealized Islamic state and divine sovereignty to replace 'man-made' laws. Elaborating on this point in *Milestones*, he argued:

> Thus jihad needs to be directed against ruling structures that withhold from individuals the freedom to choose Islam. No political system or material power should put hindrances in the way of preaching Islam. It should leave every individual free to accept it or reject it, and if someone wants to accept it, it should not prevent him or fight against him. If someone does this, then it is the duty of Islam to fight him until either he is killed or until he declares his submission.
>
> (Qutb 1978: 101–102)

Qutb's concept of jihad had universal applicability and related to all Muslim societies. This quality bolstered its appeal to Islamist actors throughout the Muslim world. His interpretation of Islam as a political doctrine that was capable of achieving major social revolution coincided with the failure of a number of secular–nationalist regimes to meet popular expectations, as was seen most clearly in the aftermath of the Arab defeat in the 1967 war with Israel. This conflict was a catalyst for widespread disillusionment with the secular–nationalist promises of prosperity and advancement of the Arab world. In a linked development, the imposition of secular governance in the Middle East and the embrace of secular social norms among sections of the elite were seen by many as indisputable evidence of a Western conspiracy against Islam. Concepts such as nationalism, socialism and liberalism were thus rejected by Islamists as corrupt and imported ideologies that were ill-suited to Arab society as well as unnecessary because a much more appropriate indigenous political code – Islam – already existed. In this way, a refocusing of communal life on Islamic tenets was seen as the panacea to the decline of the region in the face of Western intervention.

Following a long period of incarceration, the Egyptian state finally executed Qutb in 1966. But his ideas retained significant force for decades to come. In the late 1960s, Egypt proved a fertile ground for the Islamist critique of the state, as it was still ruled by Nasser's repressive secular–nationalist regime. Moreover, the regime was finding it impossible to deliver socioeconomic prosperity or a clear regional agenda, especially in relation to Israel. Islamists responded by questioning the role and legitimacy of the state's leadership, and they were consequently persecuted. This repression led to an ever more radical interpretation of the political potential of Islam as an alternative to the secular–nationalist project. The Egyptian Islamic Jihad (EIJ) organization serves as a prime example. This group, inspired by Qutb's theories, called for armed resistance against the existing political order of the Muslim world and the execution of the region's secular rulers (Knapp 2003: 88). It defined the Middle East's regimes as apostates for failing to uphold Islamic law and, in part, justified its assassination of Egyptian President Anwar Sadat in 1981 on these grounds, along with his role in the Egyptian–Israeli peace process.

The second key thinker of Islamism during this period was Iran's Ayatollah Ruhollah Khomeini, who offered an alternative political system based on Shia Islam. His politicization of Islam as a revolutionary doctrine was similar to Qutb's thinking. Both emphasized that Islam offered the best political solution to the challenges faced by the Muslim world, and both believed that an Islamic state based on divine sovereignty would eventually replace Western models of government, which they saw as illegitimate. However, Khomeini's doctrine departed from Qutb's in one key respect, because he insisted that society's return to Islam – and the restoration of God's sovereignty – was contingent on the clergy (Roy 1994: 173). This notion is encapsulated in his concept of *vilayat-e faqih* – or rule of the most learned Islamic scholar – which he developed while in exile in Najaf in the 1960s. *Vilayat-e faqih* stipulates that a senior cleric – the *faqih* (jurist) – must be the state's ultimate decision-maker, and this became the Islamic Republic's guiding principle after the overthrow of the Shah in 1979. The practical implications of this radical system of governance for Iranian society are explored in detail in Chapter 6.

The degeneration of political Islam into Islamic terrorism (al-Qaeda and ISIS)

This mid-twentieth-century ideological movement which aimed to reorient the societies of the Muslim world found distinct expression in the troubled state of Afghanistan in the late 1970s and 1980s. The Soviet Union invaded this Muslim-majority, tribal country in late 1979. In response to the invasion, Saudi Arabia and Pakistan, with the support of the American Central Intelligence Agency (CIA), crafted a cadre of transnational Islamist fighters to assist the indigenous Afghan mujahedeen. Religious justifications for armed conflict were presented to attract volunteers to wage jihad against the Soviet 'atheist' forces, and this propaganda campaign proved highly effective. Between 1979 and 1989, thousands of volunteers from across the globe flocked to Afghanistan, where they were soon indoctrinated in a Salafi worldview, funded and exported by Saudi Arabia's Wahhabi establishment. Hence, one of the unintended outcomes of this conflict was the emergence of the Salaf-jihadist movement, a transnational group of foreign fighters who had been drawn into the conflict. In the post-Afghan period, this movement spawned new, radicalized patterns of Islamic militancy directed towards regional Arab regimes and the West, chiefly the United States and its allies. Loosely affiliated and commonly denoted by the 'al-Qaeda' label, the Salafi-jihadist movement quickly evolved into, and remains, one of the greatest international security challenges of the twenty-first century, a point that is underscored by the emergence of the 'Islamic State' militia in 2014.

The Salafist movement developed in Sunni Islam in the late eighteenth century. It holds a literalist interpretation of the Qur'an and insists that the Prophet Mohammed's practices and *as-salaf as-salih* (first three generations) are the ultimate model to follow. Hence, it sought to rid Muslim society of practices which it viewed as inconsistent with the Prophet's teachings and a corruption of Islam. Muhammad Adb al-Wahhab (1703–1787), a religious scholar from Najd, gained prominence for his articulation of Salafism. The growth of his support base (dubbed Wahhabists) in central Arabia resulted in Wahhabism being closely associated with Salafi puritanism. While Salafism is actually a much broader movement than its Wahhabi manifestation, the political alliance al-Wahhab forged with Muhammad bin Saud, the ruler of the oasis settlement of Diriyah in the mid-eighteenth century, gave his teachings significant weight. This alliance survived a number of military and political setbacks, and served as the bedrock of political legitimacy for the ascendancy of the Saud dynasty in the early twentieth century, which culminated in the formation of the Kingdom of Saudi Arabia in 1932. Al-Wahhab's teachings are still considered to guide the kingdom in all its domestic and international affairs.

Saudi Arabia's economic boom in the 1970s allowed the kingdom to project its Wahhabi doctrine externally, and mosques throughout the Middle East and the West were offered Saudi petro-dollars and preachers. This export of Wahhabi literature and missionaries rendered the 'transnational organization of this movement ... an affective and influential force in the Muslim world' (Wiktorowicz 2001: 20). It is important to note that Salafism and Wahhabism are not inherently synonymous with violence and militancy, but in real-world applications the puritanical impulse of both traditions has often led to a confrontational worldview. During the Afghan conflict, for instance, Wahhabi teachings were utilized to foster Sunni Islamist militancy. This strategy helped the Saudi state and its Wahhabi establishment to emphasize its own Islamic credentials in the face of Iran's self-proclaimed revolutionary brand of Islamism. The transnational jihadist phenomenon that emerged in the context of resistance to Soviet rule in Afghanistan fused Salafi/Wahhabi teachings with modern Islamist theories to develop the concept of routine violence and acts of terror as legitimate political measures.

The Palestinian Abdullah Azzam (1941–1989) drafted the principal religious justification for volunteer participation in the war in Afghanistan. Although committed to the national liberation of Palestine, his theological and ideological thinking conflicted with the dominant secular–nationalist Palestinian doctrine of the time. He obtained his doctorate in Islamic jurisprudence from al-Azhar University in Cairo and went on to teach and preach in Palestine, Jordan and Saudi Arabia. Drawn to the Afghan conflict in 1980 and well known within political circles, he soon achieved fame as the 'jihad's herald' (Kepel 2004: 84). His work stressed Muslims' shared responsibility to defend any Muslim land that came under attack from non-Muslim forces. This drew on established Islamic jurisprudence but was radicalized in the context of the conflict. During the war's early years, he identified the defensive fight against the Soviet Union as a *Fard Kifayah*, which meant that most Muslims were not obliged to take up arms as long as some did (Azzam 2002: 19). As the conflict intensified, however, and the mujahedeen proved unable to repel the invading Soviet forces, he changed his opinion and labelled the conflict a *Fard Ain*, which meant that every Muslim now had a duty to join the fight (Azzam 2001: 55).

Box 5.1 Abdullah Azzam

Abdullah Azzam was born in Palestine in 1941. He joined the Muslim Brotherhood in the 1950s and went on to study and teach Islamic law in Palestine, Jordan and Damascus. After the 1967 Six-Day War, he and his family fled to Jordan. After receiving his doctorate from al-Azhar University in Cairo in 1971, he returned to Jordan to teach Islamic law at the University of Amman. During this period, he became an influential figure through his politicized and increasingly radicalized religious teachings. This led to tensions between Azzam and the Jordanian authorities, and he eventually moved to Saudi Arabia to teach at the Abd al-Aziz University in the late 1970s. The point at which Azzam met Osama bin Laden is contested. However, the two established the Maktab al-Khadamat (Service Bureau) in the city of Peshawar on the Pakistan–Afghanistan border in the early 1980s to recruit and train thousands of volunteers from across the globe to join the jihad against the Soviet forces. Azzam was considered the key ideologue for the anti-Soviet jihadist movement, with bin Laden providing significant financial support. Azzam's works drew on established Islamic jurisprudence, but he was radicalized in the context of the Soviet invasion of Afghanistan, which was widely regarded as an unjust foreign invasion of Muslim land. Azzam argued that joining the 'Afghan jihad' was a religious duty. He was killed by a bomb explosion on 24 November 1989 in Peshawar. After his death, the Service Bureau was transformed into what became known as al-Qaeda. Azzam's work continues to serve as the ideological foundation of many radicalized Islamist organizations across the region and their concepts of jihad.

From Peshawar, near the Afghanistan–Pakistan border, Azzam and Osama bin Laden recruited and trained thousands of volunteers from the surrounding region and beyond (Roy 1999). Their propaganda and recruitment network was expansive, covering over thirty-five countries (Springer et al. 2009: 41). The conceptual implications of this emerging global jihadism were significant. For instance, Quintan Wiktorowicz (2001: 26) has argued that 'Azzam's original call to defend Muslim lands was adopted to extend the jihad indefinitely, moving nomadic jihad into new countries to face infidel oppression'.

The eventual Soviet withdrawal from Afghanistan (explored in detail in Chapter 7) was celebrated by jihadists as a major victory. The jihadist phenomenon that took root in the fight against the Soviets was marked by its adherence to the puritanism of the Salafi movement and its propensity for violent action in the name of 'faith'. Azzam saw this type of jihad as a religious obligation that does not stop at national boundaries, but has a global reach. Hence, global jihadism became the governing framework for al-Qaeda, the organization of veteran jihadists which emerged from the Afghan conflict. By the time the war against the Soviet Union was over, al-Qaeda had developed the resources, networks and ideological principles it needed to engage in acts of terror anywhere in the Arab world. However, in 1991, the stationing of US troops on Saudi soil (which al-Qaeda considered sacred) precipitated a decisive change in the organization's focus. As Gilles Kepel (2004: 87) notes, 'for Bin Laden, the "cause" was now becoming clear: the secular America, with its soldiers, tanks and military bases, was befouling the land of the Muslim holy sites and was therefore the ultimate enemy that Islam must destroy'. At this moment, the United States and its allies became al-Qaeda's principal targets, dubbed the 'far enemy', as opposed to the regional Arab regimes, which were the 'near enemy'. The organization was implicated in the 1993 World Trade Center bombing, an ambush of US troops in Somalia, bombings of US targets in Saudi Arabia, the US Embassy attacks in Tanzania and Kenya, and various terrorist missions in Yemen (Wiktorowicz 2001: 18). In 1996 bin Laden issued a declaration of war against the United States, setting the ground for the attacks of 11 September 2001. The nineteen perpetrators comprised fifteen Saudi nationals, two from the United Arab Emirates, one Egyptian and one Lebanese.

The Islamic State in Iraq and Syria (ISIS), later renamed simply the Islamic State, is the latest manifestation of global jihadism. Drawing on the earlier tradition of recruiting fighters for jihad, ISIS has engaged in a proactive campaign to recruit Muslims from the Middle East and as far afield as Europe, North America and Australia. Its success in attracting foreign fighters has proven to be a serious security issue for the states concerned and continues to be a divisive topic (see Chapter 10).

Conclusion

The rise of pan-Arabism in the 1950s as the region's dominant ideological force occurred in the context of resistance to colonialism and its economic and social legacies. After the Arab states gained independence in the 1940s, both the Soviet Union and the United States vied for economic and political advantage. Pan-Arabism sought to unify the Arab world with a view to modernizing the region, often borrowing from various aspects of Western liberalism and socialism. However, internal rivalries in Syria, the inability of Nasser to deliver economic and social prosperity and the Arab states' crushing defeat in the Six-Day War shattered the vision of pan-Arab unity.

In the 1970s, Islamism eclipsed pan-Arabism as the principal revolutionary ideology in the region. Its proponents instrumentalized Islam as a revolutionary political doctrine capable of restoring authenticity and prosperity to the Muslim world in a defiant stance against the imported ideologies of secularism and nationalism. In Egypt, Islamists inspired by the teachings of Sayyid Qutb were viewed as a serious threat by the ruling secular regime and subsequently suffered harsh state repression. Conversely, the Iranian Ayatollah Khomeini was able to fuse religious fervour and anti-American sentiment to overthrow the ruling monarch, the Shah. His political doctrine of *vilayat-e faqih* subsequently served as the foundation stone for the Islamic Republic of Iran.

The Afghan conflict (1979–1989) and the instrumentalization of Islam to mobilize and attract Muslim volunteers to resist the Soviet invasion led directly to the evolution of Islamism. The movement was extended from an ideology for political action into armed militancy, even terrorism. The commitment to a campaign against the Soviet Union normalized the concept of global jihad and facilitated the merger of puritanical Salafism, resistance/liberation ideology and transnational physical militancy. Decades later, the Islamic State in Iraq and Syria capitalized on this history when it called on foreign fighters to enter a new theatre of war. However, after suffering a series of military setbacks, it quickly lost its ability to attract fresh jihadists. As a result, the movement morphed once again, inspiring individuals, some affiliated to Islamist organizations and some acting alone, to undertake terrorist atrocities from Kuwait to Paris, acts which they positioned within the paradigm of militant Islamism.

References

Akbarzadeh, Shahram and Saeed, Abdullah (2003) 'Islam and Politics', in Shahram Akbarzadeh and Abdullah Saeed (eds), *Islam and Political Legitimacy* (London: Routledge).

Azzam, Abdullah (2001) [1987] *Join the Caravan* (London: Azzam Publications).

Azzam, Abdullah (2002) [1984] *In Defence of Muslim Land* (London: Azzam Publications).

Baram, Amatzia (1991) *Culture, History and Ideology in the Formation of Ba'thist Iraq, 1968–89* (New York: St Martin's).

Bonney, Richard (2004) *Jihad from the Qur'an to bin Laden* (London: Palgrave Macmillan).

Castells, Manuel (2004) *The Power of Identity* (London: Blackwell).

Chaudhry, Mohammad A. (1998) 'Effects of World Capitalism on Urbanisation in Egypt', *International Journal of Middle East Studies*, Vol. 20, No. 1, pp. 23–43.

Cleveland, William (2000) *A History of the Modern Middle East* (Boulder, CO: Westview).

Denoeux, Guilain (2002) 'The Forgotten Swamp: Navigating Political Islam', *Middle East Policy*, Vol. 9, No. 2, pp. 56–81.

Esposito, John (1999) *The Islamic Threat: Myth or Reality?* (Oxford: Oxford University Press).

Ferris, Jesse (2008) 'Soviet Support for Egypt's Intervention in Yemen, 1962–1963', *Journal of Cold War Studies*, Vol. 10, No. 4, pp. 5–36.

Gerges, Fawaz A. (1995) 'The Kennedy Administration and the Egyptian–Saudi Conflict in Yemen: Co-opting Arab Nationalism', *Middle East Journal*, Vol. 49, No. 2, pp. 292–311.

Haddad, Yvonne (1992) 'Islamists and the Problem of Israel: The 1967 Awakening', *Middle East Journal*, Vol. 46, No. 2, pp. 266–285.

Hammel, Eric (2010) *Six Days in June: How Israel Won the 1967 Arab–Israeli War* (New York: Charles Scribner's Sons).

Jankowski, James (2002) *Nasser's Egypt, Arab Nationalism, and the United Arab Republic* (London: Lynne Rienner).

Kepel, Gilles (2004) *The War for Muslim Minds: Islam and the West* (Cambridge, MA: Belknap Press of Harvard University Press).

Knapp, Michael G. (2003) 'The Concept and Practice on Jihad in Islam', *Parameters*, Vol. 33, No. 1, pp. 82–94.

League of Arab States (1945) 'Pact of the League of Arab States', available at http://ava lon.law.yale.edu/20th_century/arableag.asp.

Meital, Yoram (2000) 'The Khartoum Conference and Egyptian Policy after the 1967 War: A Reexamination', *Middle East Journal*, Vol. 54, No. 1, pp. 64–82.

Middle East Institute (1956) 'The New Egyptian Constitution', *Middle East Journal*, Vol. 10, No. 3, pp. 300–306.

Nasser, Gamal Abdel (1955) *The Philosophy of the Revolution* (Cairo: Mondiale Press).

Qutb, Sayed (1978) *Milestones* (Beirut: Holy Koran Publishing House).

Roberts, David (2013) *The Ba'th and the Creation of Modern Syria* (London: Routledge).

Roy, Olivier (1994) *The Failure of Political Islam* (Cambridge, MA: Harvard University Press)

Roy, Olivier (1999) 'The Radicalization of Sunni Conservative Fundamentalism', *ISIM Newsletter*, No. 2, p. 7.

Sadiki, Larbi (1995) 'Al-la Nidam: An Arab View of the New World (Dis)order', *Arab Studies Quarterly*, Vol. 17, No. 3, pp. 1–22.

Springer, Devin R., Regens, James L. and Edgar, David N. (2009) *Islamic Radicalism and Global Jihad* (Washington, DC: Georgetown University Press).

Wiktorowicz, Quintan (2001) 'The New Global Threat: Transnational Salafis and Jihad', *Middle East Policy*, Vol. 8, No. 4, pp. 18–38.

6   The Iranian Revolution and pan-Shi'ism

Introduction

In 1979 Iran experienced a popular revolution with significant implications for the Middle East. Ayatollah Khomeini galvanized popular anger against Iran's autocratic ruler, Reza Shah Pahlavi, to overthrow the monarchy. This led to the birth of the Islamic Republic of Iran, marking the first case of a popularly elected Islamic regime in modern times. However, before Iran's revolutionary dust had settled, the Islamic Republic was invaded by its neighbour Iraq in September 1980. The two countries quickly descended into a brutal war of attrition that claimed between 850,000 and a million lives before its conclusion in 1988. This made it the longest-running conventional war of the twentieth century. Khomeini's synthesis of Iranian nationalism and religious zeal mobilized the people of Iran in their thousands in defence of the Islamic Republic. By the close of the war, the regime had solidified, with a loyal defence force that remains a key instrument of Iran's security apparatus today. At the regional level, Iran's revolutionary leaders championed the Islamic Republic as a model of resistance against Western oppression. This revolutionary call elicited popular support within marginalized communities throughout the region. Moreover, it facilitated the emergence of the Lebanese Islamist organization Hezbollah, which has since developed into a formidable force in support of Iran and against Israel.

This chapter will first explore the social and political context within which the Iranian Revolution took place. Specific attention is paid to Iranian discontent with US interference and influence throughout the Middle East. It will then explore the rise of Ayatollah Khomeini as the Supreme Leader of the Islamic Republic, including a thorough examination of the 1979 Iranian constitution that institutionalized the principles of his concept of *vilayat-e faqih*: rule by the most learned Islamic scholar. This analysis of the Iranian constitution will shed light on Iran's dual system of power and the ongoing tensions at play between divine authority, represented by the Supreme Leader, and popular authority, represented by the elected Iranian President. The chapter will then provide a brief account of the Iran–Iraq War and the religious and nationalist tactics employed by the Islamic regime to consolidate its power. It will conclude with an examination of Iran's foreign policy, which has been widely criticized as a source of regional instability, especially because of its efforts to export the revolution.

The Iranian Revolution

The Iranian Revolution of 1979 constituted a turning point in the political history of the Middle East. It also marked a vital moment in Washington's role in, and perception of, the region. The modern State of Iran was established in 1935; previously, the territory had been known as Persia. In the mid-twentieth century, the Iranian people embraced the democratic process, moving the country away from its traditional royalist system. Elections led to the accession of a nationalist government under the leadership of Mohammed Mossadeq. In line with many other post-colonial leaders, Mossadeq moved to nationalize the Iranian oil industry and free the state from Western economic influence. Understandably, Washington saw these developments with alarm, compounded by fears regarding Mossadeq's apparent socialist leanings. These concerns led to a coup in 1953, supported by British intelligence and the Central Intelligence Agency (CIA), which overthrew Mossadeq's government and reinstalled the pro-US Muhammad Reza Shah of the Pahlavi dynasty as the nation's ruler (Abrahamian 2001). British agents were directly involved in planning this coup, with the explicit endorsement of the United States. Hence, it came to be seen in the Middle East as a clear example of direct foreign interference by the Great Powers. This was a blatant violation of Iranian national sovereignty, carried out to protect the economic and political interests of the United States and the United Kingdom. This aggressive behaviour left a lasting impression in Iran and the broader Middle East. Interestingly, the gradual decline of the United Kingdom, which coincided with the global ascendancy of the United States in the post-war era, coloured the collective memory of the coup, with the emphasis increasingly placed on Washington as its principal architect. This perception was cemented as the reinstalled Pahlavi dynasty granted the United States a 40 per cent share in the Iranian oil consortium (Keddie 2003: 132). Thereafter, the Pahlavi regime became closely aligned with Washington.

Box 6.1 Mohammed Mossadeq

Mohammed Mossadeq (1882–1967) was the democratically elected Prime Minister of Iran from 1951 to 1953. An ardent nationalist, he rejected foreign intervention in Iranian affairs and was a key player in the nationalization of the Iranian oil industry. In the midst of a troubled period in Iranian politics, he was overthrown by a US- and UK-backed military coup. The CIA's role in the coup, codenamed Operation Ajax, is often seen as the first clear example of direct US intervention in Middle Eastern politics.

Map 6 Iran
Source: www.un.org/Depts/Cartographic/map/profile/iran.pdf

The overall context of the early Cold War undoubtedly influenced Washington's decision-making in this period. The 1953 coup can be seen as an early application of the 1947 Truman Doctrine, which held that unless the United States moved decisively, the Soviet Union would gain influence in the oil-rich region. Following the events of 1953, the public image of the United States suffered a blow in Iran as Washington offered uncritical support to the authoritarian Pahlavi regime, while 'rationalizing or ignoring the tremendous popular disaffection' with the regime (Makdissi 2002: 548).

Bolstered by his alliance with a superpower, the Shah embarked on a series of repressive measures. The state's security apparatus, especially the notorious SAVAK, enforced the Shah's grip on power. However, popular Iranian discontent seethed as the regime enacted the White Revolution, a top-down policy of secularization. Some of the measures were extremely ill-advised: for example, the Shah replaced the traditional Islamic calendar with a royalist one. As Ervand Abrahamian (1999: 26) points out, 'few contemporary regimes have been so foolhardy as to undermine their country's religious calendar'. Although broadly unpopular, such actions were perhaps not as damaging as the widespread perception that the Shah was a US puppet. In a fiercely nationalist country, the idea of a leadership that was beholden to external influences was profoundly destabilizing. The Shah imported millions of dollars' worth of high-tech weaponry as well as US military personnel to operate it. This made his dependence on American aid highly visible, so it became a source of antagonism for many Iranians and a potent opportunity for those who were keen to challenge his rule.

Box 6.2 SAVAK

SAVAK was a security and intelligence organization that operated under Iran's autocratic ruler Reza Shah Pahlavi (ruled 1953–1979). It was established in 1957 with the assistance of the United States' CIA and Israel's Mossad. SAVAK played an instrumental role in facilitating the Shah's power through its violent repression of all political opposition, especially leftist groups. It dissolved with the fall of the Shah following the 1979 Iranian Revolution.

As late as New Year's Eve 1978, US President Jimmy Carter publicly praised 'the great leadership of the Shah', which, he insisted, had turned Iran into 'an island of stability in one of the more troubled areas of the world' (quoted in Makdissi 2002: 548). But nothing could have been further from the truth. The Carter administration's support for the Shah can be interpreted through the prisms of both economic and Cold War strategies. After the Shah's return to power, the United States gained a significant foothold in Iran's oil industry. Moreover, in what would become a defining feature of US policy in the twentieth century, Washington demonstrated its preference for status quo leaderships in order to secure its economic objectives and ensure that the Soviet Union did not make inroads in the region. However, on the ground, popular discontent was growing.

As the revolutionary momentum intensified, Khomeini emerged as the embodiment of the future. His public image as an anti-Western, nationalist religious scholar stood in stark contrast to the opulent lifestyles of the ruling pro-US elite, and his charismatic power was bolstered by the deepening political crisis in Iran in the late 1970s. Dissatisfaction with the Shah led to public rallies in which thousands of people protested against the regime's close relationship with the United States. The response was harsh: the army was called in to quell protesters. Meanwhile, the Shah's government continued to reassure its American backers that it remained in control of the situation. Washington was happy to accept the Shah's reports of popular support for the regime, so it was wholly unprepared for the groundswell of anger and anti-regime protest which swept through the country in late 1978. In February 1979 the monarchy was overthrown and replaced with the Islamic Republic. On 1 April, a referendum confirmed this dramatic development, and the first Islamic state in modern history was officially established. In the course of a few months a sophisticated state machinery that had been propped up by Washington had fallen into the hands of fiercely anti-US Islamic revolutionaries.

The importance of the Iranian Revolution cannot be overstated. The Middle East appeared to be in a state of flux, with the established stalwarts and allies crumbling in the face of domestic agitation for change. To the region's young Muslims, the establishment of the new government in Iran, and its rhetoric of Islamic solidarity, seemed to portend a period of triumph in which Islam would become a significant power on the world stage. More importantly, the revolution was seen throughout the region as an effective indigenous response to external interference. Underscoring the adaptability of this movement, political Islam, as it was employed in the lead-up to the revolution, was about grassroots politics and people power, not violence.

Khomeini's triumphant return from exile in February 1979 brought an Islamic theocracy to power for the first time in modern history. However, politics was just as important as religion in this uprising. The revolutionary mood had a vehemently anti-US tone which Khomeini exploited to the full:

> America is the number-one enemy of the deprived and oppressed people of the world … It exploits the oppressed people of the world by means of the large-scale propaganda campaigns that are coordinated for it by international Zionism. By means of its hidden and treacherous agents, it sucks the blood of the defenseless people as if it alone, together with its satellites, had the right to live in this world. Iran has tried to sever all its relations with this Great Satan.
>
> (Khomeini 1985: 304–305)

Washington was still attempting to digest these changes when a further disaster erupted. Emboldened by the revolution, a group of Iranian students stormed the US Embassy in Tehran and took fifty-six US citizens hostage. Thereafter, the crisis dragged on for 444 days and the ramifications were significant for relations between the two countries for years to come. Carter's administration descended into chaos as it was unable to secure the release of the hostages, a failure that tarnished the President's reputation at home and abroad. In the Cold War period the ability to project an image of power was all-important, and the United States lost that ability in a matter of weeks at the hands of a small group of students. Carter halted oil imports from Iran and froze Iranian assets in the United States while continuing to pursue diplomatic initiatives, but all of these tactics proved fruitless. On 24 April 1980, US forces attempted a rescue mission, Operation Eagle Claw, but this ended in disaster as eight US marines lost their lives, dealing yet another crushing blow to the Carter administration's public profile. The failure to resolve the crisis contributed to the election of the Republican presidential candidate Ronald Reagan in November 1980. He campaigned on a tough security platform, but the Republican Party's clandestine dealings with Tehran were widely questioned in subsequent years. The so-called 'October

Surprise' theory suggests that the Republicans negotiated directly with Tehran to gain political advantage over the embattled Carter administration (Sick 1991).

The impact of the hostage-taking was felt well beyond Washington's halls of power. In their homes, the US public watched televised images of thousands of Iranians protesting violently against the United States. Throughout America, the political context of Western interference and the repressive rule of the Pahlavi dynasty were completely overlooked as people baulked at footage of Iranians demanding a return to what seemed an archaic system of governance. Deep mistrust on both sides only grew over the subsequent decades. American fears regarding political Islam's challenge to the United States were fed by consecutive administrations that wished to protect the status quo in the oil-rich Persian Gulf. The hostage crisis and the Iranian regime's unwillingness to compromise humiliated the United States on the world stage. A deep schism developed between Iran and the international community. Khomeini's *fatwa* (Islamic legal ruling) against the author Salman Rushdie in the mid-1980s then reinforced the public and political perception of Iran as a profoundly threatening presence.

In the post-revolutionary chaos, as factions fought bitterly for the future of Iran, Khomeini emerged as the only leader with the stature to harness and direct the new political system. As a result, he and his followers were able to centralize power in their hands and initiate the Islamization of Iranian society. Women who had taken the veil as a revolutionary political statement against the Shah's Western orientation found themselves forced to wear it by law (Afary and Anderson 2005: 113). Such laws were enforced by the Revolutionary Guards, formed in May 1979. The members of this zealous organization were committed to Khomeini's vision and brutal in enforcing the state's interpretation of Islamic law. However, for many ordinary Iranians, they were nothing more than an Islamic version of the feared and loathed SAVAK.

The early idealism of the revolution seemed to ebb away as the leadership's determination to maintain societal control increased. Schools and universities, for example, were repeatedly closed and purged of 'non-Islamic elements', always with reference to the need to maintain vigilance against Western influences. These authoritarian measures divided Iranian society and even its revolutionary leaders, but Khomeini's system of governance, *vilayat-e faqih*, allowed him and other conservative clerics to act with almost complete impunity.

Vilayat-e faqih and the rise of Shi'ism

Khomeini's religious and political trajectory in the years leading up to the revolution informed his system of revolutionary governance. He was born in 1902 and trained as a traditional Islamic cleric. His opposition to the Pahlavi regime in the early 1960s led to his exile in Iraq, where he continued to preach an empowered version of Islam. Drawing on the Shia tradition of defying 'unjust' authority, he used Islam as a political tool for mobilizing the population against the regime, which he dismissed as corrupt and illegitimate. He developed his Islamic revolutionary ideas further in the formulation of a novel concept: the supremacy of jurisprudence (*vilayat-e faqih*). In this model, the *faqih* (jurist) sits at the head of the state and is the ultimate decision-maker. *Vilayat-e faqih* marked a clear departure from earlier Shia political philosophies, which did not require a single source of authority. Indeed, as Dale Eickelman and James Piscatori point out, Khomeini's vision of *vilayat-e faqih* was regarded by many 'as an extraordinary, even heterodox, position' (Eickelman and Piscatori 1996: 49). In this way, Khomeini demonstrated the adaptable nature of political Islam, a movement that was capable of changing to meet the political requirements of a specific time and place. The need to contextualize his ideas within late twentieth-century Iran is underscored by the fact that his formulation of this system of governance was also very different to the thinking of contemporary Sunni activists, such as Sayyid Qutb. The latter did not reserve a privileged position for the Islamic clergy in their vision of the ideal Islamic state.

The 1979 Iranian constitution institutionalized the *faqih*'s ultimate power within Iranian society:

> [T]he *wilayah* [guardianship] and leadership of the *Ummah* [community of the faithful] devolve upon the *'adil muttaqi faqih* [the just and pious Islamic jurisprudent], who is fully aware of the circumstances of his age; courageous, resourceful, and possessed of administrative ability, [he] will assume the responsibilities of this office in accordance with Article 107 ...
>
> The powers of government in the Islamic Republic are vested in the legislature, the judiciary, and the executive powers, functioning under the supervision of the absolute *wilayat al-'amr* [guardianship] and the leadership of the *Ummah* [Muslim community].
>
> ('Islamic Republic of Iran Constitution' 1979: Articles 5 and 57)

Therefore, this constitution empowered Khomeini as the leader of the revolution and senior member of the clergy with supreme authority over national affairs. Enshrined within the same constitution is the people's mandate to elect the President, parliament and municipal councils (Articles 113–132). This established a dual system of power in the Islamic Republic: divine authority, embodied by the Supreme Leader; and popular authority, embodied by the President. This arrangement advanced the state's revolutionary narrative, which designates the Islamic Republic as both a democratic and an Islamic system of government. However, all presidential actions and decisions can be overturned by the Supreme Leader, who holds ultimate power. This essentially negates the concept of 'rule by the people' that is inherent in the term 'republic' and reveals a significant contradiction in the foundations of the Iranian state that has generated severe tension between Iran's religious conservatives and those seeking democratic reform.

The Islamic Republic's forty-year history has been marred by clashes between these two camps. For instance, some Iranian presidents have challenged the Supreme Leader's authority, albeit with limited success. The reformist Mohammad Khatami won a landslide electoral victory in 1997, and many observers anticipated that his presidency would usher in a new era guided by the principles of accountability and equality, civil rights and individual freedom. Indeed, Khatami advocated a progressive Islam to meet the demands of modern society. As a firm believer in the Islamic Revolution, he argued that adhering to a reformed or liberalized version of Islam would facilitate the revolution's prosperity. However, although his views were widely supported among the Iranian public, his reformist agenda was anathema to the conservative establishment. Liberalization would threaten not only the conservatives' vision of the ideal Islamic society but their grip on power. Consequently, they resisted all of his calls for reform. Following a prolonged period of obstruction and retrenchment which undermined Khatami's capacity to institutionalize meaningful change, Mahmoud Ahmadinejad was elected President in 2005 as the compromise candidate between the conservatives and the more hardline critics of the reform movement. The swing to conservatism in this period owed much to growing concern over US policy in the region, which had forced regime change on either side of Iran (Afghanistan in 2001 and Iraq in 2003).

In contrast to Khatami's reformist ideals, Ahmadinejad ruled with an iron fist: human rights were violated, freedom was repressed and opportunities for Iran's highly educated youth were scarce. His tenure met with utter disdain among large segments of Iranian society, which manifested in anti-government protests during the 2009 presidential elections in many urban centres. Hence, his re-election for a second term was greeted with disbelief and more protests by thousands of Iranian youths. This so-called 'Green Movement', which rumbled on for seven months, challenged the foundations of the Islamic Republic with calls for greater human rights, democratic reform and even the removal of the Supreme Leader. Dozens were killed, hundreds disappeared and thousands were arrested in the security crackdown. In the years that followed, Iran's security forces employed intimidation tactics and harsher repressive measures in an attempt to silence all political dissent. However, what the Green Movement signified for the Iranian Revolution as a whole should not be underestimated. The Supreme Leader was quick to publicly endorse Ahmadinejad's controversial victory. As Monshipouri and Assareh (2009: 40) poignantly note, 'when Supreme Leader Khamenei declared the election of Ahmadinejad a "divine assessment", he clearly chose the state over the people.

Box 6.3 The Green Movement

The Green Movement emerged following Iran's 2009 presidential elections. After the re-election of the incumbent President Mahmoud Ahmadinejad, thousands of protesters rallied in major cities to challenge the result. The protesters wore green armbands or headbands and demanded greater human rights, more government accountability and democratic reform. The protests were mobilized through social media and there was no clearly established leadership, although most were affiliated with the reformist camp in Iran. The movement was finally quelled by Iran's Basij militia.

The Green Movement exemplified the deep schism between Iran's state and society that has been perpetuated by the concept of *vilayat-e faqih*. This point is underscored by the reformist leadership of Ahmadinejad's successor, President Hassan Rouhani. The latter entered presidential office in 2013 with a clear foreign policy objective to bring Iran out of isolation. While Iran's nuclear deal with the United States in 2015 was a major success (explored in Chapter 11), his attempts to give more weight and authority to the popular vote have been repeatedly quashed. His re-election in 2017 reveals that there is still an appetite for democratic change within Iranian society. However, the widespread popular support for his reformist agenda has had little impact on Iran's conservative establishment, which continues to undermine his efforts to implement change. To a certain extent, this reflects the conservative leadership's perception of its own power, which it feels emanates directly from God, bolstered by Iran's security apparatus.

Hence, while Iranian presidents have attempted to push the boundaries of *vilayat-e faqih*, they have enjoyed limited success. Complete power is still vested in Iran's conservative religious leadership, as institutionalized by the state's constitution, to the detriment of those seeking democratic reform. Since the revolution, this leadership has sustained the domestic status quo despite the Islamic Republic's perpetuated state of conflict with external forces. The country's system of governance has survived a bloody conflict with Iraq and ongoing hostile relations with the United States (see Chapter 11). Indeed, as discussed below, the Iran–Iraq War helped to cement the revolutionary regime's power over Iranian society and firmly entrenched the security apparatus's loyalty to the state.

The Iran–Iraq War (1980–1988)

In 1980, fifteen months after the formal establishment of the Islamic Republic, Iran descended into all-out war with its neighbour Iraq. This provided Iran's revolutionary leadership with an opportunity to consolidate its power and simultaneously imbue a deep sense of nationalistic pride within Iranian society. The conflict broke out when a set of simmering historical and political tensions were ignited by the catalyst of the Islamic Revolution. Hence, it is important to explore these tensions before examining the conflict's profound impact on the Islamic Republic and Iranian society.

The political relationship between Iran and Iraq ebbed and flowed throughout the twentieth century. In a similar fashion to many other parts of the Middle East, disputes between the two countries tended to revolve around border demarcation, access to waterways and ethnic tension. Iran and Iraq were and remain major regional states in terms of political influence, resources, population and size. They both played leading roles in the political development of the post-Ottoman Middle East and maintained close relations with external powers, particularly the United Kingdom and the United States, for much of the twentieth century.

In 1975 Iran and Iraq negotiated a settlement known as the Algiers Accord. This aimed to resolve two long-standing points of tension between the two states: right of access to the Shatt al-Arab waterway and Iranian support for Iraqi Kurdish opposition to Baghdad. Iraq's repressed Kurdish minority (20 per cent) had long received military aid from the Shah to challenge the central government in Baghdad and undermine the Iraqi state. Under the terms of the accord, in return for a promise that Tehran would discontinue this support, Iraq agreed to a border on the *thalweg* (deep-water line) of the Shatt al-Arab waterway. In effect, this provision accepted Iran's demand for shared use of this vital route. What would later serve as a point of contention between the two countries was the agreement's clear articulation that both parties would uphold 'principles of territorial integrity, border inviolability and non-interference in internal affairs' (MidEastWeb 1975). Although it was an unpopular settlement, the agreement was an accurate reflection of the relationship between the Shah's Iran and Ba'athist Iraq – tense but functional, especially on issues of security.

This wary cooperation changed profoundly with the establishment of the Islamic Republic in 1979. This year was also significant for Iraq, as Saddam Hussein became President and quickly turned the state into a dictatorship. Initially, Iraq cautiously welcomed the new government in Tehran. However, the newly empowered Ayatollah Khomeini soon emerged as a vocal critic of Baghdad. Having spent part of his exile in Najaf, he had witnessed repression of the local Shia population at the hands of Iraqi's Ba'ath Party. As he consolidated his power in Iran, he intensified his rhetoric on the need for more Islamic revolutions throughout the Middle East. Moreover, he singled out Iraq's Ba'ath regime as particularly corrupt and called for its overthrow. Soon, the new Iranian regime signalled its rejection of the existing Iran–Iraq relationship and violated the terms of the Algiers Accord by recommencing assistance to restive Kurdish factions inside Iraq (Musallam 1996: 81).

Meanwhile, Iran's revolutionary message of resistance appealed to Iraq's Shia majority (60–65 per cent), who had suffered years of political, social and economic repression under the Ba'athist regime. Inspired by the changes in Iran, violent resistance to Saddam quickly became a popular notion among significant numbers of Iraq's Shia community. This constituted a dangerous moment for the regime, so Baghdad launched a rapid response. In April 1980, the authorities executed the influential Shia cleric Muhammad al-Sadr and expelled thousands of Shias, acts which inflamed public opinion inside Iran. Saddam was convinced that the Islamic Republic was whipping up dissent inside Iraq, so he began to agitate publicly for *Arab* unity – a clear indication that he was anticipating a conflict with Persian Iran. Although these issues of religious and ethnic difference played little part in the final decision to go to war, they provided a strong propaganda tool for the Iraqi regime. Focusing on the Persian and Shia character of Iran, Baghdad portrayed its neighbour as a threat to the entire Gulf region and positioned itself as the champion of vulnerable Arab regimes.

In a move that further fuelled Saddam's fears, Khomeini publicly declared that the Islamic Republic would liberate Jerusalem after liberating Karbala in

Iraq. Saddam viewed this as a declaration of war and proof of Iran's expansionist intent, so he launched a pre-emptive attack on 22 September 1980. He may have believed that Iran, still recovering from the chaos of the revolution, would be unable to withstand such an attack. However, this assessment proved misguided as the Iranian population mobilized to repel the invading army. Despite early Iraqi gains, by 1982 the conflict had become an entrenched war of attrition. Two years into the conflict, there were not Iraqi soldiers on Iranian territory, so Tehran could have declared a limited victory. However, each leadership appeared committed to destroying the other.

The conflict continued until 1988, which made it the longest conventional war of the twentieth century. It had a devastating impact on the societies of both countries, with a total of 1.3 million men on active duty – comprising one-half of all Iraqi and one-sixth of all Iranian men of military age. The Iran–Iraq War was also marked by the use of chemical weapons. Saddam used cyanide gas against Iranian troops on the front line in the hope of gaining a military advantage, but to no avail. He also deployed chemical weapons against his own Kurdish population, notably in the Anfal campaign of 1987–1988, to consolidate his grip on power. Samir al-Khalil (1989: 281) has suggested that the 'absence of military strategy, when shared by both sides, leads to gruelling slogging matches in which nothing is more expendable than human life'. This description perfectly captures the protracted and ultimately futile Iran–Iraq War.

External support prolonged the war. Iran received considerable aid from Syria, Libya, North Korea and China (Segal 1988: 951). Damascus's anti-Israeli and anti-Western stance made Syria an obvious ally for the newly established Islamic Republic. Hence, despite significant ideological differences between Iran's leaders and Syria's secular Ba'athist Party, the two states forged a strong strategic alliance during the war, with Syria supplying Iran with advanced military hardware. Iraq, on the other hand, received considerable assistance from the United States and the Arab sheikhdoms in the Persian Gulf. The US response was initially guarded but ultimately governed by geostrategic considerations that focused on containing Iran. Meanwhile, Saddam capitalized on Arab concerns regarding Iran's expansionism by portraying Iraq as a physical buffer between Tehran and the Gulf states. This tactic was successful and Iraq was loaned billions of dollars. By the close of the conflict, its war debts exceeded US$80 billion, at least half of which was owed to neighbouring Arab states (Freedman and Karsh 1993: 39). Iraq's inability to repay these loans led directly to the first Gulf War (1990–1991), which was sparked by Saddam's decision to invade Kuwait in August 1990. For Washington, the shock of the Islamic Revolution, the humiliation of the hostage crisis and the regional destabilization caused by the Soviet Union's invasion of Afghanistan all contributed to its desire to maintain the status quo in the oil-rich Persian Gulf region. This was a major factor in the United States' decision to supply Iraq with weapons and intelligence throughout the conflict (Pauly and Lansford 2005: 92).

In the course of the war, Tehran consistently laid out three preconditions to peace negotiations: Iraqi admission of guilt, the removal of Saddam and war reparations. The unrealistic nature of these demands demonstrated Iran's determination to perpetuate the conflict. Meanwhile, Iraq attempted to force the enemy to the negotiating table by inflicting massive civilian casualties. The United Nations and the rest of the international community, although issuing strong calls for an end to the conflict, appeared largely unable, or unwilling, to influence events on the ground, despite widespread knowledge of the use of chemical weapons. The lack of concerted international effort may be ascribed to the fact that the impact of the war was contained within the region. Despite substantial differences in size and natural resources, external assistance made Iran and Iraq well-matched adversaries, and neither state was able to gain a decisive advantage. This situation, although extremely costly in terms of human life, basically ensured that the conflict did not spread and entangle other Middle Eastern states. However, the international community was concerned about maintaining oil shipments through the Persian Gulf, especially when Iran threatened to close the routes in 1987. This threat signalled that the conflict was about to spill over into the wider region, which would affect not only the Middle East but potentially the global economy. Hence, the international community finally stepped up the pressure for peace. The danger of direct superpower involvement in particular triggered an immediate response from the United Nations: the Security Council issued Resolution 598 in 1987, which called for a cease-fire, and in August 1988 Iran and Iraq agreed to one, bringing the eight-year conflict to a close.

Iraq's invasion of Iran in 1980 was a critical moment in the history of the Islamic Republic. In a truly spectacular feat, Khomeini mobilized hundreds of thousands of Iranians and instilled a deep sense of nationalistic pride that continued to pervade Iranian society for decades to come. Central to this mobilization was Khomeini's creation of the volunteer paramilitary organization known as the Basij, which he lauded as a 'twenty-million-man army'. In fact, at its peak in 1986, approximately 100,000 Basij volunteers were stationed on the front line (Wright 2010: 61). These men were dedicated to upholding Iran's Islamic Revolution and played a crucial role in the conflict, fighting alongside the regular army and the Revolutionary Guards and contributing most of the manpower for the 'human wave' strategy, which involved clearing minefields and drawing enemy fire ahead of regular army advances. Hence, in the face of escalating casualties, the Basij volunteers were of utmost importance in sustaining Iran's war effort. Following the war, the organization evolved into a tool of social and political control which was used to enforce the regime's strict moral code of conduct.

During the war, Khomeini fused Shia-inspired traditions of martyrdom with fervent Iranian nationalism to create a military culture of self-assured superiority that proved difficult to counter. To sustain volunteer recruitment in a seemingly unending and brutal war, Iran's revolutionary leaders propagated Shia narratives of resistance, martyrdom and the 680 CE Battle of Karbala to mobilize Iranians to defend the Islamic Republic. The Third Imam of Shia, Hussein ibn Ali, and seventy-two companions were killed at the Battle of Karbala by forces loyal to

Caliph Yazid, whose legitimacy has since been rejected by the Shia. In the centuries that followed, his murder came to represent Shia resistance to tyranny and injustice. In the war against Iraq, this notion of resistance was linked to a strong commitment to martyrdom in defence of the Islamic Republic. Iraqi aggression, which was explicit in its invasion of Iranian territory, targeting of Iranian civilians and use of chemical weapons against Iranian troops, served to fuel this narrative. As a result, there was an upsurge in nationalistic pride. In the context of the war, Iran's leadership portrayed the newly created and seemingly isolated Islamic Republic as Imam Hussein and his followers, while denoting Saddam Hussein and his superior military forces, supported by the United States, as Yazid. Significantly, the Islamic Republic also glorified the role of Muslim women at the Battle of Karbala. For example, Fatimah, the daughter of Prophet Mohammed, was honoured as the righteous and pious mother of her martyred son, Imam Hussein. Another example is Zaynab, the sister of Imam Hussein, who was recognized for her courageous defiance against Yazid. Throughout the war, Iranian leaders circulated stories of these women to encourage their female descendants to support their menfolk in battle and show resilience and humility in the face of high casualties. Moreover, these narratives enabled Khomeini to transcend religious boundaries and appeal to Iran's secular audience by portraying the conflict in terms of justice fighting injustice. As Mateo Mohammad Farzaneh (2007: 87) points out:

> in the eyes of the Iranian clerical establishment and the secular Iranians and the Iranian youth, they were all fighting for Iran's territorial integrity based on the principle of right fighting and defeating wrong. In other words, one cannot give exclusive credit to either secular or religious elements in Iranian nationalism but one has to describe Iranian nationalism as containing both.

By the end of the war, nationalism was firmly entrenched within Iranian society and it remains central to the Islamic Republic's revolutionary message today. Effectively, it is still at the forefront of society, ready to be exploited in times of crisis.

Upon reflection, the Iran–Iraq War allowed the revolutionary regime to consolidate its power over Iranian society. In the first two years of the conflict, the regime took the opportunity to purge opposition groups in a brutal crackdown. Dissidents were arrested, detained and executed. In the midst of the war's chaos and uncertainty, public opinion was more sympathetic to this hardline approach. The war also entrenched the loyalty of Iran's security apparatus to the state. After the war, the Basij was upgraded to become one of the five main forces of the Iranian Revolutionary Guard Corps (IRGC). Since then, it has increasingly focused on activities relating to internal security, law enforcement, policing morals and suppressing political dissent. In light of the push for reform and to sustain support for the Basij, the state introduced a law in 1998 that encourages Iranians to join the organization in return for special privileges, such as employment and higher-education opportunities, better housing and loan facilities, and social and welfare services (Golkar 2015: 181). These volunteers now constitute one of the state's most important instruments for maintaining political control and suppressing dissent. This was particularly evident during the Green Movement in 2009. Iran's security apparatus initially struggled to contain the protests, but then the regime deployed the Basij and the Revolutionary Guards, who managed to counter the movement through violent suppression.

Exporting the revolution: the establishment of Hezbollah

During the Iran–Iraq War, Khomeini made frequent attempts to export the Islamic Revolution. This expansionist rhetoric, coupled with neglect of the Shia-centric nature of the revolution, led to exaggerated concerns among Western observers that copy-cat uprisings were about to sweep through the region. Moreover, the new regime had recurrent disagreements with Saudi Arabia, the United Arab Emirates, Egypt and Jordan as well as Iraq. All of these regional power-brokers were deeply unsettled by the revolution, which served as an inspiration to groups and individuals that hoped to subvert the status quo across the Middle East. Similar fears were also evident in the oil-rich Arab sheikhdoms of the Persian Gulf, whose leaders saw Iran as a serious threat because of the regime's frequent calls for popular uprisings. Shia communities had long been repressed politically, socially and economically in countries such as Iraq (65 per cent Shia population), Bahrain (70 per cent), Kuwait (30 per cent), the United Arab Emirates (16 per cent) and Saudi Arabia (10–15 per cent). Tehran specifically condemned the Saudi monarchs as 'palace dwellers' and questioned the validity of their claim to represent the Muslim masses. Furthermore, throughout the 1980s, Iran and Saudi Arabia engaged in a funding war, exerting influence and extending aid to organizations and individuals in the Muslim world and beyond. Indeed, the Saudis' desire to counter the doctrinal appeal of the Islamic Revolution was partly responsible for their determination to propagate their Wahhabi creed to all corners of the Muslim world.

However, the Shia-specific nature of the Islamic Republic, which was often overlooked at the time, undermined the Iranian regime's capacity to export the revolution throughout the region. The Shia community constitutes only about 15 per cent of the Muslim world, and their stream of Islam is theologically and historically distinct from the majority Sunni stream. They hold that the family of the Prophet Mohammed were his rightful successors after his death, whereas the Sunni tradition emphasizes the importance of community selection. According to Shia tradition, twelve descendants of the Prophet were blessed with divine inspiration and privy to esoteric knowledge, which enabled them to pass enlightened judgements. Ever since, the Shia community has maintained an established hierarchy of leaders. This is extremely important to under-standing the politics of the Iranian Revolution. Furthermore, as we have seen, Iran's newly crafted constitution explicitly adopted the principle of *vilayat-e faqih*, which took the traditional Shia respect for religious scholarship a step further by insisting on a unified hierarchy of leadership. This has resonated little with Islamic leaders outside of Iran, most of whom subscribe to the Sunni tradition.

To prevent Iran's revolutionary influence remaining confined to Shia constituencies, Tehran has insisted that its foreign and regional policies are informed by a revolutionary reading of Islam. Since its inception, the Islamic Republic has presented itself as the principal defender of the entire Islamic *Umma* (community). Its leaders have advanced a Manichean worldview that divides the world between the oppressors and the oppressed. From an Iranian perspective, the United States and Israel have long exploited the region's resources for their own ends and so constitute the primary oppressors of the Muslim world. This narrative has informed Iran's foreign policy for the past forty years, as expressed in Article 152 of its constitution:

> The foreign policy of the Islamic Republic of Iran is based upon the rejection of all forms of domination, both the exertion of it and submission to it, the preservation of the independence of the country in all respects and its territorial integrity, the defence of the rights of all Muslims, non-alignment with respect to the hegemonist superpowers, and the maintenance of mutually peaceful relations with all non-belligerent States.
>
> ('Islamic Republic of Iran Constitution' 1979: Article 152)

A little later, Article 154 states:

> The Islamic Republic of Iran has as its ideal human felicity throughout human society, and considers the attainment of independence, freedom, and rule of justice and truth to be the right of all people of the world. Accordingly, while scrupulously refraining from all forms of interference in the internal affairs of other nations, it supports the just struggles of the *mustad'afun* [oppressed] against the *mustakbirun* [oppressors] in every corner of the globe.
>
> ('Islamic Republic of Iran Constitution' 1979: Article 154)

This ideological trajectory has enabled Iran to expand its sphere of influence across the Middle East. It is important to note that the Iranian effort to export its revolution was not presented as a sectarian project. Rather, the Islamic Republic purported to stand for all of the powerless against tyrannical rule. However, grievances pertaining to social, political and religious marginalization were rife among Shia communities in the region, which inadvertently drew attention to the Shia nature of Iran's agenda. This has been damaging for the Islamic Republic, because sectarianism fundamentally undermines the ideological underpinnings of Iran's revolutionary message, which claims to represent the entire Islamic *Umma*. Iran's revolutionary leaders have been acutely conscious of this limitation and have thus sought to utilize their revolutionary message to cut through sectarian lines. Their relationship with the Palestinian Islamist organization HAMAS serves as a prime example. Tehran has pointed to the group's Sunni composition as proof that it is leading a revolutionary force in support of the *entire* Muslim community against Israel – an agenda that is shared by Shia and Sunni alike (Byman 2014: 89). Indeed, anti-Israeli propaganda played a significant role in the creation of Iran's self-proclaimed identity as the chief defender of Muslim interests. At the time of the Islamic Revolution, it was widely acknowledged that the Arab states had failed to liberate Jerusalem and the Palestinians from Israeli occupation. Nowhere had this been more apparent than in the Arabs' crushing defeat in the Six-Day War. Iran's revolutionary rhetoric regarding the liberation of Jerusalem and the fight against Israel reinvigorated the anti-Israeli camp, a point that was under-scored by Tehran's support for the Palestinian Islamic Jihad (founded in the early 1980s) and the Lebanese Islamist organization Hezbollah, which emerged against the backdrop of Israel's invasion and subsequent occupation of southern Lebanon in 1982.

Indeed, the Islamic Republic played an instrumental role in the formation of Hezbollah, which served two interconnected Iranian interests: exporting the Islamic Revolution and confronting Israel. Iran's revolutionary message of resistance to oppression thrived within Lebanon's Shia community. For several decades, the Lebanese Shia had been marginalized by the state's confessional system, which was biased in favour of the Christian Maronites on the basis of an outdated snapshot of the country's demographic composition. The majority of Lebanese Shia reside in southern Lebanon, a region which became home to the anti-Israeli Palestine Liberation Organization (PLO) in the 1970s. Consequently, thousands of Lebanese, many of them Shia, suffered in the face of Israeli and PLO retaliatory attacks. Israel's invasion of the region in 1982 to expel the PLO once and for all exacerbated these grievances. Thousands were killed, injured or internally displaced. Under the auspices of Damascus, Iranian Revolutionary Guards were deployed in southern Lebanon in 1982 to establish training camps and assist with the fight against Israel (Samii 2008: 35). From there, Iran utilized its revolutionary religious zeal, anti-Israeli stance and military expertise to merge several distinct Shia resistant groups into a single organization: Hezbollah. By 1985, this group had declared its allegiance to the Islamic Republic in its political manifesto: 'Open Letter to the Downtrodden of Lebanon and the World'. This document proclaimed: 'We view the Iranian regime as the vanguard and new nucleus of the leading Islamic State in the world. We abide by the orders of one single wise and just leadership, represented by *Vilayat-e Faqih* and personified by Khomeini' (cited in Levitt 2013: 12).

The Lebanese Shia's indignation at Israeli occupation, along with the Islamic Republic's provision of an ideological framework and financial support, trans-formed Hezbollah into a formidable fighting force. Although Israel withdrew from Lebanon in 1985, it continued to occupy around 10 per cent of southern Lebanon until 2000 (Deeb 2012). During this period, Hezbollah became the dominant force against Israel. Iranian Revolutionary Guards assisted the group with both training and weaponry and, as a result, Hezbollah's military capabilities far exceeded those of the other Lebanese Shia resistance movements, such as Amal. In similar vein to Iran, Hezbollah's leaders propagated the Shia narrative of Karbala to inspire martyrdom and recruit volunteers for military operations against Israeli targets. As Augustus Richard Norton (2000: 25) points out,

> since the Iranian revolution, it [Karbala] has acquired new political meaning and has been transformed from an exemplary act of suffering and sacrifice into an inspiring model for revolution and action ... reference to the Israeli occupiers as 'Yazidis' equates them to the oppressors of Imam Husayn and thereby invokes the living memory of his death and inspires courage in those who revere him.

Throughout the 1990s, Hezbollah survived several major Israeli air assaults that aimed to destroy the group's infrastructure in its southern Lebanon stronghold. Although under fire, Hezbollah sustained its rocket campaigns against Israeli targets across the border. These efforts culminated in Israel's withdrawal from southern Lebanon in 2000 – an event that generated both domestic and regional support for Hezbollah. For the leadership in Iran, Hezbollah's success was heralded as testament to the revolution and its wide-reaching influence.

Box 6.4 Amal

The Amal movement was established in Lebanon in 1974 by two prominent Shia reformists, Musa al-Sadr and Hussein el Husseini. They founded the organization in response to the marginalization of Lebanon's Shia community, who for decades had been disenfranchised, both politically and socially, by the state. Al-Sadr and el Husseini insisted on greater Shia representation in Lebanon's confessional system, which allocated far more political power to the Maronite Christian and Sunni Muslim populations on the basis of an outdated demographic census. Amal played an active role during the Lebanese Civil War (1975–1990) and gained widespread attention after al-Sadr's disappearance in Libya in 1978. Today, the group holds a prominent position inside Lebanon's political system.

After the fall of Iraqi President Saddam Hussein in 2003, the region's balance of power appeared to have tipped in favour of the Islamic Republic of Iran. The democratic election of a Shia-led government in Baghdad, which pursued friendly ties with Tehran, seemed destined to serve Iran's regional interests. In recognition of this, in 2004 King Abdullah of Jordan warned of an emerging 'Shia crescent' in the region, connecting the rising Shia power in Iraq to Hezbollah, Syria and Iran. To counter this sectarian designation, the Iranian regime once again emphasized its anti-Israel credentials and characterized its ties with Syria, Hezbollah and HAMAS as an 'Axis of Resistance' against Israel and the United States.

The strategic importance of this axis should not be underestimated, as Syria offered Iran direct access to Hezbollah in Lebanon. The July 2006 Israeli–Hezbollah War offers a prime example of how this arrangement served Iran's interests. During this conflict, Iran exported an unprecedented amount of weaponry to Hezbollah through Syrian territory (Wilkins 2013: 74). A UN-brokered cease-fire brought the conflict to an end after just thirty-four days. Nevertheless, Hezbollah declared itself victorious on the basis of its ability to withstand Israel's vastly superior airpower.

The group's direct role against Israel saw it emerge as the star player in the Axis of Resistance – one that might prove capable of boosting Iran's regional objectives. As Ray Takeyh (2009: 259) writes, 'in the end, the Shia guerrillas succeeded against Israel's formidable military far better than Arab armies had during four previous Arab–Israeli wars … thereby benefiting not just its own reputation but also the stature of its Iranian patron'. In this sense, the notion of exporting the revolution hinged on the rejection of the US/Israeli-led regional status quo rather than any religious or sectarian aspiration.

As will be explored in Chapter 11, the 2011 Arab uprisings and the ensuing political upheavals brought sectarian issues to the fore. Within this context, Iran was forced to rely upon the Shia actors in its Axis of Resistance and beyond to pursue its regional interests. This highlighted the strongly sectarian nature of Iran's international relations, which continues to threaten the Islamic Republic's credibility as the self-proclaimed champion of all Muslim interests.

Conclusion

The 1979 Iranian Revolution marked a major turning point in Iranian history as it had far-reaching domestic, regional and global implications. The new Iranian constitution contains an internal contradiction between divine and popular sovereignty. This dual system of power has proved to be a major source of tension within Iranian society, with divine sovereignty, as exercised by the Supreme Leader, invariably overriding popular authority. This point has been highlighted by the limited capacity of several Iranian presidents, such as Mohammad Khatami and Hassan Rouhani, to fulfil the democratic aspirations of the Iranian people. Tensions reached breaking point in 2009 with the outbreak of large-scale anti-government protests known as the Green Movement, which called for democratic reform before being crushed by the state's violent crackdown. This silencing of political dissent revealed the entrenched power of Iran's conservative elite, which is facilitated by the strength and loyalty of the state's security apparatus.

The impact of the Iranian Revolution was profound on a regional and even a global level. The establishment of the anti-US Islamic Republic of Iran shattered a regional status quo that had served American interests for decades. This forced a major foreign policy reassessment in Washington, prompting the

United States to adopt a stringent containment policy with respect to Iran. Meanwhile, leaders in the Persian Gulf viewed Iran as a serious threat because of Khomeini's frequent calls for regional revolution. This inflammatory rhetoric allowed Saddam Hussein to present his decision to invade Iran in 1980 as an act of self-defence. Throughout the course of the ensuing war, a seemingly endless supply of weaponry and cash poured into Iraq from neighbouring Arab states and the United States in an effort to contain and ultimately destroy Iranian influence. However, these efforts proved futile, as Iran and Iraq descended into an eight-year war of attrition. Indeed, the war allowed the Iranian regime to buttress its power and control over the state. Khomeini's fusion of religious fervour and nationalism mobilized Iranian society into a formidable fighting force that was willing to die for the revolution and the homeland. By the end of the war, the Islamic Republic had firmly entrenched itself as a viable and influential player in the Middle East.

Although Islamic revolution did not sweep across the Middle East, its message did. Iranian policies, guided by a revolutionary reading of Islam in which the Muslim *Umma* must be protected against oppression and Western exploitation, have resonated strongly with Islamist organizations across the region. Furthermore, Iran's self-proclaimed Axis of Resistance has highlighted its commitment to challenging Israel and the West. This has become a central plank of the Islamic Republic's foreign policy and it sends an important message to other Muslims in the region.

References

Abrahamian, Ervand (1999) *Radical Islam: The Iranian Mojahedin* (London: IBTauris).

Abrahamian, Ervand (2001) 'The 1953 Coup in Iran', *Science and Society*, Vol. 65, No. 2, pp. 182–216.

Afary, Janet and Anderson, Kevin B. (2005) *Foucault and the Iranian Revolution: Gender and the Seductions of Islamism* (Chicago: University of Chicago Press).

Akbarzadeh, Shahram and Saeed, Abdullah (2003) 'Islam and Politics', in Shahram Akbarzadeh and Abdullah Saeed (eds), *Islam and Political Legitimacy* (London: Routledge).

Al-Khalil, Samir [pseudonym of Kanan Makiya] (1989) *Republic of Fear: The Politics of Modern Iraq* (Berkeley: University of California Press).

Byman, Daniel (2014) 'Sectarianism Afflicts the New Middle East', *Survival*, Vol. 56, No. 1, pp. 79–100.

Deeb, Lara (2012) 'Hizbullah in Lebanon', in Shahram Akbarzadeh (ed.), *Routledge Handbook of Political Islam* (London: Routledge).

Eickelman, Dale F. and Piscatori, James P. (1996) *Muslim Politics* (Princeton, NJ: Princeton University Press).

Farzaneh, Mateo Mohammad (2007) 'Shi'i Ideology, Iranian Secular Nationalism and the Iran–Iraq War (1980–1988)', *Studies in Ethnicity and Nationalism*, Vol. 7, No. 1, pp. 86–103.

Freedman, Lawrence and Karsh, Efraim (1993) *The Gulf Conflict 1990–1991* (Princeton, NJ: Princeton University Press).

Golkar, Saeid (2015) *Captive Society: The Basij Militia and Social Control in Iran* (Washington, DC: Woodrow Wilson Center Press).

'Islamic Republic of Iran Constitution' (1979), available at www.iranonline.com/iran/iran-info/Government/constitution.html.

Keddie, Nikki (2003) *Modern Iran: Roots and Results of Revolutions* (New Haven, CT: Yale University Press).

Khomeini, Ruholla (1985) *Islam and Revolution: Writings and Declarations* (London: Mizan Press).

Levitt, Matthew (2013) *Hezbollah: The Global Footprint of Lebanon's Party of God* (Washington, DC: Georgetown University Press).

Makdissi, Ussama (2002) 'Anti-Americanism in the Arab World: An Interpretation of a Brief History', *Journal of American History*, Vol. 89, No. 2, pp. 538–558.

MidEastWeb (1975) 'The Algiers Accord', available at www.mideastweb.org/algiersaccord.htm.

Monshipouri, Mahmood and Assareh, Ali (2009) 'The Islamic Republic and the "Green Movement": Coming Full Circle', *Middle East Policy*, Vol. 16, No. 4, pp. 27–46.

Musallam, Musallam Ali (1996) *The Iraqi Invasion of Kuwait: Saddam Hussein, His State and International Power Politics* (London: British Academic Press).

Norton, Augustus Richard (2000) 'Hizballah and the Israeli Withdrawal from Southern Lebanon', *Journal of Palestine Studies*, Vol. 30, No. 1, pp. 22–35.

Pauly, Robert J. and Lansford, Tom (2005) *Strategic Preemption: US Foreign Policy and the Second Iraq War* (Farnham: Ashgate).

Samii, Abbas William (2008) 'A Stable Structure on Shifting Sands: Assessing the Hizbullah–Iran–Syria Relationship', *Middle East Journal*, Vol. 62, No. 1, pp. 32–53.

Segal, David (1988) 'The Iran–Iraq War: A Military Analysis', *Foreign Affairs*, Vol. 66, No. 5, pp. 946–963.

Sick, Gary (1991) *October Surprise: America's Hostages in Iran and the Election of Ronald Reagan* (New York: Random House).

Takeyh, Ray (2009) *Guardians of the Revolution* (Oxford: Oxford University Press).

Wilkins, Henrietta (2013) *The Making of Lebanese Foreign Policy: Understanding the 2006 Hezbollah–Israeli War* (New York: Routledge).

Wright, Robin B. (2010) *The Iran Primer: Power, Politics and US Policy* (Washington, DC: US Institute of Peace).

7   Playground of the superpowers

Introduction

The all-pervasive Cold War greatly affected the Middle East, with superpower interest in the region steadily increasing as the international tension between Washington and Moscow gained pace. In 1956, a war broke out that signalled a 'changing of the guard' in relation to external power-brokers and their influence in the Middle East. The combatants were Egypt and the tripartite allies: Israel, France and the United Kingdom. Known as the Suez War, this conflict was a watershed event in the history of the Middle East as British and French influence was eclipsed by the United States and Soviet Union.

Britain's declining influence in the region culminated in its formal departure from the Persian Gulf in 1971. This was a grave moment for Washington as Britain had long represented a protector of Western interests in the oil-rich region. To prevent the Soviet Union from making inroads, the United States sought to bolster the capacity of pro-Western regimes in the region. This strategy was governed by the binary relationship that signified the Cold War era. Consolidating ties with the oil-rich states of the Middle East and preventing the Soviet Union from expanding its influence became a key objective for the United States. This objective overshadowed all other considerations, including preservation of human rights and democracy. While the United States saw itself as the champion of democracy, rule of law and political liberalism, the imperative of keeping the Soviet Union out of the Middle East meant that these ideals had to be sidelined in the interest of bolstering US-friendly regimes. This point is underscored by Washington's enduring relations with authoritarian and unde-mocratic regimes in Saudi Arabia and Egypt, which since the Cold War era have been vital pillars of US strategy in the Muslim Middle East.

On 23 December 1979, fears of Soviet expansion were compounded by Moscow's decision to invade Afghanistan. In Washington, the impact of the Iranian Revolution in January of that year had barely subsided when it found itself confronted by the Afghan crisis. The Central Asian state of Afghanistan was quickly transformed into a Cold War battlefield, with the local rebels, the mujahedeen ('those who engage in jihad' or 'holy warriors'), predominantly backed by Pakistan, Saudi Arabia and the United States, fighting against the local communist government, backed by the Soviet Union. The conflict raged until Moscow's withdrawal in 1989, at which point the mujahedeen declared themselves the victors against the 'atheist' forces of the Soviet Union. In the conflict's aftermath, the devastated, war-torn country suffered a protracted civil war.

Washington's involvement and conduct in Afghanistan eventually emerged as a major point of tension in the complex relationship between the United States and the forces of Islamism. The case-study of the Soviet invasion of Afghanistan provides key lessons on how each superpower was prepared to overlook (and, in this extreme case, violate) all other considerations to gain an advantage over its rival. In the 1980s, Afghanistan became a theatre of proxy war between the two superpowers that had devastating ramifications for the country itself and the rest of the world, not least due to the rise of the al-Qaeda terrorist organization. Therefore, it merits special attention.

This chapter will first examine the rise of Cold War power in the Middle East during and in the aftermath of the 1956 Suez War. It will then explore the intricate alliances that Washington forged with the undemocratic regimes of Saudi Arabia and Egypt in order to advance its regional objectives. These alliances seriously undermined the United States' self-proclaimed ideological commitment to human rights and democracy. Finally, the chapter will examine the Soviet Union's invasion of Afghanistan in 1979 and the decision-making process that lay behind Washington's involvement in that conflict. This will reveal that the United States' short-sighted strategies ultimately helped to foster the forces and leadership structures of militant Islamism, which subsequently became a serious threat to US interests in the post-Cold War world.

The Suez War

In October 1956, a combined force from Israel, France and the United Kingdom captured the Egyptian-controlled Suez Canal that links the Mediterranean to the Red Sea. This operation took the rest of the world by surprise – most significantly, the United States – and it heralded the latter's arrival as the new superpower in the region.

The crisis was tied to the policies of the charismatic Egyptian leader, Gamal Abdel Nasser, and his posturing in relation to the United Kingdom. Nasser had come to power in 1953. In line with other post-colonial initiatives of the time, he was seeking to industrialize the Egyptian state, and his major project was the construction of the Aswan Dam. Nasser approached the United Kingdom and the United States for funding and received assurances of a US$250-million loan. But then Washington formally withdrew its offer of funding on 19 July 1956 and the World Bank followed suit four days later (Ricker 2001: 67), primarily in response to Nasser's recent overtures to the Soviet Union. The Egyptian President, now lacking the money he needed to complete his project, took the controversial step of nationalizing the Suez Canal. This waterway, built by Egyptian labour in the 1860s, had historically been under the control of a French and English consortium – the Suez Canal Company. Nasser's decision to nationalize it had two serious consequences: it deprived France and the United Kingdom of revenue and Israel of access to the Red Sea. This infuriated the colonial powers and led to the formation of an alliance of convenience. A secret tripartite operation, codenamed Operation Musketeer, was formulated by Israel, France and the United Kingdom, and their combined military force captured the canal on 29 October 1956.

Although the assault was a military success, it was a political disaster for the allied forces. Widespread protests in the Arab world were expected, but fierce condemnation from both the Soviet Union and the United States was not (Choueiri 2000: 185–186). The depth of Washington's anger was evident in its decision to call for 'collective military, economic and financial sanctions' against Israel unless it withdrew (Bar-Siman-Tov 1987: 54). This call was blocked in the United Nations Security Council by the dual veto of Israel's allies in the conflict – France and the United Kingdom. Underscoring the dynamics of the international system at the time, Washington quickly abandoned this tactic, as sanctions against Israel suggested the need for sanctions against Britain and France, too. In the Cold War context, Washington could not afford to penalize its own closest allies in that way.

The tension triggered by the conflict ratcheted up as the Soviets threatened retaliatory attacks on London and Paris, and Washington brought significant political and economic pressure to bear on the United Kingdom, including a threat to withhold vital support for the British currency (McNamara 2003: 59). Eventually, the allies were forced to withdraw in a debacle that contributed to the resignation of British Prime Minister Anthony Eden. By its conclusion in March 1957, between 2,500 and 3,500 people had died in the conflict, most of them Egyptians. Yet, in the aftermath of the Suez War, Nasser emerged as a hero in his country, for he had engineered a dual superpower endorsement of an Arab position. His standing as the champion of Arab interests proved instrumental for the upsurge of pan-Arabism and the formation of the United Arab Republic (1958–1961), as explored in Chapter 5.

Washington's firm stance in the Suez War boosted its reputation in the Arab world, as it was suddenly seen as an ally in the anti-colonial conflict against the United Kingdom and France. This positive impression was important for the United States' entry into the region as the new superpower. However, it proved fleeting, as will be explored below. For Nasser, Egypt's ongoing relationship with the United States was closely tied to his Aswan Dam project. Washington's refusal to back this major infrastructure project over fears of the Egyptian President's secret allegiance to the Soviet Union soured relations between the two countries. Frustrated by the continued lack of US support, Nasser turned decisively to the Soviet Union and received significant funding and military hardware. With this step, Cairo embarked on a path that would see Egypt become a virtual Soviet 'client state', notwithstanding the rhetoric of non-alignment.

Nasser's increasing disillusionment with US policy was clearly expressed in speeches he made throughout the late 1950s, such as:

America refuses to see the reality of the situation in the Middle East and forgets also its own history and its own revolution and its own logic and the principles invoked by Wilson. They fought colonialism as we fight colonialism ... How do they deny us our right to improve our condition just as they did theirs? I don't understand, brothers, why they do not respect the will of the peoples of the Arab East? ... We all call for positive neutrality. All the peoples of the Arab Middle East are set on non-alignment. Why should these peoples not have their way? And why is their will not respected?

(Cited in Makdissi 2002: 549)

In Washington, the Egyptian decision to turn to the Soviet Union produced an 'us versus them' dichotomy, with significant policy implications. The prevailing, if simplistic, political logic dictated that, if Nasser were a communist, then the United States would do well to consider his enemy, Israel, as a friend.

The Soviet–Egyptian alliance prevailed into the following decade, with Cairo largely dependent on Moscow for military assistance during Egypt's war against Israel in 1967. However, after the death of Nasser in 1970 and the subsequent election of Anwar Sadat as Egyptian President, this alliance began to wane. As will be explored in the following section, Sadat attempted to reorient Egypt away from the Soviet Union and towards the Western camp.

Dictators and despots

As the Cold War developed in the face of Britain's diminishing influence, the United States and the Soviet Union attempted to expand their spheres of influence in the Middle East. Washington and Moscow shored up their alliances based on two overarching policies: gaining strategic advantage in the region and securing access to the region's oil, which accounts for two-thirds of the world's reserves. The Cold War strategies of both superpowers were not guided by any intention to reshape the ideological undercurrents of the Middle East. Rather, both powers displayed a willingness to collaborate with regimes that supported their Cold War agendas, regardless of whether they aligned with their own values or ideological orientation. For example, America's desire to maintain its strategic hold on the Middle East and its access to the region's oil saw it cultivate extensive economic and security ties with authoritarian leaders. This proved damaging to the United States as the ideals of democracy and human rights have long been presented as cornerstones of US foreign and domestic policy. Yet maintaining the status quo in the region relegated the advancement of human rights to secondary importance for policy-makers in Washington.

The late 1960s saw the United States refine its regional strategy in the Middle East and start to focus on boosting the military capabilities of pro-Western regimes to counterbalance Soviet influence. This strategy was guided by both domestic and regional concerns. In 1969, US President Richard Nixon assumed office in the midst of America's costly military campaign in Vietnam. Anti-war sentiment ran deep during this period. The Nixon Doctrine was formulated against this background and was commonly understood as the Nixon administration's expectation that US allies would provide their own manpower to ensure their defence (Kimball 2006). In line with this, US policy-makers viewed arms transfers to pro-Western regimes as both an instrument of influence and a means to avoid 'risking the lives of American forces in Cold War battlefields throughout the world' (Washburn 1997).

In the Middle East, the implementation of the Nixon Doctrine was guided by the 1968 British decision to relinquish its power in the Persian Gulf, a decision which materialized in 1971. Fearing that the Soviet Union would move in to fill the power vacuum, Nixon's administration sought to prop up Iran and Saudi Arabia as twin pillars against Soviet influence in the oil-rich region. Washington had gained a significant foothold in both of these regional powers' oil industries since the 1950s. Enhancing their capacity to confront Soviet influence was given further impetus by US fears over improving relations between Moscow and Baghdad. In 1972, Iraq signed a Friendship Treaty with the Soviet Union which led to the exchange of Iraqi oil for large-scale access to Soviet arms (Smolansky 1991: 19). Between 1970 and 1979 the United States delivered over US$22 billion of high-tech weaponry to the Shah's Iran (Jones 2012: 212). Alongside Iran, Saudi Arabia was another reliable ally on which the United States felt it could depend to maintain regional security. Accordingly, the United States began selling arms to the kingdom in 1972; these sales totalled US$3.5 billion by 1979 (Jones 2012: 212). During this period, Iran and Saudi Arabia represented the United States' 'regional policemen', both of them well equipped and reliable in their pro-Western, anti-communist stance.

While these security arrangements allowed the United States to maintain the region's balance of power with limited direct involvement, they proved pro-blematic in light of the authoritarian nature of the regimes in Tehran and Riyadh. The rhetoric of democracy and liberty advocated by US leaders was seriously undermined by Washington's willingness to turn a blind eye to the gross violations of human rights that were perpetrated by these states. Popular discontent over the close relationship between the ruling Pahlavi monarchy and the United States was a driving force of the 1979 Iranian Revolution which deposed the pro-US regime and gave rise to an avowedly anti-US administration which continues to haunt US–Iranian relations. The extensive security and economic ties fostered by the United States with Iran in the pre-1979 period were suddenly cut. On reflection, this should have prompted Washington to readjust its Middle East strategy or at least try to bridge the gap between its democratic rhetoric and the reality of its regional policies. Yet, Washington has continued to play a key role in sponsoring pro-Western but undemocratic regimes in to the hope of safeguarding its interests in the region. To elaborate on this point, Saudi Arabia and Egypt, which came to represent the two main pillars of US strategy in the region in the post-1979 period, will be explored below. These two case-studies reflect an enduring feature of US policy in the

Middle East: a preference for aligning with authoritarian regimes and not challenging the status quo in order to protect America's security and economic interests.

The United States' close economic and security ties with Saudi Arabia have endured for several decades despite the repressive nature of the regime. The modern Kingdom of Saudi Arabia was founded in the 1930s on the basis of a fusion of politics and religion. Inside the kingdom, all domestic and foreign policy decisions are made by the ruling al-Saud family and its allied Wahhabi religious establishment. The King exercises near-absolute power over both the state and the government, and there is no legally binding constitution. Rather, the Qur'an represents the state's constitution and Sharia (Islamic law) governs the land and its people. Significantly, Islamic doctrine has been interpreted by the Wahhabi religious establishment both to legitimize the al-Saud family's personal power and to serve the state's interests (Sadiki 2003: 32). Abdullah Saeed (2003: 24) elaborates on this relationship: 'if the state wants to crush a particular religious or political opponent, the official *ulema* (religious scholar) may issue a *fatwa* stating the views of the opponent are heretical, giving the state a free hand in dealing with the problem'.

Saudi reformers and human rights activists have criticized this political arrangement and the extreme limitations it imposes on basic human rights and civil liberties for Saudi citizens. In Saudi Arabia, political dissidents, human rights activists and religious minorities have all been silenced by the state's security apparatus through intimidation, arbitrary arrest, long-term imprisonment and/or execution. In the absence of a parliament, elections or multi-party system, there is not even a pretence of government accountability. Moreover, the Saudi state's male guardianship system heavily obstructs the realization of women's rights in the country. Women must seek approval from a male guardian to travel and marry, and they are heavily restricted in their access to the state's legal system, healthcare and housing, which makes it very difficult for them to make meaningful contributions to life decisions. The ban on women driving was finally lifted in 2018 after years of campaigning both within and outside the kingdom, but Human Rights Watch (2017) continues to criticize the Saudi regime for its lack of genuine commitment to reform, suggesting that the regime merely pays lip-service to the principles of freedom and liberty when engaging with Western interlocutors.

Despite public declarations about the importance of democracy and protection of human rights, Washington has always prioritized security and economic interests in its foreign policy decisions. Saudi Arabia stood as a bulwark against Soviet influence in the Cold War period. Between 1950 and 1990, the United States delivered approximately US$70 billion of military hardware to the kingdom (Blanton 2005: 656), and the sales have continued into the post-Cold War era. Saudi Arabia views US arms as crucial to ensuring its own territorial integrity, while allowing Washington to safeguard its own interests. In contrast to Egypt, where US military support has been used to combat internal threats (see below), US defence packages to Saudi Arabia have been utilized to safeguard the kingdom from external threats, predominantly emanating from Baghdad and Tehran.

The United States actually increased its military sales to the kingdom in the 1990s, and they totalled more than US$22 billion between 1990 and 1998. US–Saudi relations were strengthened in the aftermath of the first Gulf War, when King Fahd allowed a large-scale deployment of US troops on Saudi soil to protect the kingdom from the ongoing Iraqi threat. However, this harmed the country's religious credentials because of its perceived acquiescence to Western interests, and the US forces were withdrawn in August 2003 after a string of terrorist attacks against various Western targets inside the kingdom. Nevertheless, the arms sales have continued unabated: for example, in May 2017, President Trump signed a record US$110 billion military deal with the kingdom (United States Department of State 2017b). At the time of writing, Saudi Arabia was also providing over a million barrels of oil per day to the United States, making it America's second-largest source of oil imports (United States Department of State 2017a).

Throughout the history of US–Saudi relations, American calls for the kingdom to democratize have been minimal. Indeed, until the 9/11 terrorist attacks and President Bush's subsequent democracy campaign in the Middle East, Washington refrained from pressuring the Saudis to implement any sort of democratic change. This suited the Saudi leaders, who continue to see calls for reform and a more tolerant political system as a challenge to their grip on power. In this sense, the absence of US pressure on Saudi Arabia has contributed to the perpetuation of the al-Saud family's undemocratic reign. Building on this point, Amnesty International (2016) has declared:

> key allies of Saudi Arabia, including the USA and UK, have failed to halt transfers of arms … [W]hat's particularly shocking is the deafening silence of the international community which has time and again ceded to pressure from Saudi Arabia and put business, arms and trade deals before human rights despite the Kingdom's record of committing gross and systematic violations with complete impunity.

Like Saudi Arabia, Egypt has long been a main pillar of US strategy in the Middle East. However, the Egyptian–US relationship fluctuated in accordance with the dynamics of the Cold War and Egypt's attitude towards Israel. Relations were tumultuous between Washington and Cairo under the leadership of Nasser due to the Egyptian President's anti-Israeli stance and overtures to the Soviets, but the election of Anwar Sadat after Nasser's death in 1970 ushered in a new phase of US–Egyptian relations. Sadat displayed a willingness to engage with both the United States and, more significantly, Israel. In 1972 he ordered the Soviet military to leave Egypt, and two years later diplomatic relations were restored between Washington and Cairo. Then, in 1978, Egypt became the first Arab state to normalize relations with Israel under the Camp David Accords. Brokered by US President Jimmy Carter and signed by Sadat and

Israeli Prime Minister Menachem Begin, the Accords formally ended the thirty-year state of war between the two countries. In exchange for maintaining peace with Israel, the United States established extensive security and economic ties with Egypt, which has since received almost US$2 billion of aid annually, with US$1.3 billion of that going to the armed forces (Karabell 1995: 44). Relations between the United States and Egypt were strengthened further under the leadership of President Hosni Mubarak (1981–2011), who rose to power after Sadat's assassination in 1981.

The US preference for preserving the status quo is epitomized by its relations with Mubarak. Throughout the course of his rule, Mubarak pursued strategies that were consistent with US interests, notably combating terrorism (which often affected non-militant Islamists) and maintaining peace with Israel. He relied on US military aid to implement these policies. However, the citizens of Egypt paid a heavy price for this close association as the regime was given a free hand to crush dissent and violate human rights. Mubarak's reign was characterized by corruption, nepotism, repressive implementation of political authority and systematic abuses of power in the name of national security. Furthermore, while a multi-party political system was enshrined in the constitution, successive Egyptian parliamentary elections were marred by fraud, violence, intimidation against voters and widespread arrests of opposition candidates (Human Rights Watch 2001). These fraudulent and repressive measures were defining features of Egypt's political system and helped keep Mubarak in power for thirty years.

The case of the Muslim Brotherhood in Egypt underscores this point. Founded in 1928, the Brotherhood's Islamic credentials conflicted with the secular orientation of the Egyptian state. The group was banned in 1954 and subsequently subjected to various periods of repression and persecution. Yet, it maintained a prominent presence within Egyptian society until the 2013 military coup. It provided a vast welfare system and bypassed electoral restrictions by setting up coalitions and fielding candidates as independents (Zollner 2012: 58). By the 1980s, it was the primary opposition group to Mubarak's ruling National Democratic Party (NDP), but this merely heightened the state repression. Up to the 2011 uprising in Egypt (see Chapter 9), the armed forces were instrumental in sustaining this repressive political environment. In this sense, US military support was conducive to the consolidation and maintenance of Mubarak's power. To the people of Egypt, however, the military–security apparatus represented a source of fear and contempt. This proved damaging to the United States' standing in Egypt, and indeed throughout the region. The 2011 uprising forced Mubarak from office and subsequent free elections brought the Muslim Brotherhood to power, but the Egyptian military soon launched a coup to restore the old order, whereupon the United States resumed its US$1.3 billion annual military aid package.

As the cases of Saudi Arabia and Egypt amply demonstrate, Washington's determination to secure its access to oil, combat threats emanating from Soviet communism and then Islamic extremism, and guarantee Israel's territorial integrity has always outweighed its declared foreign and domestic objectives of promoting democracy and human rights. Indeed, cooperating with the United States to maintain regional and economic security has benefited some of the region's most authoritarian dictators. As Eva Bellin (2004: 149) points out, 'playing on the West's multiple security concerns has allowed authoritarian regimes in the region to retain international support. The West's generous provision of this support has bolstered the capacity and will of these regimes to hold on.'

This tale of double standards has not gone unnoticed in the Arab world. Most damaging to the United States is the nature of local dissent against dictators. Across the region, popular opinion usually targets Washington for its role in propping up dictators to serve its inherently self-interested policies. This ultimately lends credence to the region's anti-Americanism. Moreover, as will now be explored, the Cold War policies that guided the United States' conduct in the Afghan conflict further undermined its regional standing.

The Soviet invasion of Afghanistan

The Soviet Union's invasion of Afghanistan constituted a major development in the context of the Cold War. As explored in Chapter 5, the relationship between political Islam and the United States has its roots in the early Cold War period. By the late 1970s, the Middle East was in a state of unprecedented turmoil. Following the war of 1967, the death of Nasser in 1970 and the rise of Islamic alternatives to ruling regimes, the relevance of pan-Arabism had already subsided. Then the Islamic Revolution in Iran propelled the potential of politicized Islam to organize society into popular consciousness. Up to that point, the United States had followed a policy geared towards maintaining the status quo, but this strategy now faced increasingly serious challenges. The surprise loss of a crucial ally – the Shah – shook Washington's belief in its ability to continue to shape the region in ways that served its own strategic and economic interests. Moreover, within the context of the Cold War, the Soviet decision to invade Afghanistan raised the very real spectre of Soviet domination of the whole Persian Gulf and its oil reserves. The role of the United States in the Gulf was therefore under threat from two distinct forces: communism and political Islam. Before exploring the dynamics of the Cold War within the context of Afghanistan and its ramifications, it is useful to examine the history of this Central Asian state and its political environment in the pre-war period.

The history of Afghanistan is complex. The modern state and its internal structure are products of ever-shifting tribal and ethnic loyalties. In the nineteenth century, Afghanistan's geographical position made it a linchpin in the regional balance of power between Britain and Russia. It became famous during this 'Great Game' of imperial rivalry, and it was often viewed as the principal gateway between Asia and the Middle East. This changed with the demise of British colonialism, which resulted in Afghanistan becoming something of an insignificant backwater. While the Soviet invasion propelled the country back into the international spotlight, it failed to trigger serious reassessment of its intrinsic geostrategic importance. This is underscored by the fact that the United States diverted its attention away from the country as soon as the Soviet forces withdrew in 1989. Before long, this decision would prove highly detrimental to America's standing in the Middle East.

Afghanistan borders Iran, Pakistan and a number of Central Asian states, which comprised the southern flank of the Soviet Union. Hence, the Islamic Revolution in Iran, a major threat to US interests, also constituted a serious challenge to the regional interests of the Soviet Union. Post-revolution Iran had emerged as another axis of power in the tense world of Eurasian politics, and Moscow was concerned about the possibility of an unchecked spread of religiously inspired dissent in its own Muslim territories. Although Iran's entry into a costly war with Iraq mitigated Soviet concerns dramatically in the 1980s, in 1979 political Islam seemed set to expand its influence. With the benefit of hindsight, the invasion of Afghanistan may be seen as Moscow's most disastrous Cold War decision. However, it could equally be argued that the Soviet Union probably felt it had few viable alternatives in the febrile context of 1979.

In April 1978, the People's Democratic Party of Afghanistan (PDPA) had come to power following a military coup. This fledgling government faced an

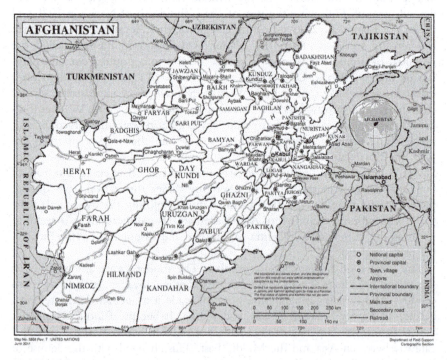

Map 7 Afghanistan
Source: www.un.org/Depts/Cartographic/map/profile/afghanis.pdf

immediate and sustained popular backlash from diverse sections of Afghan society. The resistance was based on a range of issues, including the political ambitions of local leaders and a rejection of the new regime's secular orientation. Essentially, in as much as it was inspired by ideas of modern centralized governance organized on socialist principles, the new government was at odds with the tribal and ethnic traditions of the Afghan people. It is noteworthy that, prior to the coup, Afghanistan did not have a centralized state system: power was dispersed throughout the country, with local chiefs exercising near-complete control over their respective territories. As the government struggled to maintain its grip on power, the rebels were assisted by the region's inhospitable terrain and their extensive local knowledge. The various factions were reasonably effective in their military operations and the communist government began to falter.

In addition to the armed rebellions, the situation was complicated by the unwillingness of the people of Afghanistan to submit to programmes such as forced secularization. William Maley (1988: 8) suggests that the PDPA's desire for secularization was aimed at highlighting the link between the new government and the Soviet Union. Thus, as he asserts, it is 'hardly surprising that opposition to the regime was rhetorically articulated in religious terms'. After only a few months in power, the regime felt besieged and requested help. On 5 December 1978, the PDPA and the Soviet Union signed a military cooperation agreement – or 'friendship treaty' – that both consolidated and formalized the support the communist movement in Afghanistan had received ever since the early 1950s. Maley (2002: 21) asserts the level of Soviet economic aid to Afghanistan was significant, with the state receiving US$1.2 billion from Moscow by 1979, an amount that placed it 'behind only India and Egypt' as a recipient of Soviet aid.

The 1978 treaty included a clause asserting the right of the PDPA to summon the Soviet Union for military assistance. Arundhati Roy (1987: 19) suggests that the inclusion of this clause demonstrated Moscow's awareness of the 'tenuous social base of the April revolution' and the need to institutionalize the regime without delay. The treaty sounded serious alarm bells in Washington and encouraged US planners to involve themselves more deeply in the domestic politics of Afghanistan. Indeed, there is some evidence that the United States, under a programme codenamed Operation Cyclone, was supporting the rebels in the months *preceding* the Soviet troop deployment (Maley 2002: 78). Inevitably, this reactive US interest sparked reciprocal concern in Moscow that Washington was attempting to destabilize its vital, and increasingly vulnerable, southern flank.

The battle for influence intensified, and from June to November 1979 the Soviet Union increased its number of military advisers in Afghanistan from 700 to 2,000 (Roy 1987: 21). This clearly signified Moscow's long-term commitment to assist the communist regime in Kabul. In this period, covert US support for anti-communist forces in Afghanistan was channelled through the Pakistani Inter-Services Intelligence (ISI), a tactic which helped to regionalize the conflict. As clashes between government forces and the rebels increased, the United States capitalized on the internal discontent in its efforts to destabilize the fragile communist regime. Cold War logic informed this decision, but Washington still exercised caution. The Carter administration, which was deeply embroiled in the Iranian hostage crisis, was unwilling to risk an outright confrontation with the Soviet Union at this time. Therefore, his military planners continued to send low-level weaponry and funds through the Pakistan channel, which gave the United States the key Cold War requirement of plausible deniability.

Meanwhile, the anti-communist rebellion, which was increasingly articulated in the language of political Islam – or, more correctly, anti-secularization – managed to gain support from other international actors, including Saudi Arabia and Pakistan itself. By late 1979, it was clear that the rebels had destabilized the regime and the government in Kabul would be unable to retain power without direct Soviet intervention. This situation presented the Soviet Union with a major and eventually costly political challenge. The internationalization of support for the rebellion triggered significant discontent in Moscow, and an unwillingness to accept foreign interference in a neighbouring socialist state became increasingly evident. A feature of Soviet politics for some time, this mindset had been explicitly articulated in the Brezhnev Doctrine of 1968:

> When external and internal forces hostile to socialism try to turn the development of a given socialist country in the direction of the restoration of the capitalist system this is no longer merely a problem for that country's people, but a common problem, the concern of all socialist countries.
>
> (Leonid Brezhnev cited in Ouimet 2003: 671)

Given the Cold War imperative that it must project an image of power, the Soviet Union could not afford to sit idly by while a fellow communist regime was destabilized, or even overthrown, with American assistance. To do so would have drawn the power and the prestige of the Soviet Union into question, and may have led other vulnerable Soviet-aligned states to reconsider their alliance. Hence, Moscow took the decision to intervene directly in Afghanistan. On 23 December 1979, it deployed 40,000 troops. (This figure increased over the next decade but never exceeded Moscow's self-imposed cap of 120,000.) The invasion had an immediate impact on the dynamics of the conflict. The Soviet occupation served to raise the profile of the mujahedeen struggle and Afghanistan was thrust into the centre of Cold War politics. It also became a training ground for future Islamic militancy.

Reasons for the Soviet decision to invade

Interpretations of the decision-making process that led to the Soviet invasion of Afghanistan vary. Moscow immediately justified its deployment of troops under the terms of the 1978 'friendship treaty', but the international community responded by condemning the action as an invasion. The latter interpretation rests on the nature of the government in Afghanistan and how it rose to power. As a communist regime in a religiously conservative state, the government in Kabul was strongly unrepresentative of Afghan society. In addition, its accession to power via a coup did not afford it popular legitimacy. Furthermore, after declaring that it had been invited to intervene by the Afghan government, the Soviet military ruthlessly replaced the original leadership with factions that were more pro-Soviet. Thus, the notion that the Soviet Union was responding to an invitation under the terms of the 1978 treaty is highly contentious. According to Amin Saikal (2004: 195), 'it is in relation to this fact [the killing of the President of Afghanistan] and the Soviets' post-entry behaviour that the Soviet action was nothing less than an invasion'.

The intervention in Afghanistan was unpopular in Moscow, yet, according to Willard Matthias (2001: 290), the Politburo felt compelled to move, and it justified the action on the basis of internationalism. The Brezhnev Doctrine maintained that the Soviet Union had a right and a responsibility to 'counter threats to socialism in any one state of the socialist community' (Maley 2002: 35). Moreover, the Soviet Union may have acted to prevent Islamic-orientated destabilization of its southern, Muslim-dominated regions. This theory ties into the Soviet need to contain post-revolutionary Iran.

Soviet aerial dominance placed the superpower in a position to inflict horrific causalities on the under-equipped mujahedeen rebels. Initially, only small bands of Afghans were engaged in active resistance to the local communist government, yet, as Louis Dupree (1988: 27) points out, once the Soviet forces entered Afghanistan, 'virtually the entire Afghan nation resisted the foreign invader'. Although the mujahedeen rebellion that began in 1978 was articulated in the language of a religious struggle, or jihad, it is best understood as an expression of local political aspirations. Factions were initially organized on a tribal basis. Yet, as the conflict progressed, the language of Islam was used as a unifying force by warlords who were seeking to further their own local – often repressive – agendas. At the time, the conflict was understood in the West as a battle between the forces of 'freedom' and 'totalitarianism', which reflected the worldview of the incoming Reagan administration. As US propaganda regarding the role of the Afghan 'freedom fighters' increased, a tendency to apply Western-centric political interpretations to the rebels became more evident. This was highly problematic, as the normative values of liberal democratic political participation clearly did not underpin the rebellion against the Soviet presence. The situation in Afghanistan was much more closely linked to local issues. The various rebel groups may have shared a religion, but few shared a comprehensive worldview. Instead, the groups' unity predominantly hinged on their shared commitment to resist foreign occupation. Old social disputes, ethnic rivalries, Sunni and

Shia divisions, rural–urban divides and class issues all remained important, and tribal alliances still determined the course of the resistance movement. However, as the conflict progressed and volunteers from throughout the Muslim world flocked to Afghanistan, the factions increasingly stressed their Islamic credentials in order to legitimize their struggle. As a result, the contrast between the secular, 'atheist' superpower and the Islamic resistance movement became the defining image of the Afghan War.

Regional reactions

The Soviet invasion signalled a major turning point in regional politics. For instance, Pakistan emerged from the war as an important player in the increasingly internationalized political arena of Central Asia. At the outset of the conflict, it was extremely vulnerable to Soviet expansionism as the invasion brought Soviet troops into close proximity to Pakistan's borders. Therefore, guided largely by self-interest, Pakistan strongly supported the mujahedeen. The call to arms against the 'godless' Soviets attracted scores of volunteers and Pakistan acted as the principal base for this international militia, which greatly enhanced its standing in the Muslim world. Therefore, as Maley (2002: 70) surmises, the Soviet invasion 'did not simply confront Pakistan with threats; it also provided it with opportunities'. Moreover, Pakistan benefited from the lower levels of involvement of other regional powers. Iran was soon focusing on its war against Iraq and it was acutely aware of its own proximity to the Soviet Union and the potential demands of prosecuting another war while attempting to consolidate the revolution. Hence, it largely resisted the temptation to intervene in Afghanistan. On the other hand, the repercussions of the conflict filtered through the Muslim world, and states as geographically distant as Saudi Arabia deepened their involvement. A major financier of the mujahedeen, the Saudis used the Afghan conflict to bolster their Islamic leadership pretensions. Simultaneously, the war provided them with an opportunity to strengthen their relationship with the United States on the basis of their shared need to confront the Soviet Union.

The role of the United States

Washington, having been deeply shaken by the revolution in Iran, was not prepared to cede a key Central Asian state to direct Soviet rule. Casting around for allies, it aligned itself with Pakistan and the mujahedeen in an attempt to contain the Soviet Union without the risk of a direct confrontation. As soon as the Soviet forces entered Afghanistan, the American media started to present the rebels as 'freedom fighters'. Although the mujahedeen were clearly fighting for freedom from occupation, they were not striving for the democratic liberalism that the US political imagination usually associated with this term. This misunderstanding underscores the importance of comprehending cross-cultural differences when formulating foreign policy, especially in this region. But the

United States had no illusions about what really mattered, as President Jimmy Carter explained:

> Let our position be absolutely clear: an attempt by any outside force to gain control of the Persian Gulf region will be regarded as an assault on the vital interests of the United States of America. And such an assault will be repelled by any means necessary, including military force.
>
> (Carter 1980)

Articulated in January 1980, the Carter Doctrine formed the political basis for the US decision to support the rebels in Afghanistan. At the geopolitical level, Afghanistan was becoming a major arena for the Cold War power struggle. Washington was alarmed by the seemingly endless destabilization in the region and its potential effect on oil supplies, so it felt it could not afford to let the Soviet Union gain control of Afghanistan. A White House memorandum drafted by National Security Adviser Zbigniew Brzezinski reveals the level of concern in the administration:

> The Soviets are likely to act decisively, unlike the US, which pursued in Vietnam a policy of inoculating the enemy. As a consequence, the Soviets might be able to assert themselves effectively, and [in] world politics nothing succeeds like success, whatever the moral aspects.
>
> (Cited in Brzezinski 2002: 108–110)

Despite the dire warnings reverberating around Washington, overall the United States followed a low-key policy towards the conflict until the mid-1980s. Carter focused on containing the damage and preventing the spread of Soviet control to the Persian Gulf. To avoid a superpower confrontation while making the occupation as costly as possible for the Red Army, the CIA provided limited covert support. Ironically, the weapons that were funnelled to the rebels were largely of Soviet origin (either captured by the Israeli Defence Force in Lebanon in 1982 or bought from China), and Pakistan's ISI was responsible for maintaining the flow of arms, which ensured that the United States could not be directly implicated in aiding the mujahedeen. Although this support ensured that the rebels were sufficiently well armed to harass – or 'bog down' – the Soviet forces, they never had enough military hardware to mount a serious challenge to the Red Army.

However, the change from a Democratic to a Republican administration in the United States in 1981 heralded a new, more aggressive foreign policy. The administration of Ronald Reagan, which was elected partly on the back of a widespread public perception that Carter had been 'soft' in projecting US power abroad, ultimately included the Afghan conflict in a wider policy reorientation that aimed to topple communist regimes in the developing world. The Afghan rebels received just US$50 million each year between 1980 and 1984, but the proclamation of the Reagan Doctrine in 1985 clearly articulated a change in US foreign policy and signalled the growing willingness of the United States to interpret its own 'national interest' expansively:

> We must not break faith with those who are risking their lives ... on every continent, from Afghanistan to Nicaragua ... to defy Soviet aggression and secure rights which have been ours from birth. Support for freedom fighters is self-defense.
>
> (Reagan 1985)

After intense debate in Washington, the United States declared its support for the rebels and commenced the supply of high-tech, US-made anti-aircraft Stinger missiles to the mujahedeen in 1986. This was a crucial decision because, by supplying US-manufactured arms, Washington was essentially declaring its *overt* involvement in the conflict. This ran the risk of escalating a localized war to an full superpower confrontation. A far superior weapon to those that had previously been supplied to the Afghan resistance, the Stinger was seen as capable of breaking Soviet aerial dominance (Walker 1993: 287).

In 1985 Reagan had issued National Security Decision Directive (NSDD) 166, titled 'Expanded US Aid to Afghan Guerrillas'. Although this document remains classified, it is thought to have authorized the use of 'all means available' to assist the mujahedeen; if so, it marked a radical development in US policy from assisting the rebels to actively seeking a decisive Soviet defeat. Although the impact of the Stinger missiles has been exaggerated by conservatives eager to establish a direct link between US involvement and the fall of communism (Kuperman 1999: 219), the decision to supply the weapon certainly affected the balance of power in the air, which led to a shift in the military status quo and a turning of the tide with regard to the effectiveness of the rebel campaign. The financial commitment of the United States peaked in 1987 at US$670 million (Tanner 2002: 266–267). As Soviet losses mounted, troop morale declined and the political climate in Moscow started to work against the continuation of hostilities. Before long, the Soviet presence in Afghanistan had become untenable.

After Mikhail Gorbachev came to power in 1985, Moscow increasingly viewed the continuation of the conflict in Afghanistan as an obstacle to the realization of its newly articulated domestic policies, such as *glasnost* and *perestroika*. The change in Soviet direction was underscored in February 1988 when the Politburo announced its intention to withdraw its troops from Afghanistan. As Richard Falk (1989: 144) pointed out the following year, this withdrawal was 'consistent with the overall thrust of Gorbachev's leadership ... perestroika; reducing east–west tensions; and eliminating by unilateral initiative expensive and unsuccessful Soviet commitments overseas'.

As a result of international diplomacy, the Geneva Accords formally brought the conflict in Afghanistan to a close on 14 April 1988. However, although all

Soviet forces left the country by the scheduled withdrawal date of 15 February 1989, many observers criticized the Accords for failing to represent the interests of the Afghan people (Saikal and Maley 1991: 100–117). They were essentially negotiated between Pakistan – the major backer of the mujahedeen – and the Soviet-backed Afghan regime in Kabul, while popular representation was conspicuously absent from the whole process.

Regional and global implications of the Afghan conflict

On reflection, it is clear that the Soviet Union misjudged the conflict in Afghanistan in terms of both military cost and, perhaps, willingness of the United States to commit resources to the conflict and raise the stakes. Although parallels to the American experience in Vietnam have been drawn, caution needs to be exercised when comparing the two conflicts. In both, the conventional army of a superpower struggled to cope with the guerrilla warfare tactics of its opponent. However, the Afghan War was a much smaller affair. The Soviet Union always remained within its limit of 120,000 troops, whereas the US deployment reached 500,000 in Vietnam. Although the Afghan conflict was deeply unpopular among the Soviet people, a more repressive society and tighter governmental control of the media ensured that it did not generate the powerful social changes that the United States experienced during the anti-war movement of the 1960s and 1970s. However, the impact of Soviet public displeasure with the war should not be entirely discounted. As Maley (2002: 53) points out, even in 'highly autocratic systems, significant public dissatisfaction can ... constrain' a regime's actions.

As well as exacting a heavy political price in Moscow, the war in Afghanistan tested the established international institutions. As a result of the Soviet Union's permanent seat on the Security Council, the United Nations was largely hamstrung in relation to the conflict. The General Assembly passed several resolutions condemning the conflict, such as Resolution 37/37 in 1983, which affirmed the sovereign nature of Afghanistan and called for the immediate withdrawal of all foreign troops (United Nations General Assembly 1983). However, such resolutions are non-binding, which severely limits their effectiveness in constraining the actions of major powers. As seen in the case of Afghanistan, although they express the concerns of the international community, they usually fail to influence events on the ground.

The human cost of the Afghan War was immense. Although only approximate figures are available, the death toll and damage to Afghanistan's infrastructure were staggering. It is thought that between 800,000 and a million people lost their lives – roughly 9 per cent of the total population (Saikal and Maley 1991: 135–136). In addition, World Health Organization research suggests that some 1.5 million Afghanis were left physically disabled by the conflict (cited in Maley 2002: 154). The Soviet cost was significant, too: 13,833 dead and 49,985 wounded. Moreover, the stability of the entire region was imperilled, as around six million refugees were driven into surrounding countries during the course of the war (Maley 2002: 154). The financial costs of the conflict were also devastating, with estimates suggesting that Afghanistan suffered some US$50 billion of damage – between one-third and one-half of the country's total net worth. The long-term damage to infrastructure was immense, with the majority of paved roads destroyed and over a million landmines laid throughout the country.

From Washington's perspective, and that of the international community, the subsequent instability and repercussions of the conflict were probably even more significant. Following the Soviet withdrawal, the United States increasingly distanced itself from the factions it had armed during the war. Indeed, although US funding peaked at around US$600 million per annum, it dropped substantially after the withdrawal and had ceased completely by 1992 (P.W. Rodman cited in Saikal 2004: 205). Once the Soviet threat had diminished and the Islamized nature of the tribal factions had become more evident, US planners started to realize that unquestioning support of the rebels as proxy ground forces against the Soviet Union had created its own problems. Washington's lack of operational control over the flow of funds and arms, and the faith it placed in Pakistan's ISI, also proved highly problematic. This was illuminated through post-war US concerns regarding the deployment of Stinger missiles: a reported 300 of the 1,000 supplied weapons were unaccounted for at the close of the conflict (Bradsher 1999: 226–227). It was assumed that the missiles had been stockpiled in Pakistan, sold on the black market or remained somewhere in Afghanistan. By the early 1990s, the CIA was attempting to buy back the Stingers on the black market at inflated prices (Kushner 1998: 14).

Most damaging to the United States, the decision to recruit international volunteers for the Afghan jihad incurred massive long-term costs. Some of the so-called 'Arab Afghans' were funded by the CIA through the ISI; others utilized privately raised resources. Irrespective of unresolved academic debate over the precise relationship between the CIA and Osama bin Laden in this period, Washington's willingness to fund resistance movements with little or no oversight clearly created a cadre of professionally trained, combat-ready Islamists. These men, drawn from throughout the Muslim world, were indoctrinated with the vision of undertaking a successful jihad against a superpower. The Afghan experience also encouraged individuals such as bin Laden as well as Muslim states, such as Saudi Arabia, Kuwait and Pakistan, to justify armed conflict on religious grounds. In this context, the withdrawal of the Soviet Union became mythologized throughout the Muslim world as an 'Islamic victory' against a secular superpower. This interpretation lent further credence to militant Islamism as an active, energized doctrine through which Islamic political aspirations could be attained. The emergence of several organizations, most notably al-Qaeda, provided coherence and structure to this loosely affiliated movement. As Olivier Roy (1990: 215) accurately points out, while most contemporary observers viewed the mujahedeen as rebels in an isolated battle for a country on the periphery of the international system, they were actually 'part of the movement of political revivalism which [was] sweeping through the Muslim world'.

The jihadi mindset, propagated through training centres throughout the region, began to spread and gain credibility faster than the United States had envisaged. The Afghan War therefore produced a generation of men who were convinced that united military action, undertaken by Muslims of various ethnicities and nationalities, could defeat developed world military–political power. Having returned to their home states, thousands of ex-mujahedeen turned their attention to their own ruling regimes, which they viewed as corrupt. Scattered throughout the Muslim world, with their own agendas based on their Afghan experience, many of these veterans became prominent proponents of Islamist revolution and conflict. The radicalization of political Islam in Algeria and Egypt in the 1990s, for example, may be seen as a direct consequence of the Afghan War. Hence, the war in Afghanistan contributed to the internationalization of militant Islamism, while the United States' involvement inadvertently assisted in the creation of a network of highly trained militants. The dynamics of the conflict also made legends of those who had fought with distinction against the Soviets, including Mullah Omar, Osama bin Laden and Abdullah Azzam.

Unfortunately for Afghanistan, the withdrawal of the Soviet forces did not signal a return to stability. Pre-existing tribal loyalties remained influential and post-war Afghanistan was a fractious entity, racked by warlord-based rivalry. The ensuing civil war was exacerbated by factional support provided by outside actors, including Pakistan, Saudi Arabia and Iran (Esposito 2001: 13). Adding to the suffering of the people of Afghanistan, the Taliban emerged in the early 1990s. Drawn largely from the religious schools and orphanages serving Afghan refugees in Pakistan, this organization was supported by Saudi Arabia and Pakistan. It advocated a return to 'pure Islam' – a doctrine that was understood as functioning in opposition to the factional fighting that had characterized the early post-war period. Exploiting the lack of social cohesion and experience gained in decades of conflict, the group quickly gained strength and ultimately seized power in this devastated country. As will be explored in the following chapter, although the United States removed the Taliban from power in 2001, it continues to represent a significant obstacle to peace in Afghanistan today.

Box 7.1 Mohammad Omar (Mullah Omar)

Muhammad Omar, often referred to as Mullah Omar, emerged as a major political figure in post-Soviet Afghanistan, having fought against the Soviet Union during its occupation of the country. As the local communist regime fell in 1992, Omar established the Taliban, a group whose members were drawn predominantly from Islamic religious schools. He was declared the Emir of Afghanistan in April 1996 and served as the de facto head of state until 2001. In 1997 he renamed the state the Islamic Emirate of Afghanistan. A reclusive leader who had little contact with the outside world, much of the information relating to his life remains contested. After the United States removed the Taliban from power in 2001, it is believed that Omar fled into hiding somewhere in Afghanistan or in Pakistan's North-West Frontier Province. However, he remained the Taliban's leader and continued to wage a violent insurgency against the new Afghan government and US and coalition forces inside the country until his death in 2013. He was succeeded by Mullah Akhtar Mansour.

Conclusion

The Soviet decision to invade Afghanistan in 1979 marked a decisive moment in the Cold War. The United States, still reeling from the fall of the Shah in Iran, simply could not afford to surrender Afghanistan to the Soviet Union. Accordingly, Washington (as well as Pakistan and Saudi Arabia) increasingly sought to support the mujahedeen against the local communist government, backed by the Soviet Union. The ramifications of this US support should not be underestimated. By the late 1980s, the United States was a major supporter of elements of the mujahedeen who, by that stage, comprised locals and Muslim volunteers from across the region who had travelled to Afghanistan to fight the Soviet Union. In the aftermath of the conflict, it became clear that Washington's obsession with containing the Soviet threat by any means had led to a severe neglect of local interests. Moreover, the short-sighted nature of US foreign policy in Afghanistan ultimately facilitated the radicalism and fervour of militant Islamism. The forces and leaders of that branch of Islamism came to represent the greatest global security challenge in the post-Cold War period. As will be explored in subsequent chapters, the United States and the international community continue to grapple with groups in Afghanistan, Iraq, Syria and North Africa whose jihadi mindset draws inspiration from the mujahedeen's victory against the Soviet Union.

The United States' and Soviet Union's quest for influence in the Middle East and North Africa heavily impacted the region, with the patronage of these Cold War superpowers facilitating or intensifying many regional conflicts with lasting consequences. To counterbalance Soviet influence, Washington strengthened the military capabilities of any pro-Western regime that was willing to commit to the US sphere of influence. In what would become a defining feature of US strategy in the region, successive administrations chose to back authoritarian leaders to secure access to oil and maintain a strategic hold on the Middle East, rather than run the risk of endorsing democratic experiments. This strategy dates back to the United States' relations with Iran in the 1950s.

The weight given to economic and security objectives seriously constrained the United States' promotion of democracy and human rights in the region.

This point is underscored by Washington's close relations with the authoritarian leaders of Saudi Arabia and Egypt, which have continued into the post-Cold War period. Military aid and defence packages have been utilized to secure the United States' primary objectives of guaranteeing access to the region's oil, combating Soviet communism and Islamic terrorism, and safeguarding its principal regional ally, Israel. However, Washington's willingness to turn a blind eye to systematic human rights abuses within Saudi Arabia and Egypt to achieve these aims has not gone unnoticed in the Arab world. Hence, much of the anger that is directed towards local dictators simultaneously targets the United States for its role in buttressing these regimes.

References

Amnesty International (2016) 'Suspend Saudi Arabia from UN Human Rights Council', 27 June, available at www.amnestyusa.org/press-releases/suspend-saudi-arabia-from-un-human-rights-council/.

Bar-Siman-Tov, Yaaov (1987) *Israel, the Superpowers and the War in the Middle East* (London: Praeger).

Bellin, Eva (2004) 'The Robustness of Authoritarianism in the Middle East: Exceptionalism in Comparative Perspective', *Comparative Politics*, Vol. 36, No. 2, pp. 139–157.

Blanton, Shannon Lindsey (2005) 'Foreign Policy in Transition? Human Rights, Democracy, and US Arms Exports', *International Studies Quarterly*, Vol. 49, No. 4, pp. 647–667.

Bradsher, Henry (1999) *Afghan Communism and Soviet Intervention* (Oxford: Oxford University Press).

Brzezinski, Zbigniew (2002) 'Reflections on Soviet Intervention in Afghanistan, December 26, 1979', in Barry Rubin and Judith Colp Rubin (eds), *Anti-American Terrorism and the Middle East* (London: Oxford University Press).

Carter, Jimmy (1980) 'State of the Union Address 1980', 23 January, available at www.jimmycarterlibrary.org/documents/speeches/su80jec.phtml.

Choueiri, Youssef (2000) *Arab Nationalism: A History, Nation and State in the Arab World* (Oxford: Blackwell).

Dupree, Louis (1988) 'Cultural Changes among the Mujahidin and Muhajerin', in Bo Huldt and Erland Janson (eds), *Afghanistan: The Social, Cultural and Political Impact of the Soviet Invasion* (London: Croom Helm).

Esposito, John (2001) *Unholy War: Terror in the Name of Islam* (Oxford: Oxford University Press).

Falk, Richard (1989) 'The Afghanistan "Settlement" and the Future of World Politics', in Amin Saikal and William Maley (eds), *The Soviet Withdrawal from Afghanistan* (Cambridge: Cambridge University Press).

Human Rights Watch (2001) 'Egypt: Human Rights Background', October, available at www.hrw.org/legacy/backgrounder/mena/egypt-bck-1001.htm.

Human Rights Watch (2017) 'Saudi Arabia: Leadership Change Should Prioritize Improving Rights', 22 June, available at www.hrw.org/news/2017/06/22/saudi-arabia-leadership-change-should-prioritize-improving-rights.

Jones, Toby Craig (2012) 'America, Oil, and War in the Middle East', *Journal of American History*, Vol. 99, No. 1, pp. 208–218.

Karabell, Zachary (1995) 'The Wrong Threat: The United States and Islamic Fundamentalism', *World Policy Journal*, Vol. 12, No. 2, pp. 37–48.

Kimball, Jeffrey (2006) 'The Nixon Doctrine: A Sage of Misunderstanding', *Presidential Studies Quarterly*, Vol. 36, No. 1, pp. 59–74.

Kuperman, Alan (1999) 'The Stinger Missile and US Intervention in Afghanistan', *Political Science Quarterly*, Vol. 114, No. 2, pp. 219–263.

Kushner, Harvey W. (1998) *The Future of Terrorism: Violence in the New Millennium* (London: Sage).

Makdissi, Ussama (2002) 'Anti-Americanism in the Arab World: An Interpretation of a Brief History', *Journal of American History*, Vol. 89, No. 2, pp. 538–558.

Maley, William (1988) 'Interpreting the Taliban', in William Maley (ed.), *Fundamentalism Reborn? Afghanistan and the Taliban* (London: Hurst & Company).

Maley, William (2002) *The Afghanistan Wars* (New York: Palgrave Macmillan).

Matthias, Willard C. (2001) *America's Strategic Blunders: Intelligence Analysis and National Security Policy, 1936–1991* (University Park: Pennsylvania State University Press).

McNamara, Robert (2003) *Britain, Nasser and the Balance of Power in the Middle East* (London: Routledge).

Ouimet, Matthew (2003) *The Rise and Fall of the Brezhnev Doctrine in Soviet Foreign Policy* (Chapel Hill: University of North Carolina Press).

Reagan, Ronald (1985) 'State of the Union Address', 6 February, available at www.presidency.ucsb.edu/ws/print.php?pid=38069.

Ricker, Laurent (2001) 'The Soviet Union and the Suez Crisis', in David Tal (ed.), *The 1956 War: Collusion and Rivalry in the Middle East* (London: Routledge).

Roy, Arundhati (1987) *The Soviet Intervention in Afghanistan: Causes, Consequences and India's Response* (New Delhi: Associated Publishing House).

Roy, Olivier (1990) *Islam and Resistance in Afghanistan* (Cambridge: Cambridge University Press).

Sadiki, Larbi (2003) 'Saudi Arabia: Re-reading Politics and Religion in the Wake of September 11', in Shahram Akbarzadeh and Abdullah Saeed (eds), *Islam and Political Legitimacy* (New York: Routledge).

Saeed, Abdullah (2003) 'The Official Ulema and the Religious Legitimacy of the Modern Nation State', in Shahram Akbarzadeh and Abdullah Saeed (eds), *Islam and Political Legitimacy* (New York: Routledge).

Saikal, Amin (2004) *Modern Afghanistan: A History of Struggle and Survival* (London: IBTauris).

Saikal, Amin and Maley, William (1991) *Regime Change in Afghanistan: Foreign Intervention and the Politics of Legitimacy* (Sydney: Crawford House).

Smolansky, Bettie Moretz (1991) *The USSR and Iraq: The Soviet Quest for Influence* (Durham, NC: Duke University Press).

Tanner, Stephen (2002) *Afghanistan: A Military History from Alexander the Great to the Fall of the Taliban* (Cambridge: DaCapo).

United Nations General Assembly (1983) 'The Situation in Afghanistan and Its Implications for International Peace and Security', UN Resolution 37/37, 29 November, available at www.un.org/documents/ga/res/37/a37r037.htm.

United States Department of State (2017a) 'US Relations with Saudi Arabia', 2 February, available at www.state.gov/r/pa/ei/bgn/3584.htm.

United States Department of State (2017b) 'Supporting Saudi Arabia's Defence Needs', 20 May, available at www.state.gov/r/pa/prs/ps/2017/05/270999.htm.

Walker, Martin (1993) *The Cold War and the Making of the Modern World* (London: Fourth Estate).

Washburn, Jessica (1997) 'Unethical Arms Sales', *Washington Times*, 14 May.

Zollner, Babara (2012) 'The Muslim Brotherhood', in Shahram Akbarzadeh (ed.), *Routledge Handbook of Political Islam* (New York: Routledge).

8   The US-led War on Terror

Introduction

The events of 11 September 2001 had an unprecedented and ongoing effect on the Middle East. The United States, the world's last remaining superpower, was attacked on its own soil by nineteen al-Qaeda operatives, resulting in the death of 3,000 civilians and 6,000 wounded. The operation was orchestrated by Osama bin Laden, the leader of al-Qaeda, who had received shelter from the Taliban in Afghanistan. After the attacks, US President George W. Bush initiated a significant change in America's foreign policy, evident in his launch of the US-led 'War on Terror'. This was guided by the principles of the Bush Doctrine, which emphasized pre-emptive force, America's right to act unilaterally in the face of a perceived threat or in the pursuit of US national interests, and the right to utilize the full strength of the US military in pursuit of these goals. This doctrine provided the justification for the US invasion of Afghanistan in 2001 and Iraq in 2003.

Washington presented the removal of the Taliban in Afghanistan and Saddam Hussein in Iraq as important measures in the fight against international terrorism. The War on Terror was framed in the context of US and international security. In the aftermath of regime change, Washington pledged to the people of Afghanistan and Iraq that it would bring them democratic freedom and prosperity. However, a series of policy blunders impeded the creation of nationally inclusive systems of democratic governance. These policy missteps and the absence of a strong and representative central government facilitated the re-emergence of the Taliban in Afghanistan and Sunni-led insurgencies in Iraq. This violent opposition against the newly established regimes ignited chaos and instability within Afghan and Iraqi society which remains a key obstacle to peace in the region today.

This chapter will examine the Bush administration's path to war in both Afghanistan in 2001 and Iraq in 2003. It will then explore the challenges Washington faced as it endeavoured to fulfil its pledge to bring democracy to these states. Chiefly, it will discuss the flawed policies employed by Washington to assist in Kabul's and Baghdad's post-conflict national reconstruction. This will allow for greater understanding of how, and from what conditions, the

Taliban insurgency in Afghanistan and the Sunni-led insurgency in Iraq emerged. This context is crucial to our understanding of the conflicts that continue to undermine stability in the Middle East.

Afghanistan: US responses to 9/11

In response to the 9/11 attacks, US President George W. Bush launched the War on Terror to oust the Taliban and eradicate al-Qaeda's operational capacity. The US-led invasion of Afghanistan received broad international support. The reason for this was twofold. First, from the Taliban's strongholds in Afghanistan's southern and eastern provinces, Osama bin Laden had orchestrated two attacks against the United States: the 1998 US Embassy attacks and the 9/11 attacks of 2001. In response to the first of these attacks, the United Nations passed Resolution 1267, which required the Taliban to hand over bin Laden and cease the provision of sanctuary and training for al-Qaeda operatives in areas under its control. The Taliban's failure to comply with this resolution and refusal to expel bin Laden provided the legal cover the United States needed to lead an international military assault against Afghanistan.

Second, during the Taliban's rule over Afghanistan (1996–2001), the group was roundly condemned by the international community for its repressive measures against its own civilians, especially women. Hence, the Taliban did not enjoy international recognition as a legitimate regime, which facilitated inter-national action to oust it. This absence of international recognition was important in the way events unfolded. The United States referred to the Taliban and al-Qaeda as 'unlawful combatants', not soldiers, so Washington did not have to declare war under Article 51 of the UN Convention. The Bush administration's decision to move against the Taliban for harbouring al-Qaeda won wide international support. The global community saw the US response to the shocking attacks of 9/11 as legitimate, with many countries offering to join the action against the Taliban. On 7 October 2001, Washington launched Operation Enduring Freedom against the Taliban and al-Qaeda in Afghanistan. In less than a month (by 5 November), the United States, supported by an international coalition and anti-Taliban fighters in Afghanistan, removed the Taliban from power.

In the post-war national reconstruction period, the United States continued to play a major role. This largely stemmed from two considerations. First, there was awareness in Washington that America's abandonment of the Afghan people after the Soviet withdrawal in 1989 had thrown the country into a spiral of chaos and instability. Post-Soviet Afghanistan was deeply fractured and ulti-mately became a failed state. As such, it became a haven for terrorist organizations such as al-Qaeda. Washington was determined to prevent a repetition of this scenario. Second, a central pillar of Bush's War on Terror was the dissemination of US values through democracy promotion as a means to eradicate terrorism. From that perspective, citizens in stable and free countries would not be suscep-tible to violent ideologies. This position was aligned with the neo-conservative assumption that democratic regimes would align with – and ultimately serve the interests of – the United States. As such, after the Taliban was removed from power, Washington sought to steer Afghanistan on a path to democracy.

On 27 November 2001, the Bonn Conference convened in Germany under the auspices of the United Nations to negotiate Afghanistan's post-war reconstruction and democratic transition. After eight days, the conference concluded with the Bonn Agreement, which was endorsed by UN Security Council Resolution 1383 and would serve as a blueprint for Afghanistan. The agreement stipulated the following terms: the establishment of an interim government; the creation of a constitutional assembly to formulate a new Afghan constitution; and the formation of a fully representative government through free and fair elections to be held within two years of the interim government's formation (Maley 2006: 30–31). The United States lobbied heavily for the election of Hamid Karzai, a moderate Afghan Pashtun, as Chairman of the interim government. Moreover, Karzai had spent several years in exile in the United States due to his outspoken criticism of the Taliban. By 2001, Washington saw him as a man who could be trusted. Therefore, his election as Chairman of the interim government and subsequent inauguration on 22 December 2001 were fully in line with Washington's agenda. However, the plausibility of Karzai running an effective presidential office was questionable. As Maley asserts, Karzai 'had no particular claim to expertise in policy development or implementation and his exiled years in America had isolated him from Afghan society' (Maley 2013: 259).

Box 8.1 UN Security Council Resolution 1383

Resolution 1383 was unanimously adopted by the United Nations Security Council on 6 December 2001. It specifically noted the inalienable right of the Afghan people to determine their own political future. Moreover, it noted that the provisional arrangements established under the Bonn Agreement should provide the foundations for a gender-sensitive, broad-based, multi-ethnic and fully representative government inside Afghanistan. It also called upon all Afghan groups to implement the Bonn Agreement in cooperation with the Afghan interim government, which was scheduled to take office on 22 December 2001.

Afghanistan's diverse, multi-ethnic population rendered the distribution of power an arduous task. In December 2003, the Loya Jirga ('Grand Assembly') convened to create Afghanistan's constitution. While the ensuing constitution was praised for its advancement of human rights, it was heavily criticized for the system of governance it assigned to Afghanistan. It adopted a presidential system whereby the President would serve as both head of the state and head of government (Maley 2013: 259). This strongly centralized system clashed with Afghanistan's traditional and localized system of leadership.

It is important to put this into context. The modern Afghan state is pre-dominantly Muslim and comprised of various ethnic, sectarian, cultural and linguistic groups that form distinct micro-societies. Prior to the communist coup in 1978, Afghanistan did not have a centralized state system. Rather, power was dispersed across the country, with local chiefs exercising almost complete control over their territories. Afghanistan was thus traditionally characterized as a 'weak' state with a 'strong' society. Furthermore, the Pashtuns in the southern and eastern provinces represent the country's largest ethnic group (42 per cent of the population), with the Tajiks from the north representing 25–30 per cent (Saikal 2014: 17), and the Uzbek, Hazara, Turkman, Nooristani and Aimaqui groups collectively making up the remaining 30 per cent. Karzai belongs to the Durrani Pashtun group, tradi-tional enemies of the Ghilzai Pashtuns, from which the majority of Taliban members hail.

Essentially, the centralized presidential system sanctioned by the new con-stitution proved a serious stumbling block to the establishment of an inclusive and nationally representative government. The constitution was tasked with the 'creation' of a new state – a major challenge, as was highlighted by the outcome of Afghanistan's first democratic presidential election, held on 9 October 2004. Karzai won the election with 55.4 per cent of the vote, but 'no candidate received significant support outside of their particular ethno-linguistic group' (Johnson and Mason 2008: 13). This proved highly detrimental to Karzai's political legitimacy. Amin Saikal (2014: 71), a leading scholar on Afghanistan, suggests:

> a more suitable alternative proposal was to create a somewhat decentralized parliamentary system of government, with the executive power resting with a prime minister and his/her cabinet to be drawn from the parliament that could enable citizens to connect with the central authority at different levels, from village to capital.

To ensure Afghanistan's stability, UN Security Council Resolution 1386 was endorsed on 20 December 2001. It authorized the establishment of a six-month International Security Assistance Force (ISAF) to secure Kabul, assist the interim government with rebuilding government institutions in a secure environment, and train the Afghan military. The United States deployed 10,000 troops, alongside 5,000 committed by its NATO allies (Saikal 2014: 23). The US troops were primarily focused on hunting down al-Qaeda opera-tives and Taliban leaders. As such, minimal resources were committed to the reconstruction of Afghanistan's shattered government institutions and assisting local forces with the provision of security. This proved to be a grave mis-calculation by Washington. Regional analyst Seth Jones (2006: 111) labelled it 'among the lowest of any stability operation since the Second World War'. The consequences were devastating: within two years of the US intervention, the Taliban had re-emerged in resistance against the Karzai administration and the international military forces. Moreover, the inadequacy of the military resources and personnel dedicated to Afghanistan was compounded by Washington diverting its attention to Iraq in 2003. Throughout the remainder of Bush's presidency, Iraq would take top priority at the expense of stabilizing Afghanistan.

US occupation and the Taliban insurgency

When Karzai entered Afghanistan's presidential office in 2004, he was confronted by an increasingly potent threat by a revived Taliban-led insurgency. His administration was unable to provide security outside of the major centres of population, allowing the resurgent Taliban to challenge the authority of the central government and label it a puppet of the United States. In the eyes of the Taliban, the newly established government served the US occupation of Afghanistan and merited the same treatment as the Soviets. Hence, under the leadership of Mullah Omar, the Taliban orchestrated suicide bomb attacks and planted improvised explosive devices throughout the country. In 2004, the Taliban launched only 6 suicide attacks; this number rose to a staggering 141 attacks in 2006, which caused 1,166 casualties (Rashid 2010: 229). The police force, government officials, bureaucrats and schools were increasingly targeted by the insurgency. NGOs and aid organizations were attacked to deter foreign assistance in Afghanistan. Moreover, Human Rights Watch (2006: 40) reported on the Taliban's distribution of 'night letters' which warned individuals and communities against working with the government or foreigners. These attacks undermined the ability of the central government to exert authority across the country and provide security. Equally importantly, they imperilled local and international attempts at reconstruction and development, activities which were vital if Afghan citizens were to feel they had a stake in the new system.

   The resurgence of the Taliban was a blow to the United States. To confront the rising threat, the ISAF's mandated powers were expanded by UN Resolution 1510 in October 2003. Under the terms of this resolution, NATO took over command of the ISAF and was authorized to extend its operations beyond Kabul. The ISAF defined its mission within three areas: conducting operations in Afghanistan to reduce the capacity of the insurgency; supporting the growth of the Afghan National Security Forces' (ANSF's) capacity and capability; and facilitating improvements in governance and socioeconomic development in order to provide a secure environment for sustainable stability. Hence, from 2003, US and NATO troops engaged in far more extensive combat operations in the Taliban strongholds in the country's southern and eastern provinces. Consequently, the number of troops increased from fewer than 10,000 in 2003 to 20,000 in 2005 (Jones 2006: 113). This military commitment resulted in a dramatic increase in the number of ISAF casualties. Within a year, the total number of deaths had almost doubled from 52 in 2004 to 98 in 2005 (US Defense Casualty Analysis Service 2017). These losses and the resilience of the Taliban helped to turn US public opinion against the military campaign in Afghanistan.

By the end of Bush's presidency in 2008, the security situation in Afghanistan was bleak. Karzai had failed to maintain control outside of Kabul and his administration was displaying signs of corruption, poor governance and weakness in developing and implementing detailed public policy. In the absence of a stable government, Karzai had effectively prepared the ground for the Taliban to flourish. As early as 2003, the insurgents had established 'shadow governments' and justice systems by assigning their own provincial governors, police chiefs, district administration and judges (Johnson 2013: 9). In 2009, Griff Witte reported in the *Washington Post* that, 'from Kunduz province in the north to Kandahar in the south', an increasing number of Afghanis preferred the 'decisive authority of the Taliban to the corruption and inefficiency of Karzai's appointees' (Witte 2009). However, this support was not based on ideology but on the Taliban's ability to administer better governance, such as running schools, collecting taxes and settling civil disputes. As Rashid (2010: 232) notes,

> as long as the Karzai government failed to govern effectively or provide service and jobs to the people, as long as it allowed corruption and drug trafficking to take place under its very nose, the Taliban were winning by default. The failure of the government to provide quick and effective justice to the people only further helped the Taliban cause.

The failings of the US-backed Karzai government tarnished Washington's policy of democracy promotion in the eyes of international and regional observers. The people of Afghanistan had hoped that international intervention would bring an end to the violence that had plagued their lives for decades. For example, in 2007, while insurgent attacks accounted for the majority of civilian deaths (55 per cent), 41 per cent were attributed to military operations conducted by the international coalition in support of the Afghan security forces (United Nations Assistance Mission in Afghanistan 2009: ii). This figure dropped marginally to 39 per cent in 2008. With an inadequate number of troops, the ISAF was forced to rely on airstrike campaigns against the Taliban, but

> The excessive use of airpower by US forces antagonised the local populations, since bombs frequently killed as many civilians as they did Taliban fighters and the Taliban had become adept at using civilians as shields and hostages to prevent being bombed.
>
> (Rashid 2010: 229)

Furthermore, local frustration towards the international forces increased as reports highlighted

> arbitrary arrests, extended detentions, mistreatment of civilians based on faulty information ... [and human rights] abuses at several informal detention

centers run by US forces across the country. In these centers, detainees, many of them civilians, were held without basic legal protection or access to family members.

(Ibrahimi 2014: 169)

The deadly anti-American protests that took place in Kabul in May 2006 in response to the deaths of civilians at the hands of the international forces challenged the integrity of the United States' promise to bring democracy and freedom to the Afghan people.

There was a major shift in Washington's perspective on Afghanistan with the election of Barack Obama to the US presidency in 2008. Despite the deteriorating situation in Afghanistan, the Bush administration had displayed a clear preference to focus on Iraq (see below): when Obama assumed office 20,000 US troops were stationed in Afghanistan, compared to 150,000 in Iraq (Belasco 2009). From the outset, Obama overtly criticized this focus on Iraq and pledged to make Afghanistan his top priority. He articulated his frustration during an electoral campaign address in 2008:

The Taliban has been on the offensive, even launching a brazen attack on one of our bases. Al-Qaeda has a growing sanctuary in Pakistan. That is a consequence of our current strategy. It is unacceptable that almost seven years after nearly 3,000 Americans were killed on our soil, the terrorists who attacked us on 9/11 are still at large ... if another attack on our homeland comes, it will likely come from the same region where 9/11 was planned. And yet today, we have five times more troops in Iraq than Afghanistan.

(Obama 2008)

In adherence to this electoral platform, within the first year of his presidency Obama announced: 'I have determined that it is in our vital national interest to send an additional 30,000 US troops to Afghanistan ... after 18 months, our troops will begin to come home' (Obama 2009b). After eight years of fighting a war with no apparent gains, and devastating loss of life at the hands of the Taliban, there was finally talk of withdrawal, which was scheduled for 2012. However, while many international observers at the time saw this as a positive development, many Afghans were critical of Obama's pledge. As Maley (2010: 86–87) notes:

this evoked recollections of the loss of US interest in Afghanistan after the withdrawal of Soviet forces in February 1989, and left Afghans uncertain whether the dispatch of an additional 30,000 US troops to Afghanistan that President Obama also foreshadowed in his speech represented a genuine attempt to blunt the insurgency or simply an effort to save face before withdrawal.

By 2010, the situation in Afghanistan had rapidly deteriorated. The number of US troops killed in combat reached its highest level since 2001, exceeding 400. Violent instability plagued Afghan society, with civilian casualties averaging 231 deaths per month (United Nations Assistance Mission in Afghanistan 2011: 57). Furthermore, the Taliban were increasingly targeting ANSF personnel. The resilience of the Taliban's insurgency prompted many regional observers to question the viability of a military solution. Negotiation was thus put forward as a potential means of resolution. This fundamentally undermined Washington's conventional method of conflict resolution, which rejects negotiating with terrorist organizations, but the gravity of the situation in Afghanistan seemed to merit such an approach. Hence, the Karzai administration, backed by the United States, pursued a negotiated settlement with the Taliban leadership based on their acceptance of the 2004 constitution and severing all links with al-Qaeda. In response, the Taliban 'remained steadfast that a precondition for negotiations was the withdrawal of foreign forces from Afghanistan' (Maley 2010: 87).

Obama began the withdrawal of US troops in 2011. The first 10,000 were scheduled to leave by the end of the year, with a further 23,000 set to depart in 2012. To ensure Afghanistan was adequately transitioned away from American dependence, Washington and Kabul engaged in a series of negotiations. In 2012, Obama and Karzai signed the US–Afghanistan Strategic Partnership Agreement, which outlined the US role after completion of the withdrawal in 2014. The agreement stipulated that some US forces would remain in the country to assist and train the ANSF and target al-Qaeda operatives (White House 2012). NATO expected the ANSF to take the lead in fighting the Taliban. However, as Obama endeavoured to withdraw ground troops, his efforts were undermined by a series of high-profile Taliban attacks that resulted in an unprecedented number of casualties. The United Nations Assistance Mission in Afghanistan (2014) documented at least 8,615 civilian deaths and injuries in 2013 – a 14 per cent increase from the previous year.

By 2014, US–Afghan relations had reached an all-time low. The White House was determined to establish a bilateral security agreement with Karzai, yet in the lead-up to Afghanistan's April presidential elections Karzai demonstrated a reluctance to engage with Washington. The Afghan leader went against US wishes and released several prisoners who posed a threat to the coalition forces and his office was accused of submitting false evidence to 'substantiate US collateral damage'. In a show of frustration, the White House presented Karzai with two options: the United States was prepared to leave either 10,000 troops in Afghanistan to assist with security or none at all. In response, Karzai maintained that the signing of a bilateral agreement should be left to his successor. Subsequently, Washington began to devise a total withdrawal strategy. In May 2014, Obama announced that 9,800 US troops would remain in Afghanistan at the close of the year, a figure that would fall to 5,500 in 2015, in preparation for complete withdrawal in 2016 (Holland 2014).

On 5 April 2014, Afghanistan held a presidential election that resulted in victory for Ashraf Ghani. This outcome was greeted with widespread optimism as President Ghani promised to reinvigorate peace talks with the Taliban, which had been deadlocked since 2010 under Karzai's administration. However, factional violence within the Taliban hampered Ghani's efforts. In 2015, the Taliban expanded its control across the country, with the Afghan security forces proving powerless to contain the insurgents. This placed Washington in an extremely difficult position and forced the Obama administration to re-examine its plans for complete withdrawal in 2016. More than a decade after the UN intervention to remove the Taliban from power, Afghanistan's development and future prospects were still highly questionable, and security remained a key point of concern.

Iraq: the road to war

After the United States invaded Afghanistan in late 2001, the Bush administration started to express a far more expansive foreign policy agenda. The National Security Strategy emphasized Washington's 'right' to undertake pre-emptive, unilateral military action and the need to promote US values around the world (National Security Council 2002). This led the US military and political planners to consider expanding the horizons of the War on Terror. It soon became apparent that the Bush administration was determined to lead a 'coalition of the willing' to invade Iraq and remove Saddam Hussein from power.

Unlike the path to war in Afghanistan, Bush's desire to secure regime change in Iraq was widely challenged by major world powers and the international community. Afghanistan was clear cut: the ruling regime, which was already internationally isolated, was sheltering those responsible for the 9/11 terrorist attacks, so the international community saw no other option but to remove the Taliban. By contrast, the case for invading Iraq was much more complicated and justified on the grounds of: the alleged presence of weapons of mass destruction; Iraq's failure to comply with several UN Security Council resolutions; allegations of links between Iraq and international terrorist organizations such as al-Qaeda; and a perceived responsibility to liberate the people of Iraq and democratize the state.

Neo-conservative political thinking lay at the heart of the push to remove Saddam from power. In 1998, future heavyweights of the Bush administration, including Richard Perle, Paul Wolfowitz and Richard Armitage, argued that regime change in Iraq was in the best interests of the United States and the international community. They articulated this position in an open letter to the incumbent US President, Bill Clinton, which alleged that Saddam possessed weapons of mass destruction that 'could be used against our own people', so 'strong American action against Saddam is overwhelmingly in the national interest'. The authors suggested that this should take the form of a 'systematic air campaign against the pillars of his power' (Perle et al. 1998). Baghdad's failure to comply with UN resolutions regarding Iraq's alleged stockpiling of weapons of mass destruction provided the legal basis for this neo-conservative agenda.

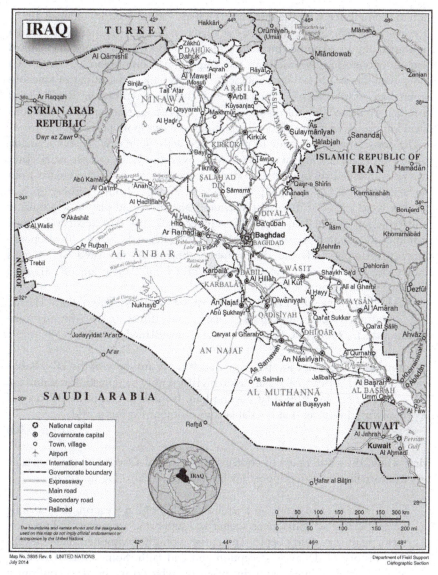

Map 8 Iraq
Source: www.un.org/Depts/Cartographic/map/profile/iraq.pdf

Washington perceived Saddam as an unpredictable actor in the Middle East following the first Gulf War in 1991. In consequence, Iraq was designated a 'rogue state' and subjected to a draconian sanctions regime by the international community. The UN Security Council moved to strengthen its stance against the country by passing Resolution 687 in 1991, which 'called for the destruction of Iraq's weapons of mass destruction and established a weapons inspection team to monitor compliance with the directive' (United Nations Security Council 1991). However, in 1998, this process failed completely as Saddam persistently obstructed the inspectors. In response, the following year the UN established the United Nations Monitoring, Verification and Inspection Commission (UNMOVIC) under Resolution 1284. This resolution explicitly linked the lifting of sanctions against Iraq with Saddam's compliance with the new commission. But Baghdad once again repeatedly stymied and stalled the inspections team and was thus considered in breach of the resolutions pertaining to its weapons programme.

The neo-conservatives came to prominence with George W. Bush's accession to the US presidency in January 2001. Moreover, the 9/11 terrorist attacks later that year provided them with a golden opportunity to shift their agenda from the periphery of US foreign policy to centre stage. Both Washington and London were aware of the role the United Nations could play in legitimizing military action against Iraq. On 8 November 2002, the UN Security Council unanimously adopted Resolution 1441, which offered Saddam a 'final opportunity to comply with the disarmament obligations' stipulated in previous resolutions, with specific reference to his breach of Resolution 687 (United Nations Security Council 2002).

The leaders of the United States and the United Kingdom both viewed Iraq's continued intransigence as a dangerous threat to the international community. In 2003, UK Prime Minister Tony Blair declared:

> at stake in Iraq is not just peace or war. It is the authority of the UN. Resolution 1441 is clear. All we are asking is that it now be upheld. If it is not, the consequences will stretch far beyond Iraq. If the UN cannot be the way of resolving this issue, that is a dangerous moment for our world.
>
> (Blair 2003)

Meanwhile, Bush attempted to conflate the actions al-Qaeda and the Iraqi state in a bid to rally domestic support for his War on Terror. He declared:

> [Iraq] possesses and produces chemical and biological weapons. It is seeking nuclear weapons. It has given shelter and support to terrorism, and practices terror against its own people. The entire world has witnessed Iraq's eleven-year history of defiance, deception and bad faith. Some citizens wonder, after 11 years of living with this problem, why do we need to confront it now? And there's a reason. We've experienced the horror of September the 11th. We have seen that those who hate America are willing to crash airplanes into buildings full of innocent people. Our enemies would be no less willing, in fact, they would be eager, to use biological or chemical, or a nuclear weapon. Knowing these realities, America must not ignore the threat gathering against us. Facing clear evidence of peril, we cannot wait for the final proof – the smoking gun – that could come in the form of a mushroom cloud.
>
> (Bush 2002)

However, the position advocated by Bush and Blair did not receive the support of other major world powers. In February 2003, a joint memorandum by France, Germany and Russia to the UN Security Council stated: 'so far, the conditions for using force against Iraq have not been fulfilled ... while suspicions remain, no evidence has been given that Iraq still possesses weapons of mass destruction or capabilities in this field' (United Nations Security Council 2003). Moreover, they concluded that Iraq was finally starting to cooperate with the international community.

Nevertheless, Bush pushed ahead with his war plans. On 17 March 2003, he stated:

> Intelligence gathered by this and other governments leaves no doubt that the Iraqi regime continues to possess and conceal some of the most lethal weapons ever devised ... The United States of America has the sovereign authority to use force in assuring its own national security. America tried to work with the United Nations to address this threat because we wanted to resolve the issue peacefully. We believe in the mission of the United Nations ... On November 8, the Security Council unanimously passed Resolution 1441, finding Iraq in material breach of its obligations, and vowing serious consequences if Iraq did not fully and immediately disarm. Yet, some permanent members of the Security Council have publicly announced they will veto any resolution that compels the disarmament of Iraq. These governments share our assessment of the danger, but not our resolve to meet it. Many nations, however, do have the resolve and fortitude to act against this threat to peace, and a broad coalition is now gathering to enforce the just demands of the world. The United Nations Security Council has not lived up to its responsibilities, so we will rise to ours.
>
> (Bush 2003)

This statement was a tacit ultimatum to the United Nations. As Mohammed Ayoob (2003: 29) suggests, the US administration made it very clear that 'unless the premier international organization agreed to act as an instrument of American policy it would be consigned to the dustbin of history'. Three days later, the United States commenced the invasion of Iraq amid the vocal opposition of many of the world's major powers and against the express wishes of most Arab states. The Iraqi forces folded quickly in the face of the US 'shock and awe' campaign of aerial bombardment and President Bush declared victory on 1 May 2003, less than six weeks after the attack had been launched.

The US invasion of Iraq failed to unearth any evidence of links between Saddam Hussein and al-Qaeda or his possession of weapons of mass destruction. Many in the international community criticized Bush over the quality of the intelligence on Iraq's alleged possession of weapons of mass destruction, which had been used to justify Washington's decision to topple Saddam Hussein (BBC 2003). Out of this criticism arose the 'war for oil' argument, which pointed to oil as the primary motivation for regime change in Iraq. This argument was underscored by decades of US foreign policy that had focused on bringing oil-rich states into the US sphere of influence through programmes of assistance, support and friendship. Economic self-interest in securing the creation of friendly regimes most likely played a part in Washington's agenda. Significantly, links between major US oil companies and individuals involved in formulating US foreign policy received much publicity. In the face of international criticism, Bush was forced to backtrack from his initial stance and articulate an agenda for Iraq that framed the United States' removal of Saddam as a necessary precondition to liberate the Iraqi people and democratize the state. The neo-conservatives' policies in Iraq revealed Washington's failure to comprehend the delicate sectarian situation in that country, which proved disastrous in the aftermath of the military victory.

After Saddam was removed from power, Washington set about creating a new political order for Iraq. In May 2003, it established the Coalition Provisional Authority (CPA) to serve as the occupation's interim government. The CPA was placed under the leadership of a neo-conservative, Lewis Paul Bremer III. Central to Bremer's policies was the 'de-Ba'athification' of Iraq, which was sanctioned eight days after Saddam was removed from power. The order aimed to eliminate the 'Ba'ath party's structures and to purge its top four ranks of membership' (Bremer 2003). This effectively created a blank canvas on which Washington might rebuild the Iraqi state. The de-Ba'athification process was supported by a subsequent order – Number 5 – issued on 25 May, which established the Iraqi De-Ba'athification Council (IDC) to work closely with Bremer. The problematic nature of this relationship was twofold. First, all members of the IDC, including the chair, Ahmed Chalabi, were previously exiled Shia Iraqi nationals whom Bremer had handpicked for the job. These men subsequently played an active role in supplying Bremer and his neo-conservative advisers with information regarding individual Ba'ath Party members. As Benjamin Isakhan (2015: 22) points out, 'the DBC implemented the CPA's de-Ba'athification in a hardline and uncompromising fashion'. Second, many Iraqis criticized the de-Ba'athification process as it failed to distinguish between active Saddam loyalists and those who had been forced to align with him out of fear.

Box 8.2 Ahmed Chalabi

Ahmed Chalabi (1944–2015) was a Shia politician born in Baghdad, Iraq. In response to Iraqi President Saddam Hussein's persecution of the country's Shia majority, Chalabi founded an opposition party, the Iraqi National Congress (INC), in exile in 1991. During this period, the INC forged close ties with members of the United States' neo-conservative movement and the

Central Intelligence Agency. Under Chalabi's leadership, the INC extensively lobbied the United States to end Saddam's dictatorship. In the years leading up to the US invasion of Iraq, Washington relied on him and his supporters for detailed information regarding Saddam's alleged weapons of mass destruction programme, and the political climate in Iraq. This information has been widely criticized as providing an inaccurate assessment of the true state of affairs inside Iraq prior to the invasion in May 2003. The United States selected Chalabi to assist the occupation's administration after the removal of Saddam. He then became interim Minister of Oil (April 2005–January 2006). Up to his death in 2015, he continued to play an active, yet sometimes controversial, role in Iraqi politics.

The consequences of this policy were devastating. Given the Sunni composition of Saddam's Ba'athist Party, de-Ba'athification soon became synonymous with the 'de-Sunnification' of Iraq. This drove a sectarian wedge deep within Iraqi society to an unprecedented level. To understand the gravity of Bremer's de-Ba'athification policy, it is important to keep in mind the Sunni and Shia divide in the Saddam era. Saddam Hussein belonged to the Arab Sunni stream of Islam. Consequently, he privileged Iraq's Sunni minority at the expense of the country's Shia majority, who make up over half of the population (the remainder, 32–37 per cent, is Kurdish, and predominantly Sunni). Iraqi's Shia were excluded from key employment fields and repressed under Saddam's rule: 'Those active in anti-regime politics were murdered, imprisoned, tortured or driven into exile and those who stayed in the country increasingly realised that survival and economic well-being were directly linked to complete political passivity' (Dodge 2007: 94). This led to high levels of discontent within Shia communities, which evolved into sectarianism following the collapse of his authoritarian rule.

Following a national referendum on 15 October 2004, Iraqi citizens took to the polls to elect a transitional national assembly on 30 January 2005. This resulted in a victory for the Iraqi National Alliance (INA), led by the Shia Islamist al-Da'wa Party. The INA nominated Ibrahim al-Jafari as Prime Minister, and he assumed office in April 2005. Thereafter, in December of the same year, the INA also won the general election for Iraq's permanent 275-seat parliament and al-Jafari continued in the role of Prime Minister. Both of these elections were hailed as a success in terms of transparency and voter turnout. However, similar to the electoral experience in Afghanistan, people tended to vote on the basis of sectarian and parochial loyalties, and once again these trends were accepted, if not actively encouraged, by the United States. This experience deepened political divisions in the country. The Shia community dominated the central government in post-Saddam Iraq, while the Iraqi Kurds were granted autonomy in the country's north. The establishment of the Kurdish regional government under the terms of the new constitution was an acknowledgement of the role Kurdish fighters had played in the fight against Saddam's regime.

These changes alienated the country's Sunni minority, who, after decades of political dominance, suddenly found themselves isolated and targeted within the new state system.

Box 8.3 Al-Da'wa

The Iraqi al-Da'wa Party is a Shia political party that was established in 1958 by Mohammed Sadiq al-Qamousee and advocated the establishment of an Islamic state in Iraq. Members of the group were arrested, imprisoned and executed under the secular rule of Iraq's Ba'athist regime. Al-Da'wa was banned in 1980 and many of its members fled to Iran. Those who remained inside Iraq operated an extensive clandestine organization that re-emerged after the fall of Saddam in 2003. In the lead-up to Iraq's first parliamentary elections in 2005, the al-Da'wa Party forged the Iraqi National Alliance (INA) as an electoral coalition with several other Shia political parties. The INA was successful and al-Da'wa's secretary-general Ibrahim al-Jafari became Prime Minister following the first parliamentary elections in post-Saddam Iraq. However, tensions between al-Jafari, Washington and other prominent Shia leaders led to Nour al-Maliki, also from al-Da'wa, succeeding him in April 2006. Al-Maliki was subsequently accused of concentrating power within his own hands and exacerbating sectarian tensions inside Iraq. Consequently, he was forced to step down due to intense domestic and international pressure. In 2014, he was replaced as both Prime Minister and leader of al-Da'wa by Haider al-Abadi.

US occupation, Sunni insurgency and Shia militia

In late 2003, a Sunni–led insurgency was launched in opposition to the occupying forces and local Shia authorities. It comprised former Ba'athists, military personnel, tribal leaders and young and impoverished men from the Sunni-dominated western province of al-Anbar.

After the Iraqi Army was disbanded, most of the soldiers simply walked off with their weapons. This led to what Sultan Barakat (2005: 579) calls a 'gun culture', which enabled the Sunni insurgents to carry out attacks against the coalition forces and Iraq's Shia population. The de-Ba'athification process and growing sectarian tension pushed Iraq onto a dangerous trajectory. Thousands of Sunnis lost their jobs, with the purge of Iraq's civil service affecting between 20,000 and 120,000 individuals, while the dissolution of the army left more than 400,000 men unemployed. Statistics released in 2004 suggested that unemployment ranged from 40 to 60 per cent in al-Anbar (Malkasian 2006: 428). Consequently, the insurgents were determined not only to reclaim political representation but to acquire greater opportunities. Hence, the Sunni uprising against the central government in Baghdad was not about Islamism;

rather, it was based on a shared sense of injury. As Ronen Zeidel (2015: 105) points out:

> being dismissed from the army, the security services or government solely for being Sunnis ... being held in secret detention centres and tortured on suspicion of terrorist activity; and suffering from discrimination in the allocation of resources. All these, and many more, advance a common secular Sunni identity, which is more relevant to Sunnis who are neither religious nor interested in the sectarian issue per se.

The Sunnis' objectives were thus markedly different from those of Islamist groups, which also emerged in this fractured and dangerous political environment. However, they were all fighting the same enemy: the Shia-dominated government in Baghdad, which was backed by the United States.

The bulk of the fighting was done by Sunnis, especially in Fallujah, al-Anbar province. This city was largely populated by ex-Iraqi military officers with Ba'athist affiliations. Tensions erupted soon after the fall of Saddam, resulting in thirteen deaths and ninety-one injuries among Iraqi civilians (Malkasian 2006: 428). In response to the deaths of four American soldiers in Fallujah in March 2004, the coalition forces launched an offensive against the city, which made it a magnet for other Sunni rebels. It is estimated that some 2,000 fighters mobilized against the coalition troops, and the fighting spread across al-Anbar. Approximately three hundred insurgents and thirteen US soldiers had been killed by the end of the following month. Moreover, the coalition's use of air strikes, artillery and tanks to combat the resistance resulted in the deaths of over five hundred civilians (Malkasian 2006: 437). This led many Iraqis to view the offensive as an unjust act committed by a foreign invader, and it marked a decisive moment for the Sunni insurgents, who proceeded to mobilize additional support and strengthen their hold over the city. The insurgents, alongside al-Qaeda in Iraq (AQI; see below), orchestrated attacks within Fallujah against Shia communities, the US troops and Iraqi security forces. In the face of this upsurge in violence, the United States and Iraqi security forces, backed by Britain, launched a second offensive into the city in November 2004, recapturing it by the close of the year. This second Battle of Fallujah was one of the bloodiest engagements of the whole Iraq War. Official reports estimate that fifteen hundred insurgents and seventy US soldiers were killed, with hundreds injured (Dale 2008: 45).

The Abu Ghraib scandal in 2004 added further fuel to the Sunni insurgents' anti-US campaign. Inside one of Saddam's most notorious prisons, the degradation and torture of Iraqi prisoners by US service personnel was captured on film. The photographs were released on 28 April and then disseminated rapidly around the world. They were viewed as clear evidence of the United States' long-standing willingness to disregard human security and dignity in the Arab world. The Bush administration attempted to mitigate the damage to its reputation, but with little success. In the eyes of many Iraqis, the US 'liberators' were irreversibly revealed as little more than oppressors.

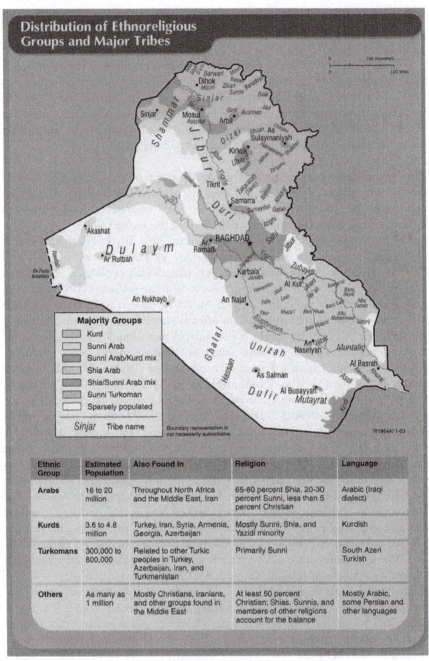

Distribution of Ethnoreligious Groups and Major Tribes

Majority Groups
- Kurd
- Sunni Arab
- Sunni Arab/Kurd mix
- Shia Arab
- Shia/Sunni Arab mix
- Sunni Turkoman
- Sparsely populated

Sinjar Tribe name

Boundary representation is not necessarily authoritative.

Ethnic Group	Estimated Population	Also Found In	Religion	Language
Arabs	16 to 20 million	Throughout North Africa and the Middle East, Iran	65-80 percent Shia, 20-30 percent Sunni, less than 5 percent Christian	Arabic (Iraqi dialect)
Kurds	3.6 to 4.8 million	Turkey, Iran, Syria, Armenia, Georgia, Azerbaijan	Mostly Sunni, Shia, and Yazidi minority	Kurdish
Turkomans	300,000 to 800,000	Related to other Turkic peoples in Turkey, Azerbaijan, Iran, and Turkmenistan	Primarily Sunni	South Azeri Turkish
Others	As many as 1 million	Mostly Christians, Iranians, and other groups found in the Middle East	At least 50 percent Christian; Shias, Sunnis, and members of other religions account for the balance	Mostly Arabic, some Persian and other languages

Map 9 Ethnic Iraq
Source: www.loc.gov/resources/g7610.ct001095/

Box 8.4 Supreme Council for the Islamic Revolution in Iraq

The Supreme Council for the Islamic Revolution in Iraq (SCIRI) was established in 1982 as an offshoot of the al-Da'wa Party. It was founded by the prominent Iraqi Shia cleric Ayatollah Sayyed Mohammed Baqir al-Hakim, who called for the establishment of a Shia state in Iraq based on Iran's revolutionary model. As a Shia organization, it emerged in resistance to Saddam Hussein's persecution of Iraq's Shia community. SCIRI was based in Tehran from its foundation before returning to Iraq after the fall of Saddam in 2003. While in Iran, its military wing, known as the al-Badr Brigade was established, which received training from Iran's Quds Force. It played an active role in support of Iran during the Iran–Iraq War and in the 1991 Shia uprising against Saddam's regime. In post-Saddam Iraq, SCIRI emerged as a serious player in Iraqi politics. In the lead-up to the country's first parliamentary elections in 2005, it worked closely with al-Da'wa to form the victorious electoral coalition, the INA. However, al-Badr played an active role against the occupying forces.

Meanwhile, the emergence of various Shia militia groups exacerbated Iraq's instability. Most Iraqi Shia supported the US-backed interim government, but the al-Badr Brigade and the al-Mahdi Army – armed wings of the Iranian-backed Supreme Council for the Islamic Revolution in Iraq (SCIRI) and the Sadrist movement, respectively – overtly rejected the US occupation and condemned the Shia-led government for its acquiescence to Washington. The leaders of SCIRI and the Sadrists both called for the establishment of an Islamic government in Iraq. However, SCIRI differentiated itself from the Sadrists on the basis of its ties to Iran and consequent desire to replicate the Iranian model. It managed to gain a foothold in Shia population centres as it filled a vacuum in social service provision, which the new central government was unable to provide. The emergence of this militia group with formal links to the Iranian government signalled a new phase in Iraq's post-Saddam experience. The reality of Iranian influence in Iraq was now an issue with which both the Americans and Iraqis themselves had to contend. Indeed, Iran emerged as the principal winner in the ill-fated US adventure in Iraq as the dynamics of sectarian conflict and the disempowerment of the country's Shia majority offered the Islamic Republic an important new sphere of influence and a much stronger voice in regional affairs.

Box 8.5 The Sadrist movement

The Sadrist movement is an Iraqi organization led by the prominent Iraqi Shia cleric Muqtada al-Sadr. The group's ideological foundations were established by Muqtada's father, Grand Ayatollah Mohammad Sadeq al-Sadr, who was assassinated by Saddam Hussein's regime in 1999. After the fall

Saddam in May 2003, the Sadrist movement gained popularity among Iraq's Shia urban poor via its provision of social and welfare services and security, while advocating for national Islamic governance. From the outset, Muqtada maintained a fierce anti-American position and consequently mobilized the al-Mahdi Army in June 2003 to resist the coalition forces. He appealed to hundreds of young, disenfranchised Shia via his preaching of Iraqi nationalism, anti-Americanism and Islamic fervour. Between 2003 and 2004, the al-Mahdi Army waged a violent insurgency against the coalition forces and the newly established – Shia-led – interim government, albeit with limited success. In the lead-up to the 2005 elections, Muqtada moderated his agenda and entered the legitimate political process.

In 2006, Baghdad and Washington faced a catastrophic upsurge in sectarian violence as both Sunni and Shia groups engaged in retaliatory and counter-retaliatory attacks which killed thousands of Iraqi men, women and children. The following year, a report issued by the United Nations claimed that 34,452 Iraqi civilians had been killed and 36,685 injured in 2006 (United Nations 2007). These figures were indicative of al-Maliki's failure to enforce law and order, and the willingness of Iraqi militias to plunge the state into civil war. Islamist forces emerged as increasingly powerful actors in this conflict, most notably al-Qaeda in Iraq (AQI). An offshoot of the global jihadist organization, AQI was established as part of a resistance strategy against the US occupation of Arab territory. The specific dynamics of the Iraqi conflict, and the ready-made sectarian environment, led to a fusion of traditional al-Qaeda doctrine and overt sectarianism, in which the organization presented itself as the champion of the now-disenfranchised Sunni community. During 2006 and 2007, AQI waged attacks against Shia neighbourhoods, the Iraqi security forces and coalition troops. It capitalized on the lack of security and anti-American sentiment and managed to gain control over several key areas in the largely Sunni province of al-Anbar. Iraq's Sunni community initially cooperated with AQI, but then largely turned against it as its brutal sectarian agenda became apparent. Furthermore, tribal leaders in al-Anbar perceived AQI's implementation of Sharia law in the areas under its control as a challenge to their authority (McCary 2009: 44).

Box 8.6 Al-Qaeda in Iraq

Al-Qaeda in Iraq (AQI) was established by the Jordanian Abu Musab al-Zarqawi in 2004. Al-Zarqawi was a veteran of the Afghan resistance against the Soviet Union and established his Jamaat al-Tawhid wal-Jihad organization in Afghanistan in 1999. After the fall of the Taliban in 2001, he fled to Iran before arriving in Iraq in 2002. After the United States invaded Iraq in 2003, the central objectives of al-Zarqawi's organization were to drive the US-led coalition forces from Iraq, reclaim Sunni political power from the Shia community and establish Islamic governance. In 2004, he pledged allegiance to al-Qaeda and renamed his group al-Qaeda in Iraq (AQI). The organization then orchestrated several attacks against US forces and inflamed the sectarian tension via brutal attacks against Iraq's Shia community. Al-Zarqawi was killed in a targeted US air strike in 2006, and AQI later changed its name to the Islamic State in Iraq (ISI).

By early 2007, Washington was divided over how to address the deteriorating situation in Iraq. The unprecedented levels of violence and instability had virtually decimated Bush's pledge to bring democratic freedom and liberty to the people of Iraq. His administration faced fierce domestic pressure to withdraw from a conflict in which dozens of American soldiers seemed to be dying for few tangible gains. The political mood was therefore squarely focused upon the need for an 'exit strategy'. Inside Washington, the Democrats urged Bush to start winding down America's involvement. In line with this, Illinois Senator Barack Obama presented the war in Iraq as one 'that never should have been authorized and never should have been waged' (Obama 2007: 4). Against these calls for a withdrawal, in April 2007 President Bush declared the deployment – or 'surge' – of an additional 30,000 troops to Iraq.

The following year, improvements in Iraq's security situation seemed to indicate that Bush's strategy had been a success. According to the United Nations, 6,787 civilians were killed and 20,178 injured in Iraq in 2008 – a significant decrease in relation to 2006 (United Nations Assistance Mission for Iraq 2008: 2). In light of these improvements on the ground, Bush declared that 'the surge has done more than turn the situation in Iraq around – it has opened the door to a major strategic victory in the broader war on terror' (Bush 2008). Observers attributed the decline in violence to the 'Anbar Awakening', a US–Iraqi tribal strategy, whereby Sunni tribesmen, in alliance with the United States, degraded AQI capabilities. This strategy consisted of US payments to Sunni tribesmen in exchange for their cooperation against AQI. By the close of 2007, AQI was seen as marginal in the Iraqi context. Despite these gains, however, many observers questioned the strategy's ability to achieve positive results in the long term. For instance, in prescient terms, Steven Simon (2008: 58) argued:

> this strategy to reduce violence is not linked to any sustainable plan for building a viable Iraqi state. If anything, it has made such an outcome less likely, by stoking the revanchist fantasies of Sunni Arab tribes and pitting them against the central government and against one another. In other words, the recent short-term gains have come at the expense of the long-term goal of a stable, unitary Iraq.

At the close of 2008, on the express wishes of the Iraqi government, President Bush and Iraqi officials signed the Status of Forces Agreement (SOFA), which required all US troops to withdraw from the country by the end of 2011.

In January 2009, the new US President, Barack Obama, declared that Washington 'will begin to responsibly leave Iraq to its people' and asserted that all US troops would be withdrawn from the country within the next sixteen months (Obama 2009a). During this period, the level of violence in Iraq remained relatively low in comparison to the catastrophic years of 2006 and 2007. In the lead-up to the US troop withdrawal, Washington and Baghdad engaged in a series of vigorous negotiations to map out US–Iraqi relations in the post-withdrawal period. These negotiations culminated at the White House on 12 December 2011, when the United States pledged to continue its assistance to Iraq's democratic institution-building and establish US-funded military programmes to train and equip Iraqi security forces without the presence of US military bases or troops in the country (White House 2012). On 18 December 2011, the United States completed its withdrawal from Iraq. After nine years in the country, it left behind a divided people, governed by a leader who displayed little interest in inclusive politics. With the escalation of tension, Prime Minister al-Maliki became a very divisive figure.

In the years that followed the US withdrawal, Iraq was gripped by widening sectarian divisions. The absence of political reform, which left the Sunni minority feeling ever more marginalized, fed into a surge of Sunni extremism. Al-Maliki was increasingly charged with exacerbating the sectarian tension. In the lead-up to the 2010 elections, he had disqualified over five hundred predominantly Sunni candidates on the grounds that they were linked to Saddam's regime. This move was widely condemned as fear-mongering to deflect attention away from al-Maliki's inability to provide economic prosperity to Iraq's citizens (Mohammed 2010). Meanwhile, international observers were drawing attention to widespread human rights violations committed by the Iraqi security forces and pro-government militias against the Sunni community (Human Rights Watch 2014). As violence, mistrust and militancy amid sectarian groups worsened, the security situation became perilous. This was underscored by the re-emergence of AQI in July 2012, when it launched a brutal campaign against Shia neighbourhoods and the Iraqi security forces. The organization was able to mobilize considerable strength by capitalizing on the inefficiency of the government and exploiting legitimate Sunni grievances. This dealt a serious blow to al-Maliki and his administration, in the eyes of both Iraqis and the international community. The following year was the bloodiest since 2008, with an average of 650 civilian deaths and 1,000-plus injuries per month due to terrorism and violent attacks (United Nations Iraq 2017).

In late 2012, mass anti-government demonstrations had broken out in predominantly Sunni areas across the country. Thousands of Iraqis protested against corruption, gross human rights violations and the state's use of arbitrary arrest, indefinite detention without trial and torture (Human Rights Watch 2014). In response, the Iraqi security forces attempted to quash the peaceful protests with lethal force. Here, it is important to note that opposition to al-Maliki's regime was not exclusive to the Sunni community. Many Shia, including the Sadrists and the SCIRI, also rejected his monopolistic rule (Arab Center for Research and Policy Studies 2014: 5). In line with this, several prominent Shia clerics publicly condemned al-Maliki's violent repression of the protests and urged the Prime Minister to implement meaningful reform. Notwithstanding these calls, al-Maliki continued to stoke sectarian tension until the end of his tenure. In the lead-up to the 2014 elections, he was placed under intense pressure to step down. Finally, he bowed to domestic and international pressure and relinquished power to another Shia politician, Haider al-Abadi, on 11 August.

The latter's electoral success was widely celebrated. Sunni, Shia and Kurdish political parties all endorsed the new Prime Minister, as did Washington and Tehran. But al-Abadi took over in a period of deep national crisis. President Obama proclaimed:

> this new Iraqi leadership has a difficult task. It has to regain the confidence of its citizens by governing inclusively and by taking steps to demonstrate its resolve. The United States stands ready to support a government that addresses the needs and grievances of all Iraqi people.
>
> (Obama 2014)

For al-Abadi and Washington, the formation of an all-inclusive government was crucial in the fight against terrorism. This view was grounded in the notion that inclusiveness prevents the marginalization of specific groups of citizens and thus dissuades them from turning to radical organizations in opposition to the state. However, this agenda was gravely challenged from the outset by the AQI, which established its so-called 'Islamic State' (discussed in Chapter 10). The Islamic State's ultra-violent campaign and its capture of large swathes of Iraqi territory in 2014 complicated Iraqi politics and eventually prompted formal re-engagement by US forces.

Conclusion

US President George W. Bush presented the US-led War on Terror within the context of America's national security. His administration argued that removing the Taliban from power in Afghanistan and Saddam Hussein from power in Iraq was crucial to ridding the world of international terrorism. Washington also linked the War on Terror to democracy promotion: democratic governance as an antidote to tyranny and terror. Hence, after achieving regime change in Afghanistan and Iraq with relative ease, Washington was confronted with the task of transitioning these states to democracy. From the outset, however, the promotion of democracy was hindered by a range of challenges, many of which stemmed from the difficulties of applying this model of governance in deeply divided societies. The strategies employed by Washington revealed a failure to comprehend the delicate social fabrics of Afghanistan and Iraq. Implementing democracy from above through regime change unleashed major social and sectarian tensions which tore the two states apart from within.

Nearly two decades after the War on Terror was launched, the US pledge to defeat terrorism and bring democracy to Iraq and Afghanistan remains far from realized. Both countries are still teetering on the edge of becoming failed states. In the absence of a central government that can protect its citizens and provide adequate services, alternative contenders continue to emerge. These contenders provide services and form their own militias to protect neighbourhoods. In times of chaos and uncertainty, they are empowered as civilians are forced to turn to them for protection. Perhaps the most destructive aspect of a state verging on collapse is the security vacuum it creates. This dangerous cyclical pattern has endured in Afghanistan and Iraq since the United States toppled the Taliban and Saddam Hussein, and it is the devastating legacy of the US-led War on Terror.

References

Arab Center for Research and Policy Studies (2014) 'The New Abadi Government: A Pre-emptive Measure against the Disintegration of the Iraqi State?', October, available at http://english.dohainstitute.org/file/Get/285227be-9a66-4496-bd5b-bbc5bf879fed.

Ayoob, Mohammed (2003) 'The War against Iraq: Normative and Strategic Implications', *Middle East Policy*, Vol. 10, No. 2, pp. 27–39.

Barakat, Sultan (2005) 'Post-Saddam Iraq: Deconstructing a Regime, Reconstructing a Nation', *Third World Quarterly*, Vol. 26, No. 4–5, pp. 571–591.

BBC (2003) 'Blix Criticises Coalition over Iraq Weapons', 6 June, available at http://news.bbc.co.uk/2/hi/2967598.stm.

Belasco, Amy (2009) 'Troop Levels in the Afghan and Iraq Wars, FY2001–FY2012: Cost and Other Potential Issues', Congressional Reserve Services, 2 July, available at https://fas.org/sgp/crs/natsec/R40682.pdf.

Blair, Tony (2003) 'Statement on Iraq', 25 January, available at www.pm.gov.uk/output/Page3088.asp.

Bremer, Paul L. (2003) 'De-Baathification of Iraqi Society', Coalition Provisional Authority, 16 May, available at http://nsarchive.gwu.edu/NSAEBB/NSAEBB418/docs/9a%20-%20Coalition%20Provisional%20Authority%20Order%20No%201%20-%205-16-03.pdf.

Bush, George W. (2002) 'President Bush Outlines Iraqi Threat', 7 October, available at https://georgewbush-whitehouse.archives.gov/news/releases/2002/10/20021007-8.html.

Bush, George W. (2003) 'President Says Saddam Hussein Must Leave Iraq within 48 Hours', https://georgewbush-whitehouse.archives.gov/news/releases/2003/03/20030317-7.html.

Bush, George W. (2008) 'Bush Remarks on Iraq War and Terrorism', *Washington Post*, 19 March, available at www.washingtonpost.com/wp-dyn/content/article/2008/03/19/AR2008031901083.html.

Dale, Catherine (2008) 'Operation Iraqi Freedom: Strategies, Approaches, Results, and Issues for Congress', Congressional Research Services, 28 March, available at https://fas.org/sgp/crs/mideast/RL34387.pdf.

Dodge, Toby (2007) 'The Causes of US Failure in Iraq', *Survival*, Vol. 49, No. 1, pp. 85–106.

Holland, Steve (2014) 'Obama Plans to End US Troop Presence in Afghanistan by 2016', Reuters, 27 May, available at www.reuters.com/article/us-usa-afghanista n-obama-idUSKBN0E71WQ20140527.

Human Rights Watch (2006) 'Lessons in Terror: Attacks on Education in Afghanistan', July, available at www.hrw.org/reports/2006/afghanistan0706/afghanistan0706web fullwcover.pdf.

Human Rights Watch (2014) 'World Report 2014: Iraq, Events of 2013', available at www.hrw.org/world-report/2014/country-chapters/iraq.

Ibrahimi, Niamatullah (2014) 'When Few Means Many: The Consequence of Civilian Casualties for Civil–Military Relations in Afghanistan', in William Maley and Susanne Schmeidl (eds), *Reconstructing Afghanistan: Civil–Military Experiences in Comparative Perspective* (London: Routledge).

Isakhan, Benjamin (2015) *Legacy of Iraq: From the 2003 War to the 'Islamic State'* (Edinburgh: Edinburgh University Press).

Johnson, Thomas H. (2013) 'Taliban Adaptations and Innovations', *Small Wars and Insurgencies*, Vol. 24, No. 1, pp. 3–27.

Johnson, Thomas H. and Mason, Chris M. (2008) 'Understanding the Taliban and Insurgency in Afghanistan', *Orbis*, Vol. 51, No. 1, pp. 71–89.

Jones, Seth G. (2006) 'Averting Failure in Afghanistan', *Survival*, Vol. 48, No. 1, pp. 111–128.

Maley, William (2006) *Rescuing Afghanistan* (Sydney: UNSW Press).

Maley, William (2010) 'Afghanistan in 2010', *Asian Survey*, Vol. 51, No. 1, pp. 85–96.

Maley, William (2013) 'State Building in Afghanistan: Challenges and Pathologies', *Central Asian Survey*, Vol. 32, No. 3, pp. 255–270.

Malkasian, Carter (2006) 'Signalling Resolve, Democratization, and the First Battle of Fallujah', *Journal of Strategic Studies*, Vol. 29, No. 3, pp. 423–452.

McCary, John A. (2009) 'The Anbar Awakening: An Alliance of Incentives', *Washington Quarterly*, Vol. 32, No. 1, pp. 43–59.

Mohammed, Muhanad (2010) 'Iraq Election Officials Confirm Sunni Candidate Ban', Reuters, 13 February, available at www.reuters.com/article/us-ira q-election-idUSTRE61C1CP20100213.

National Security Council (2002) 'National Security Strategy of 2002', available at www.whitehouse.gov/nsc/nss.html.

Obama, Barack (2007) 'Renewing American Leadership', *Foreign Affairs*, Vol. 86, No. 4, pp. 2–16.

Obama, Barack (2008) 'Obama's Remarks on Iraq and Afghanistan', *New York Times*, 15 July, available at www.nytimes.com/2008/07/15/us/politics/15text-obama.html.

Obama, Barack (2009a) 'President Barack Obama's Inaugural Address', 21 January, available at https://obamawhitehouse.archives.gov/blog/2009/01/21/president-bara ck-obamas-inaugural-address.

Obama, Barack (2009b) 'Remarks by the President in Address to the Nation on the Way Forward in Afghanistan and Pakistan', 1 December, available at https://obamawhitehouse.archives.gov/blog/2009/12/01/new-way-forward-presi dents-address.

Obama, Barack (2011) 'Remarks by President Obama and Prime Minister al-Maliki of Iraq in a Joint Press Conference', 12 December, available at https://obamawhite house.archives.gov/the-press-office/2011/12/12/remarks-president-obama-and-prime-minister-al-maliki-iraq-joint-press-co.

Obama, Barack (2014) 'Statement by the President on Iraq', 11 April, available at https:// obamawhitehouse.archives.gov/the-press-office/2014/08/11/statement-president-iraq.

Perle, Richard, Solarz, Stephen, Wolfowitz, Paul and Armitage, Richard (1998) 'Open Letter to the President', 24 February, available at www.centerforsecuritypolicy.org/1998/02/24/open-letter-to-the-president-4/.

Rashid, Ahmed (2010) *Taliban* (New Haven, CT: Yale University Press).

Saikal, Amin (2014) *Zone of Crisis: Afghanistan, Pakistan, Iran and Iraq* (London: IBTauris).

Simon, Steven (2008) 'The Price of the Surge: How US Strategy Is Hastening Iraq's Demise', *Foreign Affairs*, Vol. 87, No. 3, pp. 57–76.

United Nations (2007) 'Over 34,000 Civilians Killed in Iraq in 2006, Says UN Report on Rights Violations', 16 January, available at www.un.org/apps/news/story.asp?NewsID=21241#.WSWJyBOGP-Y.

United Nations Assistance Mission inAfghanistan (2009) 'Annual Report on Protection of Civilians in Armed Conflict, 2008', January, available at https://unama.unmissions.org/sites/default/files/unama_09february-annual20report_poc202008_final_11feb09.pdf.

United Nations Assistance Mission inAfghanistan (2011) 'Annual Report 2010 on Protection of Civilians in Armed Conflict', March, available at https://unama.unmissions.org/sites/default/files/engi_version_of_poc_annual_report_2011.pdf.

United Nations Assistance Mission inAfghanistan (2014) 'Civilian Casualties in Afghan Conflict Rise by 14 Percent in 2013', 8 February, available at https://unama.unmissions.org/sites/default/files/feb_8_2014_poc-report_2013-pr-eng-final.pdf.

United Nations Assistance Mission forIraq (2008) 'Human Rights Report', available at www.ohchr.org/Documents/Countries/IQ/UNAMI_Human_Rights_Report_July_December_2008_EN.pdf.

United NationsIraq (2017) 'Civilian Casualties', available at www.uniraq.com/index.php?option=com_k2&view=itemlist&layout=category&task=category&id=159&Itemid=633&lang=en.

United Nations Security Council (1991) 'Resolution 687', available at www.un.org/Depts/unmovic/documents/687.pdf.

United Nations Security Council (2002) 'Resolution 1441', available at www.un.org/Depts/unmovic/documents/1441.pdf.

United Nations Security Council (2003) 'Iraq Memorandum', 24 February, available at www.globalpolicy.org/component/content/article/167-attack/35224.html.

United States Defense Casualty Analysis Service (2017) 'US Military Casualties: Operation Enduring Freedom (OEF) Casualty Summary by Month and Service', available at www.dmdc.osd.mil/dcas/pages/report_oef_month.xhtml.

White House (2012) 'Fact Sheet: The US–Afghanistan Strategic Partnership Agreement', 1 May, available at https://obamawhitehouse.archives.gov/the-press-office/2012/05/01/fact-sheet-us-afghanistan-strategic-partnership-agreement.

Witte, Griff (2009) 'The Taliban Establishes Elaborate Government in Afghanistan', *Washington Post*, 8 December, available at www.washingtonpost.com/wp-dyn/content/article/2009/12/07/AR2009120704127.html.

Zeidel, Ronen (2015) 'Between Aqalliya and Mukawin: Understanding Sunni Political Attitudes in Post-Saddam Iraq', in Benjamin Isakhan (ed.), *Legacy of Iraq: From the 2003 War to the 'Islamic State'* (Edinburgh: Edinburgh University Press).

9   The Arab uprisings

Introduction

The Arab uprisings, also known as the Arab Spring, was a period of major social and political unrest which commenced in 2010. Mass demonstrations engulfed the Arab region as citizens challenged their authoritarian leaders and called for socio-political reform. The uprisings began on 17 December in Tunisia, after a young market trader, Mohammed Bouazizi, self-immolated as an act of political defiance and desperation against the ruling regime. This tragic suicide was not unprecedented (Sadiki 2014: i), but it triggered protests across the country, with thousands demanding the resignation of Tunisian President Ben Ali. In accordance with the protesters' demands, Ali stepped down, bringing an end to his twenty-three years in power. This was a truly inspirational moment in the Arab world. News of the events proliferated on social media, and within a month the protests had reached almost every Arab state across the Middle East and North Africa. Thousands of Arab youths took to the streets united by an interlinked set of grievances relating to corruption, a lack of political representation, transparency and accountability, limited social and political opportunities and repression. Significantly, this popular surge of people's power was mobilized in the absence of a leader and with little top-down organization. What mobilized the protesters was a call for immediate and profound political change.

The Arab uprisings had various outcomes across the region. Some entrenched regimes were removed from power, others fought back and successfully repressed the protesters, while yet others saw their states descend into civil war. Indeed, as the momentum of 2011 faded, many states experienced a return to repressive rule, often through a powerful reassertion of state authority. Tunisia was the only country to break away definitively from the old order. Nine months after Ben Ali was removed from office, the country held its first free and fair democratic elections since gaining independence in 1956. In a defining moment, the moderate Islamist Ennahda Party was voted into power and Hamadi Jebali was appointed Prime Minister. Ennahda proceeded to defy its secular critics by blending its Islamist traditions with the requirements of democratic governance. Despite Tunisia's economic and security challenges, the country's transition into democracy has remained on track, as is evident in the success of its second round of elections, held in 2014. However, no other Arab state was able to follow the Tunisian example, as specific national and historic factors combined to thwart the revolutionary process.

This chapter explores the Arab uprisings through both a thematic analysis and a series of brief case-studies. First, it will explore the causes of the Egyptian 'Revolution' and the political environment that transpired after the fall of President Hosni Mubarak. It will then examine two further case-studies: Libya and Bahrain. In Chapter 10, we will investigate the Syrian Civil War and its major political ramifications – the refugee crisis and the rise of the so-called 'Islamic State'. These case-studies provide insights into the various trends of Arab politics in recent years and demonstrate the significant contrasts in the political experiences of the Arab Spring countries.

Causes and the 'contagion' effect

In the early phase of the uprisings, the demands of the protest movements were diverse as a range of citizens came together to demonstrate against their ruling regimes, especially in densely populated urban environments. The protests in Egypt and Tunisia were especially notable for the participation of many women and young people. Contrary to the long-standing concerns of Western policy-makers towards the region, Islamist organizations played a very limited role in the uprisings (Pace and Cavatorta 2012: 132). As in many previous revolutionary periods, the protests centred on what ordinary people did *not* want – primarily a continuation of the existing order in which structures were seen as stagnant, corrupt, nepotistic, repressive and incapable or unwilling of providing economic, social or political opportunities. However, in most states, the turmoil did not constitute a revolution because it did not result in a radical transformation of the whole political system. In this sense, characterizing the period as 'revolutionary' is problematic. With the important exceptions of Tunisia and Libya, the Arab uprisings did not escalate into revolutions.

Indeed, in most cases, the protest movements did not articulate a clear agenda for change. In part, this was a result of the spontaneous nature of the uprisings. While past movements had been inspired by political ideologies of nationalism, anti-colonialism, socialism or Islamism, there was an ideological void on this occasion. This was partly due to the bankruptcy or irrelevance of these ideologies in the twenty-first-century Arab world. As a result, there were no obvious leaders at the helm of the uprisings. This worked in favour of the protesters, as the security apparatus struggled to target the leadership. Furthermore, in contrast to many of the historical periods explored in this volume, external support, or the perception of external interference, was not a key issue, and the protest movements challenged ruling regimes that were both pro- and anti-US in orientation.

As global public opinion rallied to the side of the protesters, a common thread that ran through the various states throughout the Arab world became evident. While the context of each protest movement was very much national, there were several shared grievances and factors that contributed to widespread discontent across the region. These included a lack of political freedom, the repressive implementation of political authority, human rights violations, high unemployment and a lack of social mobility. By 2010, these factors had generated pent-up anger over the unresponsiveness of the ruling regimes and an increasing awareness of how things could be different within the socio-political environments of the Arab region. This discontent was magnified by new mediums such as social media, which enabled young people to share their opinions outside of the traditional structures of their societies and rally others to the cause.

The role of political authority in Arab societies contributed significantly to the high levels of discontent that were felt across the region. In the years leading up to the uprisings, the Arab world was regularly characterized as devoid of political freedom, with the marginal exception of Kuwait (Diamond 2010: 95). The Arab regimes had been in power for decades, which had led academic scholarship to focus on political entrenchment of power and investigate the durability of authoritarianism in the region (Heydemann 2007). This approach to Arab politics explored how the power of the military–security complex and the strength of state-dominated economies could be employed to suppress or mitigate public discontent (Gause 2011: 83). This matrix provided support to the 'known quantities' of Arab politics – long-term rulers with whom the United States could interact in relationships that functioned in predictable and established fashions. In these relationships, the United States was prepared to overlook questions regarding human rights, gender equality and political reform in favour of ensuring continuity and stability in the region. Ensuring stability became even more critical in the context of the War on Terror. Incumbent regimes in the Arab world had demonstrated authoritarian durability and the capacity to cope with discontent. This was deemed a crucial asset in responding to the challenge of terrorism. In its determination to confront this threat, the United States turned a blind eye to ever more repressive security policies in its allied states throughout the Arab world (Carothers 2003: 85). These repressive environments that plagued most Arab societies destroyed the popular legitimacy and credibility of Arab rulers who offered their citizens little hope of reform.

The economic deprivation experienced by so many in the region was another key component of the social discontent. In the years leading up to the uprisings, youth unemployment rates were exceptionally high across the Middle East and North Africa. This was due largely to a 'youth bulge' that was evident in most Arab states. According to the UN Development Programme, the total population of Arab countries more than doubled to 314 million between 1975 and 2005. Consequently, by 2010, labour markets were simply unable to meet the increased demands for jobs from young workers (Salehi-Isfahani 2010: 10). Between 2005 and 2007, approximately 26 per cent of Arab youth were unemployed, compared to 20 per cent in middle-income countries (Salehi-Isfahani 2010: 12). Significantly, countries that experienced high levels of domestic unrest suffered high unemployment rates. For example, unemployment stood at 27.3 per cent in Tunisia, 24.8 per cent in Egypt, 16.5 per cent in Syria, 20.1 per cent in Bahrain and 22.2 per cent in Jordan. Moreover, the new job-seekers had higher expectations to match their educational attainment. By any international measure, education rates in the Arab world had sky-rocketed in the years leading up to the uprisings. Rapid urbanization and state investment in the education sector had seen an explosion of universities across the region. UNESCO estimates that literacy rates, which were low only fifty years ago, now stand at around 97 per cent in Libya, 91 per cent in Bahrain and 75 per cent in Egypt (UNESCO 2017). This represented a significant governmental and, more importantly, societal investment in education. However, this was not accompanied by structural growth. The failure of the region's economies to diversify or launch training programmes led to a generation of well-educated young people who were unable to secure employment commensurate with their educational qualifications. This had knock-on effects as the region's youth were unable to secure gainful employment and so were forced to delay marriage and parenthood.

The role of the internet and social media was significant in facilitating the Arab uprisings. Unlike earlier generations, the youth of many Arab countries had instant access to the divergent political and social environments of the outside world via the internet and especially social media. Consequently, expectations were raised as citizens witnessed how things could be done differently within their own societies. This gave rise to a combination of frustration and indignation towards Arab leaders who could not offer their citizens the prospect of a better life – politically, socially or economically. Furthermore, social media played an important role in mobilizing the demonstrations. By 2010, Arab youth, particularly in urban areas, was displaying high levels of online connectivity. Hence, opposition activists were able to disseminate information via social media to organize and publicize the protests. The effectiveness of social media during this period was underscored by the spontaneous mobilization of thousands of protesters onto the streets in the absence of any coherent leadership or organizational structure to sustain the momentum.

As the protests unfolded, the concept of pan-Arabism – or the interrelated nature of Arab politics – was reinvigorated. As we explored earlier in this volume, pan-Arabism reached its zenith in the 1960s. However, Israel's decisive victory in the Six-Day War of 1967 dealt a devastating blow to Arab unity. This was then exacerbated by subsequent political upheavals, such as the 1983 conflict in Lebanon, the 1991 Gulf War and the inability of the Arab world to halt the US-led invasion of Iraq in 2003. Despite this trend, however, the Arab uprisings demonstrated the still-powerful political, social and cultural identifications that transcend national borders in the region. As such, the protest movements, each of which was motivated by local or national challenges and influenced by a shared desire for reform, spread throughout the Arab world. In this sense, it is useful to consider a 'contagion effect' in the spread of discontent.

Revolution? Egypt, Mubarak and the Muslim Brotherhood

The emergence of organized public protests in the bellwether state of Egypt against a long-standing US ally, President Hosni Mubarak, marked an important moment in the Arab uprisings. On 25 January 2011, demonstrations erupted in Cairo and millions of people from across the Egyptian political spectrum called for Mubarak's resignation. He had been in power for three decades and was widely believed to be grooming his son, Gamal Mubarak, as his successor (El-Bendary 2013: 61). The protesters' grievances were multifaceted, including food-price inflation, unemployment and the concentration of wealth and economic opportunity in the hands of an elite that was closely linked to the regime (Anderson 2011: 4). In addition, widespread political concerns were evident. Most powerfully, the protesters rejected the enduring use of Emergency Law 162 (1958), which had remained in place since Sadat's assassination in 1981, leading to an increase in police brutality, failings in the justice system and an absence of political accountability (El-Bendary 2013: 36–39).

Box 9.1 Emergency Law 162 (1958)

Egypt's state of emergency was first declared in 1967 on the outbreak of the Arab–Israeli War and lasted until 1980. It was reinstated the following year after the assassination of Egyptian President Anwar Sadat and then repeatedly extended every three years until its final expiration in 2012. It enabled Egyptian President Hosni Mubarak (1981–2011) to enact Emergency Law 162, drafted in 1958 to eliminate 'threats to national security'. Under this law, Mubarak was granted wide-ranging powers, including the right to detain citizens indefinitely without trial or charge, restrict freedom of speech and prohibit freedom of assembly. This enabled him to eliminate political opponents, government critics and members of religious organizations such as the Egyptian Muslim Brotherhood, through arbitrary arrests, imprisonment and execution. The continuous state of emergency contributed to popular unrest inside Egypt, which in turn triggered the 2011 uprising.

As the public demonstrations spread throughout the state, the United States began to question the capacity of the regime to hold on to power. The Obama administration, caught largely unprepared by this new challenge in Arab politics and mindful of the disastrous consequences of previous US interventions in the region, tried to keep its distance from the unfolding situation, but Obama himself was left in a near-impossible position. For decades, Washington had viewed its alliance with Mubarak's Egypt as vital to regional security and US interests. Throughout the course of his rule, Mubarak had displayed a commitment to combating terrorism, securing the Sinai and maintaining Egypt's 1979 peace treaty with Israel – Washington's staunchest ally in the region. In exchange, Washington had provided the Egyptian military with US$1.3 billion of aid annually, making the United States the primary benefactor of the Egyptian armed forces. While this arrangement certainly served US interests in the region, Washington was repeatedly criticized for turning a blind eye to Egypt's appalling human rights record. The outpouring of public contempt for the regime meant the United States, once again caught by its own rhetoric regarding the importance of democracy and political representation, was unable to declare its public support for one of its oldest allies in the Arab world. By early February 2011, Obama had distanced himself from Mubarak and was calling for the will of the Egyptian people to be respected (Bassiouni 2016: 60–61). The Egyptian military also withdrew its support for the embattled President, which left his regime in an untenable position. For several decades, the armed forces had wielded extensive influence via their control of the state's political and economic structures. In this sense, and similar to many other Arab states, they had played a key role as protector of the ruling regime. As the protests grew more insistent and violent, though, the army was faced with a stark choice: either forcefully suppress the demonstrations and probably incur mass casualties or allow the regime to fall. The army decided to side with the 'nation' and Mubarak was swept aside on 11 February 2011.

The Egyptian Supreme Council of the Armed Forces (SCAF) then assumed political power and assured all Egyptians, under the watchful eyes of the international community, that it would act as a transitory authority until a new government could be elected. This promise was fulfilled when 2011's free and fair parliamentary elections were contested by a host of new parties, most notably the Muslim Brotherhood's Freedom and Justice Party (FJP), which secured nearly half of the seats (Milton-Edwards 2016b: 55). The rapid pace of political change in Egypt in this period offered a significant advantage to the Brotherhood, which, unlike many of the other opposition movements, had a long organizational history and well-established hierarchy. Unsurprisingly, then, the FJP's candidate, Mohamed Morsi, was elected President in the June 2012 presidential elections. For the Brotherhood, this was a truly historic moment. Since its establishment in 1928, its Islamic orientation had placed it at odds with Egypt's secular leadership. To maintain influence within Egyptian society and its political institutions, the Brotherhood was therefore forced to adapt its ideological foundations to a fluctuating environment. This led to periods of accommodation and political participation within the state, punctuated by moments of repression and persecution. From the outset, the international community and the Arab world speculated as to how the FJP would reconcile its Islamist traditions with the requirements of modern governance, especially in an environment so fraught with economic and political tension. The Egyptian military also observed the whole process carefully, as it still viewed itself as the final arbiter of political change within Egypt.

Morsi's accession to power was to prove a key moment for the Brotherhood, Egyptian politics and the early phase of the Arab Spring as a whole. However, the FJP struggled as a governing political party. There are two main streams of analysis regarding the failure of the Brotherhood's rule in Egypt. The first focuses on the FJP's efforts to reinvigorate the Egyptian economy. It bears mention that the economic environment in which the Morsi government came to power was little short of diabolical. Egypt's economic growth in the final years of Mubarak's rule had hovered around 4.5 per cent, short of the 5 per cent needed to sustain the country's growing population (World Bank 2016). The political upheavals of 2011 proved costly, too, with tourism, foreign investment and manufacturing all plummeting. As a result, economic growth dipped to just 1.8 per cent in that year (World Bank 2016). In this sense, the capacity of the new government to make meaningful steps towards economic recovery, and thus increase opportunities, was systemically limited. This was complicated by the fact that, after a long history in opposition, much of it spent outside the Egyptian legal and political system, the Brotherhood had no experience of government.

The second key line of analysis revolves around the intrinsic nature of the FJP and the Brotherhood itself. The capacity of an Islamist organization to 'play by the rules' was an open question for many observers, and the FJP struggled to exhibit the transparency expected of a legitimate political party. A series of political missteps culminated in a November 2012 presidential edict in which Morsi attempted to centralize power in his own office. This was taken, and publicized, as evidence of the authoritarian nature of the new President, the FJP and the Brotherhood itself, which led to public protests against Morsi's rule. In response, Morsi repealed the edict the following month, but that did little to appease the protesters or, arguably, the factions in Egyptian politics that were committed to a restoration of secular rule. This tense political environment provided an opportunity for the armed forces to reassert their authority. The military, which had allowed Mubarak to fall, still retained control of the economic structures of the state. In this sense, the 'deep state' – the complex hierarchy of which Mubarak had been the figurehead – was ultimately left untouched by his downfall, revealing that the Egyptian 'Revolution' was actually far from complete.

Once the top brass noted a few cracks in the Brotherhood's ability to govern, the army formulated a plan to restore the status quo and protect its own position in Egyptian politics. It overthrew the Morsi government on 3 July 2013 under the pretext of preserving the 'revolution' (Sadiki 2014: 260). This was a highly contentious move. In the view of many observers, toppling a democratically elected leader constituted a military coup. However, the army's removal of Morsi was undertaken with international acquiescence or even support. This point is underscored by Washington's position on Morsi and the FJP. The Brotherhood's rise to power in Egypt had been particularly worrisome for the United States. Washington could not afford to see Morsi's Islamist party disrupt the pre-2011 political and strategic alignments that had served US interests in the region. Throughout the course of the Brotherhood's rule, Washington had therefore maintained an uncomfortable relationship with Egypt as it did not wish to afford Morsi any more legitimacy. Despite moments of rapprochement with him, most notably over Egypt's involvement in mediating a cease-fire in the 2012 conflict between HAMAS and Israel, Washington remained sceptical of the Brotherhood as a conventional political actor. In a clear display of preference for a return to the pre-2011 era, the United States declined to refer to the military takeover as a 'coup'. This was significant as congressional law precludes the provision of foreign aid to any government which attains power via a coup (Talib 2014: 452).

As the military asserted its control of the Egyptian state, a surge in secular–nationalist fervour became evident. The military's principal 'strong man', Commander-in-Chief Abdel Fattah el-Sisi, swiftly crushed the Brotherhood and its supporters, then resigned from the army in order to run in Egypt's 2014 presidential elections, which saw him emerge as the victor. El-Sisi's administration rapidly moved forward with its agenda to restore security in Sinai, decimate the tunnels upon which HAMAS relied to counter the Israeli siege of Gaza and criminalize the Brotherhood (Herman 2016: 103). The new government systematically killed and imprisoned scores of Brotherhood members (Human Rights Watch 2014), while Morsi himself was sentenced to death in May 2015, although this had yet to be carried out at the time of writing (January 2018). The crackdown was openly supported by Saudi Arabia, a major benefactor of the Egyptian military, which also moved to criminalize the Brotherhood (al-Sharif 2014). Meanwhile, the Obama administration raised few, if any, objections. El-Sisi moved to turn the clock back to the Mubarak era through the unrestrained suppression of protesters, especially those supporting Morsi. This caused outrage both inside and outside Egypt, but international calls for restraint had little impact on the new regime (Human Rights Watch 2015).

The 'revolution' in Egypt had come full circle. The democratic installation of a military regime that was striking in its repressive stance on religiously orientated opposition symbolized a return to the Mubarak era. Regionally, Egypt served as a potent example of the challenges of this period. The simple reality was that this particular state, by virtue of its standing and history, was simply too important to fail. This is evidenced by the massive levels of international support which poured into Egypt after Morsi's fall. Within a month of el-Sisi entering the presidential office, the United States resumed its provision of military aid, demonstrating Washington's preference for the predictability of military-endorsed rule in an increasingly unstable region (BBC 2014). The upswing in violence in Syria and the disintegration of the Libyan state made these concerns more pressing. The Gulf states also provided significant aid packages to el-Sisi's government. The Gulf Cooperation Council alone swiftly pledged in excess of US$12 billion to the new administration (Ulrichsen 2014: 90).

Egypt's 'revolution' serves as a powerful example of the international preference for stability in international relations. However, the economic challenges which plagued the country under Mubarak remain, with unemployment peaking at 13 per cent in 2014 (it had been 9 per cent in 2010) and the population growing rapidly (United Nations Data 2017). For the Egyptian Brotherhood, the Arab uprisings proved catastrophic. The organization took advantage of what seemed to be a promising opportunity to prove its credentials as a legitimate democratic actor, but a combination of structural factors, political ineptitude and poor decision-making led to its swift demise.

The cases of Bahrain and Libya

The Arab uprisings, as we have suggested, are best viewed as a rolling series of distinct national events that were inspired by a popular desire for reform across the Arab world. As such, we shall now offer two brief synopses of the events in Bahrain and Libya. These two case-studies are markedly different from each other and demonstrate the distinct national factors at play. They highlight both the state-centric nature of the protests and generic grievances. To aid a comparative analysis with the Egyptian experience, outlined above, we explore a number of key themes: the role of political authority (dictatorships or absolute monarchy), human rights violations, corruption, nepotism and wealth disparity.

Bahrain: the failed uprising

Soon after the fall of Mubarak, protests spread to the Arab Kingdom of Bahrain in the Persian Gulf. On 14 February 2011, protesters demonstrated against the ruling al-Khalifa family and called for the implementation of promised reforms, greater political freedoms and respect for human rights. In comparison with other regional cases, this protest movement was initially non-violent and the regime's response was relatively mild. However, Bahrain is a much smaller state than Egypt or Syria, and it is enmeshed in a very delicate regional balance within the Gulf.

By late February, the protests both for and against the Sunni al-Khalifas had become routine. However, the relatively peaceful stand-off was shattered when the police and security forces countered the protesters with lethal force, resulting in the deaths of several civilians. By this time, the protest movement was drawn in large part from the state's Shia majority. Therefore, the al-Khalifas attempted to link the domestic disturbances to external interference, blaming Iran for the unrest and casting the protest movement within the broader narrative of Sunni–Shia tension. Unlike Mubarak, Bahrain's ruling family was well supported internationally, and the al-Khalifas' relationship with Saudi Arabia and the United States proved vital to the regime's ability to suppress dissent. For the Saudis, the potential for a protest movement to unseat a neighbouring friendly regime was unacceptable, so Riyadh utilized the GCC framework to deploy troops in support of the ruling family. This deployment effectively ended Bahrain's uprising and secured the continuation of al-Khalifa rule. This was yet another watershed moment for the region. The Saudi-led military response was a clear demonstration that Riyadh would protect the absolute rule of any Sunni elite against calls for enhanced popular political participation. While the Arab uprising in Bahrain was overshadowed by the magnitude of the violence in other states (notably Libya and Syria), it highlighted the importance of geopolitical interests in shaping actions.

Washington's response to these events reflected the conflicted goals of US policy, especially the pursuit of democracy, the desire for regional stability and the protection of friendly regimes. The United States had maintained a small operational presence in Bahrain for decades. Indeed, this had been vital to the US deployment in Iraq in 2003, which relied heavily on the US 5th Fleet, based in Bahrain. In 2010, the US Navy commenced a major expansion project to double the size of its facility in Bahrain. This commitment was indicative of the long-term relationship between the two states. Calls for reform, while ideologically compatible with US rhetoric on democracy, were risky for US geostrategic interests as they threatened to replace the friendly al-Khalifa regime with one that was potentially inclined towards Shia Iran. This was extremely problematic for Washington. The United States could not afford to see its interests in the region undermined by a popular revolt, so Obama's response to the crushing of the Bahraini uprising was muted, at best.

Intervention: NATO in Libya

The NATO-led international intervention in Libya was unique in the Arab uprisings period. After protests against Libyan President Muammar Gaddafi's regime commenced in mid-February 2011, the situation quickly descended into armed conflict. Despite international calls for restraint, the regime publicly indicated that it would use extreme force to crush the protest movement. These declarations provided a justification for international intervention. On 26 February 2011, the United Nations Security Council, galvanized by a broad international consensus regarding the brutality of Gaddafi's security forces, passed Resolution 1970, which endorsed freezing the regime's assets and restricting travel while the case was referred to the International Criminal Court for investigation of crimes against civilians (Bartu 2015: 36). By the following month, this international condemnation of the Libyan regime had solidified into Resolution 1973, which authorized a no-fly zone and empowered a NATO mission to use 'all means necessary to protect civilians'. The drafting of this resolution was spearheaded by the United States, which then opted to lead the campaign from the rear. NATO took the operational lead, although the bulk of the air missions were flown by US pilots. The implementation of Resolution 1973 has been widely criticized. By late March, the focus of the NATO air sorties had shifted from disabling the regime's air defences to targeting its ground forces, a development which led many observers to question if the intervention had moved into the realm of regime change (Campbell 2013: 75–88). In October 2011, Gaddafi was captured and killed alongside many of his relatives and closest associates.

In the aftermath of the ousting of Gaddafi, Libya descended into political chaos. The emergence of multiple governments, warlords and armed Islamist and tribal factions pushed the state into a multi-front conflict for control of its natural resources. It disintegrated into a series of warring city-states, supported to varying degrees by regional and international players. In a further blow to

Libyan unity, since 2015 various coastal areas have pledged allegiance to the Islamic State (Chivvis 2016: 115). In April 2016, a national unity government was declared, but there has yet to emerge any real sense of sovereign control or authority. Libya also serves as a launch pad for refugee flows into southern Europe, with thousands of migrants dying on the difficult sea crossing. By mid-2016, the United Nations High Commissioner for Refugees had detected a significant rise in the number of refugees arriving on the shores of Italy and Greece (UNHCR 2016). This indicated that, as alternative routes were blocked, ever more refugees were prepared to make the hazardous crossing. Despite rising international concern over the abysmal lack of human and political security in Libya, including the emergence of 'slave markets' (International Organization of Migration 2017), at the time of writing there were no concrete plans to reconstruct the country.

In relation to the broader Arab uprisings, and especially the international response to Syria, the Libyan conflict provides vital context for Russian and Chinese positions. These two international powers, both of which are well known for their assertion of the primacy of state sovereignty, allowed the adoption of Resolution 1973 to protect civilians in the Libyan crisis. Advocates of this resolution focused on the norms of the Protection of Civilians (PoC), established in 1999, and Responsibility to Protect (R2P), established in 2005. These norms reflect a global commitment to the protection of civilians from genocide, ethnic cleansing and crimes against humanity, and, in many ways, Libya was seen as a test case for them. However, as the NATO mission moved from protecting civilians to assisting rebel factions, both Russia and China viewed the intervention as a bid to secure regime change rather than a legitimate attempt to protect civilian life in a conflict zone. Indeed, the Russian President Vladimir Putin denounced the NATO-led operation as a violation of Resolution 1973, while his Foreign Minister Sergey Lavrov declared that Moscow 'would never allow the Security Council to authorize anything [in Syria] similar to what happened in Libya' (Kuperman 2015: 75). This provides vital context for understanding the international impasse that obstructed the United Nations from addressing the Syrian crisis (discussed in Chapter 10).

As we can see from the above discussion, the triggers, conflict patterns and ramifications of the Arab uprisings in Bahrain and Libya were manifestly different from one another. This is reinforced by contrasting them to the experience of Egypt. This diversity of experiences, however, should not mask the similarities that highlighted the systemic challenges facing most Arab states in this period.

Political authority

Prior to the Arab uprisings, Bahrain and Libya functioned under very different political systems. The tiny state of Bahrain has long been seen as an adjunct to its much more powerful neighbour, Saudi Arabia. The island, linked to Saudi Arabia by a causeway, has a Shia majority which comprises roughly two-thirds of the national population (Matthiesen 2013: 2). It was a British protectorate from the late nineteenth century until the formal declaration of independence in 1971. Since then, the Sunni al-Khalifa family has ruled as an absolute monarchy. It has permitted active Shia political engagement but has maintained a strong grip on power by filling most of the few political posts with members of the royal family. In relation to foreign policy, Bahrain has mirrored the Saudi position by forging strong links with the United States and eschewing the rise of Iran.

The North African state of Libya had a very different recent history. In 1969, the twenty-seven-year-old colonel Muammar Gaddafi seized power in a coup. Thereafter, his regime forged a path based on religion, socialism and authoritarianism. He suspended all secular laws in favour of a loose interpretation of Sharia and developed a massive surveillance and intelligence network which ruthlessly suppressed all political dissent. However, Libya was able to provide its citizens with a relatively good standard of living by exploiting the country's significant oil and gas reserves. Gaddafi's foreign policies were openly confrontational to the West, and Libya was regularly cited as a state sponsor of terrorism and paramilitary groups (Manji and Ekine 2012: 193–194). This was moderated somewhat in the last five to ten years of Gaddafi's rule as he toned down his rhetoric against America and the United Kingdom.

Despite these different orientations, Bahrain, Libya and Egypt were all characterized by their authoritarianism. As noted above, they had little desire to subject their authority to popular critique and they considered their privileges as beyond public scrutiny. The absence of political participation, combined with these states' unwillingness to offer meaningful reform, emerged as a key grievance.

Human rights violations and participation

In Bahrain, the politically active Shia majority forced the regime to engage in political debate. However, any agitation against the royal family was treated harshly and opposition factions were granted a very limited role in the political process. The eagerness of the regime to link internal issues to external players such as Iran also proved problematic. Similar to other Arab sheikhdoms on the Persian Gulf, political dissent incurred stiff penalties in Bahrain, and the regime employed repressive measures to shore up its control. A period of liberalization began in 1995 with the crowning of a new king, Hamad bin Isa al-Khalifa, and Bahrain consequently developed an established opposition movement, represented by formal political parties. This stood in stark contrast to the closed environments of Egypt and Libya, where all opposition was outlawed. However, by 2007, international observers were drawing attention to Bahrain's use of arbitrary arrest, detention without trial and torture against opposition voices (Amnesty International 2008: 61–62).

Under Gaddafi, Libya's human rights record was widely seen as appalling. In addition to its international support for terrorist groups, the regime utilized murder, rape and indefinite detention to secure its hold on power. As the legal system was intimately tied to the state machinery, there was no recourse for citizens and no means to mobilize as public association and protest were outlawed. In one of the more mystifying moments in UN history, Libya was given a seat on the organization's Human Rights Council in 2010 during the regime's short-lived attempt to improve its international image. Its membership of this council was suspended during the protests of 2011.

Corruption, nepotism and concentration of wealth

Like other Arab monarchies, the al-Khalifa family is extremely wealthy. While there are factional tensions within the regime, it rules as an absolute monarchy in which power, and its associated economic privileges, remains within the family unit. This nepotistic approach to the distribution of wealth and political power clearly angered the Bahraini protesters, mirroring the demonstrations in Mubarak's Egypt, where there was a widespread perception that Mubarak was grooming his younger son, Gamal, as his heir. This spoke clearly to Mubarak's dynastic ambition and the likely continuation of Egypt's deeply unpopular status quo. Similarly, in Libya, Gaddafi centralized wealth and power in the hands of his family and immediate circle, with his son, Saif al-Islam, his likely successor. This determination to retain power and maximize its benefits transcended the theoretical differences in governance across the three case-studies. Furthermore, in the years leading up to the uprisings, corruption ran deep within Bahrain's and Libya's public sectors. In a 2010 report, Bahrain was 48th and Libya 146th out of 178 countries in a 'Corruption Perception Index' (International Transparency 2010).

The above discussion demonstrates some of the key triggers at the heart of the Arab uprisings which applied to all Arab states, regardless of their system of governance, ideological orientation or geostrategic priorities. Popular discontent swelled up in the monarchical state of Bahrain, just as it did in the socialist-inspired republic of Libya and the pro-US republic of Egypt. Regardless of their formal systems of government, all of these Arab regimes showed a clear propensity for authoritarianism and the creation of an environment in which they could enrich themselves and those around them.

Conclusion

In the years leading up to the uprisings, Arab societies had been uniformly devoid of political freedom. This common feature of the Arab world was matched by the brutal deployment of military and security forces to suppress political dissent. The authoritarian nature of the Arab regimes had rendered their own citizens virtually voiceless in the face of human rights abuses, high levels of unemployment, and the inequitable and entrenched distribution of wealth and opportunities.

As the protests took hold, for the first time in decades Arab citizens took to the streets to demand reform, inclusion, liberty and respect for human rights.

Traditionally, the police and security apparatuses in the Arab region had represented forces of intimidation for the average citizen, not symbols of law and order. Nevertheless, the protesters showed resilience in their calls for their leaders to step down. Unlike earlier protests, the uprisings lacked a political ideology or clear leaders to mobilize the masses. Instead, it was the call for political accountability that united Arab youth in its demands for reform and transparency.

The spontaneous nature of the uprisings took the world by surprise. While Washington ideologically supported the protesters' calls for democracy, the uprisings placed President Obama in a difficult position. His administration was forced to reassess Washington's relations with some of America's longest-standing allies in the region on a case-by-case basis. The divergent US approaches to Egypt and Bahrain illustrate this point, with both regimes having served America's geostrategic interests in the region for several decades. In Egypt, the Obama administration supported Mubarak's decision to step down, yet remained sceptical of his democratically elected successor, Mohamed Morsi, and the Muslim Brotherhood's Freedom and Justice Party. When the Egyptian military removed Morsi from power, Washington remained acquiescent. Moreover, the United States' resumption of aid to Egypt, now under el-Sisi's government, reflects Washington's preference for stability, even when facilitated by military rule, over uncertainty. Meanwhile, Washington's muted response to the al-Khalifa regime's suppression of the Bahraini protest movement highlighted its double standards with respect to the uprisings, as it was more than willing to intervene in support of the opposition in Libya and openly condemned the Syrian regime for its brutal repression of its domestic uprising.

In the aftermath of the events of 2011, Egypt found itself under a new government which hailed from a military background and was striking in its repressive stance on political opposition. Bahrain remained under the traditional monarchical system which was affirmed by state repression and backed by foreign military intervention. And Libya was a failed state, characterized by communal violence, the rise of terrorist militias and the complete failure of the NATO-led intervention, which was premised, at least rhetorically, on the notion of protecting civilians.

All three of these outcomes were very far from the demonstrators' calls for reform, liberalization, respect for human rights and increased political participation. As the cases of Egypt, Libya and Bahrain demonstrate, national context is extremely important when reviewing the Arab uprisings. There are clear common threads, most powerfully the mass explosion of popular discontent. Yet, the contours of the national environment, and the international relationships that were in play at the time, decided the fate of each protest movement.

References

Al-Sharif, Osama (2014) 'Jordan Unlikely to Follow Saudis on Muslim Brotherhood', *al-Monitor*, 11 March, available at www.al-monitor.com/pulse/originals/2014/03/jordan-muslim-brotherhood-saudi-terrorism.html.

Amnesty International (2008) 'Amnesty International Report 2008', available at www. amnesty.org/en/documents/document/?indexNumber=pol10%2F001%2F2008&language=en.

Anderson, Lisa (2011) 'Demystifying the Arab Spring: Parsing the Differences between Tunisia, Egypt, and Libya', *Foreign Affairs*, Vol. 90, No. 3, pp. 1–7.

Badran, Margot (2016) 'Creative Disobedience: Feminism, Islam, and Revolution in Egypt', in Fatima Sadiqi (ed.), *Women's Movements in post-'Arab Spring' North Africa* (New York: Palgrave Macmillan).

Bartu, Peter (2015) 'The Corridor of Uncertainty: The National Transitional Council's Battle for Legitimacy and Recognition,' in Peter Cole and Brian McQuinn (eds), *The Libyan Revolution and Its Aftermath* (Oxford: Oxford University Press).

Bassiouni, M. Cherif (2016) 'Egypt's Unfinished Revolution', in Adam Roberts, Michael J. Willis and Rory McCarthy (eds), *Civil Resistance in the Arab Spring: Triumphs and Disasters* (Oxford: Oxford University Press)

BBC (2014) 'US Unlocks Military Aid to Egypt, Backing President Sisi', 22 June, available at www.bbc.com/news/world-middle-east-27961933.

Campbell, Horace (2013) *NATO's Failure in Libya: Lessons for Africa* (Pretoria: Africa Institute of South Africa).

Carothers, Thomas (2003) 'Promoting Democracy and Fighting Terror', *Foreign Affairs*, Vol. 82, No. 1, pp. 84–97.

Chivvis, Christopher S. (2016) 'Countering the Islamic State in Libya', *Survival*, Vol. 58, No. 4, pp. 113–130.

Dalacoura, Katerina (2012) 'The 2011 Uprisings in the Arab Middle East: Political Change and Geopolitical Implications', *International Affairs*, Vol. 88, No. 1, pp. 63–79.

Diamond, Larry (2010) 'Why Are There No Arab Democracies?', *Journal of Democracy*, Vol. 21, No. 1, pp. 93–112.

El-Bendary, Mohamed (2013) *Egyptian Revolution: Between Hope and Despair, Mubarak to Morsi* (New York: Algora Publishing).

Gause, Gregory F., III (2011) 'Why Middle East Studies Missed the Arab Spring: The Myth of Authoritarian Stability', *Foreign Affairs*, Vol. 90, No. 4, pp. 81–90.

Herman, Lyndall (2016) 'Sisi, the Sinai and Salafis: Instability in a Power Vacuum', *Middle East Policy*, Vol. 23, No. 2, pp. 95–107.

Heydemann, Steven (2007) 'Upgrading Authoritarianism in the Arab World', Analysis Paper 13 (Washington, DC: Saban Center for Middle East Policy, Brookings Institution).

Human Rights Watch (2014) 'All According to Plan: The Rab'a Massacre and Mass Killings of Protesters in Egypt', 12 August, available at www.hrw.org/report/2014/08/12/all-according-plan/raba-massacre-and-mass-killings-protesters-egypt.

Human Rights Watch (2015) 'Egypt: Year of Abuses under el-Sisi', 8 June, available at www.hrw.org/news/2015/06/08/egypt-year-abuses-under-al-sisi.

International Organization of Migration (2017) 'IOM Learns of "Slave Market" Conditions Endangering Migrants in North Africa', 11 April, available at www.iom.int/news/iom-learns-slave-market-conditions-endangering-migrants-north-africa.

International Transparency (2010) 'Corruption Perceptions Index', available at www.transparency.org/cpi2010/results.

Kuperman, Alan J. (2015) 'Obama's Libya Debacle: How a Well-Meaning Intervention Ended in Failure', *Foreign Affairs*, Vol. 94, No. 2, pp. 66–77.

Manji, Firoze and Ekine, Sokari (2012) *African Awakening: The Emerging Revolutions* (Oxford: Pambazuka Press).

Matthiesen, Toby (2013) *Sectarian Gulf: Saudi Arabia, Bahrain and the Arab Spring that Wasn't* (Stanford, CA: Stanford University Press).

Milton-Edwards, Beverley (2016b) *The Muslim Brotherhood: The Arab Spring and Its Future Face* (New York: Routledge).

Norton, Augustus Richard (2013) 'The Return of Egypt's Deep State', *Current History*, Vol. 112, No. 758, pp. 338–344.

Pace, Michelle and Cavatorta, Francesco (2012) 'The Arab Uprisings in Theoretical Perspective: An Introduction', *Mediterranean Politics*, Vol. 17, No. 2, pp. 125–138.

Sadiki, Larbi (2014) *Routledge Handbook of the Arab Spring: Rethinking Democratization* (Florence: Taylor and Francis).

Salehi-Isfahani, Djavad (2010) 'Human Development in the Middle East and North Africa', United Nations Development Programme, October, available at http://hdr.undp.org/sites/default/files/hdrp_2010_26.pdf.

Talib, A. (2014) 'Huna al-Khahirah: Messages from Cairo', in Ford Lumban Gaol, Seifedine Kadry, Marie Taylor and Pak Shen Li (eds), *Recent Trends in Social and Behaviour Sciences: Proceedings of the 2nd International Congress on Interdisciplinary Behaviour and Social Sciences 2013* (London: Taylor and Francis/Balkema).

Ulrichsen, Kristian (2014) *Qatar and the Arab Spring* (Oxford: Oxford University Press).

UNESCO (2017) *Reading the Past, Writing the Future: Fifty Years of Promoting Literacy*, available at http://unesdoc.unesco.org/images/0024/002475/247563e.pdf.

UNHCR Intelligence Analysis Unit (2016) 'Average Daily Arrivals and Trends Greece', 30 March, available at https://reliefweb.int/sites/reliefweb.int/files/resources/20160330OperationsCellDailyReport.pdf.

United Nations Data (2017) 'Country Profile: Egypt', available at http://data.un.org/CountryProfile.aspx?crName=egypt.

United Nations Security Council (2011) 'UN Resolution 1973', 17 March, available at www.nato.int/nato_static_fl2014/assets/pdf/pdf_2011_03/20110927_110311-UNSCR-1973.pdf.

World Bank (2016) 'GDP (Annual %)', available at http://data.worldbank.org/indicator/NY.GDP.MKTP.KD.ZG?end=2008&locations=EG&start=1966.

10 The Syrian War and the rise of the Islamic State

Introduction

The uncertainty sparked by the protest movements of 2011–2012 impacted the whole Arab world. Individual states experienced differing levels of challenge and change in their governance structures throughout this period. In terms of loss of human life, damage to a state structure and regional implications, the Syrian conflict has been the most devastating outcome of the uprising period.

The protest movement's demands for democratic reform in Syria were complicated by an influx of foreign powers attempting to utilize the domestic unrest to advance their own agendas. As such, the demonstrations quickly descended into a brutal civil war in which Bashar al-Assad's regime, supported by Russia and Iran, faced a determined, yet divided, opposition. Some factions of the Syrian opposition were backed by the United States and its allies while other (often more Islamist-minded) groups attracted the support of Arab regimes in the Gulf. In addition to the high death toll and staggering displacement of Syrian civilians, this conflict provided the context for the rise of the Islamic State militia, an organization which emerged from the twin incubators of the Syrian War and the anarchy of post-2003 Iraq.

This chapter will contextualize the uprising in Syria and explore the international reactions to that conflict. It will also track the progression of al-Qaeda in Iraq through the Syrian conflict and into its most recent incarnation as the Islamic State. Finally, it will explore the Syrian refugee crisis, which has emerged as a lasting consequence of both this conflict and the Arab uprisings period as a whole.

Historical context

Different states responded in different ways to the Arab uprisings that spread through the region in 2011–2012. These reactions were largely influenced by the regime type and the historical context of the state. Nowhere was this local history and context more important than in Syria. The modern Syrian state was an outcome of the colonial period, with the Mandate for the Greater Syrian region falling to the French in the 1920s (Neep 2012). The colonial power quickly allowed the separation of Lebanon, with its bare Christian majority, and by 1945 the Syrian state had gained its independence, too. The religious composition of the state was mixed, with around 70 per cent of the population Sunni Muslims, around 16 per cent other Muslims (including Shia and Alawi) and a small Christian community of around 14 per cent (Khoury 2014: 14). Syria was created as a parliamentary republic, but a significant degree of instability marked its early years, with a rolling series of coups and counter-coups.

The Ba'ath Party was central to this process and it provides an important link between the histories of Iraq and Syria in the twentieth century. It was formed in 1947 as a secular nationalist movement which focused on the shared Arab attributes of language, history and culture. In keeping with its socialist orientation, the movement limited the role of religion in its worldview. Founded by a Sunni Muslim, a leftist and a Christian, the Ba'athist worldview represented a secular alternative to movements such as Muslim Brotherhood and Hizb-ut-Tahrir, which were sweeping the region at this time. Ba'athism played an important role in the political development of Syria and Iraq and proved most powerful when utilized by state leaders from minority communities (the Sunni Saddam Hussein in Shia-majority Iraq and the Alawi regime of the Assad family in Sunni-majority Syria). In 1966, the party split into Syrian and Iraqi

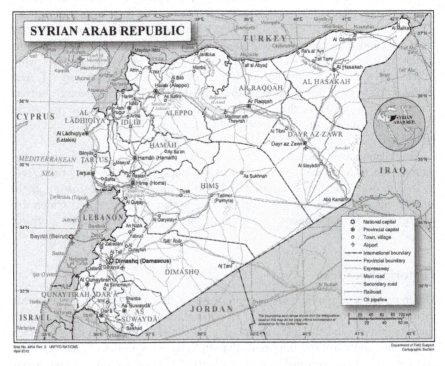

Map 10 Syria
Source: www.un.org/Depts/Cartographic/map/profile/syria.pdf

factions, and these two Ba'athist states opposed each other for the remainder of the century.

In the Syrian context, the Alawi were closely linked to the rise of the Ba'ath Party. This small community was understood as 'a people apart' in the colonial era and was incorporated into the nationalist fold during the state-building years of the 1930s (Qaddour 2013: 68). The distinct religious and cultural practices of this minority are important to understanding the dynamics of the modern Syrian state. The Alawi community is usually seen (and positions itself) as part of the Shia Muslim tradition. However, it maintains a secretive approach to its religious practice, in which Ali Ibn al-Talib, the Prophet Mohammed's son-in-law and Fourth Caliph, is venerated. The innovations in Alawi doctrine – such as the elevation of Ali and the absence of the mosque as a site for worship – have led to depictions of the community as non-Muslim by some sections of the Sunni Muslim community. In the 1970s, the secular Ba'athist ideology and the Alawi community merged due to the activities of the Assad family.

This family assumed a leadership position in the Alawi community as early as the 1920s. By the 1960s, Hafez al-Assad was the figurehead of this community and had also risen to prominence in the Ba'ath Party, of which he had been a member since the 1940s. Ba'athism was attractive to the Alawi minority as it facilitated political engagement in a secular context where their religious practices were not scrutinized by the Sunni majority. In 1970, the Assad family took control of both the party and the Syrian state with a 'corrective coup' (Roberts 2013: 102). The suppression of dissent became a hallmark of the ensuing Assad regime, with the infamous massacres of the Muslim Brotherhood's Sunni supporters in Hama in 1982 setting the tone for future atrocities. In the Cold War era, Syria aligned with the Soviet Union, and it maintained close links with Russia after 1991. It also maintained an uncompromising position in relation to Israel and continues to contest the Israeli occupation of the Golan Heights, captured in the Six-Day War in 1967. Syria's attitude towards Israel proved critical in allowing the state to forge close relations with Iran following the 1979 Islamic Revolution. By the 2000s, Iran viewed Syria as part of the 'Axis of Resistance' due to their shared position on Israel and support for Lebanon's Hezbollah. In 2000, Bashir al-Assad succeeded his father.

Despite the regime's appalling human rights record and a total lack of political freedom in the Syrian state, the young Assad was seen by many in the Arab world and beyond as a reformer. This was linked to the secular orientation of his government and his promises of liberalization and political openness. However, the promise of political reform did not materialize. Bashir al-Assad, supported by many long-serving members of his father's inner circle, continued to stifle any opposition to Alawi rule. The brutal repression of dissidents affected religious groups, most of which were affiliated with Sunni Islam. The ruling regime's intolerance of dissent was seen by many in the Sunni majority in terms of a sectarian agenda to protect the privileges of the Alawi minority. This sectarian interpretation of the political divide would prove devastating once the Arab uprisings reached Syria.

The Arab uprising in Syria

By March 2011, protesters in Syria were calling upon the Assad regime to fulfil its long-standing promises of political reform. For most observers, the Syrian state's history of violent interaction with opposition voices suggested the likely trajectory of the state's response to the protest movement (Lefèvre 2013). Hama and Homs, major population centres and Sunni-majority regions, were the epicentres of the popular protest. The regime initially fluctuated between repression and attempts at dialogue with the opposition, but within weeks the situation had slid inexorably towards open conflict. As the protests escalated across the country, Assad adopted a policy of violent repression to maintain his grip on power. Within three months, over 1,400 civilians had been killed by the state's security forces and tens of thousands arrested, detained and tortured. Furthermore, Assad displayed no reservations about using his army to crush the demonstrations. For example, on 31 July 2011, after a month of laying siege to Hama, Syrian tanks were ordered into the city to quell large-scale anti-government protests. By the end of the day, over a hundred protesters were dead and hundreds injured (Abouzeid 2011). The army attacked other restive areas across too, including towns near Damascus and Dera'a, where the protests had first ignited in March. In response to Assad's unabated use of force, the United Nations Security Council proposed its first draft resolution aimed at resolving the Syrian conflict. It 'demanded that Syrian authorities immediately stop using force against civilians and allow the exercise of freedom of expression, peaceful assembly and other fundamental rights' and called for the 'release of all political prisoners and peaceful demonstrators' (United Nations 2011). However, for reasons discussed below, Russia and China vetoed the resolution. In terms of resolving the Syrian conflict, this set a damaging precedent within the Security Council for years to come.

In response to the continued onslaught, thousands of military officers defected from the Syrian Army in protest against Assad's use of the military against civilians. On 29 July 2011, a group of these ex-soldiers declared the formation of the Free Syrian Army (FSA) with the aim of removing Assad from power and protecting Syrian civilians from his brutal crackdown. This marked a decisive moment in the Syrian uprising. In addition to ongoing, widespread, peaceful anti-government demonstrations, Assad now faced armed resistance. The FSA's command centre and headquarters were established in Turkey. By the close of 2011, it was active in several key areas across Syria, including Damascus, Homs, Hama, Dera'a and Aleppo (Syria's second-largest city). By this stage, an estimated 10,000 to 15,000 officers had defected from the army, with many then enlisting in the FSA (Burch 2011). However, despite its increasingly large presence inside Syria, the FSA lacked unity. It is best understood as a highly decentralized umbrella organization comprising hundreds of armed groups fighting against Assad under the shared FSA banner. In early 2012, regional players such as Turkey, Saudi Arabia and Qatar formed ties with different rebel groups (Lister 2016a). But this diversity of external links proved detrimental for the FSA and a unified vision for a post-Assad future as it further undermined the FSA's unity. By mid-2012, it had been pushed to the periphery of the Syrian opposition. As a result of the external funding patterns, emergent Islamist organizations soon outweighed the military capabilities of the FSA.

As the violence escalated across the country, Syrian civilians were subjected to an intolerable amount of pain and suffering. In July 2012, the United Nations estimated over ten thousand people, mostly civilians, had already been killed and tens of thousands displaced (United Nations 2012). Furthermore, human rights agencies from across the globe highlighted widespread attacks, many of which amounted to crimes against humanity, committed by the Syrian Army against civilian populations (Amnesty International 2012). In June 2012, senior UN officials declared for the first time that the Syrian conflict had descended into a full-scale civil war (Charbonneau and Evans 2012). It has raged ever since, with a staggering loss of human life: most international estimates placed the toll at around 400,000 people by 2016 (Hudson 2016). Moreover, millions of Syrians have become refugees or are internally displaced within the country.

The international reaction

United States

For Washington, the Syrian War constituted a major foreign policy challenge. The conflict erupted in the context of President Obama's failure to make any progress in addressing key challenges in the Middle East. The Israeli–Palestinian deadlock remained intractable, and the political legitimacy deficit of many US-friendly Arab ruling regimes meant that the United States was sponsoring a number of unpopular administrations. This went against the proclamations of Washington in support of democracy. This context had a bearing on how Washington responded to the Syrian crisis. While, ideologically, Obama supported the protesters' calls for democratic reform and for Assad to step down, he was reluctant to be drawn into another conflict. Several factors informed this position. First, the region was still dealing with the dire ramifications of NATO's intervention in Libya. The US-backed intervention, which resulted in the ousting and eventual murder of President Gaddafi, was a poorly thought-out military operation that threw Libya into years of armed conflict (Kuperman 2015: 67–68). In 2012, Obama declared that the United States would not intervene militarily in Syria, but 'a red line for us is … chemical weapons moving around or being utilized. That would change my calculus' (Obama 2012). Second, the historical legacy of the Afghan–Soviet War during the 1980s played a significant role in informing Washington's Syria policy. American funding of the Islamic mujahedeen fighters in their battle against the Soviets facilitated their re-emergence as a powerful regional actor in the aftermath of the conflict. This was devastating for Washington, given the mujahedeen's radical, anti-American agenda. In light of this, Obama was hesitant not only to intervene directly in the Syrian conflict but also to supply the opposition with US arms.

By 2014, Washington had played an active diplomatic role in drafting a number of broadly supported United Nations Security Council (UNSC) resolutions aimed at resolving the conflict. These tended to condemn the Assad regime and advocated a political solution, but Russia and China repeatedly blocked their passage through the Security Council as they perceived them as precursors to military action, as had happened in Libya.

Washington's position on the conflict was further challenged by the 2013 'red-line' crisis, when Assad was accused of using chemical weapons to kill 1,400 civilians in the Damascus suburb of Ghouta. Despite international pressure to launch an offensive, the increasingly complex nature of the conflict hampered Washington's ability to foresee the possible outcomes if it were to intervene. Obama was unwilling to run the risk of exacerbating the fighting and drawing the United States into conflict with other regional powers, such as Iran and Russia. In the end, he refrained from ordering military intervention, even though the use of chemical weapons against civilians was a clear breach of the 'red line' that he himself had established the previous year. Instead, the United States endorsed a Russian-brokered deal in which Assad agreed to hand over Syria's reserves of chemical weapons (Averre and Davies, 2015: 821).

However, the sheer scale of the Syrian War, along with its capacity to draw in neighbouring states, made the conflict too significant to ignore. The Obama administration was increasingly pressured by domestic voices, the Syrian opposition and Saudi Arabia to assume a more direct role. This manifested in the question of whether Washington should arm the rebels in their fight against the Syrian Army. Assad and his backers repeatedly positioned the war as a conflict between the state and Islamist terrorist organizations, some of which were formally affiliated with al-Qaeda (Merz 2014: 30). This greatly complicated Obama's options, as extending patronage to rebel forces carried the very real possibility that such support would be funnelled either deliberately or via the fluid dynamics of conflict to al-Qaeda offshoots. Nevertheless, in June 2014, Washington announced a US$500-million 'train-and-equip' programme to support 'moderate' Syrian rebels against extremist groups inside the country. The training courses were then launched in Jordan and Turkey. A year later, however, the United States deemed the programme a failure and quietly shut it down. US funds were subsequently directed to Syrian rebel groups that were already engaged in the war (Stewart and Holten 2015).

Turkey

Turkey has played a major role in the Syrian conflict. When the protests erupted, the Turkish government's early calls for reconciliation quickly gave way to condemnation of Assad's repressive regime. This anti-Assad position solidified as Turkey sheltered, trained and assisted the rebel militias in the formation of the FSA in July 2011 (Gunter 2015: 107). Turkey, supported by Saudi Arabia, Qatar and the United States, also became a major conduit for arms and financial assistance to the Syrian opposition. Its position came under intense international scrutiny as the war in Syria turned into a sectarian conflict that some parties presented as a jihad against the Assad regime. The cry of 'jihad' turned Syria into a magnet for Islamist volunteers from neighbouring states and further afield who passed through Turkey to reach the battlefields. This situation became more fraught with the emergence of the Islamic State of Iraq and Syria (later renamed simply the Islamic State) and increasing international concern that many of the foreign jihadists were being recruited by that group. Initially, Turkey ignored the Islamic State (IS) and continued to focus on Assad, but a series of terrorist attacks in Turkish cities forced a reassessment of its strategy. Thereafter, Turkey attempted to implement a seemingly contradictory policy against Assad and the Kurds.

The situation was extremely complicated for Ankara as it had long-standing security concerns in relation to its own Kurdish population. The government was very sensitive to the prospect of renewed calls for autonomy from this community, which seemed sure to gain inspiration from the Syrian Kurds' fight against the dual threats of the Assad regime and IS. Turkey also feared that Kurdish-controlled territory in Syria would serve as a safe haven for its own Kurdish militants. These concerns led to some highly inconsistent behaviour. For example, in September 2014, Turkish tanks stationed on the border with Syria gave IS forces free rein to continue their bombardment of the besieged Kurdish town of Kobane.

The other aspect of this conflict which has been central to Turkish politics is the refugee crisis, with 2.7 million refugees crossing into Turkish territory by mid-2016 (Baban *et al.* 2017: 41). Finally, in July 2016, Turkey began a formal intervention in the Syrian War. However, its targeting of IS, Kurdish *and* regime strongholds (Larrabee 2016: 70) merely served to illustrate the inherent contradictions of the Turkish position.

Saudi Arabia

Saudi Arabia viewed the Syrian War through a geostrategic lens. However, the Saudi position on the Arab uprisings was inconsistent. Riyadh condemned the popular unrest in Egypt and Bahrain, citing the need for political stability. This was underscored by a religious imperative, the rejection of *fitna* (literally, 'chaos' or 'division') amid Muslim communities (al-Rasheed 2016: 79–80). This public opposition to the uprisings sent a clear message that Riyadh would not tolerate challenges to its own authority within the kingdom. This was important as the issues of nepotism, lack of political representation and reform which had triggered unrest throughout the region were endemic in Saudi Arabia. In line with this approach, Riyadh supported the secular Egyptian military and the Bahraini royal family as they faced increasing levels of domestic unrest. However, this policy was not applied universally as Riyadh was more than happy to support the revolt against Assad. This had much to do with Saudi Arabia's ongoing rivalry with Iran. From a Saudi perspective, the fall of Assad would deal a massive blow to Iran's regional standing because Syria had been central to facilitating Iran's entry into the Levant. Destroying the Syrian–Iranian alliance would therefore be a very effective means of limiting Iran's capacity to project its influence.

The Saudi government was quick to champion the protest movement in Syria and, once armed conflict broke out, it funded many of the militia movements that were leading the fight against the Assad regime (Phillips 2016: 139–140). This policy was mirrored by many other Arab sheikhdoms, with states such as Kuwait and Qatar also becoming deeply embroiled in the Syrian War. As mentioned earlier, the radicalizing impact of Saudi and US support for the mujahedeen in Afghanistan in the 1980s should have served as a potent warning against Saudi funding for the Syrian rebels. Indeed, while US policy towards the region may be criticized, it could be argued that Washington, unlike Riyadh, absorbed the hard lessons of Afghanistan and consequently pursued a more cautious approach in Syria. By contrast, for Saudi Arabia, the opportunity to exploit the conflict to undermine Iran seemed to trump all other concerns between 2011 and 2014. However, as the war dragged on and al-Qaeda established a firm foothold in Syria, followed by the emergence of IS, the Saudi position became much more complicated. Riyadh did not want to be seen as a sponsor of IS, but it remained determined to remove Assad from power.

Iran

The Syrian state has been central to Iran's foreign policy since the early 1980s. Syria's strong anti-Israeli stance, its willingness to challenge the US-dominated regional status quo and its nominally Shia leadership has placed it firmly within the Iranian sphere of influence. This alone provides an interesting insight into the nature of Middle Eastern politics, as the revolutionary Shia ideology of Iran and the Ba'athist secular nationalism of Syria do not seem likely bedfellows. Yet, their shared antipathy to Israel, and by extension the United States, has proved sufficient to cement the alliance. Their joint determination to confront Israel has meant that Syria has acted as a conduit for Iranian support for Hezbollah, with arms and money flowing through the country en route to Lebanon (DeVore and Stähli 2015: 341). This has attracted the ire of the Israelis on many occasions, with cross-border aerial attacks against weapons transfers common over the last two decades. Yet Assad was never persuaded to abandon the alliance, and the Syrian–Iranian relationship proved vital to his regime as its position weakened in the early stages of the civil war. The Iranians not only sent military support but also encouraged Hezbollah's decisive deployment in Syria from 2013. This tactical assistance reversed the regime's early losses and bolstered the fighting capacity of its armed forces.

The Assad regime's history of repression against the Sunni opposition has meant that its rule has long been depicted in sectarian terms. Hence, the early phase of the uprising, which was characterized by calls for reform and inclusion, was short-lived and quickly turned into a battle for survival between Sunni rebels (both moderate and Islamist) and the Alawi (Shia) regime. Into this volatile mix came the Sunni-led Arab sheikhdoms, most notably Saudi Arabia. This key development changed the dynamics of the Syrian conflict for Iran. Once external Sunni players became active in Syria, Iran was forced to increase its commitment to Assad not just to safeguard its regional interests in relation to Hezbollah and the conflict with Israel but also to counter a perceived wave of Sunni militancy, which Tehran saw as a conduit for increased Saudi influence in the Middle East.

Russia

Despite its late entry into the conflict, Moscow was consistent in its support for the Assad regime in Syria. This support rested on historical and strategic foundations. Historically, Russia and Syria were Cold War partners, united in their rejection of the US–Israeli-enforced status quo. In a more strategic sense, Syria remains important to Russia as it represents Moscow's final foothold in the Middle East. The Russian naval facility at Tartus, built in 1971, is Russia's sole port in the Mediterranean and therefore vital to its ability to project its influence in the region and towards southern Europe. Finally, it is important to note an ideological component in the Russian–Syrian dynamic. For Moscow, the conflict in Syria was not about political reform or enhanced representation. Rather, it saw the civil war as an Islamist challenge to a partner secular state. This interpretation was consistent with Moscow's own experience with Islamic opposition groups. Since the 1990s, the Russian state has been challenged by an Islamist insurgency in its Northern Caucasus region, and some of those Chechen insurgents joined the fight against Assad. There were also reports of volunteer fighters travelling to Syria from former Soviet Central Asian republics. This presented further justification for Moscow to rush to the defence of Assad.

As the Syrian War gathered pace, Russia became a major player and resisted all international attempts to encourage Assad to step aside. Moscow's involvement became more pronounced as it became clear that the Obama administration was unsure of the best course of action. In an echo of their old Cold War rivalry, Russia sought to capitalize on this US indecision. Nowhere was this clearer than in the 'red-line' crisis of 2013. This was viewed as a PR triumph for Moscow at the time, notwithstanding many claims that Syrian forces employed chemical warfare against rebel-held areas (Sorenson 2016: 39–40). The long-standing Russian diplomatic, military and financial assistance to the regime peaked in September 2015, when Moscow launched a formal, direct intervention in the form of an aerial campaign in response to a request from Assad. This was justified on the grounds that the Russian planes were targeting IS militia groups (Kozhanov 2016: 66–67). However, it was not sanctioned by the international community and it has been broadly criticized for focusing on rebel positions rather than IS strongholds (Souleimanov 2016: 109).

Israel

Israel's attitude towards the turbulence associated with the Arab uprisings has been characterized as restrained, cool pragmatism. The wave of uprisings that spread throughout the Arab world served to shift attention away from the protracted Palestinian–Israeli dispute. This rare opportunity meant that Israel could pursue its policy of building Jewish settlements on Palestinian land while the world was focused on what was happening over the border. Its self-imposed restraint in relation to the uprisings paid off. In Egypt, the course of revolution and counter-revolution eventually resulted in the government of Abdel Fattah el-Sisi, who reaffirmed his country's commitment to the peace deal with Israel. He also acted decisively against both HAMAS and the militants in Sinai, which served Israel's security interests.

In relation to Syria, Israel's policy revolved around guarding against any spillover of the conflict into its territory and keeping a close eye on the activities of Hezbollah, which joined Assad's fight against the rebels. Israel had a vested interest in the future of the Assad regime, as Syria had never accepted the Israeli occupation of the Golan Heights and it remained close to Israel's ideological nemesis: Iran. As a result, Israel largely supported the removal of Syria's President, even though the alternative was unknown and potentially even more risky. However, aside from the occasional incursion to bomb military stockpiles and prevent them from falling into the hands of Hezbollah, Israel maintained its distance from the civil war that was raging across the border.

Summary

The range of international reactions to the Syrian conflict highlights several important points. First, the fate of Syria is central to the geostrategic balance in the region. Second, unlike earlier periods, such as the Cold War, many regional states have enhanced capacity and willingness to engage in regional disputes to further their own foreign policy agendas. Finally, the international community has been unable to resolve the conflict or reconcile the competing agendas. At the core of these challenges stand the Syrian people, who have been killed, displaced and impoverished in their millions.

It was within this chaotic, violent environment that the Islamic State was formed. The emergence of this organization may be traced to the mayhem that followed the 2003 invasion of Iraq and, subsequently, the inability of the Syrian regime to contain the anti-Assad rebellion. The following section will contextualize its rise and provide a brief overview of the organization itself before exploring the international community's response.

Al-Qaeda in Iraq, Jabhat al-Nusra and the Islamic State

The back story of the Islamic State begins in US-occupied Iraq in the aftermath of the 2003 conflict. Al-Qaeda, as a Sunni Salafi-jihadist movement, had no presence in Iraq prior to that date. However, following the overthrow of Saddam Hussein and the de-Ba'athification of the state, Iraq's Sunni community found itself politically and physically vulnerable within the new, Shia-led, state. As the new Iraq tilted ever more clearly towards Iran, this sense of vulnerability increased. In response to their social and political marginalization, segments of Iraq's Sunni community launched an insurgency against the US occupation and the Shia-led government. This provided the perfect opportunity for al-Qaeda to engage in Iraq, mobilize support for its cause and subsequently establish an organization named al-Qaeda in Iraq (AQI) in the 2003–2004 period (Byman 2015: 115–117). This group initially focused on resisting the occupation, a stance that was clearly consistent with traditional al-Qaeda perspectives vis-à-vis the United States. However, the specific sectarian dynamics of the Iraq conflict also led AQI to present itself as a protector of Sunni interests in the post-2003 environment. In addition to this pro-Sunni focus, the militia strove to implement Sharia law in the areas it controlled, even though this was resisted by many ex-Ba'athist Sunnis who were not ideologically inclined towards an overtly religious perspective. Moreover, as AQI's methods became more brutal and its anti-Shia focus became more pronounced, it alienated significant Sunni tribal factions within Iraq. Despite this opposition from the community it claimed to represent, in 2006 AQI declared the founding of the Islamic State of Iraq (ISI).

Box 10.1 De-Ba'athification

In 1966, the transnational Ba'ath movement split into Iraqi and Syrian wings. After the Iraqi Ba'ath Party strengthened its control of the state, power was increasingly concentrated in the hands of Saddam Hussein. He assumed leadership of the party in 1979 and then enforced a brutal dictatorship until the United States invaded the country and removed him from power in April 2003. After the US invasion, Washington established the Coalition Provisional Authority (CPA) to serve as the occupation's authority and interim government. An American, Lewis Paul Bremer III, was appointed to lead the CPA. Under Executive Order No. 1, he enacted the CPA's first and central policy – de-Ba'athification – on 16 May 2003. This policy was designed to rid the state of its ties to Saddam via the elimination of Ba'ath Party structures and a purge of its top four ranks of membership. To assist Bremer with its implementation, the Iraqi De-Ba'athification Council (IDC) was established on 25 May under Order No. 5. As a result, thousands of Iraqis lost their jobs, which ultimately fuelled anti-American sentiment in the country. Bremer's de-Ba'athification policy has been widely criticized for making no distinction between Saddam loyalists and those who simply worked under him to survive. Moreover, allegations have been made that it indiscriminately targeted Iraqi Sunnis and consequently exacerbated sectarian tension in the post-Saddam period.

For the United States, the Iraqi government and large sections of Iraq's Sunni community, AQI represented a serious security challenge. In 2006, the al-Maliki administration, with an endorsement from Washington, sought to mobilize Sunni tribes against al-Qaeda. The Anbar Awakening demonstrated the depth of ordinary Sunnis' disdain for the Islamist organization. By late 2007, the Sunni tribesmen, in alliance with the United States, had decimated AQI's ranks and the organization was seen as marginal in the Iraqi context. However, the Syrian slide into civil war along increasingly sectarian lines after 2011 gave the remnants of AQI an opportunity to re-emerge, with far-reaching consequences for the Arab world and the wider international community.

Box 10.2 The Anbar Awakening

The United States' invasion and occupation of Iraq in 2003 was not unanimously welcomed inside Iraq. Al-Qaeda in Iraq (AQI) emerged during this period to expel the US forces and install an Islamic state. The group launched a violent campaign against the coalition forces, the new Shia-led government and Shia communities, and managed to gain control of large swathes of territory. In 2006, Sunni tribes from the province of Anbar formed the Anbar Awakening to fight against AQI. Although the tribes sometimes identified with AQI's anti-US and anti-Shia orientation, they were against the enforcement of strict Islamic law in areas under AQI control. The tribal leaders also rejected AQI's vision of installing an Islamic state in Iraq by violence means. This resulted in an alliance of convenience with the United States to drive out AQI. By 2007, the Anbar Awakening had regained control of a number of Sunni cities, including Ramadi and Fallujah.

AQI and the Syrian War

In 2012, AQI's leadership sent envoys across the border to engage in the Syrian conflict. Drawing on AQI's experience, funds and techniques, a Syrian organization, Jabhat al-Nusra (JN; also known as the al-Nusra Front) was quickly formed with the specific aim of overthrowing Assad and establishing an Islamic state in Syria. JN was declared a terrorist organization by both Assad and the United States. As a consequence of the leadership's experience in combat, recruitment and the dissemination of propaganda, the group rose to prominence quickly and soon became a major player in the Syrian opposition. It attracted some foreign fighters, but its strongly Syrian agenda (the overthrow of Assad) limited its appeal to the young jihadis who were pouring into Syria from the Gulf region, Europe and the rest of the world.

Meanwhile, in Iraq, AQI tracked the fortunes of its new Syrian offshoot with close interest. The Syrian War proved a fertile ground for recruitment as the AQI dogma regarding the protection of Sunni communities found significant support in an environment where the Iranian-backed Assad regime was pounding the largely Sunni rebels. As a result of its long history in Iraq's conflicts, AQI itself had moved on from 'classical' al-Qaeda ideology, particularly in relation to the focus on sectarianism. This serves as a profound reminder of the importance of context in the formulation of ideology, as AQI morphed in response to the violent sectarian conflict in which it was a major player. Of equal importance, a new AQI leader had emerged in 2010. Abu Bakr al-Baghdadi was the *nom de guerre* of a young, formally trained Islamic scholar who claimed titular descent from the tribe of the Prophet Mohammed. As JN continued to make advances in Syria, al-Baghdadi crossed the border and changed the name of his organization to the Islamic State in Iraq (Byman 2015: 167). Subsequently, he claimed that his faction had merged with JN, but the latter group was now well established in Syria with its own leadership, recruits and resources, and it publicly disavowed the merger (Lister 2016b: 115–119).

Box 10.3 Abu Bakr al-Baghdadi

Abu Bakr al-Baghdadi was born in Iraq in 1971 and received his Ph.D. in Islamic Studies from the Islamic University in Baghdad. In 2004, he joined AQI's insurgency against the coalition forces inside Iraq. After the deaths of several AQI leaders in 2010, he assumed control and then played a significant role in reinvigorating the organization, which had been degraded during 2007 and 2008. On 4 October 2011, he was labelled a terrorist by the United Nations Security Council pursuant to Resolutions 1267 (1999) and 1989 (2011) and placed on the United States' 'Specially Designated Nationals List'. The following year, he orchestrated a large-scale AQI campaign known as 'Breaking the Walls'. This targeted Iraqi special forces, Shia groups and the Iraqi government. During the campaign, AQI broke into the Abu Ghraib Prison, which led to the escape of hundreds of AQI members. As a result, al-Baghdadi's reputation rose within the organization. In 2013, he moved to Syria, where he exploited the fragile state of the war-torn country to enlist recruits and expand his organization. In April 2014, he declared the formation of the Islamic State of Iraq and al-Sham (ISIS), which later became known simply as the Islamic State (IS). He also declared himself Caliph (leader) with a view to creating an Islamic state throughout the Arab world via the elimination of the borders that currently divide the region's Muslim countries. Since then, his organization has been responsible for thousands of deaths in the Middle East and across the globe.

The events of early 2014 are central to the modern history of Sunni Salafi-jihadism in the Arab world. Al-Qaeda, as a transitional terrorist organization, was experiencing a profound period of change and adaptation in which local franchises were fast becoming the most powerful expressions of the movement. This served to extend the reach of the organization while also rendering it vulnerable to context-specific alterations. In the Syrian and Iraqi environments, this translated into a form of overt sectarianism that had been largely absent from earlier incarnations of the organization. When al-Baghdadi's attempt to assert his control over JN was rebuffed, the stage was set for a showdown between the two militias. Al-Qaeda's formal leader, Ayman al-Zawahiri, attempted to mediate between the two powerful factions, which were now vying with each other for pre-eminence in the Syrian context. After a brief power struggle in which al-Qaeda attempted to compel al-Baghdadi to move back across the border, his renamed organization, the Islamic State of Iraq and al-Sham (ISIS), broke with al-Qaeda and JN and established itself as an independent actor in the region. In response, al-Qaeda recognized JN as its sole formal affiliate in Syria. Despite this endorsement, JN and other rebel militias lost ground, supporters and prestige to al-Baghdadi's ISIS militia as it launched a dramatic and violent sweep through Syria.

Box 10.4 Ayman al-Zawahiri

Ayman al-Zawahiri succeeded Osama bin Laden as the leader of al-Qaeda in 2010. Born in Cairo on 19 June 1951, from an early age al-Zawahiri dedicated his life to Islamic activism in opposition to Egypt's secular government, which he viewed as immoral, heretical and subservient to Israel, the United States and the West. In the late 1970s, he founded the Egyptian Islamic Jihad (EIJ) movement, which was responsible for several attacks against Egyptian citizens and Western tourists as well as several assassination attempts against leading Egyptian political figures in the 1980s and 1990s. In 1979, he moved to Afghanistan to join the mujahedeen, although he continued to orchestrate attacks on Egyptian soil. After the mujahedeen's victory in 1989, he played a central role, alongside bin Laden, in establishing and then expanding the al-Qaeda organization and planning its activities throughout the region.

ISIS distinguished itself from other Islamist groups by virtue of its virulent anti-Shia stance, its lack of interest in overthrowing Assad and its determination to establish Sharia governance structures in areas under its influence. A constant flow of foreign volunteers empowered the organization, which, for a revivalist group bent on restoring seventh-century norms, displayed remarkable facility with modern technology, such as social media. As ISIS continued to grow, it became evident that al-Baghdadi had no intention of remaining confined to the Syrian context as his militia swept back across the border to claim territory and recruits in Iraq. The potent mix of Sunni empowerment, sectarian outrage and military success gained considerable traction in Iraq, where some ex-Ba'athists chose to privilege sectarian affiliation over ideological differences. This enhanced ISIS's tactical capacity and led to ever more significant victories on the battlefield. The US-funded and trained Iraqi military, whose rank and file were disenfranchised Sunnis with little motivation to fight and die for a state that had alienated them, melted away in several key battles, which served to enhance the militia's prestige (Cronin 2015: 89).

A year after its formation, in April 2014, the ISIS pronounced al-Baghdadi as the global Caliph of all Muslims (Isakhan 2015: 223). This constituted a significant turning point in modern Sunni Islamism. The declaration of a new Caliph and the linked call for Muslims to migrate to the newly declared state met with a range of responses. The overwhelming majority of the world's Muslims rejected IS and its ideology as completely incompatible with Islamic norms and history (Byman 2015: 165). For Assad, the declaration fitted neatly into his narrative that the Syrian Civil War was a battle between a secular state and powerful terrorist organizations. For regional Sunni supporters of the Syrian opposition, the rapid emergence of IS, which was already extending its rhetoric and operations to other locations, demanded a swift reconsideration of policy (Lister 2016b: 221–222). For international Islamists, the universalist pretensions of the organization proved highly attractive and its ranks swelled in consequence (Baxter and Davidson 2016: 1302).

The influence of Ba'athist military planners was immediately evident in IS's adept use of captured territory. Supply routes and roads were quickly taken and the militia's version of Sharia law was uncompromisingly applied within areas under its jurisdiction. The newly acquired territory provided a basis upon which the new 'state' could be declared as well as access to natural resources and dominion over populations. IS enriched itself through a mixture of extortion, kidnapping for ransom and black-market sales of natural resources (Rajan 2015: 127). As mentioned, the organization's mastery of the internet was significant as the IS message was propagated online, leading to IS-directed or -inspired terror attacks in France, Turkey, Iraq, Kuwait and elsewhere. Moreover, Islamist militias around the world heeded the call and pledged their allegiance to al-Baghdadi, most damagingly in Libya (Chivvis 2016: 115). In this sense, IS emerged as a major competitor to its parent organization, al-Qaeda. The latter, while retaining its strongholds in Pakistan and on the Arabian Peninsula, certainly lost the PR battle with this new expression of Sunni jihadism.

Back in Iraq, as IS forces pushed towards the Kurdish areas and threatened genocide against the Yazidi minority, Washington was forced into military action. In September 2014, in a limited reversal of the 2011 withdrawal and in response to an invitation from the Iraqi government, the United States commenced air strikes against IS positions in Iraq. In time, it was backed by an international coalition, including many Arab states. This provided a convenient pretext for international players such as Turkey and Russia to intervene more directly in the Syrian War.

There is no simple explanation for the Islamic State's rise to prominence, but it is vital to identify the influence of Salafism, given the organization's determination to rule in accordance with Prophetic norms and its wanton destruction of tombs and holy sites. Such actions can be justified by the Salafi notion (militant or not) of 'purification of the faith'. In this sense, the Islamic State is clearly part of the Sunni tradition of Salafism – and more profoundly Salafi-*jihadism* – and thus the broader patterns of the faith. However, IS's overt sectarianism, complete disregard for human rights (particularly of minorities), explicit use of violence and deep misogyny also speak to the power of historical and political context. The anarchy that has engulfed Iraq since 2003 and the brutal and protracted nature of the Syrian Civil War provided the context for the emergence of this organization at this time. Put another way, the emergence of an overtly violent, misogynistic, intolerant and nihilistic organization was facilitated by the particular set of political circumstances that prevailed in the Middle East in the early twenty-first century.

In Syria, the establishment of the Islamic State provided the international community with a powerful distraction from Assad and his future. The conflict continued with various shifts within the opposition, including JN's decision to break away from al-Qaeda in mid-2016 and rename itself Jabhat Fateh al-Sham. Most Western observers saw this rebranding as an attempt to send the continuing Western-led air strikes towards other targets rather than a meaningful reorientation (*Guardian* 2016). Russian and US efforts finally secured a cease-fire in September 2016, albeit without any concrete decision on Assad's future, which remains a key grievance of the opposition. By this point, some 400,000 Syrians had been killed and many more left as refugees either within Syria or elsewhere.

Refugees: the consequences of war

As the Syrian conflict erupted, a small group of civilians sought refuge outside the state. By 2012, their numbers had started to increase, and by 2016 several million had fled their homes. This mass exodus triggered a much broader migration crisis with global impacts as people sought shelter from conflicts in places as far afield as Afghanistan and Sudan. In the specific context of the Syrian crisis, over 4.8 million Syrian refugees have registered as such in the Middle East and Europe, while an estimated 6.5 million have been internally displaced (UNHCR 2017). However, according to the UNHCR (2017), these startling statistics tell only half the story, because the war has exacted a terrible price on Syria: 'a quarter of schools have been damaged or shut down, and more than two thirds of all hospitals have been destroyed. Life expectancy has dropped by 20 years.' The cumulative damage of the war is almost impossible to assess at this stage.

The flow of Syrian refugees sparked media and political interest, especially as arrivals in Europe peaked. This new – international – consequence of the conflict triggered a range of political responses, from Germany's short-lived open-door policy to the increasingly assertive rejection of all refugees by far- and even centre-right political parties across Europe (Heisbourgm 2015: 9–12). However, Europe's complex responses to the arrival of the refugees pales into insignificance in comparison to the massive population flows in the Middle East itself. Lebanon has received over 1.5 million Syrian refugees (UNHCR 2016a). For a country with a population of just 7 million, beset with its own challenges, this has proved a major political and infrastructural challenge. Meanwhile, Turkey, with the support of international aid agencies, has faced the prospect of housing 2.5 million refugees in camps (UNHCR 2016b). Other regional states, such as Iraq and Jordan, have also seen huge influxes from Syria. While much of the media focus has been on Europe's response to the refugees, the impact of these mass movements will have profound and lasting economic, political and social ramifications throughout the Arab world, especially if meaningful resolution and reconciliation in Syria remains elusive.

Conclusion

The Syrian Civil War has seriously tested a generation of global leaders, politicians, policy-makers and humanitarians. At the time of writing, the report card was damning. In addition to the devastation inflicted on the Syrian state itself, the failure of national players and the international community to contain and resolve the crisis has resulted in two key outcomes: the rise of the Islamic State and the triggering of an unprecedented refugee crisis. After five years of war, 400,000 Syrians had lost their lives and millions more were refugees. The prospects of the Syrian state remaining intact, or recovering in an economic, social or political sense, seemed extremely slim.

The international interest in the Syrian War was multifaceted, with some states jumping into the conflict to further their own geostrategic agendas while others were dragged into it by the dynamics of the war itself. This served to perpetuate an increasingly violent conflict which the international community seemed unable to curtail. In the process, emergent global norms, such as R2P, have proven weak against the vested interests of individual players operating within a traditional pragmatic political framework.

The rise of Islamic State drew on a century of modern Salafi-jihadism, then sharpened and brutalized it in the crucible of two civil conflicts: the Iraq War, triggered by the US-led invasion; and the Syrian conflict, which was largely a result of the internal dynamics of the state itself, inflamed by regional interests. This led to the emergence of a new, overtly sectarian interpretation of militant Islamism with which the international community now has to grapple.

Finally, the carnage across Syria, and the sense of disillusionment across the whole region, prompted a tide of people to seek safety, security and opportunity in foreign lands. In this sense, the Syrian War, alongside the Libyan conflict, represents one of the darkest outcomes of the Arab Spring – a moment when calls for change, inclusion and progressive reform gave way to violence, repression, reassertion of the authoritarian state and rampant sectarian tension. The reasons for this are complex and entwined with national context and history. The long-term social, political, economic and security consequences are not yet apparent.

References

Abouzeid, Rania (2011) 'Syrian Military Attacks Protesters in Hama', *Time*, 1 August, available at http://content.time.com/time/world/article/0,8599,2086062,00.html.

Al-Rasheed, Madawi (2016) *Muted Modernists: The Struggle over Divine Politics in Saudi Arabia* (New York: Oxford University Press).

Amnesty International (2012) 'Deadly Reprisals: Deliberate Killings and Other Abuses by Syria's Armed Forces', available at www.amnesty.org.uk/files/deadly_reprials.pdf.

Averre, Derek and Davies, Lance (2015) 'Russia, Humanitarian Intervention and the Responsibility to Protect: The Case of Syria', *International Affairs*, Vol. 91, No. 4, pp. 813–834.

Baban, Feyzi, Ilcan, Suzan and Rygiel, Kim (2017) 'Syrian Refugees in Turkey: Pathways to Precarity, Differential Inclusion, and Negotiated Citizenship Rights', *Journal of Ethnic and Migration Studies*, Vol. 43, No. 1, pp. 41–57.

Baxter, Kylie and Davidson, Renee (2016) 'Foreign Terrorist Fighters: A 21st Century Threat?', *Third World Quarterly*, Vol. 37, No. 8, pp. 1299–1313.

Burch, Jonathon (2011) 'Exclusive: War Is Only Option to Topple Syrian Leader: Colonel', Reuters, 7 October, available at www.reuters.com/article/us-turkey-syria-colonel-idUSTRE79640Q20111007.

Byman, Daniel (2015) *Al Qaeda, the Islamic State, and the Global Jihadist Movement* (Oxford: Oxford University Press).

Charap, Samuel (2013) 'Russia, Syria and the Doctrine of Intervention', *Survival*, Vol. 55, No. 1, pp. 35–41.

Charbonneau, Louis and Evans, Dominic (2012) 'Syria in Civil War, UN Official Says', *Reuters*, 12 June, available at www.reuters.com/article/us-syria-idUSBRE85B0D Z20120612.

Chivvis, Christopher S. (2016) 'Countering the Islamic State in Libya', *Survival*, Vol. 58, No. 4, pp. 113–130.

Cronin, Audrey Kurth (2015) 'ISIS Is Not a Terrorist Group: Why Counterterrorism Won't Stop the Latest Jihadist Threat', *Foreign Affairs*, Vol. 87, No. 2, pp. 87–98.

DeVore, Marc R. and Stähli, Armin B. (2015) 'Explaining Hezbollah's Effectiveness: Internal and External Determinants of the Rise of Violent Non-state Actors', *Terrorism and Political Violence*, Vol. 27, No. 2, pp. 331–357.

Guardian (2016) 'Al-Nusra Front Cuts Ties with al-Qaida and Renames Itself', 29 July, available at www.theguardian.com/world/2016/jul/28/al-qaida-syria-nusra-split-terror-network.

Gunter, Michael M. (2015) 'Iraq, Syria, ISIS and the Kurds: Geostrategic Concerns for the US and Turkey', *Middle East Policy*, Vol. 22, No. 1, pp. 102–111.

Heisbourgm, François (2015) 'The Strategic Implications of the Syrian Refugee Crisis', *Survival*, Vol. 57, No. 6, pp. 7–20.

Hudson, John (2016) 'UN Envoy Revises Syria Death Toll to 400,000', *Foreign Policy*, 22 April, http://foreignpolicy.com/2016/04/22/u-n-envoy-revises-syria-death-toll-to-400000/.

Isakhan, Benjamin (2015) *The Legacy of Iraq: From the 2003 War to the 'Islamic State'* (Edinburgh: Edinburgh University Press).

Khoury, Philip Shukry (2014) *Syria and the French Mandate: The Politics of Arab Nationalism, 1920–1945* (Princeton, NJ: Princeton University Press).

Kozhanov, Nikolay (2016) *Russia and the Syrian Conflict: Moscow's Domestic, Regional and Strategic Interests* (Berlin: Gerlach Press).

Kuperman, Alan J. (2015) 'Obama's Libya Debacle: How a Well-meaning Intervention Ended in Failure', *Foreign Affairs*, Vol. 94, No. 2, pp. 66–77.

Larrabee, F.Stephen (2016) 'Turkey and the Changing Dynamics of the Kurdish Issue', *Survival*, Vol. 58, No. 2, pp. 67–73.

Lefèvre, Raphaël (2013) *Ashes of Hama: The Muslim Brotherhood in Syria* (New York: Oxford University Press).

Lister, Charles (2016a) 'The Free Syrian Army: A Decentralized Insurgent Brand', Brookings Institute, November, available at www.brookings.edu/wp-content/uploads/2016/11/iwr_20161123_free_syrian_army.pdf.

Lister, Charles R. (2016b) *The Syrian Jihad: Al-Qaeda, the Islamic State and the Evolution of an Insurgency* (Oxford: Oxford University Press).

Merz, Fabien (2014) 'Adversarial Framing: President Bashar al-Assad's Depiction of the Armed Syrian Opposition', *Journal of Terrorism Research*, Vol. 5, No. 2, pp. 30–44.

Neep, Daniel (2012) *Occupying Syria under the French Mandate: Insurgency, Space and State Formation* (New York: Cambridge University Press).

Obama, Barack (2012) 'Remarks by the President to the White House Press Corps', 20 August, available at https://obamawhitehouse.archives.gov/the-press-office/2012/08/20/remarks-president-white-house-press-corps.

Phillips, Christopher (2016) *The Battle for Syria: International Rivalry in the New Middle East* (New Haven, CT: Yale University Press).

Qaddour, Jomana (2013) 'Unlocking the Alawite Conundrum in Syria', *Washington Quarterly*, Vol. 36, No. 4, pp. 67–78.

Rajan, G.V. Julie (2015) *Al Qaeda's Global Crisis* (New York: Taylor and Francis).

Roberts, David (2013) *The Ba'th and the Creation of Modern Syria* (New York: Taylor and Francis).

Sorenson, David S. (2016) *Syria in Ruins: The Dynamics of the Syrian Civil War* (California: Praeger).

Souleimanov, Emil Aslan (2016) 'Mission Accomplished? Russia's Withdrawal from Syria', *Middle East Policy*, Vol. 23, No. 2, pp. 108–118.

Stewart, Phil and Holten, Kate (2015) 'US Pulls Plug on Syria Rebel Training Effort: Will Focus on Weapons Supply', Reuters, 9 October, available at www.reuters.com/article/us-mideast-crisis-syria-usa-idUSKCN0S31BR20151009.

Tarock, Adam (2016) 'The Iran Nuclear Deal: Winning a Little, Losing a Lot', *Third World Quarterly*, Vol. 37, No. 8, pp. 1408–1424.

UNHCR (2016a) 'Vulnerability Assessment of Syrian Refugees in Lebanon 2016', September, available at https://data.unhcr.org/syrianrefugees/country.php?id=122.

UNHCR (2016b) 'Turkey Winter Assistance External Update', November, available at https://data.unhcr.org/syrianrefugees/country.php?id=224.

UNHCR (2017) 'Syrian Crisis Appeal', available at www.unrefugees.org.au/emergencies/current-emergencies/syria-crisis-urgent-appeal.

United Nations (2011) 'Security Council Fails to Adopt Draft Resolution Condemning Syria's Crackdown on Anti-government Protestors, Owing to Veto by Russian Federation, China', 4 October, available at www.un.org/press/en/2011/sc10403.doc.htm.

United Nations (2012) 'UN Human Rights Council Condemns Violence in Syria', 6 July, available at www.un.org/apps/news/story.asp?NewsID=42409#.WTS-HPmGOUk.

United Nations (2017) 'Security Council Veto List', available at http://research.un.org/en/docs/sc/quick.

United States Department of State (2016) 'Foreign Terrorist Organizations', available at www.state.gov/j/ct/rls/other/des/123085.htm.

11 Iran emerging from isolation

Introduction

The US invasion and subsequent occupation of Iraq in 2003 had a tremendous and ongoing effect on Iran. From a geopolitical standpoint, after the fall of Saddam Hussein, Iran was wedged between two countries occupied by the United States: Afghanistan on its eastern border and Iraq on its western border. This was perceived by the Iranian leadership as confirmation that Washington was trying to undermine and ultimately destroy the Islamic Republic. This assumption was reinforced by the public declarations of US President George W. Bush, who threatened Iran with regime change. This was based on fears that Iran was developing nuclear weapons in a clandestine programme. Over the subsequent decade, US–Iranian relations were marked by antagonistic rhetoric and an inability to find common ground. Throughout the presidencies of Bush and Barack Obama, Washington tried different methods of dealing with Iran – from isolation and containment to engagement. After the election of Iranian President Hassan Rouhani in 2013, the world witnessed a major shift in US–Iranian relations which culminated in the signing of the 'Joint Comprehensive Plan of Action' (JCPOA) nuclear deal in July 2015.

This chapter will contextualize the JCPOA deal and explore the policies of Iranian Presidents Mahmoud Ahmadinejad and Hassan Rouhani, noting how the former isolated Iran and the latter brought the country out of isolation. It will also examine the regional responses to the nuclear deal, with a particular focus on the reaction in Saudi Arabia, as this reflected ongoing concerns in Riyadh and many other Arab capitals about Iran as a source of instability at a time when the Arab world was undergoing major political upheavals. We shall see that the acrimonious Iran–Saudi relationship has exacerbated sectarian tensions in the region and pushed the Middle East down a dangerous path.

The nuclear deal

Iran commenced its nuclear programme during the 1960s and ratified the international Non-Proliferation Treaty (NPT) in 1970. This treaty granted Iran the right to develop a civilian nuclear programme with International Atomic

Energy Association (IAEA) verification (UNODA n.d.). The IAEA is an international body mandated to administer safeguards that are designed to detect and deter the use of nuclear material for non-peaceful purposes and increase the transparency of a state's nuclear programme (Berman 2016: ix). In 2002, evidence emerged that Iran was developing a clandestine nuclear pro-gramme. At least six sites were identified with nuclear-related activities, including research reactors in Tehran, Isfahan, Bonab and Ramsar and two partially completed reactors on the coast of the Persian Gulf. Moreover, the Iranian government confirmed international reports that it had built two addi-tional nuclear facilities in Natanz and Arak, south of Tehran (Sadr 2005: 59). As the international community grew increasingly concerned about Iran's nuclear intentions, the IAEA released its first report in 2003, which revealed the country's failure to uphold its safeguards implementation. Despite this, Iran maintained that its nuclear programme was for civilian use and had no military objectives. It insisted that the NPT entitled it to 'enrich uranium for civilian use and that nuclear-powered electricity would release its oil and gas reserves for higher value-added purposes' (Amuzegar 2006: 91). However, Tehran's ensuing lack of transparency regarding its nuclear programme set the stage for an escalation of acrimony between the United States, Iran and the international community for years to come.

In response to the exposure of Iran's nuclear activities, US President George W. Bush (2001–2009) stated in his 2002 State of Union address, 'Iran aggres-sively pursues those weapons [of mass destruction] and exports terror'. In line with this view, he also declared that Iran, North Korea and Iraq 'constitute an axis of evil' (quoted in Sanger 2002). This speech, as well as repeated references to the possibility of pushing for 'regime change' in Iran, had a lasting impact on US–Iran relations and on US views of Iran. Relations were further strained after the election of Iranian President Mahmoud Ahmadinejad in 2005, who came to office with a fierce anti-American agenda. From the Iranian point of view, the development of a nuclear programme was a national right. Since the Iranian Revolution, the country's experiences of war, sanctions and isolation from the international community had created a sense of vulnerability in a hostile region. Moreover, this was fuelled by US activities in the broader region at the time. Washington had recently established naval bases in Kuwait, Bahrain and Qatar, and its naval carriers, equipped with nuclear technology, were patrolling the Persian Gulf (Milani 2009: 48). The geopolitical standing of Iran added weight to its ideological narrative that positioned the Islamic Republic in perpetual danger from external forces. As Ehsaneh Sadr (2005: 68) points out, 'having been included in George W. Bush's "Axis of Evil", having witnessed the ease with which the Taliban and Saddam were swept militarily aside', and in full knowledge of the United States' desire for regime change, Tehran could not help but be concerned that the Washington might soon turn its attention to Iran. This unfavourable environment provided the background to Ahmadinejad's antagonistic posturing in relation to Washington and his elevation of the nuclear issue into a matter of national pride.

As Iran continued to develop its nuclear facilities, Washington increasingly relied on the IAEA to monitor and report on its nuclear activities. Between 2003 and 2013, the United States maintained the pressure on Iran in relation to the nuclear issue and argued that Iran's failure to comply with IAEA guidelines suggested a deliberate attempt by Tehran to divert its nuclear programme to military purposes. IAEA reports provided the best cover for the United States to push for international action. In response to various violations, Washington, the European Union and the UN Security Council imposed economic sanctions in an effort to curtail Iran's nuclear activities. The United States imposed the 'most sweeping' sanctions (Katzman 2016: 42). As Kumuda Simpson (2015: 130) notes, 'in many ways, sanctions were regarded as the ultimate weapon, short of war, that remained in the US foreign policy box'.

In January 2009, the new US President, Barack Obama, delivered a promising inaugural speech. While acknowledging US errors in the region, he expressed a willingness to engage with the Middle East. Four months later, at a conference in Prague, he asserted his ambition to rid the world of nuclear weapons. With regards to Iran's nuclear programme, he claimed: 'my administration will seek engagement with Iran based on mutual interests and mutual respect. We believe in dialogue' (Obama 2009). As such, many international observers at the time anticipated Obama would implement a new and less aggressive US foreign policy, particularly towards the Middle East. However, Iran's continued lack of transparency regarding its nuclear facilities and failure to comply with IAEA protocols left Obama with little room to engage with Tehran. Indeed, the new administration moved to strengthen and expand the sanctions regime, as is evident in the Comprehensive Iran Sanctions, Accountability and Divestment Act, which Obama signed in 2010 (United States Department of the Treasury 2010). The following year, the IAEA released a report that deepened concerns in Washington and throughout the international community. It reiterated Iran's responsibility to cooperate fully with the IAEA on all issues, 'particularly those which give rise to concerns about the possible military dimensions to Iran's nuclear programme, including by providing access without delay to all sites, equipment, persons and documents requested by the Agency' (IAEA Board of Governors 2011: 8). It also stated that Iran had failed to engage 'in any sub-stantive way' with the IAEA since 2008 and that 'after assessing carefully and critically the extensive information available to it, the Agency finds information that indicates Iran has carried out activities relevant to the development of a nuclear explosive device' (IAEA Board of Governors 2011: 10). This led Obama to sign a second piece of legislation to increase economic sanctions against Iran in 2012 (White House 2012).

International sanctions against Iran had a devastating impact on the country's economy. By the end of Ahmadinejad's presidency in 2013, its economy had deteriorated significantly due to the sanctions, corruption and mismanagement. Its crude-oil exports had fallen from 2.5 million to 1.1 million barrels per day since 2011. This was disastrous for Iran's economy, given that oil exports constitute almost 80 per cent of the country's foreign earnings. Between 2012 and 2014, the economy shrank by 10 per cent (Katzman 2016: 1).

Nuclear negotiations

A marked shift in US–Iran relations began with the election of President Hassan Rouhani in 2013. His electoral success was seen by both Iranians and international observers as a step towards reform and moderation. He was determined to rebuild the Iranian economy, and this agenda had a profound impact on his foreign policy calculations. In Rouhani's view, economic prosperity rested entirely on the removal of sanctions, which necessitated negotiations with the international community, chiefly the United States. He thus opted for open dialogue, which immediately differentiated him from his predecessor. By November 2013, a mere three months after Rouhani had entered the presidential office, formal negotiations were under way and a 'Joint Plan of Action' was signed by Iran and the 'P5 + 1' countries (that is, the five permanent members of the UN Security Council – the United States, the United Kingdom, France, Russia and China – plus Germany). In exchange for Iran's commitment to this interim agreement, sanctions relief was afforded to Iran's crippled economy. This outcome was welcomed by Iran's Supreme Leader, Ayatollah Khamenei, who expressed his gratitude in an open letter to Rouhani.

The international community's dedication to these negotiations was profound. For twenty months, the United States, Russia and the other powers engaged with Iran around the negotiating table. Several rounds of foreign ministers' talks were held between Iran's Javad Zarif, the United States' John Kerry and Russia's Sergey Lavrov. As the talks fluctuated between progress and deadlock, mixed reactions emerged within the US and Iranian domestic constituencies. This was hardly surprising given the long history of hostility that coloured perceptions of the other in US–Iranian relations. In the face of thawing relations between Obama and Rouhani, many criticized the negotiating teams on the basis of their mistrust of the other side. Later, in the lead-up to the final agreement, US Republicans and neo-conservatives argued that the nuclear deal and the prospect of Iranian sanctions relief would facilitate 'Iranian imperialism' and 'enhance Tehran's support for destabilizing groups in the region' (Hanna and Kaye 2015: 176). Meanwhile, in Iran, hardline critics lamented that the nuclear deal undermined Iran's 'national dignity' (Nouri 2015).

On 14 July 2015, the nuclear deal was finalized, marking a historic moment in US–Iranian relations. After almost three weeks of intense talks during the final negotiations in Vienna, and following two major extensions of the interim agreement, Iran and the six world powers signed the Joint Comprehensive Plan of Action, which was then endorsed by the UN Security Council. Under the deal, Iran affirmed that it would not seek to develop nuclear weapons under any circumstances and asserted a commitment to limit its nuclear programme. In exchange, it received sanctions relief from the UN with respect to its financial, energy, shipping, automotive and other sectors. The deal also enabled

Iran to export crude oil freely and access foreign exchange reserves held in foreign banks that totalled almost US$60 billion. The IAEA was requested to verify and monitor Iran's implementation of its commitments, and 16 January 2016 was designated 'Implementation Day' (Katzman 2016: 1).

Regional responses to Iran

In contrast to the generally positive reaction to the deal in Iran and Western capitals, the regional response was mixed and included many voices of protest. The key criticism was that the deal would liberate Iran from the shackles that had constrained it for nearly a decade. Concern over Iran's regional ambitions was especially high in Tel Aviv and Riyadh. Israel and Saudi Arabia had both endured a difficult relationship with Tehran since the 1979 Islamic Revolution. Now they felt that the removal of sanctions would give Iran a boost and the resources it needed to expand its influence in the region at their expense. Additionally, both regional powers criticized the short duration of the deal, which stipulated only a fifteen-year freeze on enrichment. From a Saudi and Israeli perspective, this did not allow sufficient time to destroy Iran's nuclear capabilities.

Israel

The long-standing security and military partnership between the United States and Israel endured considerable strain during the nuclear negotiations. Israel fiercely objected to a nuclear deal with Iran as it saw the latter's nuclear pro-gramme as a direct threat to its survival. Since the 1980s, Israel has viewed Iran as a state sponsor of international terrorism via its support for groups such Hezbollah and HAMAS. It has also persistently expressed fears over the possibility of Iran either launching an attack itself or transferring nuclear weapons to these groups. These fears have been constantly reinforced by the antagonistic rhetoric emanating from Iran towards Israel. The Iranian leadership has consistently portrayed Israel as illegitimate, an occupier of Muslim land and an agent of US imperialism in the Middle East. In this sense, Israel fits into Iran's Manichean worldview and is perceived, alongside the United States, as an oppressor of the Muslim world.

This rhetoric fed into perceptions of insecurity in Israel and provided the justification for closer security ties with the United States. In the 2000s, several deals were concluded between Tel Aviv and the Washington to enhance Israel's security in the face of the perceived Iranian threat. However, these agreements did little to allay Israel's concerns, as is evident in its fierce objection to the 2015 nuclear negotiations. The gravity of this opposition was epitomized by Israeli Prime Minister Benjamin Netanyahu's 2015 address to the US Congress. During his speech, Netanyahu urged Washington to implement new sanctions against Iran and abandon the nuclear deal. His address was highly controversial as it was coordinated with the US Republicans without the approval of the

White House. As such, the Democrats criticized the Republicans for attempting to undermine the presidency. In line with this criticism, fifty Democrats boycotted Netanyahu's address and Obama sent no delegates to Capitol Hill (Baker 2015).

Israel saw the conclusion of the nuclear deal as an act of betrayal by the United States. While Obama assured Netanyahu that the agreement would thwart a nuclear-armed Iran, the Israeli Prime Minister expressed his concern over what sanctions relief would mean for Iran in terms of emboldening its proxies in the region. Shortly after the nuclear deal was announced, he declared:

> In the coming decade, the deal will reward Iran, the terrorist regime in Tehran, with hundreds of billions of dollars. This cash bonanza will fuel Iran's terrorism worldwide, its aggression in the region and its efforts to destroy Israel, which are ongoing.
>
> (Cited in Kershner 2015)

In a bid to appease Netanyahu's security concerns, a landmark deal was finalized between Washington and Tel Aviv in September 2016. Under the agreement, the United States committed US$38 billion of military aid to Israel between 2019 and 2028. This marked a significant increase on the 2007–2018 period, when the United States committed US$30 billion of military aid (Spetalnick 2016).

Gulf Cooperation Council

The United States has explicitly committed itself to protecting member states of the Gulf Cooperation Council (GCC). But the prospects of a rapprochement between Tehran and Washington caused unease in the GCC capitals.

Comprising Saudi Arabia, Kuwait, Qatar, the United Arab Emirates (UAE), Bahrain and Oman, the GCC was established in 1981 to form a united front against the newly established Islamic Republic of Iran. With the bloody Iran–Iraq War raging in the background, the GCC bolstered Iraq's military capabilities in its fight against what was generally perceived as Iranian expansionism. The United States welcomed the GCC as a mechanism for enhancing regional security and containing Iran. As Gregory Gause (1994: 140) put it, 'the GCC states want to be protected, and the United States wants to protect them. Their shared interests are clear: oil and political stability.' Since then, the United States has provided significant military support to the Gulf in an effort to keep the region secure. For example, after Iraq's invasion of Kuwait in 1990, it supplied the GCC states with over US$30 billion of military equipment. Furthermore, between 2005 and 2009, it sold up to US$22 billion of arms to GCC states (United States Government Accountability Office 2010). Significantly, in 2010, the United States pledged to sell a record figure of US$60 billion of military equipment to Saudi Arabia, with US officials stressing the importance of bolstering Saudi capabilities amid increasing fears over a nuclear-armed Iran (Quinn 2010).

The GCC's position on Iran's nuclear programme was articulated clearly in 2005. Rather than openly confronting Iran, GCC leaders demonstrated a preference for diplomatic engagement and economic measures to prevent Tehran from establishing its nuclear programme. At a GCC summit held in Abu Dhabi in 2005, Gulf state leaders called for a 'nuclear-free Gulf' for the first time and urged Iran to endorse the initiative. The GCC's close proximity to Iran and its nuclear facilities informed this position. According to the UAE's Foreign Minister, Abdullah al-Nuaimi, 'we are in a region very close to the [Iranian] nuclear reactor in Bushehr. We have no guarantees or protection against any leakage [from the reactor] which is on the Gulf coast' (cited in Hasan 2005). The GCC leaders were concerned about military flare-ups in the region, given the intensity of the hostile rhetoric among Iran, the United States and Israel. In the event of open conflict, they feared that Iran might target them due to their close association with Western powers. In 2009, GCC leaders praised international efforts to resolve the Iranian nuclear crisis through diplomatic means (Gulf Cooperation Council Supreme Council 2009). At successive GCC summits, the Gulf leaders repeatedly reiterated the 'importance of reaching a peaceful solution to this crisis' while urging Iran to 'continue international dialogue and full cooperation in this regard with the … IAEA' (Kingdom of Saudi Arabia Ministry of Foreign Affairs 2010).

However, as the nuclear negotiations intensified in 2015, the GCC was divided on how to respond to the prospect of an agreement that would free Iran of international sanctions. The UAE and Saudi Arabia were most critical of the deal and questioned Washington's commitment to their security in the face of an increasingly assertive Iran (al-Jazeera 2015). International observers also questioned the implications of the agreement for regional security. It was recognized, on the one hand, that the deal would prevent Iran from manufacturing nuclear weapons. On the other hand, it was argued that sanctions relief would inevitably offer Iran more resources to support its proxies in the ongoing conflicts in Syria and Lebanon. In the lead-up to the final agreement, the GCC leaders requested a meeting with Obama in a bid to reassert their strategic partnership. This summit was held at Camp David on 14 May 2015, and all parties expressed a commitment to forge closer ties in 'all fields, including defense and security cooperation, and develop collective approaches to regional issues in order to advance their shared interest in stability and prosperity'. Furthermore, the GCC leaders and Obama emphasized that the nuclear negotiations were in the 'security interests of GCC member states as well as the United States and the international community' and that they would work together to 'counter Iran's destabilizing activities in the region'. Finally, Obama stressed the United States' commitment to GCC security, declaring that 'in the event of such aggression, or the threat of such aggression, the United States stands ready to work with our GCC partners to urgently determine what actions may be appropriate' (White House 2015). In April 2016, US Secretary of Defense

Ashton Carter declared that the United States had provided the GCC with over US$33 billion of critical defence equipment since the Camp David summit (Carter 2016). This marked a significant increase in the United States' commitment and it helped to allay concerns in the GCC by reassuring the Arab states that Washington was not going to abandon them.

Saudi Arabia

Saudi Arabia has long viewed Iran's nuclear programme as an existential threat. This perception is informed by the intense rivalry that has permeated relations between Saudi Arabia and Iran since the Islamic Revolution. Both countries have attempted to assert ideological and religious leadership over the Muslim world. Saudi Arabia perceives itself as the natural leader of the Sunni Muslim world on the basis of its history and because two of Islam's holiest sites (Mecca and Medina) lie within its territory. These religious credentials, coupled with the Saudi state's instrumentalization of Wahhabi doctrine, adds weight to its self-proclaimed religious legitimacy over the Sunni Muslim world. Meanwhile, across the Persian Gulf, the Islamic Republic of Iran is home to 90 per cent of the world's Shia population and adheres to the Twelver School of Shia Islam, which constitutes a minority sect in Islam. The Iranian leadership has been acutely conscious of the limitations this presents and has highlighted its revolutionary message in a bid to overcome the sectarian divide.

US policies in the region have played an influential role in shaping Saudi Arabia's and Iran's perceptions of each other. The former's close links to Washington, especially in the spheres of oil and security, have drawn sharp criticism from Tehran. The al-Saud family views warm relations with the United States as crucial for its domestic and regional security. Tehran's leadership, on the other hand, views the United States as an oppressor of the Muslim world and it has persistently criticized Riyadh for acting as a vehicle for US interests in the region. As Hobbs and Moran (2013: 30) point out, 'each country thus views each other as a threat in terms of regional hegemony and this perception forms a permanent back-drop to Saudi–Iranian relations'.

Box 11.1 Wahhabism

Wahhabism is an Islamic movement formed by the Islamic preacher Muhammad ibn 'Abd al-Wahhab (1703–1792). This puritanical movement focuses on absolute monotheism and advocates a return to the Islamic texts. It also rejects all cultural accretions to the faith, including Sufi traditions, such as saint veneration. The movement came to prominence after it was adopted by the al-Saud family in 1744. Following the family's rise to power in the Arabian Peninsula in the twentieth century, Wahhabi doctrine formed the political basis of the modern state of Saudi Arabia.

The prospect of a nuclear deal that would free Iran from international sanctions worried Saudi Arabia. Riyadh feared an unchained Iran would redouble its efforts to assert regional hegemony. These concerns had a domestic dimension as Saudi Arabia is home to a 10–15 per cent Shia minority who reside predominantly in the kingdom's Eastern Province. This Shia population also identifies with the Twelver School of Shia Islam, which puts them at odds with the stringent enforcement of Sunni Wahhabism in Saudi Arabia. Furthermore, there is evidence of discrimination against them in key areas such as government, the police force, the foreign and security services, the military and the lucrative oil industry (Matthiesen 2013: 55). Hence, high levels of discontent towards the Saudi state run deep within the country's Shia communities. Since the Iranian Revolution, the Saudi elite has grown increasingly concerned over Tehran's capacity to mobilize Shia protest against the kingdom.

Box 11.2 The Twelver School

The Shia community represents approximately 15 per cent of the world's total Muslim population. The theological differences between the Shia and Sunni sects stem from the early Islamic community, focusing on the question of leadership. Shia Muslims understand succession to the Prophet Mohammed to be based on bloodline, whereas Sunni Muslims hold that the community should determine his successors. Hence, Shia reject the first three Caliphs who were elected to lead the Muslim community after the Prophet's death in 632 and insist that Ali (Mohammed's cousin and son-in-law) was the first legitimate leader. The largest group of Shia Muslims, known as 'Twelvers', reside primarily in Iran, Iraq and Lebanon. They believe that the twelve descendants of the Prophet Mohammed carried his divine inspiration, so they were both divinely inspired and infallible. In 874, the Eleventh Shia Imam died and Twelvers believe that his infant son (the Twelfth or Hidden Imam) then entered a state of occultation and will one day return to deliver peace and justice to the world.

It is important to put the Saudi reaction into context. In the aftermath of the 2003 US invasion of Iraq which removed Saddam Hussein from power, Riyadh had become very sensitive to Iran's expanding influence in the region. For Saudi Arabia and the other GCC states, Saddam's leadership in Iraq had been a shield against Iran. Tehran had viewed the Shia of Iraq as an ideal constituency for its revolutionary ideology, so it had supported several Iraqi Shia resistance groups during Saddam's brutal regime in the 1980s and 1990s. Saudi Arabia thus viewed Saddam's fall as 'catastrophically upsetting the balance of power' in the region as it effectively opened the door to the rise of Shia power in Iraq, with the inevitable consequence of closer ties with Tehran (Wehrey et al. 2009: 2). Meanwhile, Tehran's support for Hezbollah in Lebanon heightened fears of an expansionist Iran. In late 2004, these fears were encapsulated by King Abdullah II bin al-Hussein of Jordan, who warned of the emergence of a 'Shia crescent' in the form of a Shia government in Iraq, Hezbollah in Lebanon and the Islamic Republic of Iran. The political ascendancy of the Shia majority in Iraq in the 2005 general election seemed to confirm Saudi fears. Thereafter, closer ties between Baghdad and Tehran deepened Riyadh's concerns over Iranian expansionism as well as its disillusionment with the United States for facilitating it.

In terms of Iran's nuclear programme, Saudi Arabia maintained a less aggressive stance than the United States under the Bush administration. Rather than opting for open confrontation, it chose engagement with Iran. While the neo-conservatives in Washington were sabre-rattling and calling for regime change, Riyadh did not advocate military action. As Banafsheh Keynoush (2016: 163) points out, 'Riyadh felt that if the United States attacked Iran it would leave the region after a while, whereas the Kingdom had to live with the consequences given it was Iran's neighbor.' In 2006, Saudi King Abdullah bin Abdulaziz al-Saud asked US Vice President Dick Cheney to 'give diplomacy more time'. The following year, Abdullah invited Iranian President Ahmadinejad to the annual GCC summit in Doha, Qatar. This was highly significant as it was the first time that an Iranian President had attended a GCC summit. It also stood in stark contrast to the Bush administration's policy of isolating Iran. However, it had little impact on Tehran's reluctance to cooperate with the international community on the nuclear issue.

Barack Obama's accession to the US presidency in 2009 changed the dynamics. Under the Obama administration, Washington expressed a willingness to engage with Iran, which generated considerable concern among the Saudi leadership about the possibility of a US–Iranian rapprochement. The Saudis feared that such a rapprochement would enhance Iranian credibility and inevitably allow Tehran to play a larger and more legitimate role in regional affairs. These concerns were expressed in a 2009 cable (published later by WikiLeaks), in which the kingdom urged Washington to 'cut the head off the snake'. This notable contrast between the official and unofficial Saudi positions towards Iran emerged again in the aftermath of the JCPOA nuclear deal in 2015. According to Norman Cigar (2016: 188), while Saudi King Salman bin Abdulaziz al-Saud had told Obama that he would support any deal that 'guarantees that Iran will be prevented from acquiring nuclear weapons', the final deal was bluntly criticized in Saudi Arabia:

[T]he overall results, from the Saudis' point of view, were not seen as positive, as they often felt that they would pay the price in terms of a strengthened and emboldened Iran, which may well acquire nuclear weapons in the long run.

Hostility between Saudi Arabia and Iran reached its zenith with the former's execution of the prominent Shia religious leader Sheikh Nimr al-Nimr, alongside three other Shia prisoners, in January 2016. The Shia community in

Iran and elsewhere mourned the deaths of these men and condemned Saudi Arabia. Repressive measures against the Shia were nothing new, but the timing was catastrophic. The executions poured fuel on the sectarian fire that was already engulfing the region. Iranian hardliners vehemently denounced Saudi Arabia for 'the unlawfully shed blood of this innocent martyr' and accused Saudi Arabia of being 'an extension of US–Zionist will in the region' (Kayhan News 2016). Moreover, on the day of the executions, Saudi Arabia's consulate general in Mashhad and its embassy in Tehran were stormed and set ablaze by Iranian mobs and some members of the Basij security force. These incidents were condemned by the GCC as 'barbaric', and Saudi Arabia, along with Bahrain and Sudan, severed diplomatic relations with Iran. This breakdown in diplomatic relations was devastating for President Rouhani and his efforts to normalize Iran's relationship with the international community. Furthermore, the hardliners' grouping of Saudi Arabia with the United States and Israel was seen as an attempt to discredit his relationship with Obama. Therefore, less than six months after the signing of the historic nuclear deal, relations between Iran and Saudi Arabia were at an all-time low.

Escalating crisis

The tumultuous events of 2011 and 2012 in the Arab world aggravated relations between Iran and Saudi Arabia. The anti-government protests that spread through the region, dubbed the Arab Spring, was a cause for celebration in Iran and a serious concern in Saudi Arabia. Iran greeted the uprisings as a vindication of its revolutionary message against pro-US regimes, while Saudi Arabia feared regional instability and the potential loss of friendly allies across the Arab world. The fall of Hosni Mubarak in Egypt (2011) and the subsequent political ascendancy of the Muslim Brotherhood was a worrying development for Riyadh. Furthermore, the history of Shia grievances in the Eastern Province of Saudi Arabia made it a suspect community in the eyes of the government. Efforts to organize mass rallies in the Eastern Province, therefore, were met with brutal force. The problem in the province went much further than sectarianism. Limited employment opportunities and the repressive political system were the main sources of discontent. As Fredrick Wehrey (2013: 4) has argued, 'it would be wrong to interpret dissent in the Eastern Province as a purely localized or narrowly Shia issue'. In fact, calls for protest were prompted by a young Saudi *Sunni*, Mohammed al-Wadani, who uploaded a YouTube video declaring his disdain for the regime. Indeed, 'the Saudi response to the whole Arab Spring, both at home and abroad, was based on the fear that an opposition to the ruling family could emerge that would unite Sunni and Shia' (Matthiesen 2013: 22). As such, the Saudi regime presented the opposition as a 'Shia conspiracy', led by Iran and intent on creating chaos and instability. Al-Rasheed (2011: 520) contends that religion was utilized by the Saudi elite as the main strategy to prevent the spread of protests. This strategy was also pursued by Saudi Arabia during the 2011 Bahraini uprisings.

Riyadh was concerned about anti-government protests that threatened the survival of the al-Khalifa ruling family in Bahrain. The majority of the protesters were Shia who called for an end to the ruling family's discriminatory policies that had marginalized them for decades. The al-Khalifas adhered to the Sunni interpretation of Islam and maintained close ties with Saudi Arabia. The popular challenge against them was therefore seen as a challenge against a Sunni state. This sectarian view of the popular uprising in Bahrain proved damaging for political reform. The protests were increasingly painted as sectarian in nature by the al-Saud and al-Khalifa families, and Iran was accused of meddling in Bahrain. In response to an escalation of demonstrations, the GCC – led by Saudi Arabia – deployed over a thousand troops at the request of the al-Khalifa family to assist the Bahraini security forces with the crackdown. The operation was largely successful and the al-Khalifa family survived the popular challenge. By implying that the Bahraini uprisings were a foreign-inspired plot orchestrated by Iran, the al-Saud and al-Khalifa families justified the suppression as necessary for the protection of the regional stability.

The Arab Spring hardened the Saudi position on Iran. In April 2011, Saudi Arabia urged the UN Security Council and the international community to take the necessary measures to 'stop Iranian interference and provocations aimed at sowing discord and destruction' among the GCC states (Kamrava 2012: 99). The Iranian leadership dismissed these accusations of interference and warned the GCC that it was 'playing with fire' by sending 'occupation troops' to Bahrain. Such accusations and counter-accusations between Riyadh and Tehran have become the norm over the past four decades, but they are a very destabilizing feature of regional politics that encourage a sectarian perspective. In October 2013, the Saudi Ambassador to the United States, Prince Turki al-Faisal, denounced Iran during a speech he delivered to the 22nd Arab–US Policymakers' Conference in Washington. He claimed:

> the other concern we need to address in the coming decade is the Iranian leadership's meddling and destabilizing efforts in the countries with Shia majorities, Iraq and Bahrain, as well as those countries with significant minority Shia communities, such as Kuwait, Lebanon and Yemen ... [T]his must end. Saudi Arabia will oppose any and all of Iran's interference and meddling in other countries.
>
> (Al-Faisal 2013: 5)

Syria and Yemen

Against the backdrop of this diplomatic rift, conflicts in Syria and Yemen exacerbated the sectarian divide and created a deeply polarized region. Many regional observers describe these two civil wars as proxy conflicts fought between the Shia (led by Iran) and the Sunni (led by Saudi Arabia). Following the escalation of the rebellion against the Assad regime in Syria, Saudi Arabia committed resources and support to anti-Assad fighters who adhered to Sunni Islam. This support for the rebels was matched by logistical and material support from the United States, Turkey and Qatar. Iran viewed this loose international coalition to topple Assad as a major threat to its regional interests. The Assad regime, which adheres to Alawite doctrine, is much closer to the Shia branch of Islam than the Sunni, and it has been a long-time ally of Iran. Most significantly, Syria serves as the bridge between Iran and Lebanon, giving Tehran access to the Hezbollah. Iran could not accept the loss of this significant piece on the regional chessboard, so it sprang to Assad's defence. In addition to committing the Islamic Revolutionary Guard Corps (IRCG) to Syria, Tehran asked Hezbollah and Shia militia in Iraq to mobilize in defence of Assad, too. However, it tried to avoid the language of sectarianism, notwithstanding its reliance on these Shia fighters, and projected its efforts in Syria as bolstering the 'Axis of Resistance' against Western imperialism.

The Yemeni Civil War was also born out of the 2011 Arab uprisings and has since been framed increasingly along sectarian lines. This proxy conflict between Riyadh and Tehran has been played out primarily in Sana'a, Yemen's largest city in the north. In response to the protesters' demands in January 2011, the GCC brokered a deal that brought President Ali Abdullah Saleh's thirty-three-year reign to an end. He was replaced by the Saudi-backed Abd Rabbu Mansour al-Hadi, who acceded to power in February 2012. Despite this transition, though, the conflict continued to rage as armed groups sought to exploit the government's inability to maintain control and deliver adequate political and economic reforms. The Houthis, formed by Zaydi Shia Muslims from Yemen's northern Sana'a Province, are perhaps the most powerful of these rebel militias. Since their formation in 1990, they have demanded greater autonomy and recognition of their cultural and religious practices in the face of Yemen's dis-criminatory, Sunni-led government. As the northern province borders Saudi Arabia, the Saudi leadership viewed the Houthis' demands as a serious threat to the Sunni-led status quo in the region. Furthermore, they denounced the Houthis as agents of Tehran. While the Saudi concern over the Houthis in Yemen predates the Arab uprisings and the growing Iranian interest in the conflict, it has come to serve as another theatre of regional rivalry. In March 2014, the Houthis were designated a terrorist organization by Saudi Arabia. From the Saudi perspective, they cannot afford to see a Shia group, backed by Iran, rise to power in a neighbouring country.

As the Yemeni conflict deepened in 2014, Saudi Arabia grew increasingly concerned over the Houthis' progress. In September, they seized the northern Saada Governorate, declared de facto authority and advanced on Aden, the country's second-largest city. Moreover, President al-Hadi resigned in January 2015 due to his unpopularity and the failure of his administration to deliver economic prosperity to the nation. As the balance of power continued to shift in favour of the Houthis, Saudi Arabia launched the 'Decisive Storm' air-strike campaign in March 2015 in an attempt to counter their advance and reinstall a Saudi-friendly government led by al-Hadi. Morocco, Jordan, Egypt, Pakistan, Sudan and the GCC states (with the exception of Oman) supported the campaign. Although Saudi Arabia predicted the military operation would be swift and decisive, it was far from over at the time of writing (January 2018) and has been internationally criticized for worsening the dire humanitarian conditions engulfing Yemen. Meanwhile, Tehran has refuted claims that it has provided financial and military support to the rebels in Yemen, but it has openly praised the Houthis as members of its 'Axis of Resistance'.

Conclusion

The international community was deeply concerned over Iran's clandestine nuclear programme for more than a decade. Tehran made repeated assurances that its programme was for civilian purposes only, but in the absence of independent verification from the IAEA, Washington and other major powers suspected a weaponization agenda. Hence, the signing of the nuclear deal with the P5 + 1 in 2015 marked an extraordinary moment in the history of US–Iranian relations. The deal placed Iran's nuclear programme under a stringent inspections regime and was thus presented as a significant step forward in the enhancement of international security. With the lifting of economic sanctions that had crippled the Iranian economy for years, the Rouhani administration managed to bring Iran out of isolation.

However, the nuclear deal was not greeted with enthusiasm by Washington's principal allies in the region. Indeed, Israel and the GCC states saw it as an act of betrayal by the United States. They expressed their concern that a US–Iranian rapprochement would enhance Iran's credibility and allow it to play a more aggressive role in regional affairs. Moreover, they were worried that a sanctions-free Iran would extend its sponsorship of proxies in the region. In the post-deal period, Iran's activities have only served to heighten these fears.

Rouhani's attempts to bring Iran out of isolation have been challenged by its role in the region's major ongoing conflicts. Nowhere is this more apparent than in Syria. Iran's unequivocal support of Syrian President Assad and its reliance on Hezbollah and Iraqi Shia militia to facilitate that support have placed it at odds with the regional powers of Saudi Arabia, the GCC and their Western allies. Its close relations with the region's Shia groups have been denounced by Saudi Arabia as strong evidence that Iran is pushing a sectarian agenda. These claims fundamentally undermine the revolutionary message espoused by Iran's leadership, who since the revolution have recognized the shortcomings of belonging to a minority sect and have thus sought to project an image that transcends sectarian differences. However, this image has been tainted by the acrimonious diplomatic rift between Tehran and Riyadh, which has widened the sectarian divide in the region. In turn, this has hampered Rouhani's attempt to normalize Iran's international standing in the post-deal period. Iran certainly gained a major economic boost with the removal of sanctions in 2016, but its tainted image remains a source of instability in the region.

References

Al-Jazeera (2015) 'Why Saudi Arabia and Israel Oppose Iran Nuclear Deal', 14 April, available at www.aljazeera.com/news/2015/04/saudi-arabia-israel-oppose-iran-nuclear-deal-150401061906177.html.

Al-Faisal, Turki (2013) '22nd Annual Arab–US Policymakers' Conference', King Faisal Center for Research and Islamic Studies, 22 October, available at https://ncusar.org/programs/13-transcripts/2013-10-22-hrh-prince-turki-keynote.pdf.

Al-Rasheed, Madawi (2011) 'Sectarianism as Counter-revolution: Saudi Responses to the Arab Spring', *Studies in Ethnicity and Nationalism*, Vol. 11, No. 3, pp. 513–526.

Amuzegar, Jahangir (2006) 'Nuclear Iran: Perils and Prospects', *Middle East Policy*, Vol. 13, No. 2, pp. 90–112.

Baker, Peter (2015) 'In Congress, Netanyahu Faults "Bad Deal" on Iran Nuclear Program', *New York Times*, 3 March, available at www.nytimes.com/2015/03/04/world/middleeast/netanyahu-congress-iran-israel-speech.html?_r=0.

Berman, Ingrid (2016) *Verification and Monitoring of the Nuclear Agreement with Iran: Resources and Challenges* (New York: Nova Science Publishers).

Carter, Ashton (2016) 'Opening Statement as Delivered at US–GCC Defense Ministerial Joint Press Conference, Riyadh, Saudi Arabia', US Department of Defense, 20 April, available at www.defense.gov/News/Transcripts/Transcript-View/Article/739082/opening-statement-as-delivered-at-us-gcc-defense-minesterial-joint-press-confer.

Cigar, Norman (2016) *Saudi Arabia and Nuclear Weapons: How Do Countries Think about the Bomb?* (New York: Routledge).

Gause, Gregory (1994) *Oil Monarchies: Domestic and Security Challenges in the Arab Gulf States* (New York: Council on Foreign Relations).

Gulf Cooperation Council Supreme Council (2009) 'The Final Communiqué of the 30th Session', 14–15 December, available at www.gcc-sg.org/en-us/Statements/SupremeCouncil/Pages/The30thSession.aspx.

Hanna, Michael Wahid and Kaye, Dalia Dassa (2015) 'The Limits of Iranian Power', *Survival*, Vol. 57, No. 5, pp. 173–198.

Hasan, Syed Qamar (2005) 'GCC Calls for Nuclear-free Middle East', *Arab News*, 20 December, available at www.arabnews.com/node/277642.

Hobbs, Christopher and Moran, Matthew (2013) *Exploring Regional Responses to a Nuclear Iran: Nuclear Dominoes?* (London: Palgrave Macmillan).

IAEA Board of Governors (2011) 'Implementation of the NPT Safeguards Agreement and Relevant Provisions of Security Council Resolutions in the Islamic Republic of Iran', 18 December, available at www.iaea.org/sites/default/files/gov2011-65.pdf.

Kamrava, Mehran (2012) 'The Arab Spring and the Saudi-led Counterrevolution', *Orbis*, Vol. 56, No. 1, pp. 96–104.

Katzman, Kenneth (2016) 'Iran Sanctions', 21 January, available at www.hsdl.org/?view&did=789713.

Kayhan News (2016) 'Nimr's Execution Will Bring About Saudi Undoing', 3 January, available at http://kayhan.ir/en/news/22297/nimr%E2%80%99s-execution-will-bring-about-saudi-undoing.

Kershner, Isabel (2015) 'Iran Deal Denounced by Netanyahu as "Historic Mistake"', *New York Times*, 14 July, available at www.nytimes.com/2015/07/15/world/middleeast/iran-nuclear-deal-israel.html?_r=0.

Keynoush, Banafsheh (2016) *Saudi Arabia and Iran: Friends or Foes?* (London: Palgrave Macmillian).

Kingdom of Saudi Arabia Ministry of Foreign Affairs (2010) 'Summit Issues Final Communiqué', available at www.mofa.gov.sa/sites/mofaen/ServicesAndInformation/dataAndstatements/Letters/GulfCooperationCouncil/Pages/NewsArticleID58305.aspx.

Matthiesen, Toby (2013) *Sectarian Gulf: Bahrain, Saudi Arabia, and the Arab Spring that Wasn't* (Stanford, CA: Stanford University Press).

Milani, Mohsen M. (2009) 'Tehran's Take: Understanding Iran's US policy', *Foreign Affairs*, Vol. 88, No. 4, pp. 46–62.

Nouri, Bozorgmehr Sharafedin (2015) 'Iran's Conservatives Take Aim at Nuclear Deal', *Reuters*, July 16, available at www.reuters.com/article/us-iran-nuclear-idUSKCN0PQ1TQ20150716.

Obama, Barack (2009) 'Remarks by President Barack Obama Ii Prague as Delivered', 5 April, available at https://obamawhitehouse.archives.gov/the-press-office/remarks-president-barack-obama-prague-delivered.

Quinn, Andrew (2010) 'US Announces $60 Billion Arms Sale for Saudi Arabia', Reuters, 20 October, available at www.reuters.com/article/us-usa-saudi-arms-idUSTRE69J4ML20101020.

Sadr, Ehsaneh I. (2005) 'The Impact of Iran's Nuclearization on Israel', *Middle East Policy*, Vol. 12, No. 2, pp. 58–73.

Sanger, David E. (2002) 'The State of the Union: The Overview', *New York Times*, 30 January, available at www.nytimes.com/2002/01/30/us/state-union-overview-bush-focusing-terrorism-says-secure-us-top-priority.html.

Simpson, Kumuda (2015) *US Nuclear Diplomacy with Iran: From the War on Terror to the Obama Administration* (Lanham, MD: Rowman & Littlefield).

Spetalnick, Matt (2016) 'US, Israel Sign $38 Billion Military Aid Package', *Reuters*, 15 September, available at www.reuters.com/article/us-usa-israel-statement-idUSKCN11K2CI.

United Nations Office for Disarmament Affairs (UNODA) (n.d.) 'Treaty on the Non-proliferation of Nuclear Weapons (NPT)', available at www.un.org/disarmament/wmd/nuclear/npt/.

United States Department of the Treasury (2010) 'Comprehensive Iran Sanctions, Accountability, and Divestment Act', 1 July, available at www.treasury.gov/resource-center/sanctions/Documents/hr2194.pdf.

United States Government Accountability Office (2010) 'US Agencies Need to Improve Licensing Data and to Document Reviews of Arms Transfers for US Foreign Policy and National Security Goals', 20 September, available at www.gao.gov/products/GAO-10-918.

Wehrey, Frederic, Karasik, Theodore W., Nader, Alireza, Ghez, Jeremy J. and Hansell, Lydia (2009) *Saudi–Iranian Relations since the Fall of Saddam: Rivalry, Cooperation, and Implications for US Policy* (Santa Monica, CA: Rand Corporation).

Wehrey, Frederick (2013) 'The Forgotten Uprising in Eastern Saudi Arabia', *Carnegie Endowment for International Peace*, June, pp. 1–25.

White House (2012) 'Fact Sheet: Sanctions Related to Iran', 31 July, available at https://obamawhitehouse.archives.gov/the-press-office/2012/07/31/fact-sheet-sanctions-related-iran.

White House (2015) 'US–Gulf Cooperation Council Camp David Joint Statement', 14 May, available at https://obamawhitehouse.archives.gov/the-press-office/2015/05/14/us-gulf-cooperation-council-camp-david-joint-statement.

12 Conclusion

Since the collapse of the Ottoman Empire, the modern Middle East has been impacted by an ongoing battle between external powers vying for influence in the region and those striving for self-determination. Under the 1916–1917 Sykes–Picot Agreement, the colonial powers divided the crumbling empire into smaller states. The seeds of future crisis were sown. These newly created political entities were determined on the grounds of British and French economic and strategic interests, often with scant regard for local characteristics or the ethnic make-up of the region. This had major repercussions for future developments in the region. The newly created borders and the political structures that emerged from this process were not representative of the region's people. The political systems that were imposed from the top often enjoyed little popular support, which meant that the local populations sought for alternatives to capture and give meaning to their lived experiences. The political events that followed in the course of the twentieth and twenty-first centuries were the result of the tension between the indigenous search for self-expression (and ultimately self-rule) and the interests of colonial and post-colonial powers in pursuing their agendas in the region. This tension set the Middle East on a course of crisis and upheaval.

The 1956 Suez War irrevocably altered the region's status quo. Egyptian President Nasser's war with of the tripartite powers of Britain, France and Israel signalled a 'changing of the guard', whereby the influence of the old colonial powers was eclipsed by that of the two new superpowers. Thereafter, the Middle East was impacted by the dynamics of the Cold War, with both the United States and the Soviet Union keen to maximize their economic and political power in the region. To advance their interests, the superpowers developed patronage relationships with regional regimes. The rivalry between Washington and Moscow was exacerbated by the region's natural resources and the withdrawal of British forces from the oil-rich Persian Gulf in 1971. By this point, US foreign policy was dominated by the need to contain and prevent Soviet influence and enhance its own influence over the region. Washington's relations with the pro-Western regimes of Iran and Saudi Arabia were consistent with this policy objective. From an ideological point of view, these Cold War policies set a damaging precedent for the United States' standing in the region. It has long presented itself as a beacon of democracy and freedom and a champion of self-determination. Yet, throughout the twentieth century, these concerns were of secondary importance when dealing with authoritarian and intolerant but pro-US states in the Middle East, such as Saudi Arabia and Iran before the 1979 revolution. The gap between the US-espoused ideals of democracy and civil liberty and its support for regimes with chequered records on human rights and political accountability has led many critics to accuse Washington of hypocrisy. Ultimately, such criticism has been detrimental to US interests. Social and political dissent in the Middle East has generally included an anti-American dimension, especially in the twentieth century, as the United States was the key sponsor of many unpopular and undemocratic political rulers.

The formation of the State of Israel with international support was greeted with shock and disbelief by the region's Arab population. As far as the Arabs were concerned, the new state was a foreign transplant facilitated by the machinations of Western powers. This political setback, coupled with the military defeat of 1948 and the consequent Palestinian refugee crisis, heightened the Arabs' sense of vulnerability and gave impetus to the doctrine of pan-Arabism. With the consolidation of new states in the wake of the Second World War, pan-Arabism captured the explicit popular desire for modernity, prosperity and independent development in the Arab world. President Nasser became the most distinguished champion of pan-Arabism. However, his efforts to unite the Arab world politically were ultimately unsuccessful. Most devastating to the idea of pan-Arabism was Israel's crushing defeat of the combined Arab forces in the Six-Day War of 1967. This military humiliation was a rude awakening for the Arab population. Not only had their full military power been defeated by Israel, but the remaining Palestinian populations of the Gaza Strip and the West Bank fell under direct Israeli rule.

Pan-Arabism was not without its critics. Some suggested that the explicitly secular concept ignored the historic role religion had played in the public life of Muslim communities, but it was the shock of the 1967 defeat that opened the door for an Islamist critique of pan-Arabism and other political ideologies. Islamism was predicated on the idea that Muslims had grown weak and unable to defend themselves because they had allowed Islam to drift to the periphery of public life. The solution, therefore, was a forceful return to Islam. This political reading of Islam insisted that it is more than a religion: it is a political agenda and a blueprint for action. Articulated most succinctly by Sayyid Qutb, Sunni Islamism rejected the secular nation-state and contemporary political ideologies as illegitimate because they did not respect the sovereignty of God. Hence, bringing about the sovereignty of God by establishing a state that followed Islamic principles became the mission and defining feature of Islamism, also widely known as 'political Islam'. This trend was bolstered by events in the Shia world, where Ayatollah Khomeini merged a fiery interpretation of Shia theology with Iranian nationalism to harness the revolutionary sentiments of the Iranian populace, which had come to resent the Shah and his Western backers. This culminated in the formation of the Islamic Republic of Iran in 1979.

The pre-1979 Iranian state's response to political Islam established a pattern that was repeated throughout the late twentieth century and across the Muslim world. Against the backdrop of the Cold War, the Iranian state security agencies were primarily concerned with leftist and Soviet-aligned movements. While suppression of dissent was extensive, and the SAVAK intelligence agency became synonymous with brutality and torture, Islamic scholars were able to preach and conduct religious ceremonies. This allowed Islamist ideas to spread under the radar, with mosques becoming centres of political agitation.

The revolutionary regime that emerged in 1979 turned popular distrust of the United Sates, inculcated by Washington's support of the deposed dynasty, into a pillar of its foreign policy. Iran's anti-Americanism, as well as its claim to speak for the whole Muslim world and its stance against Israel (seen by many as an occupying power in Palestine), made a lasting impact on regional politics and continues to destabilize the Middle East. The Islamic Revolution was a watershed in the region as it served as a beacon of hope for other Islamist groups that sought opportunities to put their political ideas into practice. The Islamic Republic of Iran also launched a propaganda campaign to foment revolution against ruling regimes that were seen as too accommodating of US interests. Hence, its revolutionary fervour was watched with concern and trepidation in neighbouring capital cities. Baghdad and Riyadh were singled out for special attention in the Iranian propaganda and consequently felt most vulnerable. The Iraqi attack on Iran in 1980, and the subsequent formation of the Gulf Cooperation Council to contain Iran's influence, took place against this background of insecurity.

Iran's promotion of Islamism was bolstered by its commitment to 'liberate' Islam's third holiest site: Jerusalem. Tehran highlighted its support for what it called the 'resistance movement' in Palestine and Lebanon to boost its own Islamic credentials and condemned other states, most notably Saudi Arabia, for their failure to stand up for Muslim interests. The regional crisis generated by the emergent Islamist challenge to the region's status quo deepened throughout the remainder of the twentieth century. Simultaneously, the US-led Western powers sought to isolate Iran from regional and international affairs. Iran advocated its ideology of Islamism as a panacea to all the ills of economic underdevelopment and socio-political stagnation in the Muslim world. Many of its neighbours saw this as a threat to their hold on power and sided with the United States in its efforts to contain Iran.

In an ironic twist, the US commitment to authoritarian ruling regimes, especially in key states such as Saudi Arabia and Egypt, served to vindicate the Islamist critique. These regimes ruled with an iron fist and showed no tolerance for dissent. They had no respect for human rights or democracy, but they did align with US interests. Consequently, as their political legitimacy continued to ebb away, the United States was ever more closely associated with the deepening crisis. Yet, at the same time, a counter-trend appeared to bolster the United States' standing. The mobilization of the Muslim Middle East against the Soviet invasion of Afghanistan enjoyed the full support of the United States. In this scenario, Washington was an active partner with Islamists and Muslim states against its principal Cold War foe. But this alliance of convenience proved temporary. Indeed, in an unprecedented manner, it highlighted the detrimental impact of superpower interference in the region. The political landscape seemed to deteriorate with every experience of foreign intervention, opening new fissures and political fault-lines.

The anti-Soviet mobilization elevated the ideological zeal and infrastructure of Islamism, and led to the emergence of a new phenomenon: global jihadism. While Islamism was primarily focused on challenging incumbent regimes and aimed to establish an Islamic state within existing territorial boundaries, the notion of jihad against foreign occupation of a distant Muslim land normalized *transnational* action against non-Muslim interests. Islamism has traditionally been a national project; global jihadism, by contrast, is not confined by national borders. The rise of al-Qaeda, as an outgrowth of the conflict in Afghanistan, marked the start of this new era. Its interpretation of jihad drew on the Islamist ideals of rejecting human authority as illegitimate and recognizing God's sovereignty. It emphasized that the militant form of jihad was the only way to achieve this, and that jihad was transnational. Predictably, given that al-Qaeda's leader, Osama bin Laden, hailed from Saudi Arabia, this interpretation was couched in the puritanical language of Wahhabism. The integration of Islamism and Wahhabism, with an emphasis on the crucial role of militant jihad, would prove costly for the Arab world and beyond as Islamist challenges to the state continued to emerge.

On 11 September 2001, Al-Qaeda carried out a series of coordinated attacks that led to the deaths of thousands of civilians in the United States. The impact of these attacks was devastating. Soon after, an international coalition led by the United States toppled the Taliban regime that had given shelter to al-Qaeda in Afghanistan. Public opinion around the world supported this response, but it energized the interventionist instinct in the US political establishment and two years later the United States launched another operation, this time to overthrow Saddam Hussein in Iraq. The world is still suffering the consequences of these actions. For instance, they triggered a securitization of the complex relationships among the Western powers, Islamist organizations and Middle Eastern states. As part of this process, many repressive regimes were given free rein to quash dissent, with a consequent empowerment of state security agencies and the often brutal application of 'security legislation' in the region. This served to deepen the crisis.

In Iraq, itself a creation of the colonial period with a diverse sectarian and religious community, the post-Saddam regime has had to contend with rampant sectarian conflict, empowered ethno-nationalism among its Kurdish population, and the emergence of global jihadism in the form of the ISIS/IS movement. The US intervention in 2003 was not solely responsible for creating these challenges, but it had a major role in establishing the political conditions for their eruption into the open and rise in significance.

One of the unintended outcomes of the US interventions in Afghanistan and Iraq under the rubric of the 'War on Terror' has been to open up political space for Iran. For decades, the United States had sought to isolate Iran. But its post-9/11 policy of regime change removed two serious, anti-Iranian security threats: the Taliban in Afghanistan and Saddam Hussein in Iraq. Their elimination allowed Iran to forge better relations with the new regimes in both countries and expand its sphere of influence. This was especially true with respect to Iraq, as the post-Saddam administration was dominated by the Shia majority, at the expense of the Sunni community. Unsurprisingly, the region's Sunni regimes viewed the increasingly close links between the Shia communities in Iraq and Iran with mounting concern. In a region where political boundaries were drawn with little regard to the religious or ethnic composition of the population, and where incumbent leaders routinely ignored popular wishes, a vocal Shia population emboldened by Iran's public declarations of support presented a serious threat to stability. In 2005, King Abdullah of Jordan expressed the ruling regimes' anxiety when he warned against the rise of a 'Shia Crescent' that would stretch from the Levant to the Persian Gulf.

Since the Islamic Revolution, Iran has attempted to champion Muslim interests against the United States and Israel, not just *Shia* Muslim interests. But its links to and support of Shia organizations (Hezbollah in Lebanon and various Shia militias in Iraq as well as the Assad regime in Syria) have left it vulnerable to accusations of sectarianism, notwithstanding the fact that this is incompatible with Tehran's worldview. The scourge of sectarianism arrived with a vengeance in the wake of the Arab uprisings of 2011. These tumultuous popular upheavals, which began as a series of protests against corruption and the lack of political accountability in Tunisia, touched a raw nerve and soon spread across the region like wildfire. However, in general, the end result was not more inclusive, democratic government. With the remarkable exception of Tunisia itself, the Arab world suffered further authoritarianism and/or collapse into civil war. The Syrian experience was the most devastating in terms of loss of life and property. Bashar al-Assad responded to popular demands for reform with a disproportionately heavy hand, triggering the deeply held historical antipathy many Syrian Sunnis felt towards the regime. In the consequent escalation of tension and eruption of violence, the regime's Alawite (or Shia) identity served as a marker of its illegitimacy in the largely Sunni state.

The Syrian Civil War quickly became a theatre of regional rivalry as Saudi Arabia and its allies declared their support for the rebels. Riyadh condemned Iran for its support of Assad and once again accused Tehran of advancing a sectarian agenda. In practice, Saudi Arabia's support for the Sunni rebels – who increasingly claimed to be waging a jihad against an illegitimate regime – had the same effect. Hence, an uprising for more political accountability swiftly degenerated into a sectarian war. The deterioration of the security situation in Syria, and the sectarian fault-lines which emerged, paved the way for the emergence of the Islamic State of Iraq and Syria (ISIS) and its message of global jihad. This catastrophic development turned Syria into melting pot of overlapping trends: sectarianism, inter-state rivalry between Iran and Saudi Arabia, and global jihadism.

The Middle East has suffered a series of crises over the last century. While the manifestations of each crisis may differ, the key ingredients have always been remarkably similar: the vulnerability of state boundaries that were imposed arbitrarily in the colonial period; the uneasy relationship between religion and governance; the political and economic gap between the rulers and the ruled; a lack of political accountability and transparency; the willingness of external players, both regional and international, to intervene in conflicts to further their own interests; and, finally, the impact of US foreign policy which at one point secured the status quo to eliminate threats to its interests and at another sponsored regime change for the same reason. These key factors have triggered innumerable crises since the early twentieth century and they remain prevalent in the Middle East today, propelling the region from one calamity to the next.

Bibliography

Abrahamian, Ervand (1999) *Radical Islam: The Iranian Mojahedin* (London: IBTauris).

Abrahamian, Ervand (2001) 'The 1953 Coup in Iran', *Science and Society*, Vol. 65, No. 2, pp. 182–216.

Afary, Janet and Anderson, Kevin B. (2005) *Foucault and the Iranian Revolution: Gender and the Seductions of Islamism* (Chicago: University of Chicago Press).

Akbarzadeh, Shahram and Saeed, Abdullah (2003) 'Islam and Politics', in Shahram Akbarzadeh and Abdullah Saeed (eds), *Islam and Political Legitimacy* (London: Routledge).

Al-Khalil, Samir [pseudonym of Kanan Makiya] (1989) *Republic of Fear: The Politics of Modern Iraq* (Berkeley: University of California Press).

Al-Rasheed, Madawi (2011) 'Sectarianism as Counter-revolution: Saudi Responses to the Arab Spring', *Studies in Ethnicity and Nationalism*, Vol. 11, No. 3, pp. 513–526.

Al-Rasheed, Madawi (2016) *Muted Modernists: The Struggle over Divine Politics in Saudi Arabia* (New York: Oxford University Press).

Amuzegar, Jahangir (2006) 'Nuclear Iran: Perils and Prospects', *Middle East Policy*, Vol. 13, No. 2, pp. 90–112.

Anderson, Lisa (2011) 'Demystifying the Arab Spring: Parsing the Differences between Tunisia, Egypt, and Libya', *Foreign Affairs*, Vol. 90, No. 3, pp. 1–7.

Averre, Derek and Davies, Lance (2015) 'Russia, Humanitarian Intervention and the Responsibility to Protect: The Case of Syria', *International Affairs*, Vol. 91, No. 4, pp. 813–834.

Ayoob, Mohammad (2004) 'Political Islam: Image and Reality', *World Policy Journal*, Vol. 21, No. 3, pp. 1–14.

Ayoob, Mohammed (2003) 'The War against Iraq: Normative and Strategic Implications', *Middle East Policy*, Vol. 10, No. 2, 27–39.

Azzam, Abdullah (2001) [1987] *Join the Caravan* (London: Azzam Publications).

Azzam, Abdullah (2002) [1984] *In Defence of Muslim Land* (London: Azzam Publications).

Baban, Feyzi, Ilcan, Suzan and Rygiel, Kim (2017) 'Syrian Refugees in Turkey: Pathways to Precarity, Differential Inclusion, and Negotiated Citizenship Rights', *Journal of Ethnic and Migration Studies*, Vol. 43, No. 1, pp. 41–57.

Badran, Margot (2016) 'Creative Disobedience: Feminism, Islam, and Revolution in Egypt', in Fatima Sadiqi (ed.), *Women's Movements in post-'Arab Spring' North Africa* (New York: Palgrave Macmillan).

Barak, Ehud (2005) 'The Myths Spread about Camp David Are Baseless', in Shimon Shamir and Bruce Maddy-Weitzman (eds), *The Camp David Summit: What Went Wrong?* (Brighton: Sussex Academic Press).

Barakat, Sultan (2005) 'Post-Saddam Iraq: Deconstructing a Regime, Reconstructing a Nation', *Third World Quarterly*, Vol. 26, Nos. 4–5, pp. 571–591.

Barnett, Michael N. (1995) 'Sovereignty, Nationalism, and Regional Order in the Arab States System', *International Organization*, Vol. 49, No. 3, pp. 479–510.

Bar-Siman-Tov, Yaaov (1987) *Israel, the Superpowers and the War in the Middle East* (London: Praeger).

Bartu, Peter (2015) 'The Corridor of Uncertainty: The National Transitional Council's Battle for Legitimacy and Recognition', in Peter Cole and Brian McQuinn (eds), *The Libyan Revolution and Its Aftermath* (Oxford: Oxford University Press).

Bassiouni, M. Cherif (2016) 'Egypt's Unfinished Revolution', in Adam Roberts, Michael J. Willis and Rory McCarthy (eds), *Civil Resistance in the Arab Spring: Triumphs and Disasters* (Oxford: Oxford University Press)

Baxter, Kylie and Davidson, Renee (2016) 'Foreign Terrorist Fighters: A 21st Century Threat?', *Third World Quarterly*, Vol. 37, No. 8, pp. 1299–1313.

Bellin, Eva (2004) 'The Robustness of Authoritarianism in the Middle East: Exceptionalism in Comparative Perspective', *Comparative Politics*, Vol. 36, No. 2, pp. 139–157.

Berman, Ingrid (2016) *Verification and Monitoring of the Nuclear Agreement with Iran: Resources and Challenges* (New York: Nova Science Publishers).

Bizhara, Azmay (1999) 'The Uprising's Impact on Israel', in Joel Beinin and Zachary Lockman (eds), *Intifada: The Palestinian Uprising against Israeli Occupation* (London: South End Press).

Black, Ian and Morris, Benny (1996) *Israel's Secret Wars: A History of Israel's Intelligence Services* (Cambridge: Cambridge University Press).

Blanton, Shannon Lindsey (2005) 'Foreign Policy in Transition? Human Rights, Democracy, and US Arms Exports', *International Studies Quarterly*, Vol. 49, No. 4, pp. 647–667.

Bocco, R. (2009) 'UNRWA and the Palestinian Refugees: A history within a History', *Refugee Studies Quarterly*, Vol. 28, Nos. 2–3, pp. 229–252.

Bonney, Richard (2004) *Jihad from the Qur'an to bin Laden* (London: Palgrave Macmillan).

Bradsher, Henry (1999) *Afghan Communism and Soviet Intervention* (Oxford: Oxford University Press).

Bregman, Ahron (2000) *Israel's Wars, 1947–1993* (London: Routledge).

Bregman, Ahron (2003) *A History of Israel* (London: Palgrave Macmillan).

Brown, Leon Carl (1984) *International Politics and the Middle East: Old Rules, Dangerous Game* (London: IBTauris).

Brzezinski, Zbigniew (2002) 'Reflections on Soviet Intervention in Afghanistan, December 26, 1979', in Barry Rubin and Judith Colp Rubin (eds), *Anti-American Terrorism and the Middle East* (London: Oxford University Press).

Byman, Daniel (2014) 'Sectarianism Afflicts the New Middle East', *Survival*, Vol. 56, No. 1, pp. 79–100.

Byman, Daniel (2015) *Al Qaeda, the Islamic State, and the Global Jihadist Movement* (Oxford: Oxford University Press).

Campbell, Horace (2013) *NATO's Failure in Libya: Lessons for Africa* (Pretoria: Africa Institute of South Africa).

Carothers, Thomas (2003) 'Promoting Democracy and Fighting Terror', *Foreign Affairs*, Vol. 82, No. 1, pp. 84–97.

Charap, Samuel (2013) 'Russia, Syria and the Doctrine of Intervention', *Survival*, Vol. 55, No. 1, pp. 35–41.

Chaudhry, Mohammad A. (1998) 'Effects of World Capitalism on Urbanisation in Egypt', *International Journal of Middle East Studies*, Vol. 20, No. 1, pp. 23–43.

Chivvis, Christopher S. (2016) 'Countering the Islamic State in Libya', *Survival*, Vol. 58, No. 4, pp. 113–130.

Choueiri, Youssef (2000) *Arab Nationalism: A History, Nation and State in the Arab World* (Oxford: Blackwell).

Cigar, Norman (2016) *Saudi Arabia and Nuclear Weapons: How Do Countries Think about the Bomb?* (New York: Routledge).

Cleveland, William (2000) *A History of the Modern Middle East* (Boulder, CO: Westview).

Cronin, Audrey Kurth (2015) 'ISIS Is Not a Terrorist Group: Why Counterterrorism Won't Stop the Latest Jihadist Threat', *Foreign Affairs*, Vol. 87, No. 2, pp. 87–98.

Dalacoura, Katerina (2012) 'The 2011 Uprisings in the Arab Middle East: Political Change and Geopolitical Implications', *International Affairs*, Vol. 88, No. 1, pp. 63–79.

Davis, Richard (2016) *Hamas, Popular Support and War in the Middle East: Insurgency in the Holy Land* (London: Routledge).

Deeb, Lara (2012) 'Hizbullah in Lebanon', in Shahram Akbarzadeh (ed.), *Routledge Handbook of Political Islam* (London: Routledge).

Denoeux, Guilain (2002) 'The Forgotten Swamp: Navigating Political Islam', *Middle East Policy*, Vol. 9, No. 2, pp. 56–81.

Dershowitz, Alan (2003) *The Case for Israel* (New York: John Wiley and Sons).

DeVore, Marc R. and Stähli, Armin B. (2015) 'Explaining Hezbollah's Effectiveness: Internal and External Determinants of the Rise of Violent Non-State Actors', *Terrorism and Political Violence*, Vol. 27, No. 2, pp. 331–357.

Diamond, Larry (2010) 'Why Are There No Arab Democracies?', *Journal of Democracy*, Vol. 21, No. 1, pp. 93–112.

Dodge, Toby (2007) 'The Causes of US Failure in Iraq', *Survival*, Vol. 49, No. 1, pp. 85–106.

Dupree, Louis (1988) 'Cultural Changes among the Mujahidin and Muhajerin', in Bo Huldt and Erland Janson (eds), *Afghanistan: The Social, Cultural and Political Impact of the Soviet Invasion* (London: Croom Helm).

Eban, Abba (1988) 'Israel's Dilemmas: An Opportunity Squandered', in Stephen Roth (ed.), *The Impact of the Six Day War: A Twenty Year Assessment* (London: Macmillan).

Eickelman, Dale F. and Piscatori, James P. (1996) *Muslim Politics* (Princeton, NJ: Princeton University Press).

Elam, Yigal (2002) 'On the Myth of the Few against the Many', *Palestine–Israel Journal of Politics, Economics and Culture*, Vol. 9, No. 4, pp. 50–57.

El-Badri, Hassan, El Magdoub, Taha and Dia El Din Zohdy, Mohammed (1978) *The Ramadan War, 1973* (New York: Dupuy Associates).

El-Bendary, Mohamed (2013) *Egyptian Revolution: Between Hope and Despair, Mubarak to Morsi* (New York: Algora Publishing).

Elgindy, Khaled (2011) 'Palestine Goes to the UN: Understanding the New Statehood Strategy', *Foreign Affairs*, Vol. 90, pp. 102–113.

Elhadj, Elie (2006) *The Islamic Shield: Arab Resistance to Democratic and Religious Reforms* (Boca Raton, FL: BrownWalker Press).

Esposito, John (1999) *The Islamic Threat: Myth or Reality?* (Oxford: Oxford University Press).

Esposito, John (2001) *Unholy War: Terror in the Name of Islam* (Oxford: Oxford University Press).

Falk, Richard (1989) 'The Afghanistan "Settlement" and the Future of World Politics', in Amin Saikal and William Maley (eds), *The Soviet Withdrawal from Afghanistan* (Cambridge: Cambridge University Press).

Farouki, Suha Taji (1996) *A Fundamental Quest: Hizb al-Tahrir and the Search for the Islamic Caliphate* (London: Grey Seal).

Farsoun, Sami and Landis, Jean (1999) 'The Sociology of an Uprising: The Roots of the Intifada', in Jamal Raji Nassar and Roger Heacock (eds), *Intifada: Palestine at the Crossroads* (New York: Praeger).

Farzaneh, Mateo Mohammad (2007) 'Shi'i Ideology, Iranian Secular Nationalism and the Iran–Iraq War (1980–1988)', *Studies in Ethnicity and Nationalism*, Vol. 7, No. 1, pp. 86–103.

Ferris, Jesse (2008) 'Soviet Support for Egypt's Intervention in Yemen, 1962–1963', *Journal of Cold War Studies*, Vol. 10, No. 4, pp. 5–36.

Flapan, Simha (1979) *Zionism and the Palestinians* (London: Croom Helm).

Flapan, Simha (1987) *The Birth of Israel: Myths and Realities* (New York: Pantheon Books).

Freedman, Lawrence and Karsh, Ephraim (1993) *The Gulf Conflict 1990–1991* (Princeton, NJ: Princeton University Press).

Galnoor, Itzhak (1995) *The Partition of Palestine: Decision Crossroads in the Zionist Movement* (Albany: State University of New York Press).

Ganin, Zvi (1979) *Truman, American Jewry and Israel 1945–1948* (New York: Holmes & Meier).

Gause, Gregory (1994) *Oil Monarchies: Domestic and Security Challenges in the Arab Gulf States* (New York: Council on Foreign Relations).

Gause, Gregory F., III (2011) 'Why Middle East Studies Missed the Arab Spring: The Myth of Authoritarian Stability', *Foreign Affairs*, Vol. 90, No. 4, pp. 81–90.

Gerges, Fawaz A. (1995) 'The Kennedy Administration and the Egyptian–Saudi Conflict in Yemen: Co-opting Arab Nationalism', *Middle East Journal*, Vol. 49, No. 2, pp. 292–311.

Golkar, Saeid (2015) *Captive Society: The Basij Militia and Social Control in Iran* (Washington, DC: Woodrow Wilson Center Press).

Gross, Aeyal (2017) *The Writing on the Wall: Rethinking The International Law of Occupation* (Cambridge: Cambridge University Press).

Gunter, Michael M. (2015) 'Iraq, Syria, ISIS and the Kurds: Geostrategic Concerns for the US and Turkey', *Middle East Policy*, Vol. 22, No. 1, pp. 102–111.

Hammel, Eric (2010) *Six Days in June: How Israel Won the 1967 Arab–Israeli War* (New York: Charles Scribner's Sons).

Haddad, Yvonne (1992) 'Islamists and the Problem of Israel: The 1967 Awakening', *Middle East Journal*, Vol. 46, No. 2, pp. 266–285.

Hanna, Michael Wahid and Dassa Kaye, Dalia (2015) 'The Limits of Iranian Power', *Survival*, Vol. 57, No. 5, pp. 173–198.

Hasan, Naseer (2003) *Dishonest Broker: The US Role in Israel and Palestine* (London: South End Books).

Hass, Amira (2004) 'Israeli Colonialism under the Guise of the Peace Process, 1993–2000', in Dan Leon (ed.), *Who's Left in Israel? Radical Political Alternatives for the Future of Israel* (Brighton: Sussex Academic Press).

Hassassian, Manuel (2004) 'Why Did Oslo Fail? Lessons for the Future', in Robert Rothstein, Moshe Ma'oz and Khalil Shikaki (eds), *The Israeli–Palestinian Peace Process: Oslo and the Lessons of Failure* (Brighton: Sussex Academic Press).

Heisbourgm, François (2015) 'The Strategic Implications of the Syrian Refugee Crisis', *Survival*, Vol. 57, No. 6, pp. 7–20.

Heller, Joseph (1995) *The Stern Gang: Ideology, Politics and Terror 1940–1949* (London: Frank Cass).

Helmreich, Paul C. (1974) *From Paris to Sevres: The Partition of the Ottoman Empire at the Peace Conference of 1919–1920* (Athens, OH: Ohio State University Press).

Herman, Lyndall (2016) 'Sisi, the Sinai and Salafis: Instability in a Power Vacuum', *Middle East Policy*, Vol. 23, No. 2, pp. 95–107.

Hobbs, Christopher and Moran, Matthew (2013) *Exploring Regional Responses to a Nuclear Iran: Nuclear Dominoes?* (London: Palgrave Macmillan).

Hogan, Matthew (2001) 'The 1948 Massacre at Deir Yassin Revisited', *Historian*, Vol. 63, No. 2, pp. 309–333.

Hroub, Khaled (2000) *HAMAS: Political Thought and Practice* (Washington, DC: Institute for Palestinian Studies).

Hughes, Matthew (1999) *Allenby and the British Strategy in the Middle East 1917–1919* (London: Frank Cass).

Huneidi, Sahar (2001) *A Broken Trust: Herbert Samuel, Zionism and the Palestinians* (London: IBTauris).

Ibrahimi, Niamatullah (2014) 'When Few Means Many: The Consequence of Civilian Casualties for Civil–Military Relations in Afghanistan', in William Maley and Susanne Schmeidl (eds), *Reconstructing Afghanistan: Civil–Military Experiences in Comparative Perspective* (London: Routledge).

International Crisis Group (2012) 'Report on Israel's Arab Minority and the Israeli–Palestinian Conflict', *Journal of Palestine Studies*, Vol. 41, No. 4, pp. 185–191.

Isakhan, Benjamin (2015) *Legacy of Iraq: From the 2003 War to the 'Islamic State'* (Edinburgh: Edinburgh University Press).

Jacoby, Tami Amanda (2005) *Bridging the Barrier: Israeli Unilateral Engagement* (London: Ashgate).

Jankowski, James (2002) *Nasser's Egypt, Arab Nationalism, and the United Arab Republic* (London: Lynne Rienner).

Johnson, Thomas H., and Mason, Chris M. (2008) 'Understanding the Taliban and Insurgency in Afghaistan', *Orbis*, Vol. 51, No. 1, pp. 71–89.

Johnson, Thomas H. (2013) 'Taliban Adaptations and Innovations', *Small Wars and Insurgencies*, Vol. 24, No. 1, pp. 3–27.

Jones, Seth G. (2006) 'Averting Failure in Afghanistan', *Survival*, Vol. 48, No. 1, pp. 111–128.

Jones, Toby Craig (2012) 'America, Oil, and War in the Middle East', *Journal of American History*, Vol. 99, No. 1, pp. 208–218.

Kamrava, Mehran (2012) 'The Arab Spring and the Saudi-led Counterrevolution', *Orbis*, Vol. 56, No. 1, pp. 96–104.

Karabell, Zachary (1995) 'The Wrong Threat: The United States and Islamic Fundamentalism', *World Policy Journal*, Vol. 12, No. 2, pp. 37–48.

Karmi, Ghada (2011) 'The One-state Solution: An Alternative Vision for Israeli–Palestinian Peace', *Journal of Palestine Studies*, Vol. 40, No. 2, pp. 62–76.

Karsh, Efraim (2000) *Arafat's War: The Man and his Battle for Israeli Conquest* (New York: Grove).

Karsh, Efraim and Karsh, Inari (1999) *Empires of the Sand: The Struggle for Mastery in the Middle East 1789–1923* (Cambridge, MA: Harvard University Press).

Keddie, Nikki (2003) *Modern Iran: Roots and Results of Revolutions* (New Haven, CT: Yale University Press).

Kepel, Gilles (2004) *The War for Muslim Minds: Islam and the West* (Cambridge, MA: Belknap Press of Harvard University Press).

Keynoush, Banafsheh (2016) *Saudi Arabia and Iran: Friends or Foes?* (London: Palgrave Macmillian).

Khalidi, Rashid (2001) 'The Palestinians and 1948: The Underlying Causes of Failure', in Eugene Rogan and Avi Shlaim (eds), *The War for Palestine: Rewriting the History of 1948* (Cambridge: Cambridge University Press).

Khomeini, Ruholla (1985) *Islam and Revolution: Writings and Declarations* (London: Mizan Press).

Khoury, Philip Shukry (2014) *Syria and the French Mandate: The Politics of Arab Nationalism, 1920–1945* (Princeton, NJ: Princeton University Press).

Kimball, Jeffrey (2006) 'The Nixon Doctrine: A Sage of Misunderstanding', *Presidential Studies Quarterly*, Vol. 36, No. 1, pp. 59–74.

Knapp, Michael G. (2003) 'The Concept and Practice of Jihad in Islam', *Parameters*, 33, Vol. 33, No. 1, pp. 82–94.

Kostiner, Joseph (1995) 'Prologue of the Hashemite Downfall and Saudi Ascendency: A New Look at the Khurma Dispute 1917–1919', in Asher Susser and Aryeh Shmuelevitz (eds), *The Hashemites in the Modern Arab World* (London: Frank Cass).

Kozhanov, Nikolay (2016) *Russia and the Syrian Conflict: Moscow's Domestic, Regional and Strategic Interests* (Berlin: Gerlach Press).

Krasno, Jean E. (2004) 'To End the Scourge of War: The Story of UN Peace Keeping', in Jean E. Krasno (ed.), *United Nations: Confronting the Challenges of a Global Society* (Boulder, CO: Lynne Rienner Publishers).

Kuperman, Alan (1999) 'The Stinger Missile and US Intervention in Afghanistan', *Political Science Quarterly*, Vol. 114, No. 2, pp. 219–263.

Kuperman, Alan J. (2015) 'Obama's Libya Debacle: How a Well-meaning Intervention Ended in Failure', *Foreign Affairs*, Vol. 94, No. 2, pp. 66–77.

Kurz, Anat (2005) *Fatah and the Politics of Violence: The Institutionalization of a Popular Struggle* (Brighton: Sussex Academic Press).

Kushner, Harvey W. (1998) *The Future of Terrorism: Violence in the New Millennium* (London: Sage).

Larrabee, F. Stephen (2016) 'Turkey and the Changing Dynamics of the Kurdish Issue', *Survival*, Vol. 58, No. 2, pp. 67–73.

Lefèvre, Raphaël (2013) *Ashes of Hama: The Muslim Brotherhood in Syria* (New York: Oxford University Press).

Levitt, Matthew (2013) *Hezbollah: The Global Footprint of Lebanon's Party of God* (Washington, DC: Georgetown University Press).

Lister, Charles R. (2016) *The Syrian Jihad: Al-Qaeda, the Islamic State and the Evolution of an Insurgency* (Oxford: Oxford University Press).

Makdissi, Ussama (2002) 'Anti-Americanism in the Arab World: An Interpretation of a Brief History', *Journal of American History*, Vol. 89, No. 2, pp. 538–558.

Maley, William (1988) 'Interpreting the Taliban', in William Maley (ed.), *Fundamentalism Reborn? Afghanistan and the Taliban* (London: Hurst & Company).

Maley, William (2002) *The Afghanistan Wars* (New York: Palgrave Macmillan).

Maley, William (2006) *Rescuing Afghanistan* (Sydney: UNSW Press).

Maley, William (2010) 'Afghanistan in 2010', *Asian Survey*, Vol. 51, No. 1, pp. 85–96.

Maley, William (2013) 'State Building in Afghanistan: Challenges and Pathologies', *Central Asian Survey*, Vol. 32, No. 3, pp. 255–270.

Malkasian, Carter (2006) 'Signalling Resolve, Democratization, and the First Battle of Fallujah', *Journal of Strategic Studies*, Vol. 29, No. 3, 423–452.

Manji, Firoze and Ekine, Sokari (2012) *African Awakening: The Emerging Revolutions* (Oxford: Pambazuka Press).

Masri, Mazen (2017) *The Dynamics of Exclusionary Constitutionalism: Israel as a Jewish and Democratic State* (Oxford: Bloomsbury).

Matthiesen, Toby (2013) *Sectarian Gulf: Saudi Arabia, Bahrain and the Arab Spring that Wasn't* (Stanford, CA: Standford University Press).

McCary, John A. (2009) 'The Anbar Awakening: An Alliance of Incentives', *Washington Quarterly*, Vol. 32, No. 1, pp. 43–59.

McNamara, Robert (2003) *Britain, Nasser and the Balance of Power in the Middle East* (London: Routledge).

Meir, Hatina (2001) *Islam and Salvation in Palestine: The Islamic Jihad Movement* (Tel Aviv: Tel Aviv University).

Meital, Yoram (2000) 'The Khartoum Conference and Egyptian Policy after the 1967 War: A Reexamination', *Middle East Journal*, Vol. 54, No. 1, pp. 64–82.

Merz, Fabien (2014) 'Adversarial Framing: President Bashar al-Assad's Depiction of the Armed Syrian Opposition', *Journal of Terrorism Research*, Vol. 5, No. 2, pp. 30–44.

Middle East Institute (1956) 'The New Egyptian Constitution', *Middle East Journal*, Vol. 10, No. 3, pp. 300–306.

Milani, Mohsen M. (2009) 'Tehran's Take: Understanding Iran's US Policy', *Foreign Affairs*, Vol. 88, No. 4, pp. 46–62.

Milton-Edwards, Beverley (1999) *Islamic Politics in Palestine* (London: IBTauris).

Milton-Edwards, Beverley (2016a) *Muslim Brotherhood* (London: Routledge).

Milton-Edwards, Beverley (2016b) *The Muslim Brotherhood: The Arab Spring and Its Future Face* (New York: Routledge).

Monshipouri, Mahmood and Assareh, Ali (2009) 'The Islamic Republic and the "Green Movement": Coming Full Circle', *Middle East Policy*, Vol. 16, No. 4, pp. 27–46.

Musallam, Musallam Ali (1996) *The Iraqi Invasion of Kuwait: Saddam Hussein, His State and International Power Politics* (London: British Academic Press).

Mutawi, Samir (2002) *Jordan in the 1967 War* (Cambridge: Cambridge University Press).

Nasser, Jamal R. (1991) *The Palestine Liberation Organization: From Armed Struggle to the Declaration of Independence* (New York: Praeger).

Neep, Daniel (2012) *Occupying Syria under the French Mandate: Insurgency, Space and State Formation* (New York: Cambridge University Press).

Norton, Augustus Richard (2000) 'Hizballah and the Israeli Withdrawal from Southern Lebanon', *Journal of Palestine Studies*, Vol. 30, No. 1, pp. 22–35.

Norton, Augustus Richard (2013) 'The Return of Egypt's Deep State', *Current History*, Vol. 112, No. 758, pp. 338–344.

Nusse, Andrea (1999) *Muslim Palestine: The Ideology of HAMAS* (London: Routledge).

Obama, Barack (2007) 'Renewing American Leadership', *Foreign Affairs*, Vol. 86, No. 4, pp. 2–16.

O'Leary, Brendan (2016) 'Power-sharing and Partition amid Israel–Palestine', *Ethnopolitics*, Vol. 15, No. 4, pp. 345–365.

Ouimet, Matthew (2003) *The Rise and Fall of the Brezhnev Doctrine in Soviet Foreign Policy* (Chapel Hill: University of North Carolina Press).

Pace, Michelle and Cavatorta, Francesco (2012) 'The Arab Uprisings in Theoretical Perspective: An Introduction', *Mediterranean Politics*, Vol. 17, No. 2, pp. 125–138.

Pauly, Robert J. and Lansford, Tom (2005) *Strategic Preemption: US Foreign Policy and the Second Iraq War* (Farnham: Ashgate)

Phillips, Christopher (2016) *The Battle for Syria: International Rivalry in the New Middle East* (New Haven, CT: Yale University Press).

Pogodda, Sandra and Richmond, Oliver P. (2015) 'Palestinian Unity and Everyday State Formation: Subaltern "Ungovernmentality" versus Elite Interests', *Third World Quarterly*, Vol. 36, No. 5, pp. 890–907.

Qaddour, Jomana (2013) 'Unlocking the Alawite Conundrum in Syria', *Washington Quarterly*, Vol. 36, No. 4, pp. 67–78.

Qassem, Naim (2005) *Hizbullah: The Story from Within* (London: Saqi).

Quandt, William B. (2001) *Peace Process: American Diplomacy and the Arab–Israeli Conflict since 1967* (Berkeley: University of California Press).

Qutb, Sayyid (1978) *Milestones* (Beirut: Holy Koran Publishing House).

Rabinovich, Itamar (2003) *Waging Peace: Israel and the Arabs 1948–2003* (Princeton, NJ: Princeton University Press).

Rajan, G.V. Julie (2015) *Al Qaeda's Global Crisis* (New York: Taylor and Francis).

Raphel, Gideon (1988) 'Twenty Years in Retrospect: 1967–1987', in Stephen Roth (ed.), *The Impact of the Six Day War: A Twenty Year Assessment* (London: Macmillan).

Rashid, Ahmed (2010) *Taliban* (New Haven, CT: Yale University Press).

Ricker, Laurent (2001) 'The Soviet Union and the Suez Crisis', in David Tal (ed.), *The 1956 War: Collusion and Rivalry in the Middle East* (London: Routledge).

Roberts, David (2013) *The Ba'th and the Creation of Modern Syria* (London: Routledge).

Rogan, Eugene L. (1999) *Frontiers of the State in the Late Ottoman Empire* (Cambridge: Cambridge University Press).

Roy, Arundhati (1987) *The Soviet Intervention in Afghanistan: Causes, Consequences and India's Response* (New Delhi: Associated Publishing House).

Roy, Olivier (1990) *Islam and Resistance in Afghanistan* (Cambridge: Cambridge University Press).

Roy, Olivier (1994) *The Failure of Political Islam* (Cambridge, MA: Harvard University Press)

Roy, Olivier (1999) 'The Radicalization of Sunni Sonservative Fundamentalism', *ISIM Newsletter*, No. 2, p. 7.

Roy, Sara (2012) 'Reconceptualizing the Israeli–Palestinian Conflict: Key Paradigm Shifts', *Journal of Palestine Studies*, Vol. 41, No. 3, pp. 71–91.

Rosen, Steven J. (2012) 'Why a Special Issue on UNRWA?', *Middle East Quarterly*, Vol. 19, No. 4, pp. 412–437.

Rostow, Eugene V. (1975) 'The Illegality of the Arab Attack on Israel of October 6, 1973', *American Journal of International Law*, Vol. 69, No. 2, pp. 272–289.

Roy, Sara (2013) *Hamas and Civil Society in Gaza: Engaging the Islamist Social Sector* (Princeton, NJ: Princeton University Press).

Rubenstein, Amnon (1984) *The Zionist Dream Revisited: From Herzl to Gush Emunim and Back* (New York: Schocken Books).

Sachar, Howard (2005) *A History of the Jews in the Modern World* (New York: Vintage).

Sadr, Ehsaneh I. (2005) 'The Impact of Iran's Nuclearization on Israel', *Middle East Policy*, Vol. 12, No. 2, pp. 58–73.

Sadiki, Larbi (1995) 'Al-la Nidam: An Arab View of the New World (Dis)order', *Arab Studies Quarterly*, Vol. 17, No. 3, pp. 1–22.

Sadiki, Larbi (2003) 'Saudi Arabia: Re-reading Politics and Religion in the Wake of September 11', in Shahram Akbarzadeh and Abdullah Saeed (eds), *Islam and Political Legitimacy* (New York: Routledge).

Sadiki, Larbi (2014) *Routledge Handbook of the Arab Spring: Rethinking Democratization* (Florence: Taylor and Francis).

Saeed, Abdullah (2003) 'The Official Ulema and the Religious Legitimacy of the Modern Nation State', in Shahram Akbarzadeh and Abdullah Saeed (eds), *Islam and Political Legitimacy* (New York: Routledge).

Sahliyeh, Emile F. (1986) *The PLO after the Lebanon War* (Boulder, CO: Westview Press).

Saikal, Amin (2004) *Modern Afghanistan: A History of Struggle and Survival* (London: IBTauris).

Saikal, Amin (2014) *Zone of Crisis: Afghanistan, Pakistan, Iran and Iraq* (London: IBTauris).

Saikal, Amin and Maley, William (1991) *Regime Change in Afghanistan: Foreign Intervention and the Politics of Legitimacy* (Sydney: Crawford House).

Samii, Abbas William (2008) 'A Stable Structure on Shifting Sands: Assessing the Hizbullah–Iran–Syria Relationship', *Middle East Journal*, Vol. 62, No. 1, pp. 32–53.

Segal, David (1988) The Iran–Iraq War: A Military Analysis', *Foreign Affairs*, Vol. 66, No. 5, pp. 946–963.

Sher, Gilead (2005) 'Lesson from the Camp David Experience', in Shimon Shamir and Bruce Maddy-Weitzman (eds), *The Camp David Summit: What Went Wrong?* (Brighton: Sussex Academic Press).

Shlaim, Avi (2000) *The Iron Wall: Israel and the Arab World* (London: Penguin Books).

Shlaim, Avi (2001) 'Israel and the Arab Coalition in 1948', in Eugene Rogan and Avi Shalaim (eds), *The War for Palestine* (Cambridge: Cambridge University Press).

Sick, Gary (1991) *October Surprise: America's Hostages in Iran and the Election of Ronald Reagan* (New York: Random House).

Simon, Steven (2008) 'The Price of the Surge: How US Strategy Is Hastening Iraq's Demise', *Foreign Affairs*, Vol. 87, No. 3, pp. 57–76.

Simpson, Kumuda (2015) *US Nuclear Diplomacy with Iran: From the War on Terror to the Obama Administration* (Lanham, MD: Rowman & Littlefield).

Sinora, Hanna (1988) 'A Palestinian Perspective', in Stephen Roth (ed.), *The Impact of the Six Day War: A Twenty Year Assessment* (London: Macmillan).

Smolansky, Bettie Moretz (1991) *The USSR and Iraq: The Soviet Quest for Influence* (Durham, NC: Duke University Press).

Sorenson, David S. (2016) *Syria in Ruins: The Dynamics of the Syrian Civil War* (California: Praeger).

Souleimanov, Emil Aslan (2016) 'Mission Accomplished? Russia's Withdrawal from Syria', *Middle East Policy*, Vol. 23, No. 2, pp. 108–118.

Springer, Devin R., Regens, James L. and Edgar, David N. (2009) *Islamic Radicalism and Global Jihad* (Washington, DC: Georgetown University Press).

Takeyh, Ray (2009) *Guardians of the Revolution* (Oxford: Oxford University Press).

Tal, David (2004) *War in Palestine 1948: Strategy and Diplomacy* (London: Routledge).

Talib, A. (2014) 'Huna Al-Khahirah: Messages from Cairo', in Ford Lumban Gaol, Seifedine Kadry, Marie Taylor and Pak Shen Li (eds), *Recent Trends in Social and Behaviour Sciences: Proceedings of the 2nd International Congress on Interdisciplinary Behaviour and Social Sciences 2013* (London: Taylor and Francis/Balkema).

Tanner, Stephen (2002) *Afghanistan: A Military History from Alexander the Great to the Fall of the Taliban* (Cambridge: DaCapo).

Tarock, Adam (2016) 'The Iran Nuclear Deal: Winning a Little, Losing a Lot', *Third World Quarterly*, Vol. 37, No. 8, pp. 1408–1424.

Thomas, Baylis (1999) *How Israel Was Won: A Concise History of the Arab–Israeli Conflict* (Lanham, MD: Lexington Books).

Salibi, Kamal (1993) *A House of Many Mansions: The History of Lebanon Reconsidered* (London: IBTauris).

Shlaim, Avi (1995) *War and Peace in the Middle East* (London: Penguin).

Smith, Charles D. (2004) *Palestine and the Arab–Israeli Conflict* (Boston: Bedford/St Martin's).

Spiegel, Steven (1988) 'American Middle East Policy', in Stephen Roth (ed.), *The Impact of the Six Day War: A Twenty Year Assessment* (London: Macmillan).

Sprinzak, Ehud (1991) *The Ascendance of Israel's Radical Right* (New York: Oxford University Press).

Sprinzak, Ehud (1999) *Brother against Brother: Violence and Extremism in Israeli Politics from Altalena to the Rabin Assassination* (New York: Free Press).

Ulrichsen, Kristian (2014) *Qatar and the Arab Spring* (Oxford: Oxford University Press).

Vital, David (1982) *Zionism: The Formative Years* (Oxford: Clarendon Press).

Vital, David (1987) *Zionism: The Crucial Phase* (Oxford: Clarendon Press).

Walker, Martin (1993) *The Cold War and the Making of the Modern World* (London: Fourth Estate).

Waxman, Dov (2006) *The Pursuit of Peace and the Crisis of Israeli Identity: Defending/ Defining* (New York: Palgrave).

Wehrey, Frederic, Karasik, Theodore W., Nader, Alireza, Ghez, Jeremy J. and Hansell, Lydia (2009) *Saudi–Iranian Relations since the Fall of Saddam: Rivalry, Cooperation, and Implications for US Policy* (Santa Monica, CA: Rand Corporation).

Wiktorowicz, Quintan (2001) 'The New Global Threat: Transnational Salafis and Jihad', *Middle East Policy*, Vol. 8, No. 4, pp. 18–38.

Wilkins, Henrietta (2013) *The Making of Lebanese Foreign Policy: Understanding the 2006 Hezbollah–Israeli War* (New York: Routledge).

Wilson, Mary C. (1991) 'The Hashemites, the Arab Revolt and Arab Nationalism', in Rashid Khalidi (ed.), *The Origins of Arab Nationalism* (New York: Columbia University Press).

Wright, Robin B. (2010) *The Iran Primer: Power, Politics and US Policy* (Washington, DC: The US Institute of Peace).

Zeidel, Ronen (2015) 'Between Aqalliya and Mukawin: Understanding Sunni Political Attitudes in Post-Saddam Iraq', in Benjamin Isakhan (ed.) *Legacy of Iraq: From the 2003 War to the 'Islamic State'* (Edinburgh: Edinburgh University Press).

Zollner, Babara (2012) 'The Muslim Brotherhood', in Shahram Akbarzadeh (ed.), *Routledge Handbook of Political Islam* (New York: Routledge).

Index